YOUTH ENGAGING WITH THE WORLD
MEDIA, COMMUNICATION AND SOCIAL CHANGE

Yearbook 2009

YOUTH ENGAGING WITH THE WORLD

MEDIA, COMMUNICATION AND SOCIAL CHANGE

EDITORS: **THOMAS TUFTE & FLORENCIA ENGHEL**

The International Clearinghouse
on Children, Youth and Media

United Nations
Educational, Scientific and
Cultural Organization

With the support of
**Communication and
Information Sector**

NORDICOM
University of Gothenburg

Yearbook 2009
Youth Engaging With the World
Media, Communication and Social Change

Editors:
Thomas Tufte & Florencia Enghel

© Editorial matters and selections, the editors; articles, individual contributors

The authors are responsible for the choice, the presentation of the facts contained in these articles, and the opinion expressed therein, which are not necessarily those of UNESCO and do not commit the organization. The designations employed and presentation of material throughout the publication do not imply the expression of any opinion whatsoever on the part of UNESCO concerning the legal status of any country, territory, city or area or of its authorities, or concerning the frontiers or boundaries.

ISSN 1651-6028
ISBN 978-91-89471-82-5

Published by:
The International Clearinghouse on Children, Youth and Media
Series editor: Ulla Carlsson

Nordicom
University of Gothenburg
Box 713
SE 405 30 GÖTEBORG
Sweden

Cover by:
Karin Persson

Printed by:
Livréna AB, Göteborg, Sweden, 2009
Environmental certification according to ISO 14001

Contents

Acknowledgement 7

Foreword 9

Thomas Tufte & Florencia Enghel
Introduction:
Youth Engaging with Media and Communication.
Different, Unequal and Disconnected? 11

SETTING THE SCENE

Rossana Reguillo
The Warrior's Code? Youth, Communication and Social Change 21

MEMORY AND IDENTITY: YOUTH COMMUNICATING FOR THEIR RIGHTS

Antonieta Muñoz-Navarro
Youth and Human Rights in Chile.
Otherness, Political Identity and Social Change 43

Florencia Enghel, Cecilia Flachsland & Violeta Rosemberg
Youth, Memory and Justice.
The Cromañón Case and Communication in an Age of Precariousness 61

Iryna Vidanava
From Pages to Pixels. Belarus' Unique Youth Multimedia Magazine 81

Jiwon Yoon
The Power of Voice. North Koreans Negotiating Identity
and Social Integration via Mediated Storytelling 101

VOICES OF THE YOUTH: COPING, CRITICIZING AND CALLING FOR CHANGE

Rashweat Mukundu
Alternative Voices under Repression. Zimbabwe's Youth Media Projects 121

Lise Grauenkær Jensen, Mette Grøndahl Hansen & Stine Kromann-Larsen
Young Voices Driving Social Change 137

*Thomas Tufte, Aran Corrigan, Ylva Ekström, Minou Fuglesang
& Datius Rweyemamu*
From Voice to Participation?
Analysing Youth Agency in Letter Writing in Tanzania   155

Ece Algan
"There Is No Permission to Love in Our Urfa".
Media, Youth Identities and Social Change in Southeast Turkey   173

YOUTH AS SUBJECTS – OF CONTENT, PROGRAMS, PROJECTS AND REGULATIONS

Peter Lemish & Elke Schlote
Media Portrayals of Youth Involvement in Social Change. The Roles
of Agency, Praxis, and Conflict Resolution Processes in TV Programs   193

Johan Lagerkvist
Contesting Norms on China's Internet?
The Party-state, Youth, and Social Change   215

Nkosi Martin Ndlela
Critical Voices.
Student Activism, Communication and Social Change in Zimbabwe   233

Robert Huesca
Ethical Challenges in U.S. Youth Radio Training Programs   249

YOUTH IN PROCESSES: PARTICIPATORY PRODUCTION

Karen Greiner
Participatory Communication Processes as Infusions of Innovation.
The Case of 'Scenarios from Africa'   267

Ana Zanotti
Views in Progress, Views in Process. A Participatory Video Experience
with Young People in a Space of Borderlands   283

Claudius Ceccon
Learning to Change the World Right Here.
Youth, Educommunication and Social Change in Rio de Janeiro, Brazil   301

José Paulo de Araújo
Communication School for Children. Connecting Caves to the World   323

The Authors   339

Acknowledgement

We would like to acknowledge the support of UNESCO in producing this publication.

Foreword

The media are among the most powerful social forces of our time, and whether we are talking about the political, economic or cultural sphere, we cannot avoid taking the media into account. Media, and not least Internet, represent social and cultural resources that can empower people, in both their personal development and their development as members of society. An important prerequisite for empowerment of citizens is a concerted effort to improve media and information literacy. Such skills that strengthen citizens' critical faculties and ability to communicate, both of which enable them to use media and communication as tools and as a way to articulate processes of development and social change. In short, media and information literacy empowers people to influence and improve their lives – while promoting a well-oriented, democratic and sustainable society. But, we often tend to forget how crucially important such skills are for both democracy and development.

Media and information literacy is needed for all citizens, but it is of decisive importance to the younger generation – to their performance as citizens, their participation in society, and to their learning, cultural expression and personal fulfilment. Throughout history, young people have often been active participants in the manifestation of social change, and most times their creative uses of media and innovative practices of communication have been crucial in the process. Youth have had key roles in citizen media, in alternative media that stimulate public debate, or in campaigning for particular causes such as HIV/AIDS prevention, political freedom, freedom of expression, fair trade, etc. Different Internet platforms like Facebook, Youtube and blogs have become rapidly growing virtual sites that give shape to new forms of social networking, communication and mobilization, primarily amongst youth.

At the core of this creativity and these innovative practices is media and information literacy. Young people's competence in using media, their ability to produce, understand and interact with the multiplicity of both new and old media formats and technologies have been instrumental in the manifestation of social processes of change. This book seeks to explore theoretical assumptions as well as empirical evidence of media and information literacy in action. But it also gathers examples of how youth in developing countries have used their skills to bring about change.

We at the International Clearinghouse on Children, Youth and Media are pleased to have been able to engage two well established researchers within communication for social change: Dr. Thomas Tufte, Professor in Communication at the Roskilde University, Denmark, and Florencia Enghel, Lecturer in Communication for Development at the Malmö University College, Sweden, and Communication and Development Consultant in Buenos Aires, Argentina. She is also editor of the web magazine *Glocal Times*. The editors have brought together a good number of scholars who present conclusions based on their experience and the research to date on youth and media, media and information literacy, and social change.

Our frame of reference is too often the Western world, even though we know there are major differences across cultures, political systems and faiths, and that all these factors influence media culture. Thus, there is an urgent need to open the agenda to non-Western thought and intercultural approaches to a greater extent than is the case today. The authors in this book set the stage for such an agenda, contributing a variety of perspectives and including different cultures.

On behalf of the Clearinghouse, let me conclude by thanking the editors and all the contributors who have made this yearbook possible. We also wish to express our great appreciation of the support provided by UNESCO, without which this publication would not have been possible.

Göteborg in September 2009

Ulla Carlsson
Director
Nordicom
University of Gothenburg

Youth Engaging with Media and Communication: Different, Unequal and Disconnected?

Introduction by Thomas Tufte & Florencia Enghel

> 85 per cent of the world's young people live in developing countries; this simple demographic factor alone is enough to define global youth policy as being fundamentally a question of development (World Youth Report 2003)

Youthful realities

In recent years, youth have increasingly become the focus of the development policies of states, multi- and bilateral donor agencies, NGOs and CSOs. Not only are they perceived as key to economic, democratic and socio-cultural development, but young people worldwide are also understood as decisive agents with regard to peace processes and political stability on a local and global scale.

The fact that the vast majority of the world's young people live in developing countries underscores the relevance of connecting a focus on youth, agency and social change to contemporary debates in development. We may easily agree on a post-colonial perspective on development, where a multiplicity of voices and a critical approach to the Western development discourse inform the debate. We would also like to agree wholeheartedly with the fact that powerful youth agency and dynamic youth movements can be identified in most parts of the world. However, as editors of a yearbook embracing cases from more than 13 different countries in South America, Europe, Asia, Africa and North America, we find it important to outline some of the common socio-economic denominators that inform the global condition of youth in our contemporary world.

In recent years, those socio-economic conditions have been altered by large-scale social, economic and political changes that reinforce the marginal and vulnerable situation of youths, who are considered soon-to-be-adults, though in many cases they have long assumed adult responsibility. Economic globalization, pandemics such as HIV/AIDS, political transitions and repressive regimes, conflicts, climate change, the recent financial crunch and its obvious impact in terms of job destruction and unemployment, as well as changing intergenerational relations in a post-modern world – all of these factors have enormous impacts on the conditions of youth worldwide.

A few facts from the final report of the Ad Hoc Working Group for Youth and the Millennium Development Goals from 2005 clearly illustrate this:

- "Globally, the situation of young people today is characterized by extreme disparities in terms of economic, technological, social and cultural resources, which vary enormously across regions, countries, localities and population groups".

- "Despite rapid urbanization, the majority of youth still live in rural areas, primarily in developing countries. Young men outnumber young women (525 million versus 500 million), and 57 million young men and 96 million young women remain illiterate".

- "In addition to inadequate education, youth face increasing insecurity in the labor market. Sixty-six million young people throughout the world are unemployed, making up nearly 40% of global unemployment. Hundreds of millions more work fewer hours than they would like, while still others work long hours with little gain and no social protection".

- "Overall, current avenues for political participation are insufficient and consequently youth in many places are perceived as apathetic or disengaged. (...) Meanwhile, many young people are organizing locally and via the Internet and informal youth volunteerism is at record levels. This means that young people are breaking through the mold of traditional political avenues and moving beyond voting as their sole civic responsibility" (Youth & MDGs, 2005).

Facts such as these are having a significant impact on the lives of youth worldwide. Such social realities result in unequal living conditions and disparities, marginal and vulnerable rural livelihoods in poor areas of the globe, illiteracy, inadequate education, unemployment, and apathy and disengagement vis-à-vis political participation. These negative consequences speak to the highly unjust and difficult conditions faced by many young people. Thus, in pulling together a yearbook about youth engagement through media and communication, primarily in so-called developing nations, the contextualization of each case study is fundamental. Promoting an understanding of the local socio-economic, political and cultural conditions in which youth become engaged, mobilize, narrate their experiences, produce their stories and influence the lives of their communities and peers has been the overall objective of this compilation.

Youth agency via media and communication

This yearbook focuses on youth as a generation of actors and citizens who are increasingly exposed to and making use of media/ICT for entertainment and informational purposes, for social networking and mobilization, and for knowledge sharing. The mobile phone boom in recent years, observable, e.g., in many African countries, underlines the eagerness with which young Africans seek to appropriate the new digital media, even under the constrained socio-economic conditions that the majority of local youth face. Likewise, the way in which youth have embraced new social media such as Facebook, blogging and Twitter reflects a similar orientation. Involvement in both new and pre-existent forms of media and communication practices is addressed in the yearbook.

We focus our attention primarily on the role of youth as engaged and frequent media users, consumers and producers, as well as key players in the development processes. However, we are at the same time critical and sceptical concerning the growing celebratory attitude towards youth agency owing to the new social media. The increasingly intensified technological and economic exchanges call for new ways in which differences can be acknowledged, inequalities can be corrected, and majorities can be connected to globalized networks (García Canclini 2006). Global interconnectedness does not only produce new opportunities. In fact, it also simultaneously creates new differences, inequalities and forms of exclusion, or disconnections – and their social consequences seem to affect youth in important ways. Hence, the cases chosen for this book contextualize youthful media and communication practices within these overall development trends.

While 'youth' is a socially constructed conception of age and not just a biological given (Kahn and Kellner 2008), the cases in this book contextualize the ways in which and means with which youth engage in the world via media and communication. It is crucial that the social, economic and political contexts they live in are factored into the overall equation.

Mexican media scholar Rossana Reguillo, who sets the scene for this book with her article "The warrior's code? Youth, communication and social change", emphasizes some of the lived realities of youth, especially Latin American youth. The author stresses that:

> The analysis of the relationship between youth, communication and social change must take place in the context of this paradoxical tension: more and better media; increasingly powerful technological devices; the 'availability' of vast information and knowledge resources, hand in hand with the increasing impoverishment of several parts of the planet; an aggravation of the conditions of social exclusion; and the euphemistically named 'digital divide', which condemns millions of young people to new forms of communicational illiteracy.

Recognizing the social construction of youth as a category opens up for a diversity of interpretations and explanations as to who they are, what they do and how they are getting involved in media and communication, and in what ways they are influencing processes of social change through such engagement. Each in its own way, the chapters in this book speak to the relationship between youth, communication and social change. It is a fact that youth today are involved in social change processes in a multitude of ways, through their use of media and communication. The crosscutting approach to development and social change sketched out by Nestor García Canclini (a researcher born in Argentina and based in Mexico, noted for his in-depth study of popular culture and globalization) helps us fixate the analysis of youth engagement.

As mentioned above, García Canclini speaks about 'differences', 'inequalities' and 'disconnections' (Canclini 2006: 81-82). By 'differences' he refers to ethnic, national or gender differences – all categories considered to inform many identity-oriented projects, for example the North Korean youth living and blogging in South Korea, a case dealt with by Jiwon Yoon in this yearbook. By 'inequalities', Garcia-Canclini is referring to the socio-economic inequalities across the globe, as well as within nation-states and locally, that are based on asymmetries produced over time in local contexts. And by 'disconnections', he is referring to the divides that prevent majorities worldwide from connecting to the so-called information society and the globally expanded cultural, health and wellbeing repertoires.

According to García Canclini (2006: 81), "We still know little regarding productive ways of acting simultaneously in these three scenes, and about how they boost one another", a state of things that we took into account in collating the articles for this yearbook.

Inclusive citizenships

As John Gaventa, head of the poverty and social policy team at the Institute of Development Studies (IDS) in Sussex, UK, has said, "engaging with the world is about articulating citizenship" (Gaventa 2005: xii). Enhancing citizenship is about being the 'claimants of development' rather than the beneficiaries. This is precisely the prism through which we propose the case studies in this book should be viewed. In telling their stories, engaging in media production or by using media to establish counter-publics, youth become involved as self-determined subjects pursuing objectives they themselves define, often times regarding social justice.

Approaching the cases in this book from a citizenship perspective is not a question of citizenship in the liberal sense of solely exploring legal rights to vote or to express oneself. We define citizenship as a social practice grounded in everyday experiences, "an emergent concept whose realization will vary across contexts and historical moments" (ibid.). We subscribe to Gaventa's position that citizenship is not just a set of rights and responsibilities "bestowed by the state", but rather "a multi-dimensional concept which includes the agencies, identities and actions of people themselves" (ibid.). Thus, analysing youth as 'claimants for development' in their quest to use media and communicative practices to open spaces of debate, in claiming their rights and representing themselves, becomes the focus of this book.

Naila Kabeer, professorial fellow at IDS and editor of the book 'Inclusive Citizenship – meanings and expressions' (Kabeer, 2005), coined the term 'inclusive citizenship'. In her view, citizenship refers to the strategies of inclusion that people – in our case, youth – apply. Such strategies in action express a set of values and meanings, with cultural, social and economic rights that provide substance to both political and civil rights. Citizenship as a concept concerns justice, recognition, self-determination and solidarity (Kabeer 2005: 3-8).

In this light, we can assess our understanding of communication, more specifically how we conceive of youth-centred communication for the articulation of social change and social justice. We propose to inscribe this question into the growing debate surrounding the concept of 'communication for social change' (Gumucio-Dagron and Tufte 2006). 'Communication for social change' represents a new approach to certain principles derived from the field of participatory communication as developed in Latin America- and also applied in Africa- from the '60s onwards'. To articulate solutions to the development challenges of the 21st century, be they issues of unemployment, political repression, HIV/AIDS or environmental degradation, the best practices of communication for social change will be those that address the root causes of these problems, and that are based on the underlying values of inclusive citizenship.

Four perspectives upon youth, communication and social change

A broad range of questions informs this yearbook's core interest in exploring the dynamic relationship between youth, communication and social change. What is the current situation of youth, particularly marginalized youth, primarily but not exclusively in developing countries? How do governments, media and civil society act in response to the situation of young people? How do youth experience, make use of and engage in civil-society-driven media and communication platforms? What do these media and communication platforms generate/produce, and how socially inclusive are their production processes? What mechanisms are developed to hold governments accountable and transparent regarding youth-related development challenges? And what advocacy strategies do the involved civil society organizations employ, if any?

In organizing the yearbook, we have structured the contributing chapters around four dimensions of youth's engagement with the world through media and communication, offering perspectives on rights, on voice and being heard, on articulating ownership (i.e., youth as subjects in communicative process), and on participation in production processes.

In her chapter, Rossana Reguillo sets the scene by arguing that youth does not comprise a homogeneous aggregate or universal category, regardless of the shared experience of a globalized world that expands the cultural offerings while reducing the possibility of having access to them. Reguillo proposes that analysis of the relationship between youth, communication and social change must take place in the context of the above-stated paradoxical tensions that characterize globalization. Moreover, the author makes a case for reflecting upon the diverse strategies, conditions, contexts and socio-cultural configurations on whose surface communication's sense as a practice, process and product in youth worlds is organized, modelled and modulated. From a situated and historical perspective that draws on Latin American and transnational examples, her chapter explores a diversity of problems and realities relevant to the contemporary youth condition, and their links with communication and social change processes.

Memory and identity: youth communicating for their rights

This section of the yearbook examines different ways in which young people are communicating about and for their rights.

Using a qualitative approach, Antonieta Muñoz-Navarro explores the work of a Chilean NGO to promote human rights among youth, identifying the characteristics of the political identity of a group of young people through a discussion of public participation, the media's representation of human rights issues and the potential of developing their own media.

Florencia Enghel, Cecilia Flachsland and Violeta Rosemberg elaborate on the struggles for justice and memory of the survivors of the Cromañón catastrophe of 2004, in which 194 young people died in a fire during a rock concert in Buenos Aires, Argentina. Identifying the communicational instances drawn from the survivors' efforts, the authors raise questions regarding youth's agency and the role of communication – and rock music – in voicing their needs.

Taking us from South America to Eastern Europe, Iryna Vidanava investigates the role of new media in the context of the repression of civil society and independent media in Belarus through a case study of a popular multimedia magazine developed by young people and aimed at encouraging a young audience to get involved civically. The author suggests that new media is a field in which youth-led democratic opposition has outperformed the regime despite restrictions.

Jiwon Yoon transports us to the border between North and South Korea, and focuses on how youth emigrating from North to South Korea deal with the challenge of adjusting to the cultural and political differences between the countries and cope with discrimination through mediated communication. The author highlights how North Korean refugees use the Internet and the production of documentary films to tell their stories.

Voices of the youth: coping, criticizing and calling for change

This section of the yearbook examines the importance of voice in youth's involvement in social change.

Framing his work within citizen journalism, Rashweat Mukundu looks into the potential to promote empowerment and counteract governmental propaganda through the media of two underground community newsletters developed by Zimbabwean youth.

Based on an empirical study of a series of workshops held by an anti-AIDS youth club in Malawi, Lise Grauenkær Jensen, Mette Grøndahl Hansen and Stine Kromann-Larsen explore to which extent community-based dialogue and expression can foster collective identity and help redress the HIV/AIDS epidemic.

Thomas Tufte, Aran Corrigan, Ylva Ekström, Minou Fuglesang and Datius Rweyemamu take on the HIV/AIDS epidemic from a different perspective, providing an assessment of young people's 'readers' letters' to two NGO-driven magazines widely distributed in Tanzania. The authors examine the relationship between media, voice and change, critically assessing the letters as an incipient expression of articulating voice among Tanzanian youth.

In a shift from Africa to Eurasia, Ece Algan considers the importance of a radio programme and associated fan club in encouraging youth to pursue romantic relationships in Şanlıurfa, Southeast Turkey. Using an ethnographic approach, the author examines the tensions between local traditions, cultural restrictions and openings for change provided by the media.

Youth as subjects – of content, programs, projects and regulations

This section is concerned with youth as subjects within different contexts: discourse, practice and interventions – at the nation-state, student organization or NGO level.

Peter Lemish and Elke Schlote analyse how different types of youth involvement in social change are portrayed in a selection of quality TV programming produced for young audiences in different parts of the world, and suggest that certain depictions may be more likely to support learning about social change processes.

Johan Lagerkvist maps the paradoxical landscape of youth's Internet use in China, which is characterized by the coexistence of civic creativity, innovation and experimentation with self-expression and identity, side by side with what is deemed by many observers to be the world's most sophisticated Internet censorship regime. The author discusses blogging and self-censorship in connection with such a paradox.

Nkosi Martin Ndlela provides an additional view of Zimbabwean youth and their engagement with media for social change, examining how the Zimbabwe National Students Union uses communication to promote good governance, human rights and the empowerment of underprivileged young people. From that perspective, the author explores the role of word-of-mouth mobilization and public rallies.

Robert Huesca calls our attention to the ethical challenges posed by youth-radio training programmes in the US, an area of practice overlooked by research despite its enormous growth during the '90s. Through in-depth interviews with young participants, the author identifies the problems and challenges raised by their experiences.

Youth in processes: participatory production

The final section is a window into young people's participation in media and communication production processes.

Karen Greiner discusses the extent to which the "Scenarios from Africa" process, aimed at educating young people about HIV/AIDS through scriptwriting and film production, has generated youth engagement. Based on research conducted in Senegal, the author aims at demonstrating that allowing participation among youth promotes their agency with regard to health issues.

Ana Zanotti reflects on her practice as facilitator of a project for youth carried out in Misiones, Argentina, the aim of which is to train young people to make videos and create a series of one-minute long pieces on the theme of their rights. The author argues for the importance of dialogue and group-work in teaching media skills to youth.

Claudius Ceccon discusses the work of a Brazilian NGO that provides media education to youth with the aim of raising consciousness regarding their rights as citizens and empowering them to express their voices. The author highlights the relevance of hands-on training and access to technology for media literacy.

In the last chapter, José Paulo de Araújo proposes a framework for assessing youth participation through a case study of yet another Brazilian NGO that offers a communication school for young people, and explores the initiative's impact in terms change at the individual and community level.

Bibliography

Ad Hoc Working Group for Youth and the Millennium Development Goals. Final Report.
García Canclini, Néstor (2006) *Diferentes, desiguales y desconectados/Mapas de la interculturalidad*. Barcelona: Gedisa Editorial.
Gaventa, John (2005) 'Foreword', in Kabeer, Naila (ed.) *Inclusive Citizenship. Meanings and Expressions*. London: Zed Books.
Gumucio-Dagron, Alfonso & Thomas Tufte (eds) (2006) *The Communication for Social Change Anthology. Historical and Contemporary Readings*. New Jersey: The Communication for Social Change Consortium.
Kabeer, Naila (2005) 'Introduction. The Search for Inclusive Citizenship: Meanings and Expressions in an Interconnected World', in Kabeer, Naila (ed.) *Inclusive Citizenship. Meanings and Expressions*. London: Zed Books.
Kabeer, Naila (ed.) (2005) *Inclusive Citizenship. Meanings and Expressions*. London: Zed Books.
Kahn, Richard & Douglas Kellner (2008) 'Youth Culture', in Donsbach, Wolfgang (ed.) *The International Encyclopedia of Communication*. Blackwell: Blackwell Publishing. Reference Online, retrieved 01 July 2008 from http://www.communicationencyclopedia.com/subscriber/tocnode?id=g9781405131995_chunk_g978140513199529_ss2-1
United Nations (2004) *World Youth Report 2003*. New York: United Nations.

Setting the Scene

The Warrior's Code?
Youth, Communication and Social Change

Rossana Reguillo

Abstract

Youth does not comprise a homogeneous aggregate or universal category, regardless of the shared experience of a globalized world that expands the cultural offer while it reduces the possibility of having access to it. The analysis of the relationship between youth, communication and social change must take place in the context of this paradoxical tension: more and better media; increasingly powerful technological devices; the "availability" of vast information and knowledge resources, hand in hand with the increasing impoverishment of several parts of the planet; an aggravation of the conditions of social exclusion; and the euphemistically named "digital divide", which condemns millions of young people to new forms of communicational "illiteracy".

Thus, it is essential to reflect upon the diverse strategies, conditions, contexts and socio-cultural configurations that constitute the platform organizing, modeling and modulating communication's sense as a practice, process and product in youth worlds.

This chapter explores, from a situated and historical perspective, a diversity of youth problems and realities that schematically articulate certain general (non-pure) forms in the contemporary youth condition and its links with communication and social change processes.

Time precedes existence (Ilya Prigogine)

The noun is formed through the accumulation of adjectives (Jorge Luis Borges)

Youth does not respond to a universal category that can include, describe, shape the enormous diversity and asymmetries through which actual young people construct their biographies. Despite the expansion of the globalized world and the increasing interaction between different regions and zones of the planet, youth is far from representing a homogeneous whole.

Youth – as a socially constructed category which is situated, historical and relational – implies that young people are configured as social actors in quite different ways. This matter tends to be rendered invisible by the major international organizations, the national states and the mass media, which name them by alluding to "a subject" that seems to share traits, characteristics, knowledge and experiences explained as from their age range – i.e., youth understood as a biological category limited to an age range.

The complexity of youth worlds requires that we carefully problematise the elements that intervene in the configuration of the youth condition – from the structural dimensions to the subjective ones. If we assume that "being young" is fundamentally a social classification, then the classification implies the establishment of a (complex) system of differences. The articulation of those differences is what gives precise characteristics, contents, limits and meaning to "being young". Grossberg (1992) indicates that "Articulation is the construction of one set of relations out of another; it often involves delinking or disarticulating connections in order to link or rearticulate others. Articulation is a continuous struggle to reposition practices within a shifting field of forces, to redefine the possibilities of life by redefining the field of relations -the context- within which a practice is located[1]".

Youth cannot be disconnected from the context or the confrontation between multiple actors (the state, the school, the churches, political parties, the media, academia, and in a privileged way, the market) aimed at rearticulating the meaning of "being young". Besides allowing the necessary de-essentializing of the concept of "youth", this perspective contributes to introducing the principle of complexity and combating the strong tendency towards metropolitan ethnocentrism. Through categories such as "social moratorium"[2], metropolitan ethnocentrism assumes that, because of their condition, all young people enter a space of privileges and exceptions that entitle them to living on the fringes of the responsibilities, commitments, anguishes of the adult world.

Today, young subjects face a paradox. On the one hand, globalization, jointly with technological development, has undoubtedly increased the cultural offers. But on the other hand, it is equally true that the possibilities for access are reduced or restricted. In that sense, the thinking and analysis regarding the relationship between youth, communication and social change must be located precisely in the tension produced by this paradox. I.e., more and better means for communication, increasingly powerful technological devices, "availability" of enormous resources for information and knowledge, in coexistence with the increasing impoverishment of large areas of the planet, the aggravated conditions of exclusion, and the so called "digital divide". The divide condemns millions of young people to new forms of communicational "illiteracy", or to put it in other terms, to the emergence of two types of youth, paraphrasing García Canclini (2004). One is "disconnected and unequal", with limited or no access to the instruments of the net and technology, and even more serious, to health services and job security. Informalized, its demands and needs belong to a fully structural logic: employment, education, housing; or in other words, basic aspirations of social justice and wellbeing. The other one is well situated, connected and globalized, with access to technology and fundamental satisfier factors such as education, employment and health.

How should we tackle the question regarding social change and youth leadership when we know that e.g. in Latin America and the Caribbean youth population is the one more affected by poverty defined by the level of familial income? In 2002, 41% of the young people aged 15 to 29 lived in poverty, and 15% in extreme poverty. In Bolivia, Guatemala, Honduras, Nicaragua, Paraguay and Peru, over 50% of the young people live in poverty. That said there are important differences between urban and rural areas: One of each three young urban residents was poor, in contrast with half in rural areas. Moreover, the probability of rural youth being poor was 64% higher than for those in urban areas in the region (OPS, 2007). Such data becomes crucially important when crosschecked against figures indicating that 28% of the region's population are young people aged 10 to 24 (OPS, 2007). These young people represent a high proportion of the total population in the region's poorest countries, such as Haiti and Nicaragua (35% of the total). In Guatemala, Honduras, Paraguay and Dominican Republic, 30% to 35% of the population is young, compared with 23% in Cuba, Puerto Rico and Uruguay.

This demographic composition indicates that young people represent an enormous challenge for the educational, health, labour, legal and recreational systems, and certainly an unavoidable task for national states. The State of the World Population 2007 report states: "…the battle for the Millennium Development Goals is being fought in the cities of developing countries. Young people will be in the forefront. Success depends on how well cities, countries and the international community strengthen and support them" (UNFPA 2007).

The militaristic metaphor used by the United Nations is absolutely revealing; the assumption is that there is a war and that the soldiers in the first line of combat are and will be young. Inasmuch as there is no innocent metaphor, it is worrisome – to say the least- that the UN, through its Population Fund, considers youth as "soldiers", "warriors" in a war that they did not ask for. Military experts know about the importance of the first line of combat and of what it means. It is a strategic line of defence (or attack), made of the toughest but also the more expendable combatants. The Liberian child soldiers gathered in the "Small Boys Unit" of the National Patriotic Front of Liberia (NPFL) know it all too well. The NPFL recruited more than 5,000 child soldiers during the country's first civil war between 1989 and 1996[3].

The metaphor of the battle that humanity will have to fight with youth at the forefront is also distressing in that it raises questions regarding what experts[4] term "strategic battle", waged in a foreseen and calculated way, and prepared through the setting of important, clear and decisive objectives, and a subsequent strategy. The diversity, complexity and multidimensionality of the battlefronts in which youth must fight, and the intermittent, ambiguous and many times lukewarm calls from the international organizations vis-à-vis these scenarios raise serious doubts regarding this battle being strategic. In that sense, I find the metaphor unfortunate, especially in that it places an enormous responsibility on young people.

> More than 1 billion girls and boys around the World are in their second decade of life. About 85 per cent of these young people live in developing countries. Young people face enormous challenges to learn, form relationships, shape their identities and acquire the social and practical skills they need to become active and productive adults. Adults, parents, decision makers and the world community at large have a moral and legal obligation to ensure the rights of adolescents and help them develop their strengths in a supportive and safe environment (UNICEF, UNFPA, WHO, 2003).

The challenges listed, which it is assumed young people face, pales in front of the realities that many of them experience, whereby the "acquisition of practical and social abilities to become active and productive adults" is not enough to open up a horizon. They barely live in a state of the most elemental survival[5].

Beyond this, the way in which these organizations represent young people as subjects in transit towards becoming "productive adults" is perhaps the greater obstacle to intervening in an adequate, respectful and efficient way on the situations affecting them. For that reason, many governmental and non-governmental organizations choose to implement compensatory strategies or policies, such as e.g. temporary study grants or labour training. All those approaches do is temporarily rebalance the adverse conditions for youth. In other cases, institutions intervene to adjust youth trajectories to the dominant models – e.g. technical schools that make them eligible for precarious or "flexible" jobs.

This perspective, instrumental and myopic, fails to incorporate as a reflexive element the fact that young people do not experience their condition as "transitory" or as a rite of passage[6] towards what "really matters" – i.e., from the perspective of these organizations, to become a productive adult. Urban youth usually experience their condition as a "state" and not a "process". They usually settle themselves in a constant present, largely because their ability to imagine a future has been expropriated by the recurring structural crises (Reguillo 2000; Valenzuela 2008). Throughout my by now long research trajectory around youth cultures in different regions, I have found that both their narratives and their aspirations are characterized by such belief in the present – being sometimes joyful, and at other times distressed or resigned, depending on their place in the social structure.

Young people are not "outside" the social realm: their forms of identity adscription, their representations, their aspirations, their dreams, their bodies, are constructed and configured in the "zones of contact" with a society to which they belong. Bourdieu (1990) said that "youth is but a word". Regrettably, contemporary signs seem to indicate that that "noun", in Borges' terms, is increasingly turning into the accumulation of excluding adjectives, and is increasingly held responsible for facing a battle in disadvantageous conditions.

That is why I consider it fundamental to stand up to these normative and adult-centric perspectives through the analysis of the (differential) scenarios. Three strong dimensions cannot be ignored in any serious attempt to think about youth and their potential leadership in contexts of social change:

a. the processes of precarization/informalization of youth's biographies, dynamics, circuits and ideals;

b. the withdrawal of the social state, and the strengthening of the punitive state;

c. the discredit of modern institutions – the school, political parties, labour unions, businesses- as guarantors of "successful" socializing.

These processes have been widely documented through different instruments, both qualitative and quantitative, and their impact on the construction of youth identities is differential, as I have tried to emphasize, depending on young people's place in the social structure.

In the first case, it is essential to assume that structural precariousness is also vital, subjective precariousness. The instability and contingency of many of the structural processes set the limits and define the horizon of possibilities in terms of constructing a biography, one's self. The worst precariousness is the one that prevents the subject from expressing him or herself with certainty.

As regards the state's role, we see how every day social policies weaken and the role that the state should have becomes blurred. To the same extent, the so-called "zero tolerance" policy grows, criminalising youth (mainly the poor ones) and turning them into the object of vigilance and sanction. This logic underlies the discussion in different countries regarding the reduction of the age of criminal responsibility, already passed as a law in Chile and Brazil. In Chile, e.g., a young person can be convicted as from the age of 14, while you are still not considered a citizen at that age. The option is for the police "solution", leaving aside, or paying little attention to, everything related with guarantees and access for young people. Such a punitive logic embeds this century's atmospheres.

Last, when I point to discredit and distrust in institutions as a third dimension central to understanding and articulating youth leadership, I am referring to the difficulty of imagining processes of democratic change when young people do not find reasons to become involved in formal mechanisms.

Instability and contingency

It is impossible to leave aside the evidence of a large measure of exclusion of (certain) numerous youth actors from the spaces considered crucial and substantive for the sphere of social reproduction. The unemployment index[7], school desertion, the straightforward impossibility to access formative spaces[8], and the strengthening of governments' punitive policies on the one hand, and on the other hand the attribution of guilt to young people, accused in general of hedonism, non-involvement, lack of interest and of defendable motives, tend to the configuration of a "normative" thinking. Such thinking is quite concerned with producing strategies and answers to counteract exclusion, as well as with intervening youth's ideals. Its core is connected to the discussion around the breakup of the "traditional" spaces of youth participation/inclusion: school, the working world and formal politics.

I do not disregard the fact that until further notice, the workplace and school remain central institutions for the production/reproduction of social life, and that electoral democracy is an important platform to foster the transformation of our societies. Notwithstanding, I perceive a tendency to situating these three dimensions as a given, thus shifting the full weight of the analysis (or the intervention) towards what I will provisionally call "inclusion no matter how". This ends up in a pact with the model or project of society that had provoked the exclusion and marginalization of youth in the first place. In that way, we fall into an instrumental characterization that proposes "education for the workplace; work as the means to achieve a normalized citizenship; citizenship as a stable category of rights and duties". Such position would be unquestionable if we were in what Bourdieu termed "the period of stable trajectories" (1990), and/or if the trilogy education-work-citizenship was available to most of the world's youth population.

Two issues are relevant here. First, the lack of problematization or critical void – usually prevalent in these positions- as regards the structure, as if the school, the working world and the sphere of politics were homogeneous and static contents and the problem was how to expand their reach, criticising their deficiencies and "bringing" youth into those spheres. Second, an insufficient discussion around the depletion of the meaning placed by societies on those instances, which causes, among other effects, the invisibility in the debate of young people's right to say no to school, to work, to politics, in their current characteristics and expressions[9].

The excessive stress given to "inclusion no matter how" ends up stifling youth's criticism – not always explicit- of the prevailing socio-political model, and by extension holds off the (urgent and necessary) critique of the institutions.

The "not in this way" expressed by many young people calls for more and deeper analyses, since it must also reach the institutions – school, market, political parties, government areas- which accept interpellation as regards their structural deficiency but are unable to take on the deeper crisis of meaning that is shaking them up[10].

Precariousness and inadequacy of the self

Within this logic, and always aiming at arguing for the need for a complex analysis of the youth condition, I propose that, without denying the increasing leadership of many young people in projects and processes of social and cultural change, it is important to examine the intersections among the above-mentioned dimensions. I will emphasize them again, given their centrality in order to understand the contemporary youth condition:

a. the structural (poverty, exclusion, bio-insecurity) and subjective precariousness, which refers to the enormous difficulties experienced by many young people in order to construct their biographies, linked to an accelerated deinstitutionalisation and disaffiliation from the dynamics and institutions that in the course of modernity operated as spaces for access and inclusion;

b. the withdrawal of the social state, and

c. the constant failures of institutions (school, political parties, family) as guarantors of social inclusion or makers of successful socializations and construction of citizenship.

Structural precariousness, self precariousness, deficiency of social policies and breakup of the institutions, intersecting in different ways according to local contexts, gender, urban or rural settings, religious dimensions, shape and materialize the dynamics through which young people become political actors and subjects.

It is not easy to apprehend these processes. Thus, it is necessary to disaggregate them in areas that allow grounding the analysis and possible interpretation. Vis-à-vis the epochal moment that we are going through, there are five key areas for the analysis of the youth condition:

a. Access to education (unequal in terms of socio-economic sector and gender)

b. The market's inability to generate "formal" employment for the increasing youth demand

c. Spatial segregation

d. Combined discrimination

e. Circuits of violence, organized crime and drugs

f. Cultural atmospheres

The first three refer explicitly to one of the most pressing problems for youth, access, which is a determining factor for their participation in processes of social change. Without equal access to education, work, health and dignified housing, or to put it briefly, to biosecurity (what guarantees life), it is difficult for youth to take up a citizen leadership which is structurally denied to them.

E.g., as regards the pair education-employment, the impact of unemployment is higher among those young people with fewer studies. Although data from different international organizations (OIT, OCDE, among others) indicate that the relationship between studies and employability has decreased, it is also true that access to education helps counteract labour vulnerability. The crisis of the educational field in the more impoverished countries, which leaves many young people out of any chance to pursue high school studies, combines with a labour market that tends to grant higher security to those with professional knowledge. But the other side of this problem is the possibility that faced with employment reduction, young people with high qualifications will choose to leave their home country and try their luck in other places. That poses a perverse problem for national communities, which will loose that capital for the projection of better structural conditions for their societies[11].

In the case of Latin America and the Caribbean, according to the Economic Commission for Latin America (CEPAL 2004), the youth unemployment rate was 16.6%, while the rate for adults was 5.4%. It is obvious that the market's conditions make youth vulnerable more strongly, and that there are serious problems in terms of guaranteeing youth's social inclusion through work. The question we must ask here is: if they are not at school because school cannot attend to them, and they are not in the labour market because it cannot absorb them, then where are these young people – 26.8% of youth aged 20 to 24- that do not study nor work?

The high spatial marginalization to which many young people are doomed adds to this chain of restricted accesses. The segregation is both urban and rural – each with their own specificities- and translates into higher difficulties in terms of accessing minimum satisfier factors, as well as an increase of violent interactions, crime and vulnerability.

Combined discrimination has to do with the convergence of factors that add to the chain of poverty and exclusion among youth: age mainly, but also gender, looks and/or belonging to an ethnic group. All available data corroborates that age is a factor that determines precariousness in terms of employment. The International Labor Organization (OIT 2004) provides evidence of the fact that, in a crisis, businesses fire mainly those newly arrived to the labour market. As regards gender, data indicates that for Latin America and the Caribbean the regional unemployment rate is 22% for young women and 14% for young men, without comparing these figures with those for adult men and women. The threefold marginality (Reguillo 2003) indicates that being young, poor and a woman increases the risk of discrimination in processes of social inclusion.

On the other hand, data indicates that a country's ethnic majority is better suited in order to find employment. In the US, e.g., estimates indicated that approximately one third of young male workers and one fourth of black teenagers were unemployed in 1999 – a much higher rate than for youth in general (OIT 2004).

The less visible side of the problems of access and combined discrimination is the atmosphere that surrounds them: the discourse, accepted and taken as a common opinion, that tends to make youth fully responsible for this situation. The prevailing reasoning tends to blame young people for the precariousness of their own lives.

In my research work I have verified how youth from different social strata assume as their own deficiency, as a punishable deficit, their "aspect", their "style", their lack of "disposition" and "capital" (in Bourdieu's sense) and their difficulties to accommodate the logics of the dominant society. Many young people are dragged into accessory or resigned acceptance of those things that stigmatise them, marginalize them, lead them to precariousness, and exclude them (Reguillo 2004).

That is why, in order to understand the youth condition and its complex web of dimensions and elements, we must point to the weight of culture in the subjective and inter-subjective configuration of social actors. In that sense, the biggest adversary for youth empowerment is their own and fatalist assumption of their social, political and occupational "inadequacy".

I have intentionally left for the end of this path the issue of circuits of violence, because I am convinced that, if current tendencies are to continue, it is and will be one of the main problems that young people in a situation of precariousness will face.

Today, the monopoly of the legitimate violence exerted by national states stands opposite to the outburst of several violent "dialects", which are entering the social scene and contesting the social pact. I'm referring to the violence integrated to structural problems, such as the pair poverty-exclusion, but also to those generated and managed as from a challenge to legality and the crisis of legitimacy. That is to say, violence that cannot be explained merely through the structural factors already discussed, but which is rather connected to a severe crisis of the social pact.

In other words, we are facing an increasing disintegration of the social bond, which strikes in different ways, never gentle, the sphere of youth conviviality (society communicating, the "ways of being together")[12].

Worldwide, the highest violence rates among youth are to be found in Africa and Latin America. Studies reveal that for each young person killed, 20 to 40 non-fatal victims of the same age require hospital treatment (OMS 2006).

How can we explain for instance the 468 children and teenagers killed in Guatemala in 2007? We cannot isolate this violence against children and teenagers from the history of the armed conflict in the country, the state genocide[13] and the poverty rates. During the first four months of 2008, 420 people have died a violent death, including 11 high-school students. Between January and February 2008, 2.024 Guatemalans were deported while trying to emigrate towards better conditions of life, and the Mutual Support Group (in Spanish Grupo de Apoyo Mutuo) (GAM 2008) reports the return of militias in that country and documents that in just one municipality, San Juan Sacatepequez, 150 paramilitary groups have been detected. In Solalá, 6 people were lynched in February 2008[14].

In Brazil, the main cause of death among young males aged 5 to 19 is homicide (40% of the total). The same cause is placed second among women in the same age range (OPS 2007).

In Mexico (although this also happens in other countries in the region), the drug cartels are fighting heavily for the control of territories and new routes for moving drugs. In this battle, the recruitment of young people is an important strategy, which according to certain experts in organized crime is provoking a more violent scene, given the lack of experience of the new hit men. "The new hit men are young people aged 15 to 20"[15]. "The drug cartels have taken advantage of the lack of values and family integration in order to nurture their criminal ranks; in regions such as Nuevo Laredo and Matamoros (Tamaulipas), in Badiraguato and Culiacán (Sinaloa), the delinquents are good and the police is bad", says Paulino Jiménez Hidalgo, a researcher of the Police Higher Academy. "The life of a drug lord is an example for them and they aspire to the economic power and recognition of the group they have joined (drug trafficking); however, their lack of experience becomes apparent through the excessive violence they exert on their victims", according to Hidalgo. He adds: "the lifespan of the new recruits is very short…; they are killed by members of a hostile organization or sent to jail, and that is why they accept to act as hit men, and the violence they exert is in order to prove their worth"[16].

I do not share the idea that young people enter drug trafficking because of a lack of values and familial disintegration, as repeated tediously by some experts and many politicians. Such a "moral" and psychology-ridden understanding is simplistic and myopic, in that it denies, avoids or renders invisible the structural conditions in which many young people try to put together and construct their biographies, because it remains unaware of the context or atmosphere in which drug-trafficking grows and becomes more powerful.

The drug lord grows where the state has deserted its responsibilities and poverty, lack of opportunities and the survival of the fittest rule. Its power lies not only in its power to kill, but also in the fact that it proposes a life, a future that, even if short and dated, warrants a minimum of access for many young people in the region. For many young people located "south of modernity", to paraphrase Martín-Barbero, these scenarios are not apocalyptic or catastrophic, but rather "everyday life"[17].

From warriors to citizens

So far, I have focused mainly on Latin America. At this point, I would want to propose a geopolitical displacement and look into youth's tiredness and disenchantment in relation to institutions and reality from a global framework that goes beyond the "quantitative" problem of the lack of spaces or access – even if that represents a crucial problem. To think about youth participation in processes of democratization and strengthening of human rights and citizenship does not imply merely solving issues of exclusion or marginalization of an economic or structural character. The severity and complexity of the contemporary situation call for linking reflection (and action) to the sphere of culture and communication.

The cultural ebullience in many youth collectives which are increasingly visible within broader social movements (indigenous, ecological, pro-peace, etc.) – e.g. musical expressions, the production of literature and poetry, artisan small businesses, the return of graffiti as a tool for protesting and the constant aesthetic invention- is an indication of a political will that does not express itself in politics' usual languages.

To be able to grasp and foster these alternatives, the first task is to denaturalize the concept of youth and take responsibility for the diversity it encloses, in connection with both their identity choices and the type of society in which they function. Youth does not come down to a biological category of a lineal type.

In my view, the challenge at this level is to analyze youth participation within social change in the context of the critical theory of reflexive modernity (Lash, 1997) that describes present time as a moment in which modernity, with all its excesses, is capable of reflecting upon, and critiquing, itself (18). In other words, I think that the analysis and understanding of youth leadership, usually understood more as "action" than as a position[19], cannot remain centred in the uncritical reproduction of modern structures whose structural and symbolic capacity are reaching the point of exhaustion.

Undoubtedly, despite the difficult situation that many young people are experimenting, youth participation is increasing in diverse social processes in which they are speaking up and have seized communication's tools to put them to work in ways that defy the dominant understanding of "politics". Perhaps, in line with Beck (2002), we could say that today youth practices a negation of politics that is highly political.

Three analytical instruments are essential to illuminate (in Walter Benjamin's sense) the horizon against which these warriors become citizens in their search of a different society:

a. The so-called Penguins' Revolution, which in 2006 unexpectedly hit the streets in Chile to claim their rights as students and to intervene directly in national politics;

b. The growth and strengthening of the blogosphere, which has become an alternate space for communicative interaction; and

c. Youth's unquestionable participation in movements and protests with a global reach, e.g. the "no" to the Iraq war.

Taking the streets: the penguins

The protests of the Chilean high-school students in April and June 2006 point out two central issues for our discussion here.

On the one hand, their sudden irruption in the public space indicates the re-emergence of the category of "students" in Latina America, at a point in time when this form of youth aggregation seemed to be far-gone, or had been exhausted when it came to social processes beyond those strictly bound to school. The relevance of the Penguins' Revolution lies in its capacity to make prominent the mediation of student identity for political activity or social participation. In complex ways, these young students brought to the social scene an essential debate regarding the role of education as a requisite for social change.

When it seemed like the excesses in the streets (broken shop windows, looting, street lighting destroyed), which led to the arrest of 400 young people, could destroy the movement, the penguins distanced themselves from them. In a skilled political move characteristic of "high politics", by mid-June 2007 a group of them entered the UNESCO head office pacifically to deliver a document with their critical remarks and requests. That leap from the national scene to the sphere of international policies is essential, in that it reinstates the centrality of education as a privileged space for the advancement of democracy and participation. UNESCO supported the penguins' demands, acknowledged their initiative and stated: "education is a strategic public good"[20]. When I refer to "high politics", I am noting these young people's ability to identify their interlocutors in a world that goes beyond the action range of national states.

On the other hand, this movement emphasizes a type of youth agency that certain social discourse tends to obliterate: the ability to articulate and support a set of political demands and consider themselves legitimate interlocutors of the state, society, and in general other political actors with full weight. The Penguins' Revolution, to which more than 600,000 students adhered, termed as such because of the uniform worn by the students, forced President Bachelet to negotiate in public and rendered evident the fact that the understanding of systems is not alien to youth worlds.

The Chilean case, however, goes beyond the Latin American region, and its emergence is closely connected to the French case. Paris in flames in late 2005 and the subsequent crisis in March 2006 following the government's First Employment Contract legislation were events led by French young people. In the first case, it was marginal, poor, immigrant young people, eventually joined by young students, workforce and "prospective unemployed" in the second case. They all function as epochal symptoms of the same emergence: the crack of the strong monopoly of formal and factual powers in terms of defining education (as training) and work (understood as exchange value in a fierce market). Today, an increasingly critical – and despairing- voice stands up to them, which goes hand in hand with what Beck accurately and bluntly terms "the wounded dignity of superfluous populations" (2007).

This type of youth agency contests those narratives that consider young people doomed to the marginalization of their own biographies.

Seizing the word: bloggers

The cybernetic web and the blogosphere "republic" are "worlds" of youth agency that require high technological skills and have thus predominantly interested analysts. Or in other words, the technological dimension has taken over the analytical space, to the detriment of other areas that set these worlds in motion.

Vis-à-vis processes of social change, I find certain central dimensions that I will bring together under three points.

a) *The strengthening of the self as author*, which destabilizes the monopoly of knowledge either "legitimate"/"authorized" or irradiated/emitted by "accredited" centres. Bloggers, cybernauts, do not ask for permission. It is a space in which young people have access to a position of authority, of empowerment, as from a 'self' that is not shy to take the risk of making a statement. Most definitely, a counter-argument could be that there are problems and that in many cases the sites or languages of blogs end up reproducing schemes opposed to democracy, excluding, racist and xenophobic – all which is true. But even on those thresholds it is possible to find a voice introducing a critical note, a disagreement, and a calm or ignited call for another possible point of view.

Breaking the hierarchical system established by literate modernity, young bloggers find a key space to grant value to two issues that are essential for the constitution of their (new?) subjectivities. First, the possibility to choose on their own the problems, processes and/or events introduced in their individual biographies with a historical nature. Such possibility is in line with a growing tendency towards getting involved in intermittent, contingent causes, which signify, keep their distance from the institutionalized, partisan participation logics and refer to what is "personally" relevant. In that sense, one's own name (even if a *nickname*) matters. This connects to the following dimension that I deem central to these processes.

b) *The dissolution of the boundaries between what is objective and what is subjective.* Analyzing several youth blogs, it is possible to point out that there is continuity in this way of tackling this categorical separation, resulting from modernity. In that sense, if feminists said "the private is political", the blogs' movement could be characterized by the statement "subjective, personal, emotional, everyday matters shape politics". It seems to me that the relationship between everyday life and public world established through the blogs' dynamics indicates the incipient emergence of a subject that politicizes subjectivity and deconsecrates the hierarchical system through which modernity configured the space of an authority that enunciates.

c) Youth's ability to articulate relationships that go beyond territorial movements and render globalization into something other than an economic concept or a socio-cultural metaphor. The creation of cyber-identities that thrive on diversity and the planetary conversation that through a personal logbook decentre and deterritorialise the meanings produced contribute to "produce estrangement", which from my perspective is an essential requirement in order to produce reflexivity. In other words, having access to other views of the world contributes to denaturalizing the view on one's own world, which makes possible a level of reflection hard to reach when the world is circumscribed to the reproduction of local or nearby dynamics, structures and meanings.

Seizing the world: alter-egos in globalization

As regards the analyzers that I propose here as irruptions in the space disputes for the creation of new social understandings of life or the world, I find that the protest movements with a global reach, and the presence or leadership of young people in them, bring to mind the emergence of a new political cosmopolitism among youth. Its native land is the world, and its strength lies in its (seeming) absence of structure, its intermittence, and the multiple nodes in which its utopia is anchored. And we know all too well that nothing annoys or maddens power more than the lack of limits where to set its domains.

From the Seattle counter-summit in 1999, to the planetary demonstrations against the Iraq invasion in 2003, young people have shown they are capable of organizing and taking action at unimagined scales. With topics that range from economy to the environment, from peace to sustainable development, in the gigantic wave of young voices rising against the predominant state of affairs it is possible to recognize the imbrications of new and old forms of politics. Without doubt, participation in these processes has implied for many young people fast-paced and profound learning experiences in which their mastery of technology, their ability to use communication, their speed to process information, intersect the forms, languages, strategies and dynamics of more traditional politics. Even though the knowledge acquired becomes strengths, it is important to consider that the actors and institutions that hold the power against which these young people rebel resort to "conventional" containment and deprivation strategies. Using an extreme image, we could say that power responds to text messages and chat discussions with tanks, bazookas and imprisonment. Youth agency draws strength from the use of communicational and technological gadgets, and weakens when communicative mediation is exhausted and participation calls for the body.

The dilemma – the central question as regards these forms of youth empowerment – rests on the possibility of transforming such agency into citizenship potential.

In any case, the three processes that I have tried to distinguish as spaces, territories, spheres for a determined participation of youth strongly indicate the emergence of a young subject that resists becoming a warrior fighting a battle which is not his or hers. On the contrary, he/she takes on the strategies and codes of an agent that mobilises and manages, with the resources at hand, an "action" space involving identity and everyday life. From the anchored and situated student of the Chilean case to the seemingly anonymous producer and user of technologies in order to convene, support and say, we are witnessing a reformulation of culture in individual action.

However, the situation is not simple, because as I have tried to argue, the unevenness, lags and brutal differentiations among those young people that can consider themselves agents of social change, and those that are in fact sentenced to fighting daily for their survival are abysmal. On this basis, the analytical distinction is crucial.

By way of conclusion: the opaqueness of the heroic tale

In the belief that theoretical efficacy is not possible without ethnographic soundness, I return to the "Mexican situation" and the quantitative and qualitative analysis that I have been able to put together (Reguillo 2007). I do not think that Mexico is the "natural" space that would entitle me to speak without suspicion, i.e. that my territorial membership would become some sort of credential granting me reliability and truthfulness, or better still, granting trustworthiness to knowledge: on the contrary. Ethnographic density makes it possible to place the questions in a broad-spectrum socio-political framework, considering two basic issues. On the one hand, the harassment and invalidation of critical thinking by agents and policies inspired by neoliberals, which win communicative spaces and gain legitimacy[21]; on the other hand, the revision of academic knowledge's role and efficacy in the construction and configuration of the social project. Thus, when I refer to the "Mexican" situation, I am at the same time intending to set in place a map of questions that go beyond the enclosed margin of territory and nation.

Addressing an audience in Tokyo in October 1989 to discuss his study *Distinction,* French sociologist Pierre Bourdieu said: "In speaking of France, I will still be talking to you about Japan" (Bourdieu 1997). His statement does not seem to imply the sometimes-involuntary superiority that tends to be manifest in Eurocentric thinking, which takes the empirical reality of a region or a country as a parameter for universal analysis, but rather the honest concern of an intellectual for the relationships between particularism and universality, between abstraction and concreteness. It resorts to the need to "immerse oneself in the particularity of an empirical reality, historically situated and dated, as the way to grasp the deeper logic of the world" (ibid). In that sense, the invariant in that structure, that deep logic, according to Bourdieu, "is not found at first sight, especially when the gaze belongs to a lover of the exotic, i.e. of *picturesque differences*" (ibid). Thus, paraphrasing Bourdieu, I'll say: "In speaking of Mexico, I will still be talking to you about the world".

In the first place, I can confirm that, despite differences in terms of gender, age ranges and socio-economic strata, Mexican youth shares the bewilderment against political matters. In ways that are differentiated but equally dramatic, Mexican young people cannot seem to find institutional spaces where to express or channel their concerns and aspirations. This is not a minor issue, in that the lack of "representation" of youth's voice implies an absence of institutional mechanisms to stimulate and guarantee their social inclusion in the case of the more vulnerable and underprivileged. We know that the despair and disbelief shared by many young people have different faces and reaches. Taking those differences into account, it is important to consider the fact that some of them experience extremely adverse conditions.

The following is an example. On the one hand we have Mexican rural youth, which has access to consumer goods mainly through the piracy market, inclined towards self-administered justice, unsatisfied with its achievements, more conservative and authoritarian as regards cultural changes, and strongly puzzled in terms of its possibilities of action in the political sphere. On the other hand, urban youth of middle and high strata, participating in global consumption patterns, feeling confident about the future and in general satisfied with its achievements, although almost as puzzled vis-à-vis the issue of its participation in the public space.

The substantial illegitimacy of formal politics' actors, and a belief in democracy as a form of management to improve people's conditions which is barely enough, and almost nil as regards civic counterweight for factual powers set the stage in which young Mexicans become responsible for dealing with their own biographies.

The "disconnected and unequal", (García Canclini 2004) tend to seek shelter among the certainties provided by families and community, somehow more reliant on what could be called "human capital". Those favoured and already included seem to ground their certainties on the benefits derived from being connected to the globalized world. The difference becomes evident: private, emotional and sympathetic support as opposed to regulated and institutionalized support.

In this context, and despite the fact that I am referring to a "local" case, I think that the main question is how to produce, favour and circulate mechanisms that go together with social and cultural changes. How to configure a discourse that does not turn youth into warriors of the Bushido code[23], but rather provides real support to the socio-emotional, socio-economic, socio-political practices necessary to counteract the inequity in terms of the challenges faced by youth and the symbolic orientations that should function as resources for action.

To foster the heroic narrative (first line of combat soldiers) in which thousands of young people who are disconnected must fight against exclusion, marginalization and disenchantment does nothing but increase the responsibility of the isolated individual, whom only relying on his or her integrity and "military" virtues will be able to overcome adversity.

Translated from Spanish by *Florencia Enghel*

Notes

1. See also Bauman's very interesting analysis of this formulation in The individualized society (2001).
2. Alluding to the "exception" period granted to youth as an abstract and universal category, which frees them from the responsibilities of the adult world.

3. Canalsolidari.org (Communication for social change), 'Los niños soldados liberianos en primera línea de fuego' (Liberian children in the first line of combat) online at
4. E.g. Thucydides, Machiavelli, Rommel, Churchill or Bhttp://www.canalsolidari.org/web/noticies/noticia/?id_noticia=3692rzezinski.
5. E.g., according to CEPAL (2004), in Latin America there were in 2002 58 million poor young people -7,6 million more than in 1990, of which 21,2 million were in extreme poverty or destitute (800 thousand more than in 1990).
6. For a critique in this sense see Reguillo (2000).
7. According to OIT (2004), there are in the world 88 million young people unemployed -47% of which in total unemployment.
8. According to CEPAL (2004), in Latin America 80% of urban young people come from households where parents have a, educational capital which is not enough to access well-being, which tends to reproduce inequalities and educational exclusion.
9. The "outraged surprise" of political or business actors who cannot understand why young people reject training processes or enslaving and poorly paid employment constantly appears in the public space.
10. For a discussion of the crisis of meaning see Berger, P. and Luckmann, T. (1997) Modernidad, pluralismo y crisis de sentido (Modernity, plurality and the crisis of meaning), Barcelona: Paidós Studio.
11. According to PNUD, 450 thousand new Arab university graduates moved to Europe and the US.
12. In Maffesoli's early formulation (1990), then highly developed by Jesús Martín Barbero (e.g. 1998), who refers precisely to the notion of "a society's ways of being together".
13. Of the killings that took place between 1960 and 1996, 90% of the crimes were exerted by the Guatemalan army.
14. See http://www.adital.com.br/site/noticia.asp?lang=ES&cod=32059.
15. In the last 20 years Brazil has seen an increase in youth violence, mainly due to drug trafficking. During that time, the amount of young people imprisoned because of drug traffick-related crimes went from 100 in 1980 to 1,584 in 2000. See Ferraz (2006).
16. See 'Sicarios jóvenes causan violencia' (Young hit men cause violence) in Excelsior, December 9, 2007.
17. I am borrowing here the beautiful title of a book by Jesús Martín Barbero (2001) in which he discusses the gaps, differences and inequalities of the different types of modernity.
18. For an analysis of these elements see Reguillo (2002).
19. I have analyzed elsewhere these elements based on quantitative data indicating that in the Mexican case young people are much more interested in "causes" and "positions" than in participating in organizations. See Reguillo (2002b).
20. Interested readers should review the Chilean press corresponding to that period, especially the newspaper La tercera.
21. E.g., insistence on limiting university to machinery that renders students into professionals for the reproduction of members-bodies submissive to the market's needs. This happens through state policies that cut research budgets-particularly certain types of research.
22. Bushido is the code or way of the Samurai warrior, normative and strongly codified. Who chooses this path must practice a series of prescriptive virtues in order to transcend, centre don his own effort and persistence. Thus, change depends only on the individual's strength that, in embracing this doctrine, is capable of "rising above the masses of people that fear action".

References

Bauman, Zygmunt (2001) *La sociedad individualizada* [The individualized society]. Madrid: Cátedra.

Beck, Ulrich (comp.) (2002) *Hijos de la libertad* [Freedom's children]. México: Fondo de Cultura Económica.

Beck, Ulrich (2007) 'La revuelta de los superfluos', [The rebellion of the superfluous], *El País*, Madrid, November 27, available at http://www.elpais.com/articulo/opinion/revuelta/superfluos/elpporopi/20051127elpepiopi_7/Tes

Bourdieu, Pierre (1990) 'La juventud no es más que una palabra' [Youth is but a word], *Sociología y cultura* [Sociology and culture]. México: CNCA-Grijalbo.

Bourdieu, Pierre (1997) *Capital cultural, escuela y espacio social* [Cultural capital, school and social space]. México: Siglo XXI Editores.

CEPAL (2004) *La Juventud en Iberoamérica: Tendencias y urgencias* [Youth in Ibero-America: tendencies and urgent matters]. Santiago de Chile.

Ferraz, Ana Flávia (2006) *En el blanco de muchas voces. Un análisis de la criminalidad juvenil en Brasil* [The target of many voices. An analysis of youth criminality in Brazil]. Guadalajara: ITESO.

GAM (2008) *Informe sobre la situación de los Derechos Humanos y hechos de violencia ocurridos en mayo del 2008* [Report on the Human Rights situation and violent events in May 2008] online at http://www.gam.org.gt/public/gam-publica.htm

García Canclini, Néstor (2004) *Diferentes, desiguales y desconectados. Mapas de la interculturalidad* [Different, unequal and disconnected. Mapping intercultural territory]. Barcelona: Gedisa.

Grossberg, Lawrence (1992) *We Gotta Get Out of this Place: Popular Conservatism and Postmodern Culture*. London: Routledge.

Lash, Scott (1997) La reflexividad y sus dobles: estructura, estética, comunidad [Reflexivity and its Doubles: Structure, Aesthetics, Community], in Beck, U., Giddens, A. & Lash, S. *Modernización reflexiva. Política, tradición y estética en el orden social moderno* [Reflexive Modernization: Politics, Tradition and Aesthetics in the Modern Social Order]. Madrid: Alianza Universidad.

Maffesoli, Michel (1990) *El tiempo de las tribus* [The time of the tribes]. Barcelona: Icaria.

Martín Barbero, Jesús (1998) Jóvenes: des-orden cultural y palimpsestos de identidad [Youth: cultural dis-order and identity palimpsests] in Cubides, H., Laverde, M.C. & Valderrama, C.E. (eds.) *Viviendo a toda. Jóvenes, territorios culturales y nuevas sensibilidades* [Living it all. Youth cultural territorios and new sensibilities]. Bogotá: Universidad Central y Siglo del Hombre Editores.

Martín Barbero, Jesús (2001) *Al sur de la modernidad. Comunicación, globalización y multiculturalidad* [South of modernity. Communication, globalization and multiculturality]. Pittsburgh: University of Pittsburgh.

OIT (2004) *Tendencias mundiales del empleo juvenil* [Global employment trends for youth]. Geneva.

OPS (2007) *Salud en Las Américas* [Health in the Americas]. Washington: Organización Panamericana de la Salud.

Reguillo, Rossana (2000) Estrategias del desencanto. Emergencia de culturas juveniles [Strategies of disillusion. Emergence of youth cultures], in Ford, A. (dir.) *Enciclopedia Latinoamericana de Sociocultura y Comunicación* [Latin-American Encyclopedia of Socio-Culture and Communication], Buenos Aires: Norma.

Reguillo, Rossana (2002) 'Gestión del riesgo y modernidad reflexiva' [Risk Management nad reflexive modernity], in *Nómadas* No 17, Santa Fe de Bogotá: DIUC, Universidad Central, October, pp. 80-89.

Reguillo, Rossana (2002b) Jóvenes y esfera pública [Youth and public sphere], in Pérez Islas, J.A. (coord.) *Jóvenes mexicanos del siglo XXI. Encuesta Nacional de Juventud 2000* [Twenty-first century youth. National youth Survey 2000], México: IMJ.

Reguillo, Rossana (2003) Cascadas: agotamiento estructural y crisis del relato. Pensando la "participación" juvenil [Cascades: structural exhaustion and narrative in crisis], in Pérez Islas, J.A. (ed.) *Nuevas miradas sobre los jóvenes. México-Quebec* [New views on youth. Mexico-Quebec]. México: Instituto Mexicano de la Juventud/Observatorio de la Juventud de Quebec.

Reguillo, Rossana (2004) *Teens at the Border: For a Politics of Representation, en Dictionary of Teen Life in Latin America and the Caribbean*. USA: Green Wood Publishing Group.

Reguillo, Rossana (2007) Legitimidad(es) Divergentes [Diverging legitimacies], in Jóvenes *Mexicanos: membresía, formalidad, legitimidad, legalidad. Encuesta Nacional de Juventud 2005* [Mexican Youth. National Youth Survey], I, pp. 75-133. México: IMJ/SEP.

UNFPA (2007) Estado de la población mundial 2007. Suplemento jóvenes: crecer en las ciudades. *State of the World Population 2007 Report. Youth Supplement: Growing up Urban*. Suplemento jóvenes, http://www.unfpa.org.mx/SWOP07/documentos/youthswop07_spa.pdf

UNICEF, UNFPA, WHO (2003) *Adolescents: Profiles in Empowerment,* http://www.unfpa.org/upload/lib_pub_file/457_filename_adolescent_profiles_eng.pdf

Valenzuela, José Manuel (2008) *El futuro ya fue. Socioantropología de los jóvenes* [The future is over. Socio-anthropology of youth], Tijuana: COLEF.

Memory and Identity:
Youth Communicating for Their Rights

Youth and Human Rights in Chile
Otherness, Political Identity and Social Change

Antonieta Muñoz-Navarro

Abstract

In the current Chilean context, the importance of human rights for building democracy has not been actualized by the media, which stereotype youth as icons of alienation, consumerism and individualism. This article describes how a group of young people is overcoming these adversities and shaping a political identity, with human rights as its main axis, that articulates their public actions aimed at generating social change.

Within the conceptual framework of the Latin American school of communication, which describes the elements that mediate the articulation and action of such political identity, the author developed a qualitative research project based on interviews. The main findings account for elements of otherness in the life stories of the young people interviewed, who meet through a civic initiative of alternative communication. The initiative promotes the conformation of a group and strengthens the youths' knowledge of human rights.

We must investigate what gives us hope... (Jesús Martín Barbero)

In Chile, since the Pinochet dictatorship ended in 1990 and to date, public institutions in general and the media in particular have been unable to actualize the social implications of honouring human rights and highlighting them. They continue to portray human rights as a problem pertaining exclusively to the dictatorship, which has no relevance in terms of time or space in the present.

With the support of the CIA and the complicity of large sectors of the Chilean centre-right, on 11 September 1973 General Augusto Pinochet led a coup d'état that overturned the government of President Salvador Allende – the only socialist government that had achieved power democratically. This date marked the establishment of a dictatorship that lasted seventeen years: a historical period characterized by systematic violations of human rights. State agents executed, forced the disappearance of, tortured or forced into exile thousands of Chilean men and women. Moreover, during this period the Constitution was changed, and a neoliberal economic system was established.

With the return of democracy, human rights were barely addressed in the public sphere. Symbolized in two reports by two expert commissions[1] with the purpose of quantifying the violations and their impact on the victims, the matter has been confined to the realm of justice, and is covered by the media only when legal processes are too slow. At this stage, Chile has no public policy promoting human rights or their understanding and practice among younger generations. This situation does not guarantee that what happened in the country will not happen again.

In this context, the NGOs that until ten years ago worked focussing on human rights as their underlying basis have reoriented their action towards other areas. The Center for the Research and Promotion of Human Rights (Centro de Investigación y Promoción de los Derechos Humanos, referred to here as CINPRODH), located in the south of the country with its headquarters in the city of Temuco, is an exception. CINPRODH took on the challenge, working to promote human rights without state support, resorting to volunteer work and innovative social practices such as the incorporation of youth, which I will describe here.

Today, the social situation in Chile is not conducive to the development of youth participation, since neither the media nor the educational system has promoted youth citizenship or participation. Despite this, three years ago CINPRODH incorporated a group of young people who are now playing an active role in the construction of citizenship, articulated through human rights.

These young people have managed to overcome two adverse social situations – on the one hand, the invisibility and omission in the media of an issue that matters to them: human rights. On the other hand, the stereotype of youth as alienated, lazy, consumerist and individualistic, which they had to dispel in order to become agents of social change.

My research question is: how can these young people constitute a political identity given their historical condition of invisibility? To answer this question I formulated a qualitative study, aimed at describing the elements that mediate the development of this political identity.

The research project was built from the perspective of the Latin American theory of communication (Martín-Barbero 2006), which takes into account the conditions of production of the media and the cultural aspects as elements that mediate the reception process. This theory indicates that alternative forms of communication are a social response to the paradigm of domination that is characteristic of media production, and gives relevance to the relationship between culture and politics and to the development of identities. In this article, the political aspects of citizenship will be reviewed from the perspective of cultural pluralism (Requejo 2001), and the identity aspects will be understood from the perspective of the social theory of identity (Giménez 1997).

Among the results of the empirical work undertaken with these young people, a common life story stands out, mainly connected to having close family members who suffered violations of their human rights. They also share a critical perspective on the society they live in, which fostered their otherness in different areas of their daily life: the media, school, their friends, their family.

In this context, CINPRODH not only articulates an alternative form of communication that promotes human rights. It also becomes a space in which these youth can acknowledge their similarities despite the fact that they had not met before: they share a history and certain concerns, which structure a political identity expressed in terms of citizenship.

Learning more in order to understand how the value of plurality can be communicated effectively and transformed into a civic identity is an interesting approach, and an alternative vis-à-vis the serious difficulties faced in attempting to grant a space for the strengthening of civic practices in favour of diversity (Martín-Barbero 2002).

In the following section I will address the links between the three theoretical sources already mentioned. In the section Methodology I will describe the methodological framework of my research. In the following section I will present the empirical findings. To conclude, I will present new proposals that could lead to reaching an in-depth knowledge of how socially transforming identities can be formed.

Communication, political identity and citizenship

The research project was envisioned from a Latin American perspective on communication (Martín-Barbero 2006), which takes into account the existing socio-cultural framework in terms of the conditions of production of the mass media, but also in terms of the cultural aspects that imbue reception processes with meaning. These aspects have been termed mediations. Ethnic character, gender, social institutions and movements are examples of mediations.

Martín-Barbero indicates that alternative forms of communication arise as a social response to the domination paradigm characteristic of the production of the media.

In terms of the links between communication, culture and politics, this perspective has paid special attention to human rights. The body of work that explores these links frames the cultural debate in terms of social inclusion and exclusion (Reguillo 1998). Departing from an understanding of the media as fundamental social actors in the democratic process, Reguillo considers that communication's contribution would be to critically deconstruct the discourses and mechanisms that normalize exclusion and deprive women, indigenous people and youth of their right to expression.

Although Reguillo acknowledges that these are not the only social actors affected by reductionist stereotypes, "these socio-cultural identities contain clues that hold the key to transforming public space in our Latin American societies, inasmuch as they represent the otherness that can counterbalance the modernizing projects in the region" (Reguillo 1998).

The definition of democratic society put forward by Reguillo is in line with the concept of democracy that includes cultural pluralism, i.e. understands democracy and identity as dynamic and constantly under construction. Such a tendency, originating in the field of political science, challenges the fact that states that arose under the liberal-democratic philosophy have understood cultural diversity as historically neutral. According to Ferran Requejo (2001), "the current debate has come to debunk the allegedly neutral disposition of democratic states in the field of culture, and at the same time make it plural. Today we are more aware than ever of the cultural particulars that hide in the seemingly neutral and universal discourses of doctrinal liberalism".

The convergence of the Latin American perspective on communication and cultural pluralism comes from the fact that both approaches arise from acknowledging culture as political – as a source of significance on which the construction and reconstruction of meanings are based. Both approaches understand identities as dynamic; they understand politics as public action; and they perceive citizenship as overreaching the rights and duties assigned by the state, and materializing as participation. Participation is a characteristic of the democratic construction initiated by citizens.

Along these lines, Martín-Barbero (2004) highlights that, in political terms, the road towards balancing the situation between communication and human rights lies in the possibility of civic expression.

From the perspective of cultural pluralism, citizenship implies being in the public sphere and acting within it (Zapata-Barrero 2001: 48). This understanding of citizenship is broader than approaches that narrow it down to electoral participation.

In order to fine-tune the concept of political identity, I will review in what follows certain formulations of social identity theory (Tajfel y Turner 1986) as analyzed by Giménez (1997). Giménez emphasizes that identity cannot be understood merely as an attribute or intrinsic characteristic of an individual: it is relational and inter-subjective, and has an eminently social nature. Identity is an aggregate of the plurality of social selves born out of culture.

For Giménez, social identity is shaped by three discriminating factors. First, the network of social memberships that materializes in aspects such as the social role, group membership or social category. Second, the aggregate of attributes or personal characteristics. Third, a life narrative, also termed biographic identity. Giménez's definition and characterization of social identity allows us to understand that it belongs to the broad universe of social identities that incorporates, both in its construction and its expression, a precise idea of what citizenship is. With it, an actor can be identified and acts in public.

According to Martín Barbero (2002), the new ways in which youths develop identities, strongly influenced by the new information and communication technologies, lead to classifying the public sphere, in terms of building a society and local way of life, as a non-place. The multiplicity of possible identities of the *communication ecosystem* does not privilege civic identity or political participation.

However, young people constitute a diverse group and are potential agents of change. Today, the new generations are the protagonists of Chilean post-dictatorial culture. They rebel against the fear and repression internalized by their parents and other relatives, whom could hardly be their role models in terms of participating in the public space. In line with Martín Barbero (2002), we could presume that their role models when it comes to participation would be their peers and CINPRODH.

From a communication perspective, the discriminating factors stated by Giménez, on which our definition of political identity is grounded, bear correspondence with the mediations proposed by Martín Barbero – i.e., the space as from which meaning is assigned to the communication process. This theoretical dislocation allows me to focus the study on the network of social membership, the personal characteristics and the biographical accounts of the CINPRODH youth.

These are the theoretical elements that give ground to my qualitative research. In what follows I will present the methodology.

Methodology

Methodologically, this qualitative research (Sandoval 1999) consisted of two different stages. The first was defined by my interest in the participation of CINPRODH's youth in the May 2008 mobilizations against the morning-after pill. The distribution of this type of emergency contraception was forbidden in the Chilean public health services because it was considered an abortion method. Two in-depth interviews were conducted with members of CINPRODH in order to obtain details regarding the organization and its work with youth.

In the second stage, the ultimate question guiding this research was posed; the objectives were defined; the data gathering tool was selected; and contacts were made for semi-structured interviews, aimed at describing the relevance of the discriminating elements that mediate in the structuring of political identity.

Next, I will present the results reached in the first stage and show how the data gathered configured the second stage.

Promoting human rights at CINPRODH and including youth: first research stage

To swim against the tide seems to have been CINPRODH's undeclared objective since its emergence as a social organization in 1991. In the midst of the democratic transition, it was logical to think that human rights would continue to be an important drive of Chilean social action. However, the organizations that worked in the field actually fell back.

The void, and the unfinished work, especially as regards human rights violations during Pinochet's dictatorship, led the members of the Temuco Committee against Impunity (*Comité contra la Impunidad de Temuco*) to create a new organization, and this is how CINPRODH emerged. Its four lines of work were to be: investigating the cases of those who had disappeared or been killed for political reasons; giving legal support to their relatives; advocating and promoting human rights; and raising funds to finance their work. However, for almost ten years CINPRODH focused on trying to find those who had disappeared for political reasons and giving legal support to the victims' relatives. Víctor Maturana, the centre's Coordinator, ponders upon this aspect: "We got caught in it. It was the tougher side of the problem. The more serious aspect of the human rights violations. We tried to work on the other lines, but there was no continuity".

In the year 2000, CINPRODH built the Park for Peace (Parque para La Paz) in Temuco, with its memorial devoted to those who had been killed or had disappeared in the south of Chile during Pinochet's dictatorship.

Having built this public space, and as a result of reflection, CINPRODH's work changed. Víctor Maturana explains, "We needed to come to a turning point. We realized that we had to keep on working in the field of violations to human rights, but with an eye to the future – concrete action in terms of human rights. We had to work on advocacy and education, and it was important that we reached youth and children. We had to set the seeds, foster their interest in human rights, and develop their critical thinking. This was something that no one was doing".

Thus, CINPRODH devised a pilot project with youth: its human rights camp, with three editions by 2008. How did young people come to participate in this camp? Victoria Irribarra, a CINPRODH member and also part of the team of youth instructors, describes the experience: "We designed a human rights camp such that participants had to stay for four days in order to learn about human rights, sexuality, self-development and leadership, etc. We offered it to young people with some sort of connection to the issue – i.e., that had victims of the dictatorship among their relatives – or that showed responsiveness to human rights matters. We aimed at a maximum of 25 young people, because our possibilities to operate were limited".

Víctor Maturana recounts what happened at CINPRODH as a consequence of their work with youth: "Young people have taught us many things, in a dialectic imbrication. They destroyed the cliché of youth not being there... We can say that's a prejudice. They are there, and if given the opportunity, they participate".

Between the summers of 2005 and 2008, more than sixty (60) young people participated in CINPRODH's camps, a unique experience in Chile that educates its participants in human rights. Without state support, and based on voluntary

Outdoors activity in a human rights camp held by CINPRODH (2006) *Photo:* Teodoro Smith

work, CINPRODH provides these young people with elements for the development of citizenship, based on participation and with human rights as a guiding theme.

CINPRODH hopes these young people will become human rights instructors. To this end, they have made arrangements for workshops to take place in different settings. If everything goes well, the young former campers will start facilitating human rights workshops at the primary schools of Temuco in November 2008.

Despite the complexities involved in being an NGO without state support, having existed for 17 years CINPRODH has become necessary for an extended sector of the Chilean society. Among its future activities, the centre plans to inaugurate two memorials to the dictatorship's victims in the cities of Villarrica and Lautaro, combining the advancement of human rights with the rescue of memory.

Based on data obtained through the two interviews, it was possible to reconstruct part of the socio-cultural context that gave way to the creation of CINPRODH and its involvement with youth. According to the theoretical focus introduced above, such context is part of the mediations on which youths develop their political identity.

Distinctive characteristics of the construction of political identity among the CINPRODH youth: second research stage

This second stage, as indicated by Iñiguez (2001), implies the methodological possibility to apprehend both the singular experiences and the socially elaborated conceptions that produce those experiences. This is possible thanks to discourses.

I administered individual semi-structured interviews to six young people, aged 17 to 22, from CINPRODH in the city of Temuco. CINPRODH provided a list of the young people with their e-mail addresses and phone numbers, which I used to contact them and determine their interest in participating in the study, time availability and locations where the interviews were to take place.

I interviewed four (4) girls and two (2) boys, all students in their last year of high school and taking courses for university entrance exams, or starting their studies at university, from families with parents who work professionally. In Chile, such an indicator implies that they belong to the middle class in symbolic terms, which in turn signals a relevant theoretical differentiation. These young people are not the *marginalized youth* characterized by Reguillos' studies (1994) or from the *shanty towns* studied by Martín Barbero (2002). Nonetheless, they represent a break in stereotypes and the development of identity.

In line with my objective – to describe the mediations articulated in the political identity of the CINPRODH youth, the interview was developed based on three thematic lines:

Life story and human rights: determine the importance granted to human rights in the young people's daily life, and how this allocation of meaning arises.

Relationship with CINPRODH: determine how they contact the centre and become campers. Do they feel they belong to a group? What is their perception of that group? Does technology play a role in these processes of group building?

Public participation: learn about the spheres of interest and action of these young people.

The interviews were considered discourses, and the tool for their examination was discourse analysis, mainly the analysis of topics, which according to van Dijk (2000) define the main themes or subjects of speech and represent what language users find more relevant.

Since my purpose was to describe the mediations that articulate the political identity of the CINPRODH youth, I paid attention to the topics connected with these youths' particular ideas of common life and public action. These ideas are connected to their own autobiographical narrative, personal characteristics and social membership groups. Related sub-topics arise from each topic.

Moving through the topics and sub-topics will show the multiplicity of interconnected themes. Next, I will present a selection of the interviews and comment on the identitarian relationships found.

Life story in connection with human rights: here it is possible to recognize two actors relevant to the CINPRODH youth: their parents and other relatives. Next, I present some segments of the interview referring to this topic:

> ...my parents did not actively engage in politics, they are left-oriented, but silently so... my parents were always very apprehensive, they were always telling me that you must not participate, that your personal information stays registered. 'Do not get involved in one cause because it's not worth it, because you don't know what the consequences will be'... my grandfather and my uncle on my father's side participated actively in a peasants' organization. This attracts my attention, I'm curious about it, I don't know if I want to do what they did, but I like their attitude, it's a

type of leadership that comes naturally. I came to the south and could commit to causes that attract my attention, without fear (Participant 1)

My parents always went to meetings and would not tell me what they were about, because they didn't want to compromise me. I knew it had something to do with the left... I don't know how old I was when I learnt that my father had been a political prisoner, I believe I was very young, and then I wanted to go where they went... I can't say that I joined CINPRODH because of my father, it was because of my mother and my father; this was something they did. It was not out of pity, but rather because I felt it was something that I had to do (Participant 3)

In my family there are human rights violations. My aunt and uncle were exiles. As I grew up, my parents participated in student leadership; my mother threw stones. Back then, everything was quite unfair, you got killed because you thought differently. They taught me to think (Participant 4)

...Politically, I have been influenced by my elder brother. He had an interest in the matter, he talked to me about human rights, questioned the society we live in. People my age live without thinking much, apathetically (Participant 6)

These examples allow us to understand that parents and other relatives, such as uncles, aunts, grandparents, and brothers, have been an important source of mediation that configures the political identity of the CINPRODH youth.

It is interesting here to note that these actors are mainly associated with an act of social struggle: with an idea of society that was attacked through torture, freedom deprivation, exile, etc. Thus, here admiration for one's parents and relatives who were politically active is combined with pain. Both elements are constitutive of identity and at the same time of otherness, allowing these young people to feel like an "other" among their immediate peers, which will in turn facilitate their identification among the CINPRODH youth through life histories with an otherness in common.

An outstanding aspect is the way these young people resignify their parents' fear regarding participating publicly. In some cases, parents support and incentivize their daughters' and sons' political participation, but in other cases the young people interviewed acknowledge that their participation is an act of rebellion against this fearful attitude. It is here that other relatives appear as reference models.

Theoretically, the life narratives of these young people arise in family contexts characterized by an extended significance of life in common and public participation – i.e., political contexts, with social ideals that they acknowledge as pertaining to the left. However, as these young people participate at CINPRODH and learn about human rights, their ideologies become more neutral in a clearly strategic sense: they rid them of the link established in Chile between human rights and the left, thus generating the conditions required for a social empowerment of the issue.

Next, I will describe what happens with these young people within CINPRODH.

Relationship with CINPRODH: At least seven (7) related sub-topics arise from this topic, connected with, e.g., the incorporation to CINPRODH as a key stage of their social lives. The group is perceived positively and the development of strong bonds of friendships is highlighted. The young people state that they feel a strong admiration for the life histories of the CINPRODH members and the way the centre has worked. There is some criticism regarding the need to incorporate technology into the organization's practices. In what follows I will present examples of the descriptions of otherness in other reference groups, perceived only upon arrival to CINPRODH, and of the importance of the use of technology in the conformation of this group.

Otherness in other reference groups: The young people interviewed state that they were mocked, associated with communism as something negative, or simply termed different because of their ever-critical attitude towards situations they deemed unfair. These examples show elements of such otherness, connected to their interests or their stories coupled with human rights, and their valuing CINPRODH as a space for encounters.

> ... At CINPRODH it is possible to talk without fearing that I will be labelled in a certain way. This had not happened in other groups (Participant 1)

> People often link me to communism. Within the CINPRODH group, when we talk we come to the conclusion that human rights belong to all, not to a segment... I wish everyone knew what those rights are about (Participant 2)

> ...I thought that Pinochet had put my dad in jail. I singled him out and was enraged at him. During the election between Lagos and Lavín I had to do work at school and a schoolmate wrote 'dictum' instead of 'coup d'état' and placed a photograph of Pinochet on the Chilean flag instead of the star, and it affected me... I told myself 'there's the picture of the guy who almost killed my dad!' and reacted: 'if you put Pinochet's photo there, I have the right to do this' and I cut the photo. I started defending myself and realized that everyone at my school was from the right. Then I wanted to learn more. Their grandparents and parents talked to them, and I wanted to know, in order to defend myself... They bothered me; they called me 'comunacha'[2] (Participant 3)

> I'm a great fighter for freedom of expression... it is the right with which I identify more. I have a story... I like to wear my hair a bit long, and my school forced us to wear shorter hair, to be the way they wanted... I had this difficulty with school; I did not want to attend. Sometimes this made me lose self-confidence... With a friend, I wrote a letter to the administrative board that turned out to be spectacular. I was congratulated. We gave it to the director. The contentions we used were many, including human rights. The way it was received was incredible; we were supported by the president of the parents' association, who's a lawyer. The letter made us look serious, not like children's foolishness... We set a higher standard for the debate (Participant 5)

Sexuality and affectivity workshop in a human rights camp held by CINPRODH (2006)
Photo: Teodoro Smith

Technology in the group's formation: the interviewees say that technology plays a fundamental role in the group's formation. They use e-mail, chat, photo blog (Fotolog) and Facebook. Examples follow:

> ...we use mail, Messenger for activities such as going out to chill out, and also photo blogs and lately Facebook (Participant 2)

> Technology is fundamental to carry on work at CINPRODH. Today almost everybody has an e-mail address, we communicate via Messenger and mail (Participant 4)

An initial analytical approach allows me to state that CINPRODH is a reference group for these young people. Theoretically, this finding is relevant in order to describe the mediations that structure these youths' political identity, since it is here that they start practicing their particular ideas of life in common and of public participation – i.e., practicing their political identity.

The young people interviewed report that, besides being a space in which they could find interests, CINPRODH has been the space where they managed to share a part of themselves that did not come through other spheres of their lives. That otherness, structured as from their family histories, characterized in most cases by human rights violations or simply a critical view of society, made them targets for stereotypes and mockery. They experienced the condition of "being different" and feeling excluded since they were small kids, and the media and the Chilean educational system never acknowledged the situation.

The chance to participate in human rights camps and become part of a group where human rights are rid of their political connotation and presented as a fundamental pillar of democratic life triggers in the CINPRODH youth a state of inclusiveness and a disposition to become sources for the promotion of such knowledge. At the same time, they remain critical of the adults' practices, especially as regards incorporating new technologies.

The public life of the CINPRODH youth, and therefore the development of their political identity after the camps, is possible mainly due to the use of e-mail and other technological tools. In this sense, I need to highlight the work of the instructors, who must update their digital knowledge in order to motivate the young participants.

The next topic will show how these young people, once conscious that a group in which they manifest their political identity exists, make decisions regarding participation in the context of a wide array of possibilities, in which publishing through the media, participating in electoral terms and volunteering for an NGO have the same value.

Public participation: In this topic we find sub-topics in terms of possible ways of public participation, e.g. voluntary work, identification with ideas that they can turn into action, opinions regarding the significance of enrolling to vote, participation and opinions regarding the prohibition of the day-after pill, opinions regarding politics through political parties, opinions regarding the role of the media in the field of human rights, and the possibility of developing their own media.

Forms of public participation: the young people interviewed identify a broad spectrum of forms of public participation, such as volunteering in human rights organizations, poverty eradication, political parties, the environmental movement, elections and student leadership.

> At university I don't participate that much... Sometimes delegates consult with me; I give them ideas. I volunteer for 'A Roof for Chile' ('Un Techo para Chile')[3] and at CINPRODH I belong to the youth and adult groups (Participant 1)

> I participated in the youth section of 'Together we can' ('Juntos Podemos')[4]; I found that doing so represented me... although I did not have the right to vote. I have experience in political work... I was president of the student centre at school; I was chosen with very clear ideas (Participant 2)

> I worked as a volunteer in pastoral care. I don't believe in church that much, but I do believe in helping people. It ended when I left school. Perhaps I will participate in 'A Roof for Chile' ('Un Techo para Chile') and now I will be an instructor at CINPRODH (Participant 3)

> I participated in the 'Penguins' Revolution'[5] in 2006... and now I do at CINPRODH (Participant 4)

> I have offered to volunteer for Greenpeace. I've been to protests, I keep myself informed... I would like to become a public official, I find it complicated because of politics, but I would like to help, give ideas, contribute (Participant 5)

Participation in the *day-after pill* case: This sub-topic is especially interesting because the participation of these young people in the May 2008 street protests in support of the free distribution of the day-after pill was the first expression of their public participation at the social level. I wanted to get into the arguments of the CINPRODH youth for demonstrating in favour of the day-after pill. Although not all of them participated in the demonstrations, they still have opinions:

> I'm against the ruling. I have participated in the demonstrations with friends, with people from CINPRODH. Through my photo log I send information; I talk about this matter at parties. There is plenty of disinformation – especially among the people who declare themselves against it because of religious principles... the pill is not abortive. The court of law prohibiting it, which also wanted to prohibit all contraceptive methods, does not make sense, is not democratic (Participant 2)

> I agree with the delivery. I know that we are getting older; if we have not developed yet, we already have the problem that Europeans have – a low birth rate. If we look at this from a social point of view, people can choose not to have so many kids. We could slowly reduce poverty. For me, the right is against it because they will be left without a source of jobs, and there will be fewer poor people (Participant 4)

> I feel that if this discussion exists in Chile, it means that this country is extremely retrograde. We should talk about this and not assume it is obvious. Everyone should choose what to do with their lives. I can't understand how they can still have an opinion, hold so much power, and introduce the church's contentions to decide government policies. I have not participated in the demonstrations (Participant 6)

Opinion on politics bound to political parties: For the CINPRODH youth, political activity connected to parties is not transparent; it is tied to nonsensical quarrels. Although the young people interviewed empathize with ideals more connected to the left, being active in a political party is not well thought of.

> I don't like indirect democracy; I feel that today's politicians do not represent me. I have not enrolled yet, I have just turned 18. I feel that they are dirty (Participant 2)

> Talking about politics causes problems. In my class I usually listen to those debates, and no one ever gets anywhere. At my age, talking does not lead to anything. You cannot decide anything. I do not identify fully with political parties (Participant 5)

Role of the media in the human rights sphere: The Chilean media are absent as a source of mediation when it comes to human rights. Although they acknowledge that the media's role to inform is important, the interviewees are critical not only of their contents but also of their production processes.

> They have performed an irresponsible role as regards human rights. They reach social groups that are very difficult to reach. But they are not fulfilling the role of expressing an opinion. They are influenced. They are losing objectivity (Participant 1)

> For me the media are worthless, they do not dig deep. During the 'Penguins' Revolution', the media destroyed everything we tried to say. We were calm, but the TV always portrayed us as violent. Chile lacks information, the media need to be opened up (Participant 4)

> The media are important in a democracy. People must be informed in order to make decisions... In Chile there is not enough information, there are many things that I do not learn about, which might affect me in a direct way. Human rights, for instance. News is redundant, it does not look into new issues. I am concerned with the fact that there might be censorship, but I do not have a way to find out if it really exists (Participant 5)

The possibility to develop their own media: This question was highly novel for the interviewees. They acknowledge that they had not thought about such a possibility and see it as consistent with their future performance promoting human rights. They also highlight the existence of "The Camper" ("*El Campamentista*"), an in-house bulletin that disseminates their camp activities.

> We do have a channel of communication of our own that talks about what happens at camp and is called 'The Camper'. But it is in-house, it only tells about our experiences. It's printed. This time we wanted to act as the writers. It does not aim at generating opinion. We have not considered setting up or own press... The truth is that we had not thought about it (Participant 1)

> It had never occurred to us to develop our own media... now that you mention it. I believe we could do it. CINPRODH has many connections... I see it as feasible. We could start with a blog, where each person can have an opinion, and then come up with a web site and post it; this would be quite helpful for our work of promoting human rights (Participant 4)

In this topic, which refers to public participation, the CINPRODH youth expresses its political identity, stimulated by the common experiences shared.

As indicated above, the possibilities for political participation identified by the young people interviewed are wide: student leadership, publishing an opinion piece in the media, volunteering for an NGO, demonstrating, etc. On the one hand, these options for participation contradict the representation of a socially apathetic youth. On the other hand, they contradict the approaches that narrow the spectrum of participation to the electoral sphere. Even if this sphere is considered important by the young people interviewed, they do not find it essential in order to feel like actors and sources of change.

It is important to highlight that most public participation activities are undertaken following the human rights camps. This allows us to understand CINPRODH's relevance in the configuration of their political identity as a source of mediation that reinforces family history and the processes related to otherness that have taken place in their lives. In this sense I can affirm that, in a context of economic precariousness, but with great imagination in order to overcome the dominant discourses aimed at generating amnesia and lack of interest in human rights, CINPRODH is an alternative communication source that is promoting social change.

The sub-topic regarding the young people's opinions on the day-after pill case becomes relevant. In this sense, the young people interviewed are in favour of distributing the pill. Moreover, they criticize the Constitutional Court, an institution handed down by the dictatorship, for forbidding the pill and regulating people's sexual life through moral contentions.

It is important to note that the interviewees repeatedly refer to being human rights instructors, because it is through this decision that they come to consider themselves agents of change. In perceiving and verifying the void that exists in Chilean society in terms of human rights-bound knowledge, they decide to act to transform what there is.

Despite being critical of how the media represent human rights and of several situations they deem unfair, these young people did not take into account the possibility of developing their own media using daily technological resources. The media's historical omission of their life stories and of aspects that matter to them might have led them to visualize the media not as a tool for change, but rather as mechanisms that reproduce domination patterns not worth imitating as active receivers.

However, from the question and their answers they come to perceive that developing their own media is in line with their future work promoting human rights. Then sense-making takes place, and a new mediation arises. Such mediation will link their political identity with their idea of social transformation. How they envision these media, and what elements will be given new meaning through it, are questions that should be answered in future work.

A summary of the study's findings and the theoretical reflection derived from them will be presented next.

Conclusions

As regards the research question aimed at identifying the mediations that frame the configuration of the political identity of the CINPRODH youth and their action, the results of the empirical work made it possible to specify a set of components that mediate how this political identity is developed.

A history of life in common among the young people, mainly connected to human rights violations having affected their nuclear family or other close relatives, and a critical perspective on the society in which they live, stand out. The Chilean social context in which these youngsters have grown up, with the media's outdated discourse regarding human rights and portrayal of youth in a stereotyped way, implied that an important part of their lives was omitted from the public space. This turned them into an *other* in the different social groups they belong to, such as school, friends and sometimes family.

In this scenario, where public invisibility and a feeling of not belonging combine, CINPRODH's role is to act as an alternative communication source that promotes human rights. This implies that young people empathize with CINPRODH based on their own interests. Moreover, since the camp is specifically aimed at a youth group, young participants understand that CINPRODH trusts in youths' ability to understand social issues and go beyond the stereotype of alienated, individualistic consumers. Also, and perhaps even more strongly, CINPRODH becomes a space in which these young people recognize each other as similar, discover their common histories and kindred feelings, acknowledge their remote past and recent otherness, share their particular sense of life in common, and invent their way of expressing themselves publicly – i.e., configure their political identity.

In terms of communication, founded on their position as critical receivers, these young people had not visualized the possibility of developing their own media, because they link the media to spaces where practices that have omitted their history are reproduced, and that delivers a stereotyped view of their status as young. Thus, here the media act as sources of mediation with a clearly negative sense, with which there is no recognition. However, inasmuch these young people start imagining possibilities connected to the media, a new mediation arises, that will articulate their political identity with their idea of social transformation.

As regards future work, I foresee the possibility of undertaking action research with these young people in the sphere of communication and social change, particularly in terms of producing their own media, as well as of following through their work as promoters of human rights in different social and cultural contexts.

Translated from Spanish by *Florencia Enghel*

Notes

1. The first report, known as the Rettig Report, was delivered by the Truth, Justice and Reconciliation commission in 1991. Its purpose was to report human rights violations occurred during the dictatorship. In 2003, the National Commission on Political Prison and Torture had the mission of compensating victims for their suffering by offering them or their families a symbolic economic compensation.
2. Derogatory way of referring to communists.
3. A program of the Jesuitical Religious Order, aimed at developing dignified housing for people living in extreme poverty. Most of the professional work is based on volunteering.
4. Left-wing political pact achieved in 2005 for the Chilean presidential election.
5. Chilean student movement arisen in 2006, which questions the deficiencies and inequality in Chilean public education.

References

Aguirre, F., Arriaza, A., Benard, E., Caballero, A., Espinoza, V., Uribe, V., Vega, J.C. (2003) *Informe de Derechos Humanos 2002*. [Human Rights Report 2002.] Santiago de Chile: LOM Ediciones.

Araya, J., Espinoza, V., Loi, P., Natale, K.M., Ortiz, M.L., Reyes, M., Vega, J.C. (2001) *Informe de Derechos Humanos 1990-2000*. [Human Rights Report 1990-2000.] Santiago de Chile: LOM Ediciones.
Caminal, Miquel (2002) *El federalismo pluralista: del federalismo nacional al federalismo plurinacional* [Pluralist federalism: from national federalism to pluri-national federalism.] Barcelona: Paidós.
van Dijk, Teun (2000) 'Parlamentary Debates' in Wodak and van Dijk (eds.) *Racism and the Top*. Austria: Drava Verlag, Klagenfut/Celovec.
Dutrénit, Silvia (1996) 'El Frente Amplio y la reproducción de la identidad política' [The Broad Front and the reproduction of political identity.] *Nueva Sociedad* N° 144: 126-137. Published online at www.nuso.org
Fahmy, Eldin (2006) *Young Citizens: Young People's Involvement in Politics and Decision Making*. United Kingdom: Ashgate Publishing Ltd.
Giménez, Gilberto (1997) 'Materiales para una teoría de las identidades sociales' [Materials for a theory of social identities.] *Revista Frontera Norte* 9(18): 9-28. México: Colegio de Frontera Norte. Published online at www.colef.mx/fronteranorte
González, Roberto; Manzi, Jorge; Cortés, Flavio; Torres, David; De-Tezanos, Pablo; Aldunate Nerea; Aravena, María T.; Saiz, José L. (2005) 'Identidad y Actitudes Políticas en Jóvenes Universitarios: El Desencanto de los que no se Identifican Políticamente' [Identity and political attitudes among university youth: the disillusion of those not identified with politics.] *Revista de Ciencia Política* 25(2): 65-90. Santiago de Chile: Pontificia Universidad Católica de Chile. Published online at www.puc.cl/icp/revista/
Iñiguez, Lupicinio (2001) 'Identidad: de lo Personal a lo Social. Un Recorrido Conceptual' [Identity: from the personal to the social sphere. A conceptual journey.] in Crespo, E. (ed.) *La constitución social de la subjetividad* [The social constitution of subjectivity.] Madrid: Catarata.
Krauskopf, Dina (2000) 'Dimensiones críticas en la participación social de las juventudes' [Critical dimensions of social participation among youth.] in Balardini, Sergio (ed.) *La participación social y política de los jóvenes en el horizonte del nuevo siglo* [The social and political participation of youth at the dawn of the new century.] Buenos Aires: CLACSO.
Leech, Beth L. (2002) Asking Questions: Techniques for Semi-structured Interviews. *Political Science and Politics*, 35(4): 665-668. Washington D.C.: American Political Science Association.
Martín-Barbero, Jesús (2002) 'Jóvenes: Comunicación e identidad' [Youth: Communication and identity.] *Revista de Cultura Pensar Iberoamérica* N° 0. Madrid: OEI.
Martín Barbero, Jesús (2002b) *Oficio de Cartógrafo. Travesías de la comunicación en la cultura* [Officiating as cartographer: communication's journey within culture.] México D.F.: Fondo de Cultura Económica.
Martín-Barbero, Jesús (2004) Medios y culturas en el espacio latinoamericano. Revista de Cultura Pensar Iberoamérica N° 5. Madrid: OEI.
Martín Barbero, Jesús (2006) 'A Latin American Perspective on Communication / Cultural Mediation', *Global Media and Communication* 2(3): 279-297. London: Sage Publications.
McGehee, Ralph (1999) *A Model Operation – Covert Action in Chile: 1963-1973. Article 51542*. San Francisco: Institute for Global Communications.
Reguillo, Rossana (1994) 'Las tribus juveniles en tiempos de modernidad' [Youth tribes at a time of modernity.] *Estudios sobre las Culturas Contemporáneas* V, 15: 171-184. México: Universidad de Colima.
Reguillo, Rossana (1998) 'Un malestar invisible: derechos humanos y comunicación' [An invisible malaise: human rights and communication] *Revista Latinoamericana de Comunicación Chasqui* (64): 18-23. Quito, Ecuador: Centro Internacional de Estudios Superiores de Comunicación para América Latina.
Requejo, Ferran (2001) 'Ciudadanos plurales, democracias diversas' [Plural citizens, diverse democracies.] in Ricard Zapata-Barrero, *Ciudadanía, democracia y pluralismo cultural: hacia un nuevo contrato social* [Citizenship, democracy and cultural pluralism: Towards a new social contract.] Barcelona: Anthropos.

Sáez, Yanina (2005) *Análisis del discurso de la Unión Demócrata Independiente (UDI) sobre el tema de los Derechos Humanos* [Analysis of the speech of the Democrat Independent Union on Human Rights.] Temuco, Chile: Universidad de La Frontera.

Sandoval, Guillermo (1999) 'Misioneros de la libertad y peregrinos de los derechos del hombre' [Missionaries of freedom and pilgrims of humanity's rights.] in Blomeier, H., Donoso, J., Fernández, J., Hormazábal, G., Larenas, F., Sandoval, G. (eds.) *Sociedad y Comunicación, en medio de los medios* [Society and communications: amidst the media.] Santiago, Chile: Fundación Konrad Adenauer.

Sandoval, Mario (2000) 'La relación entre los cambios culturales de fines de siglo y la participación social y política de los jóvenes' [The relationship between cultural changes at the turn of the century and the social and political participation of youth.] in Balardini, Sergio (ed.) *La participación social y política de los jóvenes en el horizonte del nuevo siglo* [The social and political participation of youth at the dawn of the new century.] Buenos Aires: CLACSO.

Tuvilla, José (1997) 'Derechos Humanos y Medios de Comunicación' [Human rights and the media.] in *Comunicar* 9. Andalucía, España: Grupo Comunicar.

Yates, Miranda & Youniss, James (1998) 'Community Service and Political Identity Development in Adolescence', *Journal of Social Issues* 54(3): 495–512. Washington: SPSSI.

Youniss, James & Yates, Miranda (1999) 'International Perspectives on the Roots of Civic Identity' in Yates & Youniss (eds.) *Roots of Civic Identity: International Perspectives on Community Service and Activism in Youth*. UK: Cambridge University Press.

Zapata-Barrero, Ricard (2001) *Citizenship, Democracy and Cultural Pluralism: Towards a New Social Contract*. Barcelona: Anthropos.

Youth, Memory and Justice
The Cromañón Case and Communication in an Age of Precariousness

Florencia Enghel, Cecilia Flachsland & Violeta Rosemberg

Abstract

In December 2004, in the city of Buenos Aires, Argentina, 194 young people died in a nightclub called "Cromañón Republic" during a rock concert. The Cromañón catastrophe gave way to a collective movement with complex characteristics. The relatives and friends of the dead, and the young survivors, set their struggle for justice and memory in different spheres: judicial, political and communicational. This article analyses two communicational instances drawn from those struggles: a *shrine*, erected metres away from the location where the catastrophe took place, and a *campaign of urban interventions (graffiti* and *stencilling)* undertaken by a group of young survivors in the streets, and promoted and popularized through the Internet. Those instances raise a series of questions not easily answered. What space does youth from popular sectors have to invent cultural and political forms that aim at social change in a context in which social relationships are disrupted by precariousness? And which roles can communication have within such space? These questions will be taken up in the article.

Introduction

On 30 December 2004, in a central area of the city of Buenos Aires, Argentina, known as Once, 194 young people died in a nightclub called "Cromañón[1] Republic" during a concert by the rock band Callejeros.[2] The catastrophe was caused by a toxic gas emitted by a plastic blackout net hanging from the roof, which had been ignited by a firework.

The pain caused by the deaths was followed by perplexity: this time, the young people had not fallen prey to the state's repressive forces,[3] but been caught up in what they used to consider their own celebration. Both the band, a proponent of a style known as "neighbourhood rock", and the owner of the club belonged to an artistic scene that sought out alternatives – precarious and thus more than once unlawful – in a city characterized by a privatization and a marked absence of state policies for the inclusion of youngsters from popular sectors. Sixty per cent of the victims were from the Greater Buenos Aires area, the agglomeration surrounding the city where poor people live.

The relatives and friends of the dead and the survivors have set their struggle for justice and memory in the city of Buenos Aires. After Cromañón, the pain of those individuals who had lost a son or daughter, a relative or a friend gave way to a collective movement with complex characteristics, which was difficult to typecast in the usual political categories and had serious difficulties in articulating a discourse that would touch the rest of society.

While Argentina moved towards recovery in its economy following the institutional schism derived from the events of 2001,[4] Cromañón revealed those aspects that had become more precarious as a consequence of the deepening of capitalism in the country. According to the International Labour Organization (ILO, Organización Internacional del Trabajo, OIT), in post-crisis Argentina, characterized by four years of high growth rates and a vigorous reduction in the levels of poverty and unemployment, the subjects of youth unemployment and job insecurity are at the centre of gravity among social issues. Since 2005, the rate of youth unemployment (i.e. unemployment among 15 to 24 years old) has stagnated at around 25 per cent, while the rate of adult unemployment (i.e. unemployment among 25 to 59 years old) has continued to fall, from 9.3 per cent to 7 per cent. The youth unemployment rate has gone up from an average of 2.9 times the adult unemployment rate to 3.6 times (OIT, 2007).

The struggles derived from Cromañón take place in different spheres: judicial, political and communicational. This article analyses two communicational instances drawn from those struggles. First, the *shrine* erected metres away from the location where the catastrophe took place. And second, a *campaign of urban interventions (graffiti* and *stencilling)* undertaken by a group of young survivors and promoted and popularized in different parts of the city through the Internet and websites – the virtual space to which the youngsters returned later to reproduce photos of the graffiti and stencils and to discuss them.

These communicational practices contrast the meaning of what happened with the media's discourse, which insists on turning the pain into a spectacle and on clamouring for security and stigmatizing youth as representative of anomy. However, they are experiences deeply affected by part of that media representation. Their protagonists also demonstrate a negation of politics, but such a denial – unlike the media's – is geared to the privatization of experience, and based on mercantile logics and thus more unsettling. In our view, it requires that we enquire into how public life and communication are shaped in the contemporary world. At the same time, it provides evidence of the increasing difficulties faced by young people in terms of setting in motion certain mechanisms that not only give them at least some visibility on the social horizon, but can also generate dignified living conditions.

The Italian theorist Franco Berardi, known as Bifo (2007), characterizes new forms of politics useful for our analysis of the communicational strategies arising from the Cromañón case:

> Dialogue is no longer effective, and democracy becomes a myth and is exercised as a rite, but it is no longer the location for the free elaboration of a common discourse. The media, which delimitate the field of what is visible, produce the common discourse and the invisible, and establish the formats of the narrative organization of society. ... The imaginary scene is dominated by mythological configurations. The mythologies of belonging occupy the field of social communication and collective identity.

If, as is argued by the Mexican social scientist Rosanna Reguillo Cruz (2000), when political action vanished from the mid-1980s, youth as a subaltern sector became visible in the territory of culture and communication by "trafficking meanings", the Cromañón case forces us to raise a series of questions that are not easily answered:

- What happens when death appears in the space conceived as a *refuge* against control – that is to say rock music?
- How much was change, and how much reproduction – both discursive and social – inasmuch as both operate in our view in a dialectical relationship within that space?
- What space does youth from popular sectors have to invent cultural and political forms that aim at social change in a context in which social relationships are disrupted by precariousness?
- Which roles can communication have within such space? (This question is taken up below in order to try to establish how much change and how much reproduction there is in the shrine and the campaign of urban interventions).

These questions introduce us to one of the problematic knots established by the new reality of youth from the popular sectors, submerged in the post-work culture and void of protection. How to reflect on their practices without forgetting the precariousness of their position, and without reducing them to mere degradation? How to identify what is singular about them beyond the fact that such singularity may not respond to what is expected of them? By "what is expected of them", we refer to three representations frequently used in the social discourse on youth, synthesized by the Argentine sociologist Cecilia Braslavsky (1986): the golden youth (young people are those bearing the possibility of renewal), the white youth (young people are innocent and pure), and the grey youth (young people are apathetical).

The discussions of the French sociologists Claude Grignon and Jean-Claude Passeron with their mentor, himself a French sociologist, Pierre Bourdieu, form the background of our proposition. While Bourdieu states that there is no popular culture that is not a degraded reflection of, or a guilty response to, the legitimate culture, Grignon and Passeron take a critical stand and reply:

> If we conceive the culture of popular sectors as the symbolic production that only replies to or reflects symbolic domination, aren't we reducing it to an epiphenomenon of an external determination? Aren't we being reductionist by finding identity among the popular, the subaltern and the deficiencies or limits of poverty? What about the cultural production of popular sectors that does not arise from their state of lack or constraint and is rather the result of their creative capacity? [...] Perhaps to a certain extent the culture of popular sectors arises from "elections", and these might have a relevance and functionality not merely derived from the action of resisting. They have political value, because they do not respond to a sense of duty, nor do they arise from a project of resistance even if they exert it (Miguez and Semán 2006).

In this context, it is important to note that in the past 40 years of Argentine history, rock music has been linked to the lives of youth – initially, mainly young people from medium-income sectors, and since the 1990s those from the impoverished middle classes and the poorest sectors. Rock music became a communicational and cultural practice essential to making youth visible: it gave young people voice, a space, an embodiment and their aesthetics. From its origins, it challenged young people to think of what it means to talk about rebellion from within the weave of power. Since the 1990s, the challenge became even thornier, and the question became: what does it mean to go against a power that produces abandonment rather than disciplining? What types of protection does rock promote in a context of desertion and precariousness?

Searching for the communicational dimension: after Cromañón

Cromañón necessarily implies that we return to a key issue in the field of communication in Latin America: the tension between media cultures and popular and subaltern cultures.[5] In the region, until the 1970s, to study the media, communication and/or mass culture critically implied unravelling the ways in which the dominant ideology penetrated the communication processes, producing certain effects. Events at the end of the 1960s and the beginning of the 1970s brought full awareness of two issues in the intellectual, journalistic and artistic spheres: it was necessary to discuss mass communication, and to address politically the concrete problem posed by a monopolistic private power, which altered the imageries of vast social sectors. This critical theory, marked in Latin America by the emergence in the 1970s of Dependency Theory,[6] was connected to political projects that aimed to transform society.

The dictatorships halfway through the 1970s, the democratic experiences of the 1980s, and the disillusionment that followed in the 1990s – processes common to most of the region – transformed that viewpoint. The field of communication and culture stopped focusing mainly on emission – on questioning ownership of the media – and shifted towards reception. Instead of *what do the media do to people*, the question became *what do people do with the media*: how do people own what is massive, how do they mark their worldview in it and how do they dispute representation in search of a sense of their own?[7] In other words, culture and communication were acknowledged not merely as spaces of manipulation, but also as conflict zones. Questions regarding the connections between media and social movements, communicative practices and the plurality of cultural matrices were highlighted.

As regards Cromañón, our specific question is: can small scale action, that is, a group understood as the social sphere – these young people that somehow become organized and circulate within the streets and on the web – lead to visibility and generate an understanding that is different to that which is stated by the media?

Rock music as communicational practice

According to the anthropologist Jesús Martín-Barbero, born in Spain and a resident of Colombia since 1963, "merchandise value does not obliterate meaning; it captures it and misrepresents it, but speaks as from it – with a sensationalist and melodramatic language – for whoever wants to hear: a world of experiences and hopes that, unrecognized by high culture and politics, would be a key location for popular classes to recognize themselves" (Altamirano 2002).

As a communicational practice that moves between cultural conspiracy and mercantile design, rock music is one of the languages through which merchandise speaks, and thus a sphere that allows us to think about the tensions between the mass media, popular and subaltern cultures and the ways in which youth negotiates and expresses such tensions. This is especially the case in Argentina, since national rock has been themed as a space of resistance against the disciplinary ways imposed on youth during the period of state terrorism.

As a space in which young people from popular sectors can recognize themselves, rock contests the way in which the media discourse represents them, insistent on the juridical and repressive power models. Argentine researcher Mariana Chaves sates: "Adopting Foucalt's propositions, I maintain that youth is marked out by a big 'no'. It is denied (juridical model) or deemed negative (repressive model); its existence as a complete subject is denied (in transition, incomplete, not a child nor a grown-up) or its practices are deemed negative (problematic youth, grey youth, deviant youth, juvenile tribe, rebels, delinquents)" (Chaves 2005).

If, in the research field, popular cultures tend to be envisaged as a degraded reflection of a legitimate culture or as pure reproduction, in the field of the media, when starred by youth, such culture is denied outright. And when it appears *because there is no choice*, as in the Cromañón case, due to the severity of the event, then its protagonists are denied – portrayed as the victims, they are denied as active subjects with their own political and cultural practices. In the media discourse, youth practices are not considered interesting and are not covered.

Rock in Argentina: from counterculture to shelter

The importance we assign to the rock sphere as a conveyor of the existence of poor or impoverished youth in Argentina requires that we justify our stand. Or in other words, it leads us to chronicle its transformation.

In his book *The Age of Extremes* (2000), British historian Eric Hobsbawm states that "youth is a post-war invention", indicating the moment at which youth becomes a socially autonomous group. It is no longer a group in transit awaiting adulthood. The youth of the 1960s and 1970s aimed to transform the world in several ways, and in many cases did this in tune with rock and roll – a cultural and communicational practice born within a cultural industry, which "traffics" meanings with that which such an industry imposes, combining music, lyrics and bodies on stage.

The more countercultural side of this practice interpreted that, in the new phase of capitalism of the mid-1970s, the struggle was no longer linked to taking power: what was required was an intervention on the social imagination in its existing forms. "To circulate rapturous flows, i.e., capable of straying from the dominant message of work, order, discipline" (Bifo 2007).

In Argentina – and more specifically in its large cities – rock music arrived quite early, at the beginning of the 1960s. The phenomenon, initially industrial and originating in the so called dominant countries, became one of the most potent traditions in popular music. Argentine rock musicians gave local colour to the genre. They sang in Spanish, told their own stories and experimented with intersections with tango and folk – the two types of music considered "national".

During the 1970s, while many young people opted for different types of political organization – and even armed struggle – as the revolutionary path, part of the middle classes chose to fight against bourgeois disciplining through rock music.[8]

Rock songs gave visibility to these young people from the Argentine middle classes. Historically, the country had had an extended middle class, but started to loose it as a consequence of the economic reconversion undertaken by the military dictatorship, which was characterized by economic concentration, a move against industrialisation and a depreciation in wages.

The class composition among the youth who followed the genre, as well as among many of the musicians playing in rock bands, had changed by the mid-1990s, when the neoliberal project overturned the never achieved illusion of social integration. The middle classes became impoverished and the gap between rich and poor grew wider. Sociologists use a single phrase to refer to this process: workers turned into poor people.

According to OIT (2007), the most worrying fact in Argentina right now, derived from the scenario described above, is the high percentage of young people who neither study, work nor seek a job: a total of 756,000 in urban areas (of which 427,000 are aged 20 to 24).

The scenario since the 1990s is quite different from the one in which the rock culture started. Rock music ceases to be a countercultural experience and becomes a "shelter", a form of protection against the end of social protection. Young people from poor sectors moved by rock no longer have a disciplinary context to distance themselves from; they tend to fail at school and cannot enter the job market. These new conditions generated the phenomenon known as neighbourhood rock, or "kids rock". Its main characteristic relates to class issues. For the first time, Argentine popular sectors massively accessed rock. Argentine sociologist Pablo Semán (2006) refers to its other attributes:

- it is a phenomenon based on listening – how lyrics are interpreted is more important than lyrics as such;

- the audience's activity is as important or more important than the band's;

- it is oppositional, but not like in the 70s – the quest now is for access to the labour market rather than to denounce the exploitation of workers;

- it is nationalist, but its native land is the neighbourhood.

The culture of neighbourhood rock acknowledges among its musical influences most of national rock, certain forms of punk and heavy metal, and particularly the Rolling Stones, from whom it has inherited its musical style, seizing on their legacy to generate a culture of its own, which is called "stone" or "rollinga". Another characteristic is its tight linkage to soccer culture. In the intersection of rock and culture, the neighbourhood is a privileged space – the scene for everyday practices, and a key component of an imagination that helps to configure identity. Within this culture, each neighbourhood has a music group that aspires to represent its small community: the social realm takes the shape of a group.

In the 1990s, the number of bands singing in the neighbourhood expanded. Among those bands was Callejeros. Created in 1995 in the neighbourhood of Villa Celina, in the Greater Buenos Aires area, its original name was Green River (Río Verde), and it played cover versions of songs by the Rolling Stones, Creedence Clearwater Revival and Chuck Berry. With three records released – Thirst, Pressure and Rock and Roll Without Destiny (*Sed, Presión, Rocanroles sin destino*),[9] by December 2004 the band's concerts contained certain rituals of kids' rock: the "aguante"[10] manifested itself through enormous flags, and a large amount of fireworks and firecrackers. Some of the band's followers were organized in what were called "families" – small communities that arranged the party and aguante for each concert.

In addition to the music, followers of these bands have shared aesthetics, as well as certain preferences and consumption habits. In this way, they aim to become visible in a city that does not provide spaces for them. With their fringes, white Topper sneakers,[11] t-shirts with prints referring to the band, tattoos and marked backpacks, their own bodies are designed in a way that situates them in an interregnum somewhere between social indiscipline and the marketing trail. One of the most shattering images of Cromañón showed parents and friends identifying victims based on the tattoos on their bodies.

Devotees of kids' rock privilege face-to-face encounters and physical contact, experiencing the group as an emotional, affective space. Thus, the importance of concerts and of what they call the "run-up", as well as the privileged position granted to pogo dancing and the aguante in general. One of the most moving symbols of what happened at Cromañón was the solidarity that youngsters displayed that evening: the aguante with which they followed their band led them to enter the club again and again in order to help rescue the survivors.

Communication strategies for memory and justice

The two communicational initiatives to arise from Cromañón, in which young people – survivors, relatives or friends of the survivors and fans of the band – became involved are the shrine and the campaign of urban interventions "Stop blaming Callejeros" ("Basta de culpar a Callejeros").

The shrine

A few metres away from the burned out club, the relatives, friends and survivors of Cromañón spontaneously built a shrine to remember the victims, starting on the night on which the incident took place. They began by lighting candles, and eventually added other objects: personal memories, flowers, religious images, crosses, rosaries, soccer t-shirts, small puppets or dolls, photos, signs asking for justice or vengeance, song lyrics, flags, record covers, the burned clothes of victims and many sneakers.

Built as a form of shelter against the pain caused by so many deaths, the Cromañón shrine reveals, however, the abandonment that caused those deaths, as well as the desolation that followed them.

Popular religiosity

Even if a casual glance might see the objects as piled up and somehow abandoned, a more attentive eye will discover disquieting images of the current state of popular Argentine culture and of its youth.

The Argentine philosopher Ruben Dri (2003) indicates that the flipside of the advance of capitalism's instrumental rationality is the proliferation of religious forms that mix symbols, fetish, superstition and extravagant doctrines.

Popular religiosity sanctifies those who have a traumatic death, especially the young, and grants them the gift of miracles. An "out of place" death is worth remembering permanently, and can therefore be sanctified. If, moreover, a social conflict is identified, sanctification appears as a way of rescuing the victims from less privileged classes, which contributes to the process. Some of the relatives of the Cromañón victims have chosen this way of remembering those who suffered an injustice perpetrated by "the powerful".

What it is that popular religiosity terms powerful in the case of Cromañón is a key question. 'Who are the powerful' is a question that the relatives of the Cromañón victims still debate today, more than four years after the event. How can those responsible for what happened be identified? Or in other words, does responsibility lie within the state government, that is, the city, but also the nation; in the fact that the state government was absent, that is, the lack of an adequate response from the firefighters, the police and the emergency services; among those who benefited from the concerts in economic terms, namely the club owner and the band; in the existing corruption, which led to inadequately equipped premises being licensed; or among the audience that lit fireworks during the concert? Or does responsibility lie in the sum of all these elements?

For some relatives – grown-up parents in particular – the guilty have a name: "Ibarra, Chabán, you must pay", one of their mottos, singles out the then mayor of the city of Buenos Aires and the owner of the club. But the young mainly adopt another motto at their demonstrations: "it was not the fireworks, it was not rock and roll; our kids were killed by corruption". Youth tends to differentiate itself from grown-ups, in that it does not seem convinced about publicly pointing at guilty parties, and mottos are instead oriented towards attacking the political system as a whole and at the same time defending the space of rock and roll. In this sense, in terms of our inquiry, rock and roll acts as a surface and a framework for us to raise the question of whether these young people are proposing reproduction or resistance in their ways of communicating – to others and among themselves – about Cromañón.

From our perspective, in the Cromañón case, the powerful seem to have acted through omission rather than concrete actions, and in a sense what causes the disaster is the precariousness of social relationships: the absence of what is usually called 'the social fabric' becomes violently evident.

With regard to the role of communication, this refers us back to the above mentioned remarks by Bifo: faced with the difficulty of situating power, and therefore identifying those responsible for what happened, democracy stops functioning as the space for the free elaboration of a common discourse, and the media take its place, producing a particular narrative.

In that sense, as one of the communicational spaces in which young people try to overcome the invisibility imposed on them by the media through their

Florencia Enghel, Cecilia Flachsland & Violeta Rosemberg

Youth, Memory and Justice

The shrine built after 194 young people died divides a street in the centre of Buenos Aires. Canvas sneakers represent neighbourhood rock, the *aguante* and the presence of the dead young people
Photo:
Violeta Rosemberg

coverage of Cromañón, the sanctuary can be read as an expression of resistance.[12] Thus, the representation of the young dead in the shrine unfolds in a contested territory. These young people, who had attended a concert enthused by the promise of intensity and communion, were faced instead with proof of their abandonment. The sanctuary does not refer to glamorous rock myths. It refers to dead bodies seeking solace in low-class forms of religion, one of the last shelters still available after the fall of utopias.

Ways of interpreting the space

Within the media universe, the shrine has a small space: the discussion revolves around whether it is right or wrong for this memorial to block a street, interrupting the traffic flow and causing disruption in the life of the neighbourhood. Among the relatives and the survivors, however, it occupies a privileged space – in both their debates and their feelings.

For the young survivors, the shrine represents a space connected to death and pain. "I don't find the shrine convincing because when I go there, what I see is scattered bodies, the bodies of those kids who died. I can't see anything else. I feel calmer when I go to the Callejeros concerts, not at the shrine", says Facundo, one of the survivors and a member of the group. *Stop blaming Callejeros* refers directly to the need to keep resorting to the space of rock as a possibility for catharsis. For Juan, a member of the carnival street band, "Those who will never shut up" [Los que nunca callarán], the alternative would be to turn the shrine into a space for joy: "At first I was not convinced, but then I realized that it was our place. What I would like now is to paint it in colours, because the way it looks now it makes you fall into a state of low spirits. Paint it red, yellow, green, so that it comes alive".

The campaign: *stop blaming Callejeros*

The shrine connects us to remnants of old traditions from Argentine popular culture, and appears as a space of conflict between adults and youth. The campaign *Stop blaming Callejeros* refers specifically to youth struggles for representation, which take place in those spaces that young people want to, or can, contest: the streets, on the one hand, and the virtual space of new technologies, on the other hand.

After the tragedy, the relatives and a portion of society chose to place blame on the rock band Callejeros for what happened. Against those accusations, the band's fans somehow organized themselves as a shield and became visible to defend it. Once again, rock and roll functions here as a surface and a framework for analysis: what are these young people defending of their own social situation when they try to protect the band? What does the band represent for them under these circumstances?

The initial debates regarding how to confront those who blamed the band took place on the Internet, in blogs belonging to fans of Callejeros and on web pages that existed prior to Cromañón and had been created to exchange opinions on rock bands.[13]

Soon after the catastrophe took place, a group of fans managed to regroup and launch the campaign *Stop blaming Callejeros*. The initial idea was to go out at night and paint the city's walls. For these young people, the night hour remained the right one to express themselves. Graffiti was painted in different neighbourhoods of Buenos Aires, and in some neighbourhoods of the greater city area.

The Cromañón issue is quite difficult for Argentine society. Given its complexity – the number of elements intervening to aggravate its magnitude and the interrelationships among them – it is not easy to take a stand regarding what happened, and on where or on whom responsibility lies. To date, there is no agreement in terms of who to make responsible.

However, while the social debate continued, as the months went by the band started to face increased levels of accusations. This, in turn, led to an interesting dispute: on the one hand, a generational dispute unfolded between parents, who saw Callejeros as the guilty party, and young people, who found no reason to put the band in that position and instead saw it as yet another victim[14]. At the same time, the media provided a simplified and condemnatory image of both the band and the victims' relatives – especially of those who organized themselves after what had happened and put up a fight.

In this context, marked by the impossibility of establishing a common territory in order to reflect on the event, those passionate about the band came out to say "Stop", with the purpose, according to Sebastián in his blog, of moving "away from the violence brought into being by the lack of understanding among the different positions".[15] These young people developed a series of strategies to voice their "Stop" and become visible in the public space: they went out and painted the streets, they designed a series of yellow t-shirts with the slogan *Stop blaming Callejeros*, and they disseminated images of the graffiti and the t-shirts in the virtual space of the Internet[16]. At present, when the oral stage of the trial corresponding to the legal case is about to start, the web calls on young people to demonstrate in the streets[17].

Political graffiti has a long tradition in Argentine history: it was emphatic, raging and encouraging in the 1960s and 1970s – decades in which politics seemed to have pervaded everything; it was imaginative and humorous in the 1980s; it was connected to the dissemination of bands in the 1990s; and it was characterized by irony and inverted meanings in the wave of graffiti that covered the city of Buenos Aires in the wake of the 2001 crisis.

The graffiti *Stop blaming Callejeros* became visible in 2005 on many of the city's streets. "It worked as a form of protest, as a statement of love, resistance and 'aguante'", explains Sebastián. Perhaps its innovative aspect lies in the motto chosen. The statement works in a way as an x-ray of the youth that becomes visible through neighbourhood rock: a youth that inhabits a social fabric marked by precarious relationships, which built rock into their shelter and, once that shelter was demolished by death, asks not to be blamed.

In terms of analysis, it is possible that graffiti is a way of going against the stigma that burdens the youth. As the media labels them the "enemy within", they respond "stop blaming us". Moreover, faced with the need to adopt a denomination, they choose the band's name: Callejeros.

The form of public intervention produced by graffiti is non-institutionalized art, vandalism and mercantilism all at once, and, as such, adds to the city's visual structure. The primary idea is to generate a short message to be spread on the streets that remains in the memory of passers-by, very much like the commercial images that routinely and incessantly attack our subconscious mind.

According to Diego Garay,[18] the re-emergence of the street use of this technique, utilized by political groups in the 1930s, is connected mainly to "the proliferation of motifs through the Internet and new software that allows downloads of many of the plates that have become classics within the genre".

Putting the mottos discussed over the Internet on the street is the strategy that the band's young followers found to contest the way in which both they and their loved band were being represented in the media. It has also been a way to connect the more private space and individual level of intervention allowed by Internet access with the public space and collective action.

To fight what they consider, as expressed in many interviews, "lies produced by the media", the youth took the public space by storm and attempted to narrate their realities, which the media do not mention. Graffiti works as a particular form of intervention, presence and voice; as an appropriation of the city in an attempt to make the public space more democratic. "We did not want to go unnoticed; we wanted to catch the inattentive eye", says Martín in his blog.

Through a stencil, young people claim justice and name their dead as "our Callejeros"
Photo: Violeta Rosemberg

Prior to Cromañón, young people from popular sectors who followed Callejeros and other similar bands were invisible. Due to Cromañón, they were portrayed by the media as passive victims or guilty parties. Through the campaign, a group of them looked for and set in action an alternative to revert both representations. Establishing the extent to which they managed to achieve this would require in-depth research that goes beyond the boundaries of this study. Nonetheless, narrating their experience allows us to visualize certain possible strategies for youth from impoverished urban sectors. Grounded in communication, the campaign *Stop blaming Callejeros* seems to have a political and cultural dimension that is not fully apparent: how to conceptualize that dimension is a challenge.

Conclusions

> A change of realities, when it becomes essential, also requires a change of the instruments capable of thinking. We do not have a fixed theory to consider the change of realities, nor a fixed reality to adjust the change of theories. We have both variables changing at once without a pre-established coordination. [. . .] If in order to assess experience we need certain parameters, when an experience eliminates the parameters, there is an additional amount of disturbance. Let's call it *perplexity*. We are left without parameters to assess what happens when there are no symbolic organizing elements that can give meaning to a situation. (Ignacio Lewkowicz 2004)

We refer above to the perplexity that ensued when 194 young people caught in the Cromañón fire died on 30 December 2004. Without question, it was an experience that changed known parameters, and one which forces us to consider what new parameters to use in order to think it through.

In our view, reading the shrine and the campaign *Stop blaming Callejeros* as communicational strategies connected to the Cromañón event allows two types of operation.

In the first place, it is possible to delineate some of the current characteristics of young people from the popular sectors of the urban peripheries of Argentina and the city of Buenos Aires:

- The political dimension of their practices seems to be set partly by incorporating the stigmas burdening them into their own mottos. While public opinion pictures them as uninterested in the public sphere, they put together a campaign aimed at stepping into the public sphere. While the media's discourse establishes them as representative of anomy and insecurity,[19] they hit the streets to demonstrate and try to contest that discourse, although they have serious difficulties in disputing the media's agenda and instituting their own.

- To defy the exclusion generated by the precariousness of social relationships, they resort to what seem to be new forms of certain "traditions"; they exalt the more immediate social space and re-appropriate old popular customs, renewing them to take shelter in them. For example, the religiosity expressed in the shrine, or the notion of family transferred to attendance at concerts. The extent to which these strategies imply a call for the state government to provide new forms of protection and security, if we highlight those elements more characteristic of tradition, or to envisage new forms for social relationships, if we highlight the innovative elements, remains unclear. We propose that question for debate.

- Their practices are accompanied by an attitude identified as *aguante*. Against their increasing difficulties with holding on to long-term projects – at school, at work, in the family, in creating a common project – these young people show their character, that is, their way of inhabiting the world, by putting it all in the 'here and now'. This manifests itself in the celebrations organized in connection with each concert to support those bands that are not successful with an unseen passion, as well as in their resistance to adversity. An example is their aguante of 'Callejeros' while a large part of public opinion considers the band guilty.

- Faced with a situation of widespread abandonment, and even though Cromañón led to an abrupt decrease in the places and opportunities available for gatherings or rock concerts, some of these young people insisted on getting together. They did so in the virtual space of the web, by hitting the streets to paint their mottos in the context of the campaign, by going to concerts, at the demonstrations held on the 30th day of each month, by wearing their t-shirts with the slogan *Stop blaming Callejeros*, and when they differentiate themselves from the adults who publicly place blame – or not – in the contested territory of searching for the guilty parties. These experiences, however, cannot hide the fact that many young survivors – especially the poorest ones – are immersed in social abandonment, depressed and in some cases attempting suicide.

In the second place, it is possible to analyse the extent to which these strategies promote social change or, in other words, as put forward above, to identify the role of communication in these circumstances – what is change and what is reproduction – in discursive and in social terms in the shrine and the campaign Stop blaming Callejeros.

- More than four years after the event, these young people persevere with the debate regarding the shrine and how to relate to that space marked by pain, and with their support for the campaign. The virtual space of the Internet allows them to keep a certain form of community working. It is virtual, and thus limited, and its political impact is arguable, but it is still a community. In this sense, the search for the other seems ceaseless, and is persistently creative, in the midst of circumstances that seem designed to discourage them.[20]

Returning to Grignon, Passeron and Bordieu, we strongly believe the peculiar complexity of the Cromañón case forces us to rethink the categories available for our analysis. The shrine and the campaign combine elements of both reproduction and resistance. Even if the young people's responses are marked strongly by elements derived from popular cultures and by those characteristics typical of poverty and an absentee state government, it is possible to detect creativity in their communicative action.

To inquire into and establish the political value of such action, that is, its power to generate positive change in the conditions of their existence as a social group, is a challenge that the field of communication must face with a spirit that is open to the new. To go deeper into the characterization of rock music as a surface and a framework for analysis of the situation and the modes of expression of today's youth is part of that challenge. In our view, the task should involve tying together culture and politics from a perspective that goes beyond everyday life, that is, that understands the links between youth and rock music not merely as cultural consumption but also in terms of the convergence between everyday life, participation and citizenship.

At this stage it remains an open question whether the youth's communicative actions will remain sustainable until the trial starts, or regain momentum at that time in order to influence the process in organized ways. Connected questions include whether the tools available will be used mainly to express individual opinions and whether such expression will be limited to the virtual realm.

Nonetheless, the fact that these questions cannot yet be answered does not imply that the communicative forms used so far – whether or not by the young people directly affected – in order to analyse the circumstances are not fundamentally important. In our view, they are relevant inasmuch as they express the possibilities of the youth as well as their shortcomings and certain shared wishes – their desire to come together, to recognize themselves and be valued as a collective subject with an identity different from the one branding them as dangerous; and their desire to be present in circumstances that link, painfully and unquestionably, what is personal with what is collective, and what is private with what is public.

Translated from Spanish by *Florencia Enghel*

Notes

1. Translation note: Cromañón, pronounced Cro-Magnon, is used throughout the text to refer to the nightclub.
2. Translation note: the band's name can be translated as "Street wanderers".
3. This has happened not only in the context of the last dictatorship (1976-1983), but also during democratic times, when police forces chose to repress, sometimes resorting to fire their guns

without justification. According to Coordination against Police and Institutional Repression (Correpi), between the return of democracy in 1983 and 2007, 2,300 young people have died as a consequence of police action in police stations and jails.

4. On 19-20 December 2001, Argentina experienced two days of popular outbreaks and subsequent repression, which led to a large number of detainees and resulted in 38 deaths. This situation forced then President Fernando de la Rúa to resign, and evidenced the deterioration of a representative system that no longer managed to articulate the demands of most of society. The levels of poverty and unemployment in a society that had historically had an extended middle class, and the economic measures that confiscated the savings of small-scale proprietors in order to sustain the fiction of dollarization, triggered the outbreaks, which questioned neoliberal policies. The events marked the start of a new economic and political cycle in which the state government aimed to regain its leadership vis-à-vis the markets and concentrated capital.

5. On the debates characteristic of the field of communication in Latin America in the 1970s see e.g. Mattelart, Armand and Dorfman, Ariel (1974) *Para leer al Pato Donald/Comunicación de masas y socialismo* (How to read Donald Duck/Imperialist Ideology in the Disney Comic), Buenos Aires: Siglo XXI. On the turn experienced since the 1980s, see e.g. Landi, Oscar (1992) *Devórame otra vez/Qué hizo la TV con la gente, qué hace la gente con la TV* (Devour me again/ What people did and do with TV), Buenos Aires: Planeta.

6. Developed by Latin American thinkers, Dependency Theory analyses, from an economic, political and cultural perspective, the reasons for the region's delayed development in the 1960s and 1970s. Its main figures include Fernando Cardoso, Celso Furtado and Teotonio dos Santos.

7. See a book which is paradigmatic of the field of communication in Latin America: Martín Barbero, Jesús (1991) *De los medios a las mediaciones* (Communication, culture and hegemony: from the media to mediations), Barcelona: Editorial Gustavo Gili.

8. During the period of state terrorism (1976-1983), even if many musicians were forced into exile and others were persecuted by the police, they were not disappeared. Rock was one of the few cultural spaces that could subsist during the dictatorship, becoming an inter-generational chain between the genre's founders and subsequent generations.

9. *Señales* (Signals), their fourth record, was produced after Cromañón.

10. The idea of "aguante", which could be translated as "hanging in there", became popular in Argentine daily life by the mid-1990s. It is used e.g. to cheer a soccer team with a small chance of winning, or to encourage an unknown rock band that must come out on stage to play. Young people also use it to indicate that they will give support to someone in an unfavourable situation. According to Pablo Semán (2006), "it is a physical and mainly moral category, which accounts for people's ability to resist and/or attack when in a disadvantageous situation. Its importance, which can be observed in different popular expressions, brings together soccer and music fans. [...] You 'hang in there' in rock when you oppose the police or the market and their perverse provocations ... when you state social truths that the false adult world and the institutions cannot accept". The aguante speaks of a way of life that, while unable to project itself into the future due to adversity, does not give up – it resists. The Spanish term is used throughout the text.

11. For youth cultures, one of the keys to their identity lies in the choice of sneakers. In her book *Emergencia de culturas juveniles* (The emergence of youth cultures), Rossana Reguillo Cruz analyses the role of Nike sneakers among certain groups of young people from popular sectors. "The Nike effect indicates the pressing need to go beyond the essayistic speculation and visualize the complexity of the consumption of culture as a sphere in which many things other than the lightness of being are at stake. Youth cultures cannot be analyzed divorced from a biopolitics of consumerism as mediation between the structures and logics of capital and the cultural interpretation of value". The Topper sneakers, made in Argentina, are cheaper and more austere than Nike sneakers. After Cromañón, they became a symbol. Their image was used as the logo for the organization *The Cromañón Youngsters* and included in stencils and stickers with the motto "Justice for our Callejeros".

12. It is important to reiterate here that the shrine is a space in which both young people and adult relatives of the victims express themselves. It is not an initiative belonging to youth exclusively.

13. Resorting to communication through the Internet is something young people had done before. They organized their participation in concerts – what they would do before the concert started – as well as travel when the band played faraway, and sometimes even the playlist of the songs that Callejeros was to perform in a given concert.
14. Many of the young survivors who resorted to legal action asked their lawyers to let the band be. As a consequence, the legal proceedings were organized in different groups. One of them says clearly "We do not hold Callejeros responsible". The band, however, is being taken to trial and, in the meantime, every time it gives a concert the money earned is confiscated.
15. www.fotolog.com/guason
16. www.fotolog.com/chakita87; www.fotolog.com/angeles_cromanon
17. For an example of the materials shared online see http://www.destinovisual.com/volante_cordoba_byn.jpg
18. A member of an engraving and print art workshop at a renowned fine arts school in Buenos Aires.
19. According to researcher Mariana Chavez: "The current paradigm is [...] insecurity; in that context, the young subject becomes the inner enemy, inasmuch as he/she represents insecurity. But isn't it a contradiction in terms that danger is represented by an insecure being? No. It is actually that insecurity that frames him/her within the paradigm, and that is what is dangerous" (Chaves, 2005).
20. For an online example that combines images of the catastrophe, the shrine, the campaign *Stop blaming a Callejeros* and other related expressions with the band's music and an invitation to join one of the forums see http://foro.callejeros.com.ar/, and http://es.youtube.com/watch?v=qUCU9Q1eNjE The motto is "We are organizing these actions so that we will be heard".

References

Alabarces, Pablo (2004) *Crónicas del aguante: Fútbol, violencia y política*. [Chronicles of the 'aguante': soccer, violence and politics] Buenos Aires: Capital Intelectual.

Altamirano, Carlos (dir.) (2002)*Términos críticos de sociología de la cultura*. [Critical terms of sociology of culture] Buenos Aires: Paidós.

Berti, Eduardo (1989) *Rockología*. [Rock-ology] Buenos Aires: AC Editora.

Bifo, Berardi Franco (2007) Generación post-alfa. [Generation post-alpha] Buenos Aires: Tinta Limón.

Bourdieu, Pierre (1999) *La miseria del mundo*. Madrid: Fondo de Cultura Económica.

Braslavsky, Cecilia (1986) La juventud argentina: informe de situación. [Argentine youth: status report] Buenos Aires: Centro Editor.

de Certaeu, Michel (1999) *La invención de lo cotidiano*. [The practice of everyday life] México: Universidad Iberoamericana.

Chaves, Mariana (2005) 'Juventud negada y negativizada. Representaciones y formaciones discursivas vigentes en la Argentina contemporánea'. [Youth denied and turned negative] in *Revista Última Década* N° 23, Valparaíso: Ediciones Cidpa.

Colectivo LaVaca (2005) *Generación Cromañón*. [Generation Cromañón] Buenos Aires: Ed. LaVaca.

Dri, Rubén (coord.) (2003) *Símbolos y fetiches religiosos en la construcción de la identidad popular*. [Symbols and religious fetishes in the construction of popular identity] Buenos Aires: Biblos.

Fernandez Bittar, Marcelo (1999) *Historia del rock en Argentina*. [The history of rock in Argentina] Buenos Aires: Distal.

Gramsci, Antonio (1972) *Cultura y literatura*. [Culture and literature] Barcelona: Península

Grignon, Claude & Passeron, Jean Claude (2004) *Lo culto y lo popular: miserabilismo y populismo en la sociología y en la literatura*. [What is cult and what is popular] Buenos Aires: Nueva Visión

Grinberg, Miguel (1993) *Cómo viene la mano: orígenes del rock argentino*. [What's the story: origins of Argentine rock] Buenos Aires: Distal.

Hobsbawm, Eric (2000) *Historia del siglo XX*. [The age of extremes] Barcelona: Crítica.

Hopenhayn, Martín (coord.) (2004) *La juventud en Iberoamérica: tendencias y urgencias*. [Youth in Ibero-America: trends and urgent matters] Santiago de Chile: CEPAL.

Lewkowicz, Ignacio (2004) *Pensar sin Estado*. [To think without the State] Buenos Aires: Editorial Paidós.

Martín Barbero, Jesús (1991) *De los medios a las mediaciones*. [Communication, culture and hegemony: from the media to mediations] Barcelona: Editorial Gustavo Gili.

Miguez, Daniel & Semán, Pablo (2006) *Entre santos, cumbias y piquetes. Las culturas populares en la Argentina reciente*. [Among saints, popular dances and picket lines] Buenos Aires: Biblio.

Oficina Internacional del Trabajo (OIT) (2007) *Trabajo Decente y Juventud – Argentina*. [Decent work and youth – Argentina] Lima: OIT.

Pintos, Victor (1993) *Tanguito, La verdadera historia*. [Tanguito: the true story] Buenos Aires: Planeta.

Pujol, Sergio (2007) *Las ideas del rock. Genealogía de la música rebelde*. [Rock's ideas] Rosario: Homo Sapiens Ediciones.

Pujol, Sergio (2006) *Rock y dictadura, crónica de una generación (1976-1983)*. [Rock and dictatorship, chronicle of a generation 1976-1983] Buenos Aires: Emecé Editores.

Reguillo Cruz, Rossana (2000) *Emergencia de culturas juveniles. Estrategias del desencanto*. [The emergence of youth cultures. Strategies of disenchantment] Buenos Aires: Norma.

Semán, Pablo (2006) *Bajo continuo. Exploraciones descentradas sobre cultura popular y masiva*. [Continuous bass: off-centre explorations of popular and massive culture] Buenos Aires: Gorla.

Semán, Pablo & Vila, Pablo (1999) '*Rock chabón e identidad juvenil en la Argentina neoliberal*'. [Neighborhood rock and youth identity in neoliberal Argentina] in Filmus, Daniel (comp.) *Los noventa: política, sociedad y cultura en América Latina y Argentina de fin de siglo*. [The 90s: politics, society and culture in Latin America and Argentina at the turn of the century] Buenos Aires: Eudeba.

Williams, Raymond (1985) *Keywords: A Vocabulary of Culture and Society*. New York: Oxford University Press.

Williams, Raymond (1997) *Marxismo y literatura*. [Marxism and literature] Barcelona: Península.

From Pages to Pixels
Belarus' Unique Youth Multimedia Magazine

Iryna Vidanava

Abstract

In Belarus, "Europe's last dictatorship", civil society and independent media are heavily repressed. Internet-based "new media" offers an effective and attractive tool for democrats to inform and engage citizens, particularly young people. Due to the country's regime and isolation, little research or reporting has been done on this subject. To explore the impact and possibilities of "new media" in Belarus, this article looks at the history and development of a pioneer and leading proponent, *CDMAG*. Originally created as a print magazine by young people for young people, this independent publication was transformed into a popular multimedia magazine. It utilizes cutting edge technology to survive and flourish while chronicling and building a separate public space for creative youth in this post-Soviet state. The story of *CDMAG* provides important lessons in using "new media" to reach out to young people and inspire them to be more civically active. It offers some ideas about why "new media" is one of the few fields in which the democratic opposition is outperforming the regime.

Belarus is often called "Europe's black hole" and is known mainly for its dictator, Alexander Lukashenka, and the 1986 Chernobyl Disaster. With its statues of Lenin, KGB, socialist realist buildings and collective farms, time seems to have stopped in this part of Europe, where nostalgia for the Soviet Union still holds sway. But many young Belarusians refuse to be left in the past. Behind the country's closed borders and hidden from the secret police, a dynamic youth political and cultural scene is alive and active, underground, in dorms, NGOs, music clubs, informal groups, artistic communities and cyberspace. The story of the country's opposition and counterculture youth, the future of a free Belarus, is being told by Internet-based, independent media. But more importantly, the political and cultural activism of pro-democratic youth is being aided and abetted by cutting-edge "new media." In Belarus today, the democratic opposition and the authoritarian regime are competing for the hearts and minds the country's youth, and "new media" is playing a key role in this struggle.

Bleak picture

Being young and active in "Europe's last dictatorship" is no easy task. The regime in Belarus targets independent youth groups working for democratic change.[1] Youth leaders have been imprisoned, activist students have been expelled from schools, youth politicians drafted into the army, and youth NGOs have been closed down.[2] The situation regarding independent media is also grim. Media rights groups consistently rank Belarus near the bottom of media freedom lists.[3] Independent newspapers and radio stations have been shut down, editors have been taken to court on trumped up charges, and journalists have been beaten, jailed, murdered and made to disappear. Since 1996, more than 1,200 independent media entities, including youth publications, have been closed down (Belarusian Association of Journalists 2008). According to Reporters Without Borders' 2008 report, "the free press has virtually disappeared and been forced underground" ('Reporters Without Borders' 2008). Belarus' citizens, including young people, suffer from a dramatic lack of independent information and have become more isolated and apathetic.

After the country's 2006 presidential elections, which were not recognized as free or fair by the international community, tens of thousands of young people rejected passivity and demonstrated for democracy and freedom. More than 1,000 young people were arrested, beaten, imprisoned, fired from jobs and expelled from studies. Since the March events, the regime has feared youth most of all. Despite heavy indoctrination, disinformation and pressure, a new generation of young activists has come to the fore. A key goal of the democratic opposition and independent media is to reach out to these youth and keep them engaged in civil society.

A creative response

To counter the regime, independent media has been forced to be more inventive in devising alternative ways to present its information. The result has been a flowering of free-floating alternative media, embodied by traditional *samizdat* (underground publishing), small-scale community bulletins, online journalism, email newspapers, information websites, blogging and social networking. While only a handful of indipedent newspapers still publish, the readers of online information sources are steadily increasing. Although the circulation of the print editions of state-run newspapers is many times larger than that of the independent press, the web versions of independent newspapers have become more innovative and popular than their state counterparts. Internet statistics indicate that the opposition dominates the "new media" information field. More than a half of the twenty most popular news and information websites are produced by the democratic opposition.[4]

Dozens of regional independent newspapers and NGOs have also established their own websites; some are more popular than their state counterparts. While the regime has succeeded in monopolizing broadcast media inside the country, television and radio stations targeting Belarus are broadcasting from abroad. The websites of two, Radio Liberty (www.svaboda.org) and European Radio for Belarus (www.euroradio.fm), are also popular.

"New media" and youth resistance

Young democratic activists in particular have embraced "new media", which does not yet require state registration, can be produced at home, and is easily disseminated, making it harder for the state to control. In Belarus, youth are a key force behind the opposition's "new media". While the editors of most important websites came of age in the 1990s, young people make up the core group of techies and journalists responsible for producing most of the Internet-based media. The webmasters, designers, programmers, photographers, bloggers and editors of "new media" are mostly from the younger generation. The average age of the journalists and DJs at the European Radio for Belarus, for example, is about 22; its technical staff is all under 26. Most regional websites are also run by activists under 35. Young people are the driving force of innovation in Belarus' media field, where they are creating unique projects and adjusting the latest technologies to the needs of Cyrillic Internet users. Unlike their older colleagues, most young journalists have impressive multimedia skills – they are able to report using audio, video and Internet technology.

Young people are not only the creative force behind the opposition "new media," they also are important users and purveyors. They have taken their struggle online, merging their activism with the Internet and acting as virtual dissidents. It also works both ways; young democrats are taking virtual activism live. They are utilizing the Web to improve their organizing and increase the impact of their real world activism. After the 2006 protests were brutally put down, young activists retreated to various online communities. Like the kitchen, which was the refuge of their Soviet dissident parents, the Internet became a virtual meeting place, where young activists camped out, held fireside chats and cooked up new forms of real-world resistance, such as flash mobs, campaigns to assist persecuted young people, and other forms of cyber-assisted activism[5].

Virtual activism has become an inseparable part of Belarusian reality, especially for the country's young generation of digital natives. The percentage of Internet penetration in Belarus is more than twice that of Russia. According to one 2006 survey, a third of the population regularly uses the Internet; half of these are under 30 years old.⁶ As reported by the Ministry of Statistics and Analysis, in 2000 there were only two computers per 100 families; by 2008 the number had increased to 32. For families with children younger than 18, the figure is even higher – 52 computers per 100 households (Doroshevich, 2009). The number of Internet users 16 years or older has increased from 16.2% in 2006 to 20.7% in 2007, and the number of mobile phone users topped seven million last year (Zimina 2008).

Young people are the chief users of these hi-tech tools. In a recent survey, students cite virtual activities as second in popularity only to going to discos, clubs and movies (Belarusian Institute for Strategic Studies, 2007). While most young Internet users in Belarus consider the Net to be primarily a source of entertainment, those heading online can hardly avoid the news and other information posted on Belarusian web portals. A purported state survey of students at two universities in Gomel found that more than a third of respondents listed the Internet as their primary source of information (Belarus Partisan 2007). Young Internet users form a vibrant, influential community that spreads independent information to tens of thousands and often influences public opinion. In a country of only 10 million, Belarusian youth make up the world's 13th largest LiveJournal community, including more than 42,445 blogs.⁷

From *Thought* to action

There are a number of interesting examples of youth-run "new media" which have been able to develop successfully despite the reprehensive human and media rights situation in Belarus. The two most popular regional Internet websites, *Narodnye Naviny Vitebska* [The people's news of Vitebsk] at http://news.vitebsk.cc, and Westki.info at http://westki.info, were founded and are run by activists younger than 35 years old, as is Generation.BY (http://generation.by), Belarus' most popular student website. But perhaps the most interesting "new media" story is *CDMAG*, formerly *Студэнцкая Думка* [Students' thought], the country's pioneer youth publication.⁸

Students' Thought first appeared as a Belarusian newspaper in 1924. After a long hiatus, it was re-started in 1988 by pro-democratic students during the USSR's glasnost period and became the bulletin of the Belarusian Students' Association, one of Belarus' first NGOs. During the early years of the country's independence, the publication was unprofessional, small, irregular, not especially lively and not very political. But in 1999, the bulletin became an independent youth magazine. Despite growing repression, it developed into a regular monthly and grew from 16 black-and-white to 40 color pages. By 2005, its circulation had grown from 500 to 5,000 copies and its readership was estimated to be over 10,000 per issue. The magazine covered topics such as cultural diversity, corruption at universities, youth employment, urban-rural differences, and youth and new technologies.

Cover of one of the first issues of *Students' Thought*, September 1998. *Photo:* © CDMAG

The worsening situation in Belarus pushed the magazine to become more activist and innovative. In 2003, it launched an activism campaign for youth. "Become. A Self-Made. Person". was the first Internet civic campaign in Belarus. Its goal was to paint a portrait of a new generation as seen through the eyes of young people, as well as to convince them that it is possible to be successful by becoming more civically active. Participating teams of two to three students were asked to describe and design their idea of the Belarusian dream. More than 160 teams submitted concepts. The finalists attended creative workshops run by specialists in social advertising. By the end of the trainings, each team had completed a script for a video and audio social commercial representing their generation's dreams and aspirations. The winning slogan declared "Don't wait for the right moment! Make it yourself!" Along with a 30-second cartoon, it was shown on state TV. This nonpolitical campaign, with elements of a game and reality show, attracted broad public attention: 600 young people entered the contest, thousands voted for their favorites online, and millions saw the winning cartoon on television.

It is not surprising that the authorities, unnerved by the impact on society of a relatively small independent publication, reacted by trying to close down

Students' Thought. At the end of November 2003, two weeks after the campaign's award ceremony, the editorial office received a notice from the Ministry of Information that the magazine's legal registration had been cancelled. Forced underground, the magazine continued publishing. Unable to be disseminated via the state-controlled subscription service, it created an alternative distribution system using places popular among youth, like clothing boutiques, Internet cafes and music stores. The magazine became one of the first publications in Belarus to launch its own website.

In summer 2005, a follow-on campaign – "Become. A Self-Made. Person. ACTION!" – was organized. This time, young people were asked to identify a social challenge facing their local community and propose a plan of action to raise public awareness of and address the problem. The finalists were provided with resources and outreach support to implement their own local social campaigns in Belarus' regions. The activities were so interesting and creative that state TV featured several on news programs. On the national level, this campaign was even more interactive than the first. Thousands of youth not only followed the contest online but also submitted problems from their own communities on a specially created website and took part in debates on what could be done to improve the situation. In addition to an immediate public impact, both campaigns also had long-term effects. Several participants ended up joining the editorial team and later used their hi-tech savvy to help transform the magazine into a "new media" publication. Others joined NGOs or started their own civic initiatives. Some became professional musicians, photographers, artists and advertisers, and many attribute their current careers to the experience gained from the campaigns.

Due to its growing influence, the publication's November 2005 issue was seized by the secret police under the pretext of being printed with "poisonous ink", and the magazine was banned. A criminal case was launched against the founder and editor-in-chief. After the incident, printing houses were afraid to continue printing the unregistered, illegal magazine, since it might lead to their closure as well.

Going digital

The publication's response was to transform itself into a multimedia edition, published on compact disc. The editorial team exploited a loophole in the media law, which did not regulate materials on CDs. In January 2006, the magazine reappeared under the title of *CDMAG* (the letters "C" and "D" in Belarusian are the first letters of the two words in the title of *Students' Thought*, as well as the abbreviation for "compact disc"). Like the original magazine, *CDMAG* targets students and youth aged 18 to 25. The Belarusian-language monthly offers pieces on social, political, economic and cultural issues important to youth, such as problems of higher education, students' rights, professional opportunities for youth, international exchanges, information on youth NGOs, Belarusian youth subcultures, and European youth culture. Each issue focuses on one topic of particular relevance to youth. Regular sections of the publication include a spotlight on a unique young person who is a leader in his or her field, an in-depth analysis of Belarus' system of education or those abroad, a look at the month's most interesting cultural events, a presentation of a young artist's work, and a piece of investigative journalism.

The shift to "new media" allowed the magazine to become more attractive to youth, which is drawn to compact disc, DVD, and other computer-friendly technology. In addition to text and pictures, the CD format allows the use of catchy video, audio, music and flash animation. Original, youth-oriented video materials (short spots, reports and interviews) make up 50 to 70 percent of each issue. The CD format also allows a much more substantial publication. For example, the final print issue of *Students' Thought* included .87 MB of text (44 pages with illustrations). The average issue of *CDMAG* contains more than 600 MB of text, illustrations, video and audio clips, and flash animation. Since the CD can easily be read, replicated or disseminated on any computer, an endless number of copies can be burned and distributed underground. In fact, *CDMAG*'s slogan is "Make Your Own Copy!" The editors estimate that the number of readers of each issue is four to five times higher than the 5,000 CDs produced. Finally, *CDMAG*'s audio and video clips offer some alternative to the state's monopoly over television and radio broadcasting.

That summer, the magazine showed what the new format could do. It produced a special issue on the March presidential elections and the demonstrations that followed the rigged contest. The "Open Air Revolution" issue told the story of the revolution that took place in the minds of the young people who were active participants in, and often leaders of, the March 2006 events. It was the first multimedia chronicle of the key events surrounding the election, depicting the Election Day demonstration, the rise and fall of the protest's "tent city", the Independence Day march and the crackdown that followed, in which more than 1,000 people, mostly youth, were beaten, detained and imprisoned.

The issue told the dramatic story through more than four hours of the words, music, lyrics, pictures, poetry, videos, protest materials and text messages of young people who took part in the events. It contained audio and video interviews with participants and various video and audio materials recorded during the actions, including those smuggled out of prisons. The issue showed the many different sides of the events – the excitement, hopes, dreams, disappointment, fear, suffering and commitment to the struggle for freedom and democracy – through the eyes of youth. An English-language version was produced to allow foreigners to experience the story of the March "Rave-o-lution" as lived by Belarus' young generation.

The "Open Air" issue proved to be so popular that a follow up edition was produced and dedicated to the one-year anniversary of the 2006 events. The second issue included a new design, four original pieces on the most important trends during the 12 months after the protests, and follow-up interviews with the heroes of the first edition. An English-language version of the follow up issue was released under the title "Back to the Future". In recognition of its unique transformation and reporting on the March events, *CDMAG* was awarded the Gerd Bucerius Prize for "Free Press of Eastern Europe" in 2007.[9]

All about youth

"Youth media are in decline and extremely underdeveloped in Belarus. There is not a single influential and popular publication for youth. The only exception is *CDMAG* – the country's brightest and most progressive youth magazine", – wrote a 20-year old student of journalism at Belarusian State University in a course paper on the history, content, language and significance of *Students' Thought* and *CDMAG*. "In my opinion, *CDMAG* sets very high standards of journalism. Its editors and authors are creative and original. No other media has spoken about many of the problems covered in *CDMAG*. Like youth itself, *CDMAG* is always avant-garde, experimenting with its content and formats. It targets creative, curious and proactive young people. It is possible to say that *CDMAG* represents Belarus' most progressive youth circles."[10]

What this young scholar and *CDMAG* reader defines as progressive is derived from a key principle – the magazine is produced by young people for young people. In 1998, students formed the original editorial team of *Students' Thought*. Over the course of a decade, it has developed into a professional office which includes three editors and a designer, proofreader and programmer. Today, about 30 young activists, mainly students, contribute to producing *CDMAG*. There is no requirement that one be a trained journalist to become a contributor. Any young person with good ideas and the wish to cooperate is welcome. Together with the editorial team, contributors develop topics and materials for future issues. Given the multimedia format, authors often work together in small teams, with one person coming up with the idea for the piece, another assisting with video or flash animation production, and an editor putting it all together. The combination of a professional editorial team and freelance contributors, which are from the age group of the magazine's audience (and who often join the publication after first being its readers), helps *CDMAG* to accurately reflect new trends and stay on top of developments in youth life.

The editorial team actively communicates with its audience via email and the magazine's blog community. Each week, it receives hundreds of comments and dozens of emails. Andrus, a 20-year old reader, wrote: "I was lucky to get the "Eco" issue. Super! I liked it very much. Moreover, I'm deeply impressed! Good job! I would like to contribute to your magazine, if possible." Unlike traditional editorial offices, *CDMAG*'s team actively encourages not only feedback from readers but also their active participation in creating the magazine, thus maintaining its youthful and informal style. The magazine serves as an informal school of youth journalism. Most authors are not professional journalists; they learn by doing and are trained by experienced editors. Several contributors have moved on to other independent media as full-time correspondents.

The concept of the magazine has evolved over the last ten years, but the goal remains the same: to inform, educate and encourage young people to be more active in civil society. Knowing that young people tend to resist when told what to do, the magazine avoids providing ready answers or imposing certain views. Rather, it strives to be diverse and pluralistic, offering a broad range of opinions. Provocative, but supported by strong arguments, its materials often generate spirited debate. Born in a repressive authoritarian state, the publication's goal is to encourage young people to think for themselves and make their own choices, whether it is about the candidates they vote for or the clothes they wear.

Popularizing the counterculture

Like kids everywhere, young Belarusians are crazy about the Internet, fashion and popular culture. But unlike in the West, where all of this is readily available, in Belarus the state attempts to restrict everything independent. Here, in the middle of Europe, youth activists are detained, expelled from universities and fired from jobs. Youth NGOs have been disbanded, youth publications seized and alternative bands banned. The Lukashenka regime tries to control youth life because it fears any free ideas, whether home-grown or from the West. A "state ideology" course is taught during early school years and is required for all college freshmen. All state employees must take a special ideology exam as a part of hiring procedures. A new regulation requires that all college applicants seeking to study journalism, international relations and law must obtain letters of recommendations from their local authorities. The Ministry of Culture decides what kind of music private FM radio stations play and the Ministry of Education sets official guidelines for youth fashion.

The authorities can try to restrict, impose, threaten and repress, but they really can't determine what young people wear, listen to, read or watch. Like with jazz in the 1950s and jeans in the 1960s Soviet bloc, what is forbidden today in Belarus becomes even more trendy and desirable. Young Belarusians are no different than other youth who respond to restrictions and regulations with creative forms of dissent. Thanks to the regime, the youth counterculture is alive and well in Belarus. When peaceful meetings are broken up, young activists stage flash mobs and street performances that ridicule the absurdities of the authorities. When concerts are cancelled, youngsters go to underground night clubs, across borders and to forest festivals to listen to their blacklisted bands. When there is no officially approved venue for their works, young artists, photographers and designers show in alternative art galleries and post their works online. Independent writers and journalists publish in underground newspapers and journals, create online communities, and spread information through blogs and homemade documentary films and videos. These are the subjects being covered by *CDMAG*.

Timely topics

Each multimedia issue of *CDMAG* blends together serious and light materials. Young people can read, hear and see stories about Belarus' hippies, geeks, revolutionaries, rock stars, artists, student leaders and other nonconformist heroes. Recent issues were dedicated to the environmental movement, higher education, music censorship, and the country's regions, all key issues in authoritarian Belarus. "The Regions" issue, for example, aimed to shed light on the "unknown" aspects of youth life in the provinces, which tend not to be the focus of the mainstream media or general public. *CDMAG* managed to unearth interesting and colorful personalities and trends in the fields of civic, cultural and educational life. The materials included an audio interview with and a photo slide show on a young guy from Horki, a small town in Mahiliou region, who created a website (www.dobraja.com) for his grandmother. The site, which preserves her Soviet-era folk tales, songs and memories of village life, was his birthday present to her. Another video featured a group of young activists from the small western city of Baranavichy which transformed an abandoned school gym into the country's coolest "do-it-yourself" music club.

The "Eco Life Style" issue focused on the country's most pressing environmental challenges, not only to make young people aware of key issues but also to motivate them to be active in an environmental sense, beginning with adopting a green lifestyle and leading to joining green initiatives. It offered an in-depth look at the current public debate over nuclear power, since the Lukashenka regime plans to build a new reactor in the country that suffered most from the Chernobyl disaster. Teams of an author and environmental expert worked together on each piece. The issue contains two videos on alternative energy issues, made in an investigative reporting style, one flash comic with a person who lives according to "green principles", and several photo slideshows and podcasts, as well as texts and several designer prints with the magazine's logos and environmental slogans, so readers can make their own alternative tee shirts.

The second disc of the double issue included a ranking of the top environmentally-themed films of the last half century and four episodes of popular cartoons – "The Simpsons", "The Oblongs", "Sponge Bob" and "South Park" – on environmental issues, translated and dubbed into Belarusian. None of these cartoons have ever appeared in Belarusian. These materials were chosen because debates on environmentalism are usually presented in a somber manner and stress dire consequences in order to garner public attention. In contrast, *CDMAG* tried to portray environmental challenges and activism in a colorful and humorous way in order to attract and not turn off young people. The goal was to educate readers and promote their green activism by drawing on a variety of youth-friendly sources. Feedback from readers proved that this approach worked for some in the target audience. Tatsiana wrote: "Good job! The Eco issue had a really great design! The content is very interesting and it's also very nice that it's all done with humor. Special thanks for putting together an issue on environmental problems. Haven't seen anything like this before!"

The "Music under Pressure" issue focused on the idea that freedom of expression is an essential right for everyone, and one that is especially attractive to young people. The lead piece featured a relatively new but popular band, "Mauzer", which was banned from performing in Belarus due to its controversial lyrics, which are openly critical of the regime, and its provocative musical style. A 20-minute video was produced, using a backstage rockumentary style of reporting, focusing on human rights issues as seen through the eyes of the members of a popular but underground band. The issue also included multimedia materials on music censorship in other countries, rising music stars from around the world who promote worthy causes, historical music censorship in the Belarusian Soviet Socialist Republic, what other jobs Belarusian musicians must do besides playing music to earn a living, the musical press in Belarus, and the winner of a contest for the most creative homemade music video.

Something special

CDMAG frequently works in partnership with other youth initiatives and produces special issues when something interesting or unusual happens. For example, a student festival – "UnRealStudentLife" – took place at Minsk's Museum of Film History in February 2008. For one week, the staid museum was transformed into a place where students could show their art, music, stage performances, fashion, and homemade videos, while hanging out together in a very informal but energetic atmosphere. More than 20 young activists contributed to the exhibit. The organizer – the student initiative StudFarmat (Student Format) – set no limits in terms of artistic style or quality. The goal was to display a diverse set of pieces interesting for students, including works that inspire them to express their creativity. At a time when the regime was cracking down on young activists, hundreds of students attended the exhibit, which became one of the hit cultural events of the year and attracted broad public attention. *CDMAG* decided that the festival should be available to those who could not attend, as well as to preserve its unique exhibits for future generations. So it published an electronic catalogue of the event on compact disc as a special issue.

As a multimedia publication in an ever changing world of technological advancement, the magazine continues to experiment with other formats. Last fall, *CDMAG* released an issue on digital video disc (DVD). "Stand.BY"[11] was the magazine's first attempt to create a television-style show on disc. Since the issue was produced in a DVD format, instead of the magazine's traditional flash technology, the video materials were of a higher quality and could also be watched on big screen TVs, making the issue look like an actual TV show. The disc consisted of three video pieces, 6-7 minutes each, presented as one video block with an introduction, music theme, and special design uniting all three video spots, and a musical insert. The goal of the show was to portray irrational, marginal and unique subjects that cannot be shown on Belarusian state TV, the dictatorship's main propaganda mouthpiece.

The issue featured a video interview with a young, gay Afro-Belarusian, depicting what it is like to be a black homosexual in a country where racism and homophobia still flourish. Another report featured the most marginal band in Belarus, "UNB", which has made 104 albums but played only a dozen concerts and rarely appeared on state radio because the regime considers it to be controversial. The piece considers what it means to be an underground band for more than 25 years and why the group never became a headliner. The final video featured an artist who chooses to live and create in the basement of an apartment block. The perpetually drunk Vladimir Akulov, who produces an average of 20 paintings a day in a sparsely furnished cellar, exhibits and sells well mostly abroad. Life in a concrete bunker, where there is little fresh air but plenty of alcohol, is quite different. It is a place where news of the outside world comes only from state TV and time seems to have stopped.

As the editors expected, "Stand.BY" sparked varied feedback. The office received these two unsigned emails on the same day: "I watched the issue, but hated it. What happened to you guys? Don't you have anything else to film? I don't think anybody will find it interesting." and "Got it! Thank you! Absolutely fantastic! I've already started distributing it among my friends. I especially liked the piece on that artist." Many readers found the issue to be eye-opening. Kryscina, a 21-year old, wrote: "We received the "Stand.BY" issue. By the way, it's already being passed around among my friends. It causes mixed feelings. Some people are shocked, but the issue definitely touches the heart. And I like it! Really, people should not only see a pretty picture. They should see how life really is, even when it's brutal."

Different strokes

In Belarus, where the regime wants youth to be a passive grey mass that silently obeys state orders, *CDMAG* encourages its readers to be active individuals. "Don't be like the others, Be yourself!" is a motto of the publication, which is constantly searching for new faces, trends and phenomena. One way to help young Belarusians overcome the fear of being different in a dictatorship is to feature their peers who have already achieved something special in their lives and to share their opinions on important youth issues. In this way, many well-known musicians and artists were first featured in *CDMAG* at the start of their careers.

While trying to "keep it real", the editors realize that it can be dangerous for the magazine's authors and subjects to appear openly in an underground publication. This is when the multimedia format shines as a form and means to communicate the publication's message and promote its mission. In choosing the format of each piece (video, podcast, photo slideshow, comic or flash cartoon), the editors decide the best fit for the form, content, artistic style, risk factor, and wishes of the person featured. When appearing on film is too dangerous, flash cartoons with animated figures, but using real voices from a recorded interview, are utilized. Interactive comics and photo slide shows are also used to protect activists.

Specially designed covers and internal art work are another special feature of the magazine, which makes it stand out on the Belarusian media market. Each disc is designed and programmed specifically to reflect the topic of the issue. For example, the "Univers" issue, which examined different aspects of higher education, had the look of a student's notebook, with ink doodles serving as pathways to the materials. "Music under Pressure" appeared to be a concert stage with the silhouettes of famous musicians and used different microphones as entry points for the contents. Making every issue look different keeps readers interested and makes the magazine fun to explore.

Layout of the inside page of the "Univers" issue. *Photo:* © CDMAG

Speaking in tongues

CDMAG is on the cutting edge of the "culture wars" in Belarus. Like its predecessor *Students' Thought*, *CDMAG* is published in the Belarusian language, which is suppressed by the country's Russophile regime and often presented as a peasant language. After more than two centuries of russification when Belarus was occupied by Russia and Soviet Union, the majority of the population uses Russian,

Belarus' second state language. The russification policy has been continued by Lukashenka.[12] In Minsk, the capital with a population of two million, there are only six schools where all subjects are taught in Belarusian. Virtually all state newspapers are published and all state electronic media broadcast in Russian.

By using the country's native language, *CDMAG* strengthens national identity among young people and helps them to feel part of a diverse European community. A leading independent newspaper wrote: "*Students' Thought* writes in such sexy and modern Belarusian that it makes everyone want to begin speaking it right away" (Siarhej 2008). As with form and content, the magazine experiments with language. Its editors and authors are not been afraid to create new words to help define modern trends. "Language must be organic. This is why the language of our magazine is close to the living language and slang of the streets", believes a *CDMAG* editor. The publication also uses many English words in order to expand the borders of young Belarusians who are not able to travel freely but are passionate about transatlantic youth life and popular culture. A critic wrote that: "Whether you like it or hate it, *Students' Thought* is something new, something unseen before among Belarusian language publications."[13]

The publication targeted a new law on language requiring a standardized form of Belarusian that is closer to Russian. Since several independent newspapers and magazines use a more traditional form of Belarusian, this law may force some publications to abandon their traditional language or be closed down. Despite its problems, the law did not spark much public debate or protest, even among activists of Belarusian language and culture. *CDMAG*, which also uses traditional Belarusian and is considered to be one of the creators of modern Belarusian, decided to publish an issue on language as a cultural, social and political phenomenon. It was both a response and an attempt to draw public attention, especially of youth, to the issue. The issue includes multimedia pieces on young couples who speak Belarusian and raise their children to use Belarusian, despite the country's pro-Russian climate, youth activists who refuse to speak Belarusian on principle, minority languages and popular youth slang from other countries; the fashion of using Cyrillic symbols in art and fashion, and youth who translate foreign movies and cartoons into Belarusian as a hobby. The issue also contains a unique Belarusian-English slang dictionary and phrase book, as well as designer prints for tee shirts that promote Belarusian.

The issue generated a lively debate. An anonymous reader responded: "Your 'Language' disc really touched me. I found some of the materials quite provocative, but you made me think". *Nasha Niva*, the country's leading Belarusian-language independent newspaper, reposted a flash cartoon, "Language is Politics in Belarus", from the issue, which became one of the most popular materials on its website, garnering 175 comments.[14] The piece was promoted as the "Video of the Week" on www.belarus-live.tv, Belarus' first online TV channel. In the week following the posting, more than 1,200 people also watched it on YouTube.

Among the elite

While not overtly political, *CDMAG* encourages young people to think and make informed choices. It remains the only national publication introducing key ideas, events and people to a general youth audience. Not just a magazine, it also conducts civic campaigns, linking politically active youth with creative young representatives of the counterculture and strengthening youth activism and the Belarusian democratic movement as a whole. A Belarusian youth website posted the following assessment: "The language of this multimedia magazine is an example of very high quality journalism and the ability to prove the arguments made by the authors in a very interesting way. Every issue, published on compact disc using a flash format, is topical. The magazine is enriched with audio and visual materials. Unbelievable! By banning and persecuting independent media, the state forces them to produce even better and more competitive products. *CDMAG* is a great source of free, alternative and very interesting information. Start reading it right away!"[15]

Distributed by hand and further duplicated and passed along by readers, each *CDMAG* issue manages to reach more than 20,000 young Belarusians. To date, its 119 original video materials posted on YouTube have been viewed by at least 62,000 people.[16] Some 122,000 viewers have watched *CDMAG* videos on www.belarus-live.tv. The magazine's blog community on LiveJournal counts 220 active members and is regularly read by more than 300 bloggers.[17] But despite its growing popularity, *CDMAG* can hardly be called a mass publication. Understanding the limitations of the magazine's impact and poor growth prospects in Belarus' current unfavourable conditions, *CDMAG*'s creators by necessity focus on Belarus' young elites. The team tries to expand the minds and mentality of students and youth leaders, believing that the vanguard of this new generation will play a crucial role in bringing changes to Belarus and transforming it into a European democracy.

Not all wine and roses

Belarus is a dictatorship in which independent media and activist youth are under great pressure. *CDMAG* is an underground publication that is produced, distributed and even read at some risk. In normal countries, most media do not need to fear the secret police. Despite the security measures undertaken by the *CDMAG* team, it is impossible to exclude the possibility that the KGB will target the publication and put it out of business. Operating in conspiratorial conditions limits the magazine's growth and development. Editors and contributors must work anonymously and cannot openly build a community around the publication.

While the compact disc format makes the magazine unique and helps it to avoid persecution by the regime, it also imposes atypical challenges. Producing a multimedia publication is more demanding than putting together a print edition. Video pieces and flash cartoons are complicated and time-consuming to assemble. Just designing and programming an issue takes 7 to 10 days. Therefore in summer 2009 the magazine moved to a bimonthly production cycle but added an online version at 34mag.net (the numbers refer to third and fourth letters of the Latin alphabet that spell out CD) that is updated daily. Multimedia also calls for special skills from editors and contributors, so training demands are higher. Although the multimedia format is attractive for youth, compact discs are more difficult to read and navigate than print editions. They require access to a computer and cannot be read by students on the go. Print is tougher to read on a computer screen, so the multimedia version of *CDMAG* contains less text than the print version of the magazine. While offered free of charge, the magazine must be distributed through private channels since the state-controlled post, subscription services, and retail outlets will not accept it. Distribution by informal networks of trusted persons limits the size, geographical coverage, impact and readership of issues. It is often to difficult to insure that issues always reach subscribers and the target audience.

With independent media persecuted and marginalized by the regime, it should not be surprising that there are few surveys, articles, books or audience analysis studies available to ascertain the impact of non-state publications like *CDMAG*. Given the newness of the field and the ideological constraints of state-controlled academia, there has been little scientific research, analysis and debate on "new media" in Belarus. For *CDMAG*, reader feedback offers some indication of the publication's impact: Borys offered the following about the

Layout of a page from a special English issue. *Photo:* © CDMAG

"Language" issue: "Watched your new creative issue with great admiration. As always, cool and interesting. I have a question: What would you recommend to a Russian speaker who wants to speak Belarusian?" The editorial team included a short, anonymous electronic questionnaire in "The Regions" issue, which was automatically emailed back to the office when the disc's user went online. The humorous questionnaire was designed to provoke readers' response, allowing the editors to identify and track readers. According to the results, 82% of the audience is 18 to 25 years old, 12% is older than 25, and 5% is younger than 17. Of the respondents, 61% watched "The Regions" issue alone, 23% indicated that two or three people watched the disc and 16% declared that they had copied the issue onto a home computer network.

The existence and development of *CDMAG* is only one example of how the regime is losing the "new media" war. But the authorities are not remaining idle. In February 2009, a new law on media went into effect which could be used to control the Internet.[18] The regime understands well the bond between "new media" and youth. Lukashenka has declared: "It is time to stop the anarchy on the Internet. We cannot allow this great technological achievement of man to be turned into an information garbage heap." The first legal action taken against a "new media" outlet took place in 2005, when the regime repressed the Third Way youth NGO for displaying cartoons on its website that "insulted" Lukashenka.[19] The case was used as a pretext for the March 2008 raids against other independent media outlets. Yet despite the attempts to silence freedom of expression and suppress youth activism, creative young people continue to come up with new forms of resistance.

Breaking borders and barriers

At a time when Belarus is isolated internationally, the magazine is also developing partnerships with a number of popular youth media in the European Union, such as *Chili* (Denmark), *Plotki* (Germany), *Spunk* (Netherlands) and *Üliõpilasleht* (Estonia), as well as the European youth media projects Cafebabel.com and Europocket Television. Some of the materials from these outlets have been translated and published in different issues of *CDMAG*. Last fall, three of *Chili's* editors visited Belarus and met with youth activists, students, journalists, and human rights defenders. As a result, *Chili's* November issue included a cover story on Belarus that was read by more than 80,000 youngsters and provoked a lively discussion among readers. As part of Belarus' broader youth movement, the magazine was also featured in Estonia's *Students' Newspaper* in December 2007 and in *Eesti Ekspress*, a leading national daily, in January 2008.[20] By cooperating with popular foreign youth publications, participating in international youth and media events, and releasing annual special English issues with its best materials, *CDMAG* is introducing an unknown, freer Belarus to the Euro-Atlantic community.

CDMAG is a unique youth publication which has already made an impact on several generations of Belarusian youngsters. It is creating an alternative public space for nonconformist youth dissatisfied with a stifling regime. In "Europe's last dictatorship", the magazine is a breath of fresh air and beacon of hope for youth. As one independent paper declared: "reading it is like traveling to another Belarus..." (Martinovich, 2004). *CDMAG* has responded to complex political and economic challenges by successfully transforming itself from a print to a multimedia magazine. In terms of both format and content, the publication remains in the forefront of "new media". It continues to play a key role in bridging virtual and real youth activism. After almost a decade, *CDMAG* remains one of the most interesting and innovative independent publications in Belarus

In Belarus, "new media" is a powerful tool being wielded against authoritarianism. It is attracting "the best and brightest" of Belarus' opposition and nonconformist youth. In contrast to the oppressive regime, Belarusian cyberspace is full of energy and ideas. A core group of creative and committed young people, including those around *CDMAG*, are helping "new media" to win the online information war against the regime. "New media" initiatives, even on a small scale, are inspiring thousands of youngsters to be more active. Working together, "new media" and youth are at the forefront of creating a modern European culture that is strengthening Belarusian identity and promoting the ideals of freedom, independence and democracy.

Notes

1. On the youth situation see Iryna Vidanava and Rodger Potocki, "Out with the Old," at http://www.data.minsk.by/belarusnews/122007/208.html, and Iryna Vidanava, "Pawns on the March" at http://www.belreview.cz/articles/3188.html..

2. For information on Belarus' human rights situation, see the webpage of the country's leading monitoring organization, the Viasna Human Rights Group, at: http://spring96.org/en/about.
3. For international assessments of the independent media situation, see the annual reports of Freedom House, http://www.freedomhouse.org/uploads/FOP_Belarus.pdf, Reporters Without Borders, http://www.rsf.org/article.php3?id_article=25496, and the Committee to Protect Journalists, http://www.cpj.org/attacks07/europe07/bel07.html.
4. For the 30-day period prior to November 10th, for example, the top two Internet resources and more than half of the Top 30 were independent or opposition websites. See http://top.akavita.com/Mass_Media_and_News/Internet-media/30days/visitors/by.
5. For information about flash mobs, see "Belarus, Flash Mobs and the Ice Cream Revolution" at http://www.andycarvin.com/archives/2006/05/belarus_flash_mobs_a.html. For information about cyber activism, see "Belarus: Give Lukashenko his LuNet!" at http://www.data.minsk.by/belarusnews/102007/2.html.
6. More recent statistics on Internet penetration are contradictory. A UN study puts the number at 56.5%. See http://newmediabelarus.net/node/3. The website www.internetworldstats.com puts the number at 61.9%, with a growth of 3,233.3% from 2000-08, see http://www.internet-worldstats.com/stats4.htm#europe. What is interesting is that even under the current regime, which is quite traditional and fearful of innovation, Internet usage is rapidly growing.
7. For the LiveJournal statistics, see http://www.livejournal.com/stats.bml.
8. For an electronic archive of *Students' Thought* issues, see http://www.kamunikat.org/studenckaja_dumka.html.
9. The Gerd Bucerius Prize is awarded annually by Germany's ZEIT Foundation and Norway's Freedom of Expression Foundation to publications in the region which strive to promote press freedom and freedom of expression in the face of threats and censorship.
10. "Канцэптуальны аналіз часопіса *Студэнцкая думка* ["A Conceptual Analysis of the Publication *Students' Thought*"] http://www.referat-911.ru/referat/journalism/2_object6685.html.
11. BY is also the international abbreviation for Belarus.
12. For information about the regime's language policy, see David Marples, *Belarus: A Denationalized Nation* (Harwood Academic Publishers, 1999).
13. Interview with Siarhai Sakharau from "*Студэнцкая Думка:* часопіс, не падобны да іншых," Центр экстремальной журналистики ["*Students' Thought*: A Publication Like No Other," Center for Extreme Journalism]. http://www.library.cjes.ru/online/?a=con&b_id=571&c_id=6757.
14. Я не люблю беларускую мову, *Наша Ніва* [I Don't Like the Belarusian Language, *Nasha Niva*]. http://www.nn.by/index.php?c=ar&i=19633.
15. Мартиновіч, Виктор, "Пробило на "Думку", *Белгазета*, No.14, [Martinovich, Viktor, "Getting *Dumka*," *Belgazeta*, No. 14]. http://www.belgazeta.by/20040412.14/430460142.
16. See the 119 videos and their statistics at http://www.youtube.com/34video.
17. *CDMAG*'s LiveJournal community is at http://community.livejournal.com/4asapopi3.
18. "Despite protests, Lukashenko signs restrictive media law", Committee to Protect Journalists, http://cpj.org/2008/08/despite-protests-lukashenko-signs-restrictive-medi.php.
19. The Lukashenka quote originally appeared in the state newspaper, *Soviet Belarus*. With information about the case against the Third Way, it is cited in Sami Ben Gharbia, "Belarus: Give Lukashenko his LuNet!" Belarus News and Analysis. http://www.data.minsk.by/belarusnews/102007/2.html
20. For the Estonian publications, see http://www.yliopilasleht.ee/5554 and http://paber.ekspress.ee/viewdoc/CABBC9B16632F4CCC22573BD00808F45. In 2009, two joit issues were produced in cooperation with Lithuanian's leading youth magazine, Pravda.

References

Attacks on the Press 2007: Belarus (2008) Committee to Protect Journalists. http://cpj.org/2008/02/attacks-on-the-press-2007-belarus.php (accessed November 2, 2008).

Belarus – Annual Report 2008 (2008) 'Reporters Without Borders'.

Belarus, Flash Mobs and the Ice Cream Revolution, Andy Carvin's Waste of Bandwidth. http://www.andycarvin.com/archives/2006/05/belarus_flash_mobs_a.html (accessed November 6, 2008).

Ben Gharbia, Sami (2008) 'Belarus: Give Lukashenko his LuNet!', *Belarus News and Analysis*. http://www.data.minsk.by/belarusnews/102007/2.html (accessed November 8, 2008).

'Despite protests, Lukashenko signs restrictive media law' (2008) Committee to Protect Journalists, http://cpj.org/2008/08/despite-protests-lukashenko-signs-restrictive-medi.php (accessed November 9, 2008).

Doroshevich, Mikhail (2009) 'Belarus: 32% of Household have Computers', *e-Belarus.org*.

Freedom of the Press: Belarus (2008) Freedom House. http://www.freedomhouse.org/uploads/FOP_Belarus.pdf (accessed November 1, 2008).

'Internet Communications in Belarus' (2008) New Media Belarus. http://newmediabelarus.net/node/3 (accessed November 8, 2008).

'Internet Usage in Europe', *Internet World Stats: Usage and Population Statistics*. http://www.internetworldstats.com/stats4.htm#europe (accessed November 8, 2008).

Marples, David (1999) *Belarus: A Denationalized Nation*. Harwood Academic Publishers.

Mass Media in Belarus, 2007: Annual Report, Belarusian Association of Journalists, Minsk, 2008, p. 8. http://baj.by/index.php?module=p&type=file&func=get&tid=6&fid=pdf&pid=16 (accessed November 4, 2008).

Vidanava, Iryna & Rodger Potocki:'Out with the Old', *Belarusian News and Analysis*. http://www.data.minsk.by/belarusnews/122007/208.html (accessed November 5, 2008).

Vidanava, Iryna: 'Pawns on the March', *Belarusian Review*, Vol. 20, No. 2. http://www.belreview.cz/articles/3188.html (accessed November 3, 2008).

Зимина, Ирина (2008) 'Сколько интернет-пользователей в Беларуси? Мнения экспертов', IT.TUT.BY [Zimina, Iryna: 'How Many Internet Users are there in Belarus? Expert Opinions'] http://it.tut.by/news/97123.html (accessed November 4, 2008).

'Интернет-издания, новостные ресурсы', *Akabita*, [Internet-Media, News Resources, Akavita]. http://top.akavita.com/Mass_Media_and_News/Internet-media/30days/visitors/by (accessed November 9, 2008).

'Канцэптуальны аналіз часопіса *Студэнцкая думка*' ['A Conceptual Analysis of the Publication *Students' Thought*"] http://www.referat-911.ru/referat/journalism/2_object6685.html (accessed November 1, 2008).

Luft (2008) 'Война по законам подлости', *LiveJournal* [Luft, 'War without Rules', *LiveJournal*]. http://community.livejournal.com/lulu_gov_by/163808.html (accessed November 6, 2008).

Мартинович, Виктор (2008) 'Пробило на 'Думку', *Белгазета*, No.14, [Martinovich, Viktor, 'Getting Dumka', *Belgazeta*, No. 14]. http://www.belgazeta.by/20040412.14/430460142 (accessed November 9, 2008).

Новая информационная война. Эпизод второй", *Белорусский Партизан* (2008) [The New Information War: Episode Two, *Belarus Partisan*]. http://www.belaruspartisan.org/bp-forte/?newsPage=0&page=100&news=18614 (accessed November 9, 2008).

Студэнцкая Думка: часопіс, не падобны да іншых, Центр экстремальной журналистики [Students' thought: A publication like no other, Center for Extreme Journalism] http://www.library.cjes.ru/online/?a=con&b_id=571&c_id=6757.

Сяргей, Мэдыя-часопіс 'CDMAG – глыток свабоднай інфармацыі' (2008) [Siarhai, The Media Publication CDMAG – A Breath of Free Information]. http://gayby.org/naviny/belarus/medyya-chasopis-34-glytok-svabodnai-infarmacyi.html (accessed November 3, 2008).

Ценностные ориентации и гражданская активность белорусских студентов. Результаты социологического исследования, BISS, (2007) [*The Value Orientation and Civic Activism of Belarusian students: Results of a Sociological Survey*, Minsk, Belarus: Belarusian Institute for Strategic Studies.

'Я не люблю беларускую мову', *Наша Ніва* [I don't like the Belarusian language, *Nasha Niva*]. http://www.nn.by/index.php?c=ar&i=19633 (accessed November 4, 2008).

The Power of Voice
*North Koreans Negotiating Identity
and Social Integration via Mediated Storytelling*

Jiwon Yoon

Abstract

About 1500 to 2000 North Koreans emigrate to South Korea each year and about 13 to 15% of them range in age from nine to eighteen years. These young refugees struggle not only from the differences they experience in social, cultural and economical gaps, but also from discrimination by South Koreans. Such difficulties encourage young North Korean refugees to be less confident in direct forms of interpersonal communication, leading them to rely more on mediated communication. Unlike their parent-generation whose media experiences exclusively include mass media consumption, such as television, radio and newspaper, increasing numbers of young North Korean refugees are now not solely viewing mass media passively but rather telling their stories actively with ICTs and films. This chapter observes young North Koreans' identity negotiation and their process of social integration through their mediated storytelling.

Until the end of 2007, around 13,000 North Korean refugees settled in South Korea. Each year, about 1500 to 2000 North Koreans emigrate to South Korea and about 13 to 15% of them range in age from nine to eighteen years (Ministry of Unification 2008). When North Koreans come to South Korea, both adults and young people believe that there will be better opportunities for young North Koreans to be successful in this seemingly promising land as a result of their South Korean education. The hope is that this education will equip these youths with the necessary knowledge and grounding to get better jobs in South Korea, unlike the experience of their parents who often work for minimum wage. In reality, contrary to their expectations, it does not take these North Korean emigrants long to realize that their dream to be integrated into South Korea both socially and economically is more difficult than they expected. While many North Korean refugees intend that South Korea will be their second home country due to their same historical and cultural backgrounds, they soon come to learn that North and South Koreans have held different beliefs, ideologies, political systems and cultures for more than half a century.

In fact, North Korean refugees' position in South Korea is somewhat different from other immigrants and refugees because of their position as *both* insiders and outsiders. Most North Korean refugees look like South Koreans, have relatives in South Korea, and speak Korean. However, their strong accents distinguish them from other native South Koreans and contribute to them being perceived as "others" in South Korean society. This process of negotiating their identities as both insiders and outsiders becomes very challenging and intimidating as they go through the uneasy route of acculturation in which discrimination toward North Korean refugees is still prevalent. Therefore, North Korean refugees often choose the safe way of communication by which to learn the society: mediated communication. However, unlike their adult counterparts whose dominant media usage relies on such mass media as television, newspapers or radio, young North Korean refugees now actively create messages and tell their stories themselves through the Internet and video production. This chapter observes how young North Koreans use the Internet and film to tell their stories and how such storytelling influences their process of acculturation to their host country.

Why North Koreans emigrate to South Korea

Several reasons motivate North Korean refugees to risk their lives to escape North Korea. In the article "Causalities of North Korea Defectors and International Issues", Chung (2006) categorized the reasons for escape by North Korean refugees into four categories. First, these refugees extricate from North Korea for political reasons. Kim Il-Sung, the first leader of North Korea after Japanese Imperialism ended in 1945, conceived Juche ideology, a very unique socialism that was influenced by Marxism-Leninism and Confucianism. Juche ideology, which strongly united the North Korean people, has been the solid ideological foundation of North Korea. However, after the death of Kim Il-Sung in 1994, increasing numbers of people questioned and distrusted North Korea's ideological, political and social systems. Such dissatisfaction encouraged many North Koreans to leave their homeland.

The second reason for this exodus is tied to economic problems. Due to many natural disasters, such as the deluge in 1995-1996 and a long drought in 1997, numerous people have lost their means of livelihood. Food distribution by the government has not been extensive enough for people to survive, and the money that people have obtained from their work has not been sufficient to satisfy their basic needs. The worse the food situation has become, the more aggravated people's health conditions have gotten. People have not been able to obtain medicine for diseases that in many other countries are not even dangerous, such as tuberculosis; therefore some people have crossed the border of North Korea to procure medicine and food for themselves or for their family members.

The third motivating factor for North Koreans to escape their home country has been a socio-cultural issue. Increasingly, North Koreans are being exposed to knowledge from other socio-cultural systems, and such knowledge challenges their confidence and trust in what they see and experience in North Korea. Recently, highly educated people with professional careers also have emigrated from North Korea due to their pursuit of other socio-cultural and political systems through which they can experience and achieve what they believe.

Lastly, the fourth reason for the emigration has been North Koreans' increasing opportunities to experience other cultures. North Korea has been sending workers and students to other countries in order to earn more money or to learn from these countries. However, after experiencing different parts of the world, many of their citizens decide to emigrate to South Korea. In addition, geographic factors play an important role since North Koreans can reach China by simply crossing a river. Moreover, many Korean-Chinese reside near the border between North Korea and China. Because the Chinese government sends North Korean refugees back to North Korea, these refugees leave China to go to Mongolia, Thailand, Vietnam, Cambodia or Myanmar (Burma), and then come to South Korea from these countries. These four factors often overlap with one another as they impact why North Koreans leave their country of origin (Chung 2006; K.-N. Kim 2006).

The lives of young North Korean refugees in South Korea

Since North and South Korea have the same historical and cultural backgrounds, some might think that these two should have lots of commonalities. However, North and South Korea have carried different beliefs, ideologies, political systems and cultures for more than half a century. Even though an increasing number of North Koreans are exposed to other cultures, the majority of North Koreans still do not have the chance to experience other kinds of social, political, and economic systems until they escaped North Korea (Y.-M. Kim 2005). Therefore, most North Korean refugees go through a culture shock when they come to South Korea (Jo et al. 2006).

When North Koreans settle down in South Korea and face survival in a new society, many have to reject much of the beliefs that they have maintained for their entire lives. Many South Koreans tend to view North Korea as a poor and underdeveloped country where people are brainwashed into communism. Such negative views held by South Koreans appear to have created discrimination and hatred toward the North Korean immigrants. North Korean teenagers in particular experience more difficulties as they have to adjust to a totally different educational system, learn new subjects, and fit themselves into a dramatically different peer culture. Even though they quickly catch up with academic subjects at school, they hardly can understand what their South Korean peers are talking about because the two youth cultures are so distinct. More specifically, young North Koreans do not have much knowledge about South Korean teenagers' interests, such as computer games, celebrities, and famous television programs. Moreover, young South Koreans' widely-used slang is another challenge (M.-S. Choi, Choi, & Kang 2006; S. Choi 2006; Jeon 2000; Lee 2006). In fact, because of the high rate of school drop-out among North Korean refugees, only half of middle school-aged teenagers and a much lower 6.6 percent of high school-aged teenagers attend schools where they will attain a diploma (Chun & Cho 2006). Such challenges existing in the social context affect young North Korean refugees' personal circumstances by leaving them educationally, culturally, and socially unprepared to survive in a competitive South Korean society.

Therefore, religious groups, social activists, and government organizations have established several educational institutions exclusively for North Korean refugees in order to address the unique challenges that they face (M.-S. Choi et al. 2006; Gil, Gong, & Moon 2003; Jeong, Jeong, & Yang 2006). Most of these institutions focus on two educational goals: (1.) preparing young North Koreans to pass the school diploma certificate examinations and (2.) helping them to adjust successfully to South Korean society. While these institutions focus on these refugees' personal issues of adjustment and survival, these North Koreans have relatively few opportunities to communicate with native South Koreans.

Refugees hiding their North Korean identity

When North Koreans first arrive in South Korea, they all have to stay in Hanawon, the educational institute that helps North Korean refugees to learn not only about South Korean society, but also about possible educational and vocational opportunities. After staying in Hanawon for three months, the government connects them to public welfare facilities to better facilitate their sound adjustment. These North Koreans meet experts in Hanawon and other welfare facilitators who have much knowledge of North Korean refugees and understand their unique situation. However, as North Korean refugees expand their radii of life and meet native South Koreans, many sense inhospitality and prejudice emanating from these native South Koreans because many of them still view North Koreans as poor, brainwashed, and uneducated; these are longstanding stereotypical images. (Jo et al. 2006; Y.-M. Kim 2005).

The journey of these North Korean refugees to South Korea is tied in with other hardships as well. When North Koreans come to South Korea, they cannot simply cross the border between North and South Korea; rather they first have to go to China, the country adjacent to North Korea, where they are wanted by the Chinese police. Because Chinese police put North Koreans in prison or send them back to North Korea, these North Koreans look for an opportunity to go to other countries that exhibit less hostility, such as Mongolia, Myanmar, Thailand, or Vietnam. In these countries, they obtain help from the South Korean Embassy and the NGO people to cross over to South Korea. This process often takes North Koreans from two months to ten years to reach South Korea from the time they leave their homeland. Because their nutritional conditions are poor during this time, North Korean refugees, especially those who have experienced these hardships during a growth period, are often smaller than native South Koreans. Thus many of these refugees lose confidence in their physical appearance and feel that the majority of South Koreans look at them scornfully. Due to such factors, many North Korean refugees avoid socializing with native South Koreans or often hide their North Korean identity (M.-S. Choi et al. 2006; Jeon 2005).

As young North Korean refugees spend more time with other North Korean refugees and less with South Koreans, they experience even more situations in which they consider themselves as outsiders or aliens in South Korea, even though they all receive South Korean citizenship. Since they find it difficult to adjust their accents, many pretend that they are from the South Korean countryside or from China (M.-S. Choi et al. 2006; Jo et al. 2006). In fact, most North Korean refugees experience hardships in communicating with native South Koreans. Moreover, unlike in North Korea where neighbors naturally socialize together as a community, North Korean refugees must live in the isolating apartment culture of South Korea, another factor which makes communicating among neighbors even more challenging. Most of them view South Koreans as individualists who are very exclusive. Therefore, North Koreans' social intercourse is limited to those who are directly related to North Korean refugees or to those who want to support them, such as family members, government officials, social workers, NGO people, religious people, educators and volunteers. When North Korean refugees are with South Koreans, they realize that they are being treated as a "special" group of people. They often view such treatment as insinuating the message that that "are inferior to native South Koreans", making them feel even more fretful, anxious, and hopeless (Chae & Yhi 2004; Jeon 2000; Jo et al. 2006).

Use of media among refugees and immigrants

In the process of cross-cultural adaptation in a host country, immigrants/refugees in general endeavor to be familiar with various cultural aspects of their host country so that they can obtain a certain degree of fitness or compatibility in the new cultural environment and become effectively functional in their daily activities (Gunykunst & Kim 1997; Y.Y. Kim 1977, 1996). In this stage, immigrants/refugees who pursue interpersonal communication opportunities acquire a high degree of acculturation and intercultural communication competence by experiencing more direct and relevant information and practices (Gunykunst & Hammer 1988;

Gunykunst & Kim 1997; Y.Y. Kim 1996). Direct, interpersonal communication enables immigrants to recognize the cultural differences between their native cultures and host culture, as well as to negotiate between the two through real, direct experience. However, immigrants and refugees often feel uncomfortable about developing interpersonal relationships when they do not have an adequate level of intercultural communication competency. Therefore, mediated communication sometimes plays a more vital part in the adaptation process than does more direct means of interaction (Y.Y. Kim 1977, 1991). Television was the most common medium among immigrants/refugees when the above mentioned intercultural communication scholars observed these newcomers from the 1970s to the 1990s. However, while television is still a popular medium, the rapidly changing media environment with its prevalent Information Computer Technology (ICT) and accessibility to video and other media production, is playing a significant role in the media experiences of immigrants/refugees.

From my personal experience in teaching North Korean refugees in South Korea, I was able to view first hand that such a reliance on mass media leads to emigrants' understanding of their new society and culture. From 2002 to 2003, I helped young North Korean refugees in South Korea to prepare for their high school diploma certification. I also taught media literacy to young North Korean refugees in four different educational institutes during the summer of 2008. Because of young North Koreans' difficulties in fitting into South Korean society and in establishing intimate relationships with native South Koreans, I noted that young North Koreans often understand South Korea mainly through South Korean mass media. Nevertheless, this reliance on mass mediated images often leads to their misconceptions of South Korean society. For instance, during the class discussion about South Korean society, young North Korea refugees showed a tendency, based on news reports, to view South Korean society as a very violent and dangerous country. Moreover, young North Korean refugees often become disappointed, resentful or cynical about how North Korea or North Korean refugees are portrayed in the media. South Korean media also frequently portray the struggles and challenges that North Korean refugees experience in South Korea so that South Koreans can be aware of these problems. However, many North Korean refugees feel uncomfortable about such depictions because they feel that they are made to look deficient. Because many of them are hiding their identities as North Koreans in South Korea, they do not voice their objections in order to attempt to correct these wrong images and misconceptions of North Korea and North Korean refugees.

While many North Korean refugees hide their immigration from North Korea in order to be accepted as "real South Koreans", an increasing number of young North Korean refugees have revealed their identities with confidence and actively use the mass media to communicate their life stories and thoughts. In the next part of this chapter, I will explore how young North Korean refugees are going beyond their comfort zones to use the Internet and documentaries to vocalize their experiences to the larger society.

Research design

The data collection for this project consists of four different methods: 1.) participatory observation in the media literacy classes that I taught during the Summer 2008 in South Korea; 2.) analysis of 23 blogs owned by North Korean refugees and four online communities; and 3.) content analysis of three documentaries that were produced by young North Korean refugees. In order to better understand young North Koreans' views on media and their experiences as bloggers and video producers, I also conducted interviews with students and their teachers.

During the Summer 2008, I taught media literacy to North Korean refugees, ages from 12-20, in three different alternative education institutions. As a part of their media literacy lessons, students discussed their experiences, thoughts, and reflections on their media usage. During lunch or break times, I was able to observe my students using the Internet in the computer lab. As I interacted with my students in the computer lab, students casually shared their thoughts on media, South Korean society and their personal lives. I documented the contents of my lessons and students' reactions in a form of pedagogical documentation that allows transparent records of educational practices through students' work and teachers' documentation (MacDonald 2007; Mitchell 2003; Moss 2006). After each class, I created observation charts, which included not only a detailed description of what I taught and what students said and did in the classes, but also reflective field notes with my interpretations and thoughts about the classes. This reflective process guided my preparation of the future lessons. The participatory observation in alternative educational settings and documentation allowed me to holistically understand young North Korean refugees' mediated experiences and thoughts. It also led me to have a better insight of other parts of data collection: analysis of blogs and online communities and content analysis of three documentaries.

While I was teaching in alternative educational institutions for North Korean refugees, I was able to collect students' and their friends' blog URLs. I analyzed 24 blogs by young North Korean refugees, ages 14 to 28. I also joined and analyzed four online communities for students in these alternative educational institutions for North Korean refugees. Even though these online communities were generated by teachers who are South Koreans, most entries were posted by either current students or graduates. Analyzing the entries in these blogs and online communities allowed me to observe what stories these young North Koreans are telling online and how they are interacting with other people.

Even though video production is comparatively more demanding and complicated work compared to blog posting, some North Korean refugees participate in video production projects. I watched three movies several times by North Korean refugees, *The Long Journey I, The Long Journey II, and The Dialogue on the Road,* in order to analyze the content; in addition I searched news articles about these movies and interviewed one student who participated in producing *The Long Journey II* and *The Dialogue on the Road.* I screened these three movies in my media literacy class and was able to hear the responses of other North Korean refugees to these films. It allowed me to see how young North Korean refugees experience this video production process and how other students comprehend the content of these films.

North Korean refugees' view on South Korean mainstream media

I was allowed to teach media literacy to North Korean refugees because teachers and administrative members in these alternative schools were concerned about young North Korean refugees' media usage. Teachers considered that these students were not viewing critically, accepting the messages from mainstream media without discretion. Teachers' common anxiety was over the influence of commercialized media content in creating materialistic values in these young North Korean refugees. As I met these students in the classroom settings, such concerns by teachers seemed to be legitimate. Students showed great interest in the products that were advertised by famous stars and admiration towards the life styles of rich people. However, having taught the same age group of native South Korean students and American students, such interests and admirations are also observed by other groups of young people as well. Therefore, young people being heavily influenced by commercialized media is not a problem among only North Korean refugees but also among other young people who are saturated with commercialized media content. Even though their prior knowledge of the purpose of advertisements and their role in mainstream media was relatively small compared to that of other students whom I have taught before, these North Korean youths learned these norms very quickly and demonstrated their knowledge in class discussion and casual conversation with me.

Besides the issue of advertisements, young North Korean refugees demonstrated their critical viewing skills even before I taught anything about critical viewing or analyzing the messages. When my media literacy class covered the content of other mainstream media, such as soap operas, television dramas, non-fiction movies, television news, and articles in newspapers and magazines, students expressed their uncomfortable feelings about how North Korea and North Korean refugees are portrayed in these mainstream media. They indicated the importance of their success and good communication with other South Koreans to provide positive impressions of their people. Students also pointed out how media content which contains honest descriptions of North Korean refugees can help native South Koreans to correct misunderstandings about North Korea and North Korean refugees and improve these images. When the class covered the media industry in South Korea, students were also keen at pointing out the innate limitations of mainstream media, which are restricted by viewership and sponsors' interests. Such a class discussion on the issues of mainstream media naturally led students to consider alternative media outlets, such as the Internet, which can encompass their own voices more freely. The use of the Internet by young North Korean refugees is discussed in the following section.

Use of the Internet by young North Korean refugees

As I indicated earlier, mass communication allows rather safer communication activities to immigrants and refugees by providing indirect interaction with socio-cultural environments (Y.Y. Kim 1991). When intercultural communication scholar Young-Yun Kim (1991) published "Communication and Cross-cultural Adaptation" in the United States, she probably meant television, radio, or newspapers, as these media were among the most popular during that time period. These media may have allowed immigrants/refugees to passively watch, read or listen to media content, rather than providing opportunities to actively participate in the communication process. However, as the Internet has become more easily accessible and has allowed its users to have more direct forms of communication, providing a venue to express themselves and to hear from others, North Korean refugees are taking advantage of this new media to become a part of their host society.

Surprisingly, most young North Korean refugees whom I have met have their own blogs, albeit not all of them are active bloggers. Those with blogs had them on Cyworld (www.cyworld.com), a site that allows bloggers to decide the degree of accessibility that each of their blogs entry has to the public. For instance, if a blogger wants to indicate a certain entry as private, this means that the blogger has sole access to the entry and only she or he can read it. Because the only person who can read a private entry is the owner of the blog, blogs often can serve as personal journals or diaries. The blogger also has the potential to delineate the privacy as "open to special friends only", thus allowing only other bloggers who have Cyworld IDs and who are appointed as "special friends" to have access to these entries. When bloggers (i.e., Cyworld users) visit others' blogs, they can automatically see if each entry is open to the public or to "special friends" only. Because I have a Cyworld ID and have "special friend" relationships with many of these students, I was able to see both their open content and semi-open content which were accessible exclusively to their "special friends". I then was able to determine if the owner of the blog opened the entry either to the public or to his/her special friends only, because the blog usually announces that certain types of folders are open to special friends only. Bloggers can, of course, open their entries to the public as well.

When I was analyzing the blogs written by North Korean refugees, I first categorized the content and labeled if each entry was designated as either "open to the public" or "open to the special friends only", in order to observe their willingness to share their stories with wider audience. Among the 27 blogs I analyzed, four of them are inactive blogs, at which no entry can be found. The close examination of the 23 active blogs shows that young North Korean refugees were using their blogs to tell stories about their daily lives that included their interests and hobbies. By using the scrap function that allows bloggers to copy entries by other bloggers to their own blogs, a number of young North Korean refugees scrapped postings regarding love, friendship, proverbs, popular fashion and trends. Several students also uploaded video clips that showed North Korean popular culture and pictures of beautiful scenery of the North Korean natural world. In terms of the content that is not directly related to their privacy, such as those entries regarding love, friendship, proverbs, popular fashion and trends, all of these 23 active bloggers set these entries as open to the public. However, when it came to personal postings, such as their own pictures and journal entries, only nine students among twenty who posted their personal stories opened all of their personal entries to the public. Three students had set some personal postings as "open to the public" and other postings as "open to special friends only". These three students opened their stories and pictures at school, in church, and in other institutions, like NGOs and other private academic institutions. All of their photos with their friends were also open. They seemed not to have any problem in making their personal lives in South Korea public. However, interestingly enough, they made their family pictures as "open to special friends only", probably because they do not want to publicize their family issues. It can be also a safety issue. Many young North Koreans have some or all family members in North Korea or other countries, waiting their opportunity to come to South Korea. In this situation, such pictures can threaten their safety if their faces and stories are revealed on the Internet.

Chart 1. Young North Koreans' blog. Aged 14 to 28. Total 23 blogs

Types of Content	Private Life	North Korea Related	Hobbies/ Interests	Proverb/Essay written by Others
Open Content	9	6	13	23
Semi-Open Content "open to special friends only".	8	0	5	0
Mixed (Some Open/ Some Semi-Open)	3	0	3	0
Total	20	6	21	23

I also visited the blogs owned by those who left comments or feedback on the blogs by North Korean refugees so that I could observe their socialization. Although I was not able to distinguish on some of the visitors' blogs whether these visitors were North Korean refugees or South Koreans, I clearly could see through the uploaded pictures, writing entries and personal information. From their stories about their birth places, family, daily lives, I was able to determine that some of the visitors were North Korean refugees' and many others were native South Koreans. While most blogs by North Korean refugees have mixed visitors from both North Korea and South Korea, there were noticeable differences between college students and students in the secondary education system or alternative schools. On the one hand, students in the secondary education system and alternative schools had more North Korean refugee visitors than native South Korean visitors. However, these students also had other native South Korean bloggers indicated as "special friends", whom they had met in other social groups, religious organizations, or online communities. North Korean refugees in college, on the other hand, had more native South Korean than North Korean refugee visitors, probably because they were able to meet more native South Koreans at college and build up personal relationships with them. One of these North Korean bloggers, Sung-Eun, a 17 year-old girl who had come to South Korea in 2003, explained the reasons for her straightforward expression of her identity on the blog:

> To be honest with you, I do not always tell other people that I am from North Korea. I often try very hard to speak, dress, and behave like the South Koreans. For those whom I've known for a long time, I feel comfortable to be who I am in front of them. However, when I meet new people, perhaps 90 % of the time, I feel that people have different looks and perceptions when I tell them that I'm from North Korea... Well, I'm not saying that I feel like that all the time. Some people make me feel very comfortable and to these people, I can naturally tell my story. But when it comes to the Internet, I can reveal my identity without having to worry about others' reactions. I do not have to worry about what they would think of me because I do not have to see their faces. Well, I do not like to see people's reactions when they have found out where I am from. But I still think that native South Koreans need to understand the fact that in South Korea, there are many North Korean refugees, and we are part of this society. So I think it is important for South Koreans to have a good knowledge of North Korea and North Korean refugees, and accept us as a part of this society. I think many South Koreans still consider us as outsiders. I think they need to hear more of our stories. Perhaps, blogs by North Korean refugees can be one of the sources to educate them.

Ki-Sook, a 24 year-old female college student who came to South Korea in 2001, told me that blogging is a great way for North Korean refugees to open themselves and tell their real stories:

> I do not trust the mass media. My friend once had a press interview, but what she told the reporter was all edited and what has been broadcasted was different from what she wanted to tell. I know some filmmakers have good intentions in making our stories known to the public. The movie *Crossing*[1] is a great example. But not all media people have good intentions. They tell the story they want, not what we want. I know other North Korean refugees have produced independent films. I watched these films and they were very good. But I don't think many people watched these films. Blogging is the easiest and most efficient way to tell our stories...Well, I'm not saying that North Korean refugees have to tell educational or agitating messages.

> What I'm saying is...hmmm...I think people need to feel that we are part of this society. We have Korean citizenship, but we are always considered as 'others.' I want other South Koreans to see that we are part of their 'we.'

I interviewed Ki-Sook and Sung-Eun separately. In fact, they do not even know each other. However, what they were telling me was very similar. Both of them expressed that it is important for native South Koreans to have balanced knowledge about North Korea and North Korean refugees because their current knowledge is distorted. Both of them thought blogging can be an effective tool to tell the real stories about North Korea and North Korean refugees.

It is true that even though blogging is open to everybody, not everybody visits blogs. In fact, most visitors of North Korean refugees' blogs seemed to be the people who already knew them. Blogging thus is becoming a venue through which these refugees have built up more intimate relationships with people whom they already knew. Many online communities that they joined function similarly. In Cyworld, users can open the list of their participating online communities to the public. Among fifteen students who publicized their lists of participating online communities, five of them joined the online communities that are only for North Korean refugees. These online communities appear to be extensions of their offline lives by continuing their offline dialogue in online. These online communities are rooted in the schools or other social gatherings for North Korean refugees and they seem to continue their offline conversations in these online communities.

However, the other ten students had joined other online communities besides the ones relevant to their offline lives. They became members of these online communities to meet new people with whom they could share their personal interests, like sports, celebrities, or fashion. Four of them joined online communities so that they could learn about stocks and investments. I do not know how active these ten students are in these online communities, but in my interview with Tae-Woo, a 20 year-old male who is attending an alternative school to prepare for his school diploma certificate examinations, he shared his use of the Internet and online communities as follows:

> When I first came to South Korea, I entered the public middle school. I was 3 years older than my classmates, but I hid the fact that I was older than them...Everyday was very challenging. I was not able to catch up with my studies. And in everyday life, students used lots of vocabulary of foreign origin. It was hard for me to understand what they were talking about. Although I've met some good friends, it was hard for me to open my true self because we had so many differences. I withdrew from the school and am now attending an alternative school for students like me. Here, I feel much more comfortable in communicating with others, and the teachers here are great and really care for us. However, I think it is also important for us to know about South Korean society. I cannot stay in this school forever. Someday, I will go out and be a part of the mainstream. To do so, what I need is money. So I joined many online communities that focus on how to get rich...I've never met any

of members there. I've never written any messages there either. But I learn so much from these young people. When I read these postings, there are many words that I do not understand. However, because it is not direct personal communication, I do not have to be embarrassed. I do not have to pretend that I understand what they are saying. I can easily look up these words on the Internet. The Internet is giving me a great opportunity to learn about this society without too much cost. I admire other North Korean refugees who came to South Korea before the Internet era.

After talking with several students who are actively using the Internet in their lives, their statements suggest that the Internet is serving as a safe venue for North Korean refugees to learn about their new society and to gradually open themselves to others. Even though many North Korean refugees have their own blogs, as do their native South Korean counterparts, they might not be powerful bloggers who have a very strong influence on others. As I indicated earlier, most of the visitors who leave comments on these North Korean refugees' blogs are people whom they already know. Their efforts to open up themselves and to let others see the true image of North Korea and North Korean refugees are not reaching larger audiences. However, by using their blogs, they are able to practice expressing themselves and voice their opinions in a safe context. Even though these experiences are indirect, they are slowly expanding their radii of action through the Internet. Even though their offline personas may not be as confident as their online personas, the Internet provides North Korean refugees an unthreatening, safe, and fun venue in which to experiment with their host society. Moreover, these North Korean refugees who exhibited confidence in sharing their stories through the media broadened their use of media beyond the Internet. In the next section of this chapter, I will introduce the documentary films that were produced by young North Korean refugees.

Documentary films by young North Koreans

Indebted to the development of media technology, the producing of videos has become accessible to almost everybody. As shown in the overflowing video clips on YouTube, anybody can produce video content simply with a video camera and appropriate computer software. With such advanced media technology, young North Koreans have produced three documentaries: *The Long Journey I*, *The Long Journey II*, and *The Dialogue on the Road*. *The Long Journey* series was produced by students in one alternative school for North Korean refugees. In these videos, students retraced the route that they took to come to South Korea. The numbers of students who were listed on the ending credits are three for *Long Journey I* and eight for *Long Journey II*, but other students in this school also travelled together and assisted in the production process. During her interview with a reporter from a film magazine, Mi-Sun, a girl who participated in the *The Long Journey II*, said that she wanted to show the hardships and challenges that North Korean refugees experienced in coming to South Korea, because the stories of North Korean refugees were always told by others, not by North Koreans themselves (Hur 2005). Even though teachers at this alternative school were the ones who suggested making documentaries with their stories, it was the students themselves who wrote the script and took responsibility for each stage of the documentary.

The Long Journey series portrays the emotions and reactions of North Korean refugees when these young North Korean refugees revisited the places where they had to hide from police due to their illegal stay there. Since North Korean defectors are not recognized as refugees, they are not protected by the international agreement regarding refugees. The Chinese government sends illegal North Koreans back to North Korea, where these defectors are either executed or harshly punished. These North Korean refugees therefore never feel stable in China, due to a fear of repatriation back to North Korea. However, this time they revisited these nightmarish places with the camera and a passport from the Republic of Korea. They no longer had to hide from anybody, because their status had changed. They were not cowering anymore and thus they were able to talk comfortably with anybody, including the police.

When the students were shooting *The Long Journey II* in China, they were held for inspection by Chinese guards. Nothing happened to them because of that inspection, but the incident reminded the students of their memories of suffering. One boy injured his leg during the inspection because he was so nervous. Yet as time went by, they were able to approach Chinese guards and pass pleasantries with them. Finally, the scabs on their hearts peeled away. Using the camera, their journeys helped to heal their wounded hearts (Sinyoon 2006). In the movie, they encounter foreigners. Whenever these students tell them that they are from Korea, these foreigners ask them whether they are from North or South Korea. These students get confused about how to answer. This documentary thus does not simply trace the journeys back to their past, but also shows their current confusion regarding their identities (Sinyoon 2006).

The Dialogue on the Road was produced by two university students, one North Korean refugee student, Keum-Hee, and one native South Korean student, Min-Jee. These two students traveled through China and Mongolia together for twenty days and video-recorded what they experienced. In the film, these two college students share their own stories as they travel through these foreign countries. These places remind Keum-Hee of tough times after leaving North Korea because China was on her escape route. As Min-Jee travels for the filmmaking, she is able to connect these foreign environments to her childhood memories. This movie shows how these two young college students experience hardships, solve these problems, and open up to each other as they journey. After their travels, Keum-Hee told me that she now feels very relieved and comfortable about her past:

> I have a serious nostalgia for North Korea. Even though my whole family suffered from hunger, North Korea is and will be my home forever ... Nevertheless, my memories of China, Burma and Thailand still torture me. I left North Korea when

I was fifteen, and it took our family four years to come to South Korea. During these years, I had to hide my identity to work in a restaurant. I also stayed in a jail. Those were and are torturing memories. But after revisiting China through this documentary project, I felt so relieved. Even though the fact that I experienced such harsh times during these four years has not changed, I feel like I'm liberated from these severe memories which have tormented me.

These films thus have not simply healed the wounded hearts of students who participated in the production process; they also have been well-recognized both nationally and internationally. These movies were screened at various film festivals and received many awards. For instance, *The Long Journey I* received an award at the Seoul International Youth Film Festival (2006) and "Laudatory Mention" at the Berlin Youth Media Festival (2007). *The Dialogue on the Road* was screened at the Busan Asian Short Film Festival (2007). Even though *The Dialogue on the Road* was not officially circulated by other media outlets, such as broadcasting stations or the Internet, *The Long Journey I* and *II* can be searched and viewed in the website where Korean educators can upload their educational video sources. Moreover, when I inputted the titles of these three documentaries on Internet search engines, I was able to find numerous articles about them. Reporters, film critics, and bloggers in South Korea have posted their reviews, thoughts, and feelings after watching these three documentaries. These entries show not only others' empathy with these North Korean refugees' stories over their difficulties, challenges and grief, but also people's efforts to have insightful reflections on what we have to do in order to embrace North Korean refugees as part of "we".

Conclusion

During the Summer 2008 when I was teaching media literacy education to young North Korean refugees, all the students who had lived in South Korea for more than a year had their own blog and most of them were putting much time and effort into their maintenance. Students who recently arrived in South Korea also showed a great interest in others' blogs and wanted to start their own blog if they had not started one already. In my media literacy class with North Korean refugees, I included the issues of digital media, the Internet, blogs, and grass-roots media. Even before I was pointing these media out, students indicated how people in marginalized groups can have a voice through blogs and other forms of independent media. Many of my students pointed out the importance of openness and honesty in order to be secure and confident in their host society, and how communication through any form of media or channels can provide changes to practice storytelling in an open and honesty way. Although they started their blogs because they looked interesting, they were aware of the usefulness of blogging as a safe way to socially network. As I observed young

North Koreans' offline and online communications, these messages were more confident in disclosing their status as refugees through the media, thereby initiating a personal process of empowerment and consequently improving their integration into South Korean society. For the same reason, students liked the three documentaries produced by the young North Korean refugees. Despite their acknowledgment of these documentaries' unprofessional camerawork and editing, these students thought that these films created by their peers certainly contained some truthfulness that was lacking in other mainstream media.

As discussed in this chapter, some young North Korean refugees have turned to directly working with media professionals to tell their stories in more refined way. One educator who has worked in the shelter for North Korean refugees for ten years told me that he gets lots of contact by media professionals because they are interested in covering the stories of young North Korean refugees. After discussions with his students, he sometimes allows these media professionals to report on the students' stories if these media personnel exhibit a sincere and trusting attitude. Then, students, teachers and media professionals work together to provide the most truthful picture of themselves possible. For instance, Qchannel, the only documentary channel in South Korea, has recently produced two documentaries regarding the lives of North Korean refugees in South Korea. One of these documentaries was about a shelter in which North Korean refugees' lives with guardians who are South Korean adults. This documentary originally was screened in theaters and was then broadcasted on television. Before the formal screening in the theater, this educator had an opportunity to speak in front of the audience; he described the students' reactions when they were discussing the possibility of participating in this documentary project:

> In the beginning, many students were doubtful and hesitant about this project. Some of them had participated in such kinds of projects before, but did not like what came out as a result. The final output was often different from what we wanted to communicate through these projects. However, from these experiences, we have learned that it is still important to use media to tell our stories. By revealing their identities through media, I have seen many young North Koreans become more confident about themselves. At the same time, it is important to tell these stories, because such stories are not still heard by many South Koreans.

Of course, telling the stories of North Korean refugees through ICTs or films cannot be a panacea for solving the issues of the prevalent inequality, bias and prejudice toward North Korean refugees in South Korea. However, these efforts have the potential to facilitate meaningful changes in South Korean society. Even though these changes are being made very slowly, these North Korean refugees are paving the road not only for themselves, but for the next generation who will hopefully experience reunification of South and North Korea. Many scholars have mentioned the importance of North Korean refugees in South Korea because they function as a predictor of possible troubles and challenges when the two Koreas are unified (Jo et al. 2006; Yoo, Jeon, Hong, Jo, & Eom 2006). Therefore, such efforts by North Korean refugees are preparing South Koreans to be more aware and prepared, which in turn will encourage a more harmonious reunification of the two Koreas.

Note
1. The movie *Crossing* (2008) is a South Korean film about one North Korean refugee who had crossed the border of North Korea to get medicine for his wife. Even though this film is fictional, the story is created based on the testimonies of North Korean refugees in South Korea.

References
Chae, J.-M., & Yhi, J.-H. (2004) 'North Korean Defectors' Individuality-Relatedness Affecting their Psychological Adaptation', *The Korean Journal of Health Psychology*, 9(4): 793-814 (in Korean).

Choi, M.-S., Choi, T.-S., & Kang, J.-H. (2006) 'Psychological Characteristics of Children and Adolescents Escaped from North Korea & Seeing a Counseling Strategy', *Korean Journal of Play Therapy*, 9(3): 23-34 (in Korean).

Choi, S. (2006) *Project-I 2.0 Research Report*. Seoul, Korea: Korean Art Therapists' Association in Social Work (in Korean).

Chun, J.-S., & Cho, J.-K. (2006) *Young People in North and South Korea*. Seoul: Zeitgeist.

Chung, J.-S. (2006) 'Causalities of North Korea Defectors and International Issue', *Northeast Asia Studies*, 21(2): 117-139 (in Korean).

Gil, E.-B., Gong, Y.-G., & Moon, S.-H. (2003) *'The Realities of Young North Koreans Refugees Adjusting to South Korean Society and the Appropriate Support'*, Seoul: Korean Youth Development (in Korean).

Gunykunst, W., & Hammer, M.R. (1988) 'Strangers and Hosts: An Uncertainty Reduction Based Theory of Intercultural Adaptation', in Y.Y. Kim & W.B. Gunykunst (eds.) *Cross-Cultural Adaptation: Current Approaches* (pp. 106-139). Newbury Park, Beverly Hills, London, New Delhi: Sage Publication.

Gunykunst, W.B., & Kim, Y.Y. (1997) *Communicating with Strangers: An Approach to Intercultural Communication* (3rd ed.). New York: McGraw Hill.

Hur, J.-W. (2005, 11, 30) Documentary by North Korean Refugee Teenagers: Long Journey, *Film 2.0.* (in Korean).

Jeon, W.-T. (2000) *Social Adjustment and Mental Crisis*. Paper presented at the Korean Psychology Symposium (in Korean).

Jeon, W.-T. (2005) 'The Role of Social-Psychiatry in the Studies of the Unification of North and South Korea', *Unification Studies*, 9(2), 37-52 (in Korean).

Jeong, J.-K., Jeong, B.-H., & Yang, G.-M. (2006) 'Teenaged North Korean Refugees' adjustment to South Korean educational system', in B.-H. Jeong, W.-T. Jeon & J.-K. Jeong (eds.) *Welcome to Korea: The Lives of North Koreans in South Korea* (pp. 263-282) Seoul, Korea: Hanyang University Press (in Korean).

Jo, J.-A., Im, S.-H., & Jeong, J.-K. (2006) *Cultural Crisis and Cultural Integration for North Korean Refugees*. Seoul: Korean Women's Development Institute (in Korean).

Kim, K.-N. (ed.) (2006) 'North Korean Defectors' Human Rights and Plan to Protect their Rights', in *The Unification Strategy Society of Korea. Practical Analysis of North Korean Defectors' Problems]* (pp. 41-). Busan, South Korea: Lee Kyung (in Korean).

Kim, Y.-M. (2005) *The Reality of North Korean Refugees' Adaptation in South Korea: The Influential Factors of their Sense of Alienation and Life Qualities*. Kyung-Gi, South Korea: Korean Studies Information Co., Ltd.

Kim, Y.Y. (1977) 'Communication Patterns of Foreign Immigrants in the Process of Acculturation', *Human Communication Research,* 4(1): 66-77.

Kim, Y.Y. (1991) 'Communication and Cross-cultural Adaptation', in L.A. Samovar & R.E. Porter (eds.) *Intercultural Communication: A Reader* (6th ed., pp. 383-391). Belmont: CA: Wadsworth.

Kim, Y.Y. (1996) 'On Theorizing Intercultural Communication', in Y.Y. Kim & W.B. Gunykunst (eds.) *Theories in Intercultural Communication* (pp. 11-21). Newbury Park, London, New Delhi: SagePublications.

Lee, H. (2006) 'School Adjustments of Young North Korean Refugees', *Education Criticism,* 21: 193-207 (in Korean).

Ministry of Unification. (2008) North Korean Defectors in South Korea 2008.05.01, from http://www.unikorea.go.kr/

Sinyoon, D.-W. (2006) 'Standing again on the Road to Escape', *Hangyerae* 21, retrieved 2008.06.12, from http://h21.hani.co.kr/section-021015000/2006/12/021015000200612130639038.html (in Korean, electronic version).

Yoo, S.-E., Jeon, W.-T., Hong, C.-H., Jo, Y.-A., & Eom, J.-S. (2006) 'Life and Education', in B.-H. Jeong, W.-T. Jeon & J.-K. Jeong (eds.) *Welcome to Korea: The Lives of North Koreans in South Korea]* (pp. 422-439). Seoul, Korea: Hanyang University Press (in Korean).

Yoon, J. (2007) 'Koreans Scholars Studying North Korean Movies', *Asian Cinema,* 18(2): 160-179.

Voices of the Youth:
Coping, Criticizing and Calling for Change

Alternative Voices under Repression
Zimbabwe's Youth Media Projects

Rashweat Mukundu

Abstract

This is a descriptive study of the use of alternative media voices by youths in Zimbabwe. Alternative media can be located within the realm of citizen journalism or citizen media, as it does not follow the strict media processes and discourses of traditional media. In the context of Zimbabwe, alternative media use cultural artefacts, theatre, music and underground publications, among other things. This scenario is a response to the prevailing political, social and economic situation in Zimbabwe in which critical voices are not tolerated and the state resorts to the use of coercion to silence dissenting voices and propagate its own views. This article questions the taken-for-granted assumption that the mainstream media comprise the arena or platform for the exchange of ideas, arguing instead that certain social, economic and political situations give rise to "new media" that society can rely on to counter the dominant views. These media are not only informative but are also used as a form and mode of resistance to the dominant view.

This article is a descriptive analysis of the use of alternatives media voices of youths in Zimbabwe to confront the realities of political oppression, unemployment and the collapse of social services, as well as HIV/AIDS. Based on Jürgen Habermas' (1989) analysis of the media as constituting the public sphere, this article seeks to show that youths in Zimbabwe, largely left out of the "public sphere" as constituted by the state media and the remaining independent newspapers, are in fact creating their own means of communication and creating subcultures that are challenging the dominant views. These subcultures are premised on the need to enhance access to information by the largely poor and politically active urbanites.

This article looks at the use, motivation, and structures of youths' alternative media voices in Zimbabwe and whether these herald a new era in media use by youths from poor urban and rural areas in Zimbabwe. The discussion is located within the broader theories of media and democracy. This article focuses on youths between the ages of 13 and 25 who are involved in creating their own media products to discuss, share information and challenge issues they see as going wrong in their communities. The target youths live in three urban centres of Zimbabwe: Chitungwiza, a satellite town of the capital, Harare, is a sprawling poor suburb of over 1.5 million people. The town, which relies on Harare for virtually everything, suffers from a lack of entertainment facilities, employment and educational and vocational institutions, as well as other basic services such as water, housing and health facilities. The same is true of Highfields, the oldest suburb of Harare, and Sakubva, the oldest suburb of the Zimbabwe border city of Mutare, 350 kilometres east of Harare. In the economically deprived and politically charged environment of Zimbabwe, alternative media have become a source of entertainment, protest and hope for youths in these communities.

This study starts by analysing the history of Zimbabwe, which has a bearing on the current political, social and economic situation there. The study then maps out Zimbabwe's media landscape to offer an explanation of why alternative media voices would rise in such an environment. A theoretical perspective of issues on media and democracy, especially in relation to the role of the media and access to information, is also provided. The last part of this study analyses the alternative media voices, looking at who they are and what they say and write.

Zimbabwe historical and present context

Zimbabwe is a state under siege from what Zimbabwe's political scientist and civic activist Brian Raftopolous (2003: 217) calls state-orchestrated violence and policies of exclusion designed to preserve the political power of the ruling elite. This violence has found its expression in a racial discourse that started with white farmers and was extended to include farm workers and urban workers "without totems", or proper Zimbabwean identity (Raftopolous 2003: 217). Youths in Zimbabwe have been used as cannon fodder in the political struggles, with some as young as 12 being conscripted as political activists (Solidarity Peace Trust 2003: 20). Youths are caught up in situation in which they have to take sides, either as perpetrators of political violence or on the receiving end. Youths in Zimbabwe's urban centres are becoming increasingly politically aware as a result of witnessing and being affected by the prevailing socio-economic crisis.

Having lost a constitutional referendum in 2000 as well as 57 seats in the 2000 Parliamentary elections[1], Zimbabwe's government has sought to maintain political support by articulating what it calls a "nationalist" agenda (Raftopolous 2003). The nationalism that the ruling elite hold is based on the belief that the political and national units should be congruent and that the nation state should be identified through one political culture. The ideology of nationalism in Zimbabwe is rooted in the 1970's War of Liberation waged by the now ruling party,

ZANU PF and PF ZAPU. The current nationalism being pushed by the ruling elite while claiming that its roots are in the agenda of the liberation struggle is, however, a construction and invented permanency. One aspect of this was the implementation of a violent land reform programme that saw many white farmers and their workers killed, harassed and losing their property (Raftopolous 2003). Although the government had passed the Land Acquisition Act in 1992 (Mdlongwa 1998: 10), no process of land reform was put into motion until 2000 after the constitutional referendum.

The 2008 election, however, marked a watershed in the history of Zimbabwe, as ZANU PF lost its Parliamentary majority for the first time. A presidential runoff, boycotted by the opposition, was held in June 2008. Zimbabwe's political and economic crisis has intensified since then, resulting in the international community pushing the two parties to agree on a political settlement. This process is still underway.

Zimbabwe news media landscape

Zimbabwe has a small media industry dominated by the state media and a few privately owned media organizations (MISA 2005, www.misa.org). The country inherited a monopolistic media industry in which the current government owns not only the sole broadcasting station but also the largest newspaper publishing company (MISA 2005). The media are used by the government to promote government policies, and the private media consider their role to be to keep an eye on the government, exposing corruption and, more importantly, human rights violations (Chakaodza 2003).

News coverage in Zimbabwe is therefore characterized by a clear divide between the state-owned and private media (Chakaodza 2003). For this reason the Zimbabwe government sees the private media as rivals who have a political agenda (MISA 2005). The government has put the media under its direct control through regulations requiring media houses to be registered and journalists licensed. Four newspapers have been closed down since 2003 for failing to meet registration requirements and tens of journalists arrested for violating these laws (MISA 2005). *The Standard*, the *Zimbabwe Independent* and *The Financial Gazette* are the remaining privately owned newspapers in Zimbabwe. These newspapers have a combined reach of less than 100,000, and this mostly in urban areas[2]. The target market of these newspapers is mostly the urban middle class. The so-called "common person" stories are rarely covered in the private and state media. Media consumption in Zimbabwe can be seen as a class issue, with the costly print and Internet-based media being a working class affair. Youths in Zimbabwe have access to radio and television, which are state controlled. This control of radio and television content by the state, as well as the cost of accessing privately owned newspapers and the Internet, have resulted in the traditional media being shunned by youths in poor urban centres, who have instead turned to creating their own media. While youths are generally aware of developments in the country through radio and TV, these media, as this was discovered in this study, is not enough for entertaining and influencing their thinking on the situation in Zimbabwe; hence the rise of alternative media in the form of newsletters, poetry, theatre, etc.

Theoretical approach

Academics and philosophers have advanced several rationales for the role of the media in society, especially issues of access to information and communication. The point put forward is that access to the media/information is a vital part of the democratic process. The basic philosophical assumption underlying this rationale is that citizens of a democratic society need information upon which to base their decisions (Lichtenberg 1990; Keane 1991). A key aspect of democracy is the right of the citizens to actively participate in political processes. It follows as a logical necessity that participation requires access to information. There is clearly much substance to this statement, because without adequate information the principle of open government cannot be sustained, as there would be no facilities for rational discussion. The grounds for access to information are well articulated in Habermas' theory of the public sphere. In classical liberal theory, the public sphere is:

> A neutral zone where access to relevant information affecting the public good is widely available, where discussion is free of domination by the state and where all those participating in public debate do so on an equal basis (Curran 1991: 83).

As Habermas states:

> The citizens act as a public when they deal with matters of general interest without being subject to coercion; thus with the guarantee that they may assemble and unite freely, and express and publicise their opinions freely...We speak of a political (as distinguished from a literary one, for instance) when the public discussions concern objects connected with the practice of the state (Habermas 1989: 231).

Democracy assigns the ultimate responsibility to the public to decide how it wishes to live; it presupposes that the public is fully informed when it makes this judgement. A free press with guaranteed access to information is instrumental in fulfilling this logic. The right to access is not an individual right, directed at the self-expressive interest of an individual citizen, but is rather intended to further the collective goal of a robust public debate. The free flow of information is necessary for the creation of a robust public sphere.

The democratizing role of the media as described above is an interesting point in discussing the alternative media voices in Zimbabwe as attempts at reconstituting the public sphere. While at first sight the youth alternative media are seen as completely outside the public sphere, their impact has forced the state to respond, albeit negatively[3], and in some instances other organized social groupings are seeing the need to interact with the alternative media voices, thereby giving the voices legitimacy and influence. While Habermas' conceptualization of the "public sphere" envisions the mainstream media, this study argues that this can only be so in advanced societies where the so-called mainstream media are fully fledged. On the contrary, in poor countries like Zimbabwe, governed by authoritarian governments, youth alternative media voices, among others, become influential voices that respond directly to people's information needs. Participants say that there is an element of achievement and pride in the ability to control the content of what comes out of community newsletters, poetry and music (MISA 2007).

The major question that is often asked in the theory of public sphere concerns the conditions that would make possible rational, informed discussion of public affairs and democratic decision-making. Access to information practices is therefore crucial to the public sphere, because it determines the nature, amount and accuracy of information available for public discussion and how that information is accessed. As stated above, the state remains a dominant player in Zimbabwe's media. This scenario means that access to information as a right and practice is not given with regard to having all voices represented/heard. A large part of information accessed is therefore seen by communities as biased, unhelpful and at worst government propaganda. The flipside of this is the rise of alternative voices that provide content that communities develop themselves and use to resist the dominant views, while the dominant media in Zimbabwe, both public and private, have often been criticized for being luxuries and carriers of the elite culture, not able to achieve social action or social change. Youths interviewed in this study see alternative media as countering this scenario by attending to greater social goals.

While the public sphere as defined by Habermas would be coordinated by the mainstream media, the alternative media in Zimbabwe in fact represent an attempt at reconstituting the public sphere from a people's point of view. In the classical Habermasian view, a mixture of the state and alternative media would facilitate interaction and decision-making by providing a platform for divergent information or a marketplace of ideas. The marketplace of ideas concept draws from the philosophical arguments raised by John Milton about truth and falsehood grappling with each other in a free and open encounter. Liberal political scientists emphasize the free exchange, or marketplace, of ideas as a defining condition of democracy.

The alternative media voices in Zimbabwe see themselves as the "people's media", regulating the flow of ideas between people and their leaders. This they do, the alternative voices say, by providing the greatest range of ideas and information about the political process, economic and social issues and policy interrogation. While being denied what the alternative media activists call "relevant and empowering information" by the mainstream state and small independent media, the alternative voices say that their media offer a possible diversity of information available to citizens. Alternative media attempt to create connections between listeners and viewers (Reyes Matta 1983a; Simpson Grinberg 1986c). An assumption across the body of literature is that conscientisation leads to liberation and social solidarity, which oppose dominant power structures.

Just like people need food, shelter and health care for their physical survival, they need communication for their social welfare. Moreover, for their human dignity they need factors that are intrinsic to genuine democracy: reason, responsibility, mutual respect and freedom of expression and of conscience, all of which are mediated by communication. A prerequisite for democracy, therefore, is the democratization of communication, which in turn requires the empowerment of individual (Philip Lee 1995). The media facilitate this process by providing an arena for public debate and reconstituting private citizens as a public body in the form of public opinion.

In pursuit of the argument above, this article argues that alternative media voices, as created and run by youths in urban centres in Harare, Mutare and many other places, seek not only to achieve the above with regard to access to information, but also to broaden the debate on political, social and economic issues at the grassroots level. The alternative media are not only seeking to reconstitute the public sphere but are also competing with the dominant view on meaning-making; i.e. whose story is to be believed and whose story makes sense between that of the state media or an underground publication? Rodriguez (2002: 3) defines alternative media "in terms of the transformative processes they bring about within participants and their communities". She adds that alternative media break the dichotomy of a powerful media dominated by the mainstream media and a powerless alternative media, arguing that "...this type of binary thinking limits the potential of alternative media to their ability to resist the big media, and blinds our understanding of all other instances of social change facilitated by citizens' media" (2002: 3).

Research procedure

This study is a descriptive analysis of the operations, purposes and structures of alternative youth media voices in Zimbabwe. The sample of the youth media for this study includes two underground publications in the satellite town of Chitungwiza, which is 30 kilometres from the capital, Harare. Chitungwiza boasts being one of Zimbabwe's artistic centres, with many youths involved in all sorts of artistic enterprises from drama and poetry to stone carving, among other things. *The Voice of Chitungwiza* and *Sakubva News* are other underground publications published in the city of Mutare, 350 kilometres east of Harare. Mutare, though rich in agricultural land, tourism and recently discovered diamonds, still faces poverty and unemployment as a result of the economic collapse in Zimbabwe.

The Voice of Chitungwiza and *Sakubva News* are bi-monthly youth publications distributed secretly in pubs, on school grounds and at civic meetings. In gathering materials for this study, I interviewed the actors involved in this project: a director of an NGO in Zimbabwe that has worked closely with the youth groups, and three activists within the alternative media grouping. I also analysed stories carried by the publications. The youths interviewed for this study are aged between 15 and 25 years. The majority of youths involved in the community media projects are either in high school or have just completed high-school level education, with a few having undergone tertiary vocational training. It is also important to note that primary school children as young as 6-14 play a key role in distributing newsletters that are published, taking the newsletters home and also distributing them at shopping centres and other public places. All these interviewees and organizations are not named for security reasons; thus, for example, the director of the NGO will simply be referred to as "the NGO representative". This study presents its findings in a descriptive and narrative format. At a minimum, the study seeks to showcase the new alternative media in Zimbabwe, how it is structured and its intentions, achievements and likely future trajectory.

Alternative media voices in Southern Africa and Zimbabwe – A historical perspective

Alternative media have been used in countries such as Mozambique and have in fact become a main feature of the mainstream Mozambican media landscape. The use of fax news in Mozambique is a unique phenomenon in media work that defies traditional forms of media production. Fax newspapers have existed in Mozambique since the 1980s and have gained popularity and multiplied in numbers. Among the leading fax and e-mail news organizations are *Mediafax*, *A-TribunaFax*, *Vertical*, *Expresso* and *Alternativa Daily Newspaper*. While the examples of fax newspapers mentioned above do not necessarily inform the rise of youth media in Zimbabwe, they at least show the possibilities available for non-media players and groups opposed to certain national processes, events or issues to organize alternative channels of communication and information in order to be heard.

Why alternative voices in Zimbabwe?

A key element in the creation of youth alternative voices in Zimbabwe is a belief by the proponents that their rights and dignity have been subverted by a concerted effort by the dominant political structures to deny them a voice. According to a representative of an NGO that works closely with the communities, these media are meant to "allow communities to use all forms of communication available

Chitungwiza Voice, October 2008. This cover page of the newsletter illustrates the type of political commentary that the youth was talking about. The headline is in local language and reads "How long should we wait for the unity government to be put in place while we are dying of hunger and the present government is unconstitutional". The newsletter goes on to quote the unity agreement, translated in the shona local language. The pictures at the top are of the leadership of the main political parties and below the same leaders, empty shelves in a shop and raw sewage flowing in residential areas. This is the type that is purely political commentary by youths.

to counter the dearth of information in Zimbabwe". Alternative media are seen as a response to the limitations of the mainstream media, albeit within the state of small independent media. "Apart from this there is also a challenge of access where newspapers are sold in main urban areas and the state is the dominant player in the broadcast media", says the NGO representative. An underlying position is also that Zimbabwe's communities lack a diverse media in which one can receive diverse views on the situation in Zimbabwe.

"None of us here can afford to buy a newspaper every day, so we rely mostly on radio for news, entertainment, etc.; of course these are controlled by the government and you only receive the good news, when you see the bad right in front of you every day in your neighbourhood", says a Highfields youth identifying himself using the pseudonym Biko.

The view above is based on the belief that Zimbabwe's story or narrative since 2000 has been dominated by the ruling party and government to the exclusion of other sectors. "The intention is to tell a story that is not being told in the mainstream state and privately owned media, and also to drive people driven actions to correct social misnomers", says the NGO representative. The participation of an NGO might be interpreted to mean that the youths' media projects are donor-drive, a position that both the NGO and youths interviewed disagree with. "The community newsletter project was in fact conceptualized by youths in the high-density suburbs of Highfields and Glen View. University students who have their own newsletters also came in later", says the NGO representative.

"This is one of the few projects that we can say…came from people, unlike all our work which sometime starts at the centre and moves out, this time the people themselves simply came to us for technical assistance, and as you see the stories, distribution and other administrative issues are handled by the youths themselves", added the NGO representative. This point is interesting in this study as it points to a conjunction of civil society interests in Zimbabwe and a deliberate intervention by communities and NGO players in the social world to identify issues they see as problematic and finding ways of correcting these issues. The media are thus being used not only as a source of information but also as an empowering tool to correct social ills that according to the interviewees include a failure by local councils to collect garbage, a collapse of education and social delivery, and as a political commentary tool as well. "We are not thinking big about what the media should do, we are simply thinking of our own situation, I see litter everywhere in Highfields, I see raw sewage flowing everyday by our home, we don't have electricity most of the time, there are no teachers in our schools, and you say to yourself who else should I talk to, how else can I put a little bit of pressure on the local councillor and politicians, and the media is a little stick in our hands, no one knows where it is coming from, but everyone has to listen at the end of the day", says Biko.

Between 2,500 and 5,000 copies of each newsletter are produced bi-monthly using a printing press hidden in the capital, Harare. One person collects the newsletters after printing for onward distribution to the rest of the team and to the wider community. The newsletter is two-page, bond paper printed in colour on both sides and is comprised of stories and pictures.

Alternative voices and the journalism discourse

More often than not, the mainstream news organizations' appeal to the need to be 'objective', 'balanced' and 'impartial' as basic tenets of being 'professional'. The argument that newspapers cover issues 'objectively' and in a 'balanced' and 'impartial' manner is one that is found in many editorial policy documents of most newspapers. The processes of achieving "objectivity" in the mainstream media are in variance to the way alternative media voices source their news as well as write it. In interviews with the youths running *Sakubva News* and *The Voice of Chitungwiza* editor, it became clear that news in the alternative media voices is a content developed from group discussions, observations, commentary and directly talking to communities. News is generally defined by how it is linked first to the community, and second to an issue categorized as important, i.e. affecting the whole community and other concerns of communities, especially regarding social delivery issues and politics, both local and national.

The Sakubva and Chitungwiza community newsletters are made up of a minimum of ten youths, drawn from different social backgrounds. The youths, aged between 13 and 24, are a mixture of those with an interest in religion, civic activism, sports and other issues. They are also a mixture of those still attending school and those who have finished. Before a newsletter is produced, a meeting (newsroom diary meeting) is held at a community hall and current issues are discussed. Each member is then given a task according to their ability to investigate a story as well as their interest and knowledge about a given story. "Our newsroom is not what you are used to knowing. We do not even know what a proper newsroom looks like, we just meet to discuss what are the interesting issues that we should write about, what is happening in our community, so it is an open discussion where each one has to say something and suggest what they want write about", says the 17-year-old editor of *Sakubva News*.

Deadlines for the submission of stories are established and stories are usually written by hand on pieces of paper for transmission to the NGO for transcribing and printing. Stories written by the alternative voices are mostly personal experiences, interviews with communities, investigative pieces and opinions. The stories, according to the *Sakubva News* editor, are an expression of those issues that people cannot communicate in the mainstream newspaper. "The newsletter is about breaking the silence in Sakubva and Mutare. In general, people want to talk but don't have anywhere to talk", says the editor. While mainstream media organizations have a clear line of leadership and newsroom structure and routines, alternative media voices have an almost linear leadership in which everything is established by consensus and consultation. These publications, in the context of Zimbabwe's media laws, are illegal. The Access to Information and Protection of

Privacy Act (AIPPA 2002) says that any mass media, including newsletters distributed to a mass of people, should be registered by the government-appointed Media and Information Commission (MIC). In this regard, the newspapers fall within the category of what the MIC calls "mass media". Whilst registration is an option for the newsletters, their style of writing, objectives and funding are in variance to the MIC rules and guidelines.

For example, the MIC requires that only qualified journalists run mass media services and that all funding for mass media work should be local. In the definition and media policy of the Zimbabwe government, the newsletters are therefore part of what they would call the oppositional or adversarial media. This point is not lost on the youths working on this project, as they have faced threats from security agents and some of them have been arrested for distributing the newsletters. "*Sakubva News* gives us the power and right to speak without being traced", says the newsletter's editor.

According to the youths, the security threats make it difficult to distribute the newsletters in the open; they instead resort to what they call "underground methods". It therefore follows that when the newsletter is printed, its distribution has to be secretive. Distribution channels change from time to time. The method used most often is giving the newsletters to schoolchildren at school entrances to take home and give to their parents. In some instances, thousands of the newsletters are simply left on street corners in the busy city centre, or in bus stations for people to pick up on their way either to or from work. At weekends the newsletters can be distributed at church gates as well as in bars across the two towns.

Content analysis of stories covered by newsletters, issues around reception and feedback

While the power to tell a society's story is traditionally left to professional journalists, alternative media voices run by youths in Zimbabwe argue that the mainstream media or "professional journalist" has failed them and they need, in the words of Chitungwiza youths, "news that points at the grey areas". In this instance, the grey areas are what communities conceive as issues that are not going right in their community and need change. Below is an example of a typical community newsletter story that appeared in *Sakubva News* July 2008. The story that appeared in the vernacular, Shona, has been translated into English for this research.

Sakubva News: July 2008: Transport problems persist in the city of Mutare

> Many residents of Mutare are living a difficult and miserable life owing to the high cost of fuel which has resulted in the cost of transport skyrocketing. From our investigations we have found out that the residents most affected are those from the

suburbs of Zimunya, Feenvalley and Dangamvura who need to connect with two different buses to get into the city centre. Transport operators in these areas are demanding that commuters pay at least 700,000 to 1, 000,000 million Zimbabwe dollars (USD 3 to 5) to travel the city centre. These fares are raised in the evening, when the demand for transport is high. Transport operators are literally doing as they please in changing the bus fares. Residents of Sakubva are suffering, as many have resorted to walking long distances as they cannot afford the transport fares. Some who talked to this paper say they have no choice but to walk these long distances as they cannot afford the transport fares. Many bus crews are now a law unto themselves as they even demand bribes for one to board a bus. This means that one has to pay the bus crew a bribe and then pay the bus fare. Many residents say they have no one to complain to. Bus owners say the high fares are due to the increases in the cost of fuel.

This story is an interesting example of how news is written from what the editor of *Sakubva News* calls a "people-centred view", i.e. the story is about the residents of Mutare, distinctively poor residents who use public transport. Mutare is a sprawling town located in a valley set in mountainous and rugged terrain. The story attempts at every turn to demonstrate that it is about the views of residents and challenges they face concerning transport in Mutare. This is achieved by positioning the resident against the transport operators as well as explaining the host of problems the residents face. While the story does not call for any specific action, it clearly points at the ills of the transport operators, including bus crews who are demanding bribes and being "a law unto themselves". The *Sakubva News* editor says this story is what they would call a watered-down story as it does not specifically call for particular action to be taken like other stories do. "Our intention is to warn the bus crews as well as alert residents to these practices". "More importantly however, we place this story in the economic context of the whole country, where prices are going up. So while addressing a Mutare issue, we are also addressing a countrywide problem of skyrocketing prices in the whole of Zimbabwe", adds the editor.

The 25-year-old editor of the Highfields newsletter not only sees himself as a political activist seeking change for his community but also doubles as a people's poet, writing protest poems that are recited at youth festivals or poetry slams at nightclubs in the suburbs and other areas.

A way that is used to get feedback on the newsletters is to provide an anonymous e-mail account in the paper that people can write to, as well as having one-to-one interaction with trusted community members to get feedback on the stories covered. In Mutare, where *Sakubva News* operates, municipal workers have used the publication to highlight corruption within the city council and to mobilize city council workers on strike actions. This has resulted in efforts by the city fathers to determine who the "publishers" of *Sakubva News* are, and attempts to influence the coverage of the newsletter have been made through invitations to meetings. These, stresses the newsletter's editor, are real and tangible results coming from actions of the youths running the newsletter. More importantly, the communities covered by *The Voice of Chitungwiza* and *Sakubva News* say they cannot afford the cost of main newspapers, selling at an average of 2 US dollars per copy. According to the NGO representative who assists with the printing of the newsletters, the stories they tell are not the usual media stories that one gets in the newspapers or on the radio or television. This makes the stories unique, "people-driven" stories. The Chitungwiza newsletter has become such an important political commentary publication that one of its members campaigned and won a Parliamentary seat on an opposition ticket in the March 2008 elections. This 31-year-old former 'journalist' from the newsletter is the youngest legislator in the current Zimbabwe Parliament. A content analysis of the two issues before the March 2008 elections show that while the story covered every issue falling within community news, water and roads, health and political violence, the newsletter gave the youths a platform to articulate their political vision, not necessarily as a political party newsletter.

While this study has largely focused on the Sakubva and Chitungwiza newsletters run by youths, another interesting example of the success of the newsletters project is in Glen View, a poor Harare suburb where ten youths have teamed up to form and run *GV News*. Within its first six months, *GV News* had made headlines as one of its lead stories on how the local high school had failed to purchase a school bus despite over ten years of financial contributions from parents resulted in instant results as the school authorities bought the bus two weeks after the story.

"We were encouraged by what happened in Glen View to start our own publication", says the editor of *Sakubva News*.

The impact of the newsletters in this period is aptly captured by the reports that came from the state, especially the Ministry of Home Affairs' (www.moha.gov.zw) citing the newsletters as part of what the present government calls regime change agenda. The acknowledgment of the newsletters by security agents is an indication of their impact and of their potential as alternative sources and platforms of information.

Alternative media voices in Zimbabwe and the future

The youth community newsletters, according to the NGO representative, can come to be established as a cultural trend in Zimbabwe. This cultural trend will be premised on the actions that communities can take using information instead of waiting for the mainstream media to inform them. The key element of the community newsletters is therefore how they have inculcated a culture of freedom of expression and how the media can be used to advance access to information that is empowering and can result in certain actions being taken to correct issues in communities. The future success of the community newsletters will therefore not be based on their becoming formal, i.e. adopting the formal and professional standards and structures of professional media organizations, but rather in their remaining informal and focusing on that story which is not a story in a "normal" newsroom. The power of the newsletters is also on the basis that they are not owned by anyone; hence their sustenance is purely the interest that the youths have in making their voices heard and the feeling of having power and a voice in their hands. The editor of *Sakubva News* says they are looking at expanding the project and solicit support from communities by launching subtitles as well as hosting a blog to tell their story worldwide as an experience of youths in Zimbabwe.

"This is our own experience which we want to share with similar youths worldwide", says the editor.

"I feel that while computers and the Internet in general is not available to many of us in Mutare, we have many of our brothers and sisters in the Diaspora, the UK, and America who may want to follow what we are doing and possibly participate and help", he adds. Zimbabwe has a strong presence in the web-based alternative media, with at least 12 Internet-based news agencies run by journalists in exile in South Africa, the UK and the US. The Chitungwiza newsletter has since branched off to form *The Voice of St. Mary's*, (St. Mary's being another suburb of Chitungwiza).

Conclusion

This article sought to describe the youth newsletter project in Zimbabwe as an effort at self empowerment in a difficult political, economic and social environment. A key motivation of the youths, many of whom are still in school while others have an average education but are unemployed, are to play a part in the democratization of Zimbabwe. Youths argue that political accountability, which presupposes a high degree of openness, is not practised in Zimbabwe, and that access to information will enable people to know what the government is doing as well as why and how people can improve their own livelihood and counter the state propaganda. One can still argue that as way of 'killing time', unemployed youths are finding the media projects as something that gives them power, gives their existence meaning in an a environment where they have neither the voices nor the means to be heard. The youths in urban centres involved in the alternative media projects view their actions as empowering not only to themselves but also to the community at large, and that these actions are also political and a process of seeking 'positive' change.

This study also seeks to show that while the government has dominated the mainstream media, this has not completely crippled the capacity of youths and many other voices to use whatever means available to communicate and share information. The youth media projects are therefore projecting a new media trajectory which redefines and challenges known media trends and processes. While the state tries to transfer its own systems of signification via the media, youths are using their own voices to counter this by telling their own story in their own words and according to their own understanding. At the centre of this is the struggle for meaning-making, in which the state and youths see issues from different perspectives. The project points not only to already existing weaknesses in mainstream media work worldwide, but also to the possibilities of what citizens can do on their own. A key question answered is that which asks when mainstream news organizations channel out news, whose news is it, and whose views are carried in those stories? The youth project in Zimbabwe, in the view of the NGO participating in the project, is a starting point in revolutionizing how news is collected, written and consumed, and for what purposes. It is possible that youth media can develop into 'The Media' of the future, especially with the possibilities of these voices finding expression via new media technologies such as the Internet and spreading even wider.

This is in no way an exhaustive media study but rather a description of the situation in Zimbabwe and of what youths are doing. It is thus interesting to see what the future holds for this type of media in an era of both political and economic stability. Key questions that only the future can answer concern whether these media will survive the post-political crisis in Zimbabwe, whether this is just a case of protest media, and whether these media can transform into established and sustainable community media.

Notes

1. The ruling ZANU PF party lost 57 of 120 contested Parliamentary seats to the opposition, Movement for Democratic Change (MDC). This was the first major electoral loss by the ruling party since 1980. Before June 2000 the opposition occupied less than three seats in Parliament (Raftopolous 2003: 230).
2. Interview with an executive at *The Financial Gazette* conducted in February 2008 by Rashweat Mukundu (author).
3. Some members of the community newsletters have been arrested and others threatened with arrest and beatings. The Ministry of Home Affairs has classified the publications as hostile literature distributed on behalf of opposition political parties.

Bibliography

Article 19 (1993) *Press Law and Practice: A Comparative Study of Press Freedom in Europe and Other Democracies*, International Centre Against Censorship, UK.

Article 19 (1994) *Guidelines for Election Broadcasting in Transitional Democracies*, International Centre Against Censorship, London.

Cápriles, O. (1986) Venezuela: ¿Política de comunicación o comunicación alternativa? [Venezuela: Communication policy or alternative communication?] in Simpson Grinberg, M. (ed.) Comunicación alternativa y cambio social [Alternative communication and social change], pp. 171-185. Puebla, Mexico: Premiá editora de libros.

Chakaodza, B. (2003) 'The State of the Media in Zimbabwe', Paper presentation at the Media Institute of Southern Africa Annual General Meeting. Maseru.

Curran J. (1991) 'Mass Media and Democracy Revisited', in Curran, J. & Gurevitch, M. (ed.) (1991) *Mass Media and Society*. London: Edward Arnold.

Feltoe, G. (1995) 'Removing Legal Barriers to Press Freedom', Harare (unpublished)
FXI/MISA/ Article 19 (1996) *Media Law and Practice in Southern Africa*, Protection of Sources, No 2.
Habermas, J. (1989) *The Structural Transformation of the Public Sphere: An Inquiry into a Category of Bourgeois Society*. Cambridge: Polity Press (Translated by Burger, T. & Lawrence, F.)
Hall, S. (1997) 'The Work of Representation', in Hall, S. (ed.) *Representation. Cultural Representations and Signifying Practices*. London. Sage.
Kaulemu, D. (2004) *The Culture of Party Politics and Concept of the State in Zimbabwe: The Past is the Future*. Barry, D.H. (ed.) Harare: Weaver Press.
Keane J. (1993) 'Democracy and the Media – without Foundations', in Held, D. (ed.) (1993) *Prospects for Democracy: North, South, East, West*. Cambridge. Polity Press.
Lichtenberg J. (ed.) (1990) *Democracy and the Mass Media*. Cambridge: Cambridge University Press.
Media Monitoring Project Zimbabwe (2000) *Election 2000,* Harare.
Media Monitoring Project Zimbabwe (2000) *The Question of Balance*, Harare.
MISA (1996) *So this is Democracy? The State of the Media in Southern Africa*, Media Institute of Southern Africa.
MISA (2004) *So this is Democracy? The State of the Media in Southern Africa*, Media Institute of Southern Africa.
MISA (2005) *So this is Democracy? The State of the Media in Southern Africa*, Media Institute of Southern Africa.
O'Connor, A. (1990b) Radio is Fundamental to Democracy. *Media Development*, 4, 3-4.
O'Sullivan-Ryan, J., & Kaplún, M. (1978) *Communication Methods to Promote Grass-roots Participation: A Summary of Research Findings from Latin America, and an Annotated Bibliography*. Paris: Unesco.
Paiva, A. (1983) 'La comunicación alternativa: Sus campos de influencia, sus limitaciones, y sus perspectivas de desarrollo' [Alternative communication: Fields of influence, limitations, and future directions], in Reyes Matta, F. (ed.) *Comunicación alternativa y búsquedas democráticas* [Alternative communication and the search for democracy] pp. 29-56. Mexico City: Instituto Latinoamericano de Estudios Transnacionales y Fundación Friedrich Ebert.
Raftopolous, B. (2003) 'The State in Crisis. Authoritarian, Nationalism, Selective Citizenship and Distortions of Democracy in Zimbabwe', in Hammar, A.; Raftopolous, B.; Jensen, S. (eds.) *Zimbabwe Unfinished Business: Rethinking Land, State and the Nation in the Context of Crisis*. Harare. Weaver Press.
Reyes Matta, F. (1983a) 'Comunicación alternativa: Respuesta de compromiso político' [Alternative communication: Response of a political commitment], in Reyes Matta, F. (ed.) *Comunicación alternativa y búsquedas democráticas* [Alternative communication and the search for democracy], pp. 23-28. Mexico City: Instituto Latinoamericano de Estudios Transnacionales y Fundación Friedrich Ebert.
Rodriguez, C. (2002) 'Citizen's Media and the Voice of the Angel Poet', *Media International Australia*, 103, May 2002.
Saunders, R. (1991) *Information in the Interregnum: The Press, State and Civil Society in the Struggles for Hegemony, Zimbabwe 1980-1990*, Ph.D. thesis, University of Carleton, Canada.
Solidarity Peace Trust (2003) 'National Youth Service Training: Shaping Youths in a Truly Zimbabwean Manner', http://www.reliefweb.int/library/documents/2003/spt-zim-5sep.pdf: Accessed 24 October 2008.

Young Voices Driving Social Change[1]

Lise Grauenkær Jensen, Mette Grøndahl Hansen & Stine Kromann-Larsen[2]

Abstract

This article seeks to explore how youth can be active participants in and drivers of social change processes needed in the fight against HIV/AIDS. Based on an empirical study in a Malawian anti-AIDS youth club from spring 2007, the article analyses how a youth club can act as a mediator for social change processes.

Taking its point of departure in Clemencia Rodriguez's concept of citizens' media, the article explores the youth club and its activities as that of community media. In doing this, concepts of critical consciousness, social movements and civil society are applied.

The study shows that communication in the youth club does to some extent challenge different social norms, as well as provides a foundation for collective action. Thus, the youth club becomes an actor in the public sphere, giving voice to a group of people commonly referred to as a risk group.

> *What we did during the past and what we can do now will be totally different, because there are other things we have not known. We have learnt something – so when we go back to our youth clubs, we will be discussing other things, not only AIDS (...) and it will bring change to the community – because we are the community* (Jon Nkawile, 22 years old, Mpemba Youth Club, Malawi)

In Malawi, young people stare in the eyes of the HIV/AIDS epidemic every day. More than every seventh person is infected, and even more are affected by the epidemic. The epidemic permeates their social, family and work life. It is a fact they have to deal with every day.

In spring 2007, we worked with approximately 30 young people at an anti-AIDS youth club in Malawi. During two months, the youth club members participated in a series of workshops developing different activities within a Communication for Social Change (CFSC)[3] framework. The main purpose of these activities was for the youth club members to *"define who they are, what they need and how to get what they need in order to improve their own lives"* (Parks 2005: 3) – that is, to promote social change. In the workshops, the participants were introduced to different communicative tools and activities. The objective was to initiate community dialogue and collective action, thus encouraging them to address HIV/AIDS-related issues.

The overall purpose of this article is to explore whether youth clubs have the potential to evolve into gateways for young people to voice their opinion – and in doing so become active participants in and drivers of social change processes in their community.

The Mpemba Youth Club

The youth club participating in our study is situated in Mpemba, a semi-urban village just a few kilometres outside Malawi's largest city, Blantyre. At the time of the study, the club had existed for about five years, being established in 2002 by the NGO ADRA (Adventist Development and Relief Agency) Malawi. It was one of several anti-AIDS clubs established by ADRA as part of their *Let's Fight HIV/AIDS in Malawi* (LEFAM) programme[4].

The Mpemba Youth Club has a fairly non-formalized structure because its initial members, who had received training in peer education and HIV/AIDS transmission and epidemiology, are no longer active in the club. Several of the current members have received training from other NGOs or the local health clinic. The youth club now works independently, the ADRA programme has been phased out in this area. They meet once a week to discuss issues related to HIV/AIDS, act and play sports. The members are 12-28 years old (average age 21) and live in Mpemba village or the surrounding area, and comprise approximately 70% men and 30% women. The majority of these members have finished secondary school or at least part of it. None of them is employed, but they often help their families in their subsistence farming or small income generating activity (IGA).

The members have different backgrounds. Some members live with their parents and siblings, while most of them live with grandparents or relatives as they have lost their families to the epidemic or disease. Furthermore, the members have different religious affiliations, ranging from different Christian beliefs such as Adventist and Baptist, to Muslim. Despite these obvious differences, we observed that they were not explicit once the members were socializing at the youth club and joining each other in a more common cause – discussing HIV/AIDS. At the youth club, the members use and draw upon their individual differences as resources, and work together as a group with the common goal of fighting HIV/AIDS.

It quickly became evident to us that all these young people have first-hand experience of the epidemic. About two-thirds of the club members know at least three people living with HIV/AIDS (PLWHA), and approximately the same number of people said that they think about HIV/AIDS every day. It is no wonder, though; they live in a part of Malawi with an HIV prevalence rate among the adult population (ages 15-49) of 14-21% (NAC Malawi 2007: 18). Several have lost a friend or family member to AIDS, and have personally experienced the stigma and discrimination that comes with this. Thus, the detrimental effects of the HIV/AIDS epidemic are an integral part of their lives, and the young members of the Mpemba Youth Club are ready to deal with it. They want to make a difference.

But what can young people in an anti-AIDS youth club like the one in Mpemba do? How can 22-year-old Jon and his friends make a difference in the fight against the epidemic? An epidemic spreading at what seems to be an accelerating speed, hitting those made vulnerable by poverty, mobility or social status. An epidemic that has eroded the foundation for development in Malawian society and which many experts, state officials and international NGOs have spent a great deal of time, effort and money trying to curb – something, as of yet, they have not yet succeeded to do.

Therefore, this article attempts to explore how the club can be an example of how youth clubs can offer a chance to young people to become active participants in and drivers of social change processes.

Empirical approach

The empirical data used in this article were originally produced for our Master thesis 'Voice of Mpemba', with a focus on how small-scale empowerment processes in a Malawian youth club can be considered large-scale social changes. In the production of the data, an inherent wish was also to somehow 'test' the assumptions inherent in the CFSC theories, taking our point of departure in the Integrated Model of CFSC[5] developed by the John Hopkins Institute (Figueroa et al., 2002). The study sought to qualify the links between community dialogue, collective action, and social change assumed in CFSC. The empirical data is the result of a series of workshops carried out with the Mpemba Youth Club over the course of eight weeks. These workshops were based on CFSC principles[6] and drew on the pedagogical ideas of Brazilian educator Paulo Freire. In this sense, the data do not represent the real-life situation of Mpemba Youth Club but are rather an attempt to construct an 'ideal type' situation of a CFSC process. The idea of this short 'artificial' intervention was to produce data that would indicate the potential and shortcomings of CFSC activities and methods.

However, the data produced also constitute interesting material on the social interaction and communicative dynamics taking place at the Mpemba Youth Club, indicating what potential lies within the social setting of a youth club. Thus, the 'artificial intervention' bared open a potential that would not have manifested itself if the study had been carried out with data produced during the 'ordinary' life of the youth club. In this article, we want to analyse this potential from a theoretical perspective, and with a focus on youth clubs as community media. Before such potential is analysed, the workshops are briefly presented.

Presentation of the workshops

The objective of the workshops was to create a space for horizontal dialogue within the youth club, and to 'give voice' to the youth. In doing so, we offered the members communicative tools to address issues and reflect critically on the social circumstances of the HIV/AIDS epidemic. We conducted seven workshops: Problem Tree, Vision Tree, Photo, Storytelling, Drama, Advocacy and Most Significant Change (MSC) evaluation.

Based on Paulo Freire's idea of 'critical consciousness', we started with a Problem and Vision Tree workshop, during which the youth had to identify causes and consequences of the epidemic. They arranged them in chains of causal relation, from the 'root' causes at the bottom of the tree to the consequences at the top. These causal and circumstantial correlations were identified through a process of 'critical learning' by which participants reflect critically upon their own social situation (Freire 1974: 39).

The tree was used as a metaphor and a visualization of the causal relations. In the Vision Tree workshop, the participants had to reverse the problems into their 'visions of change'. After having identified this vision, they were to find the appropriate actions needed to realize this vision. The participants were divided into smaller groups, and chose a problem they wanted to work with in depth

Image 1. Problem and vision trees

One of the participants presents the problem and their causal relations to the group
Photo: Grauenkær Jensen, Grøndahl Hansen and Kromann-Larsen

during the next workshops. For example, one group chose the problem 'discrimination'. After having chosen a problem, they were asked to develop an 'action plan'. The action plan was a detailed plan for activities that would bring about changes in their community concerning HIV/AIDS that included consideration of the nature of the problem.

Through the next workshops, the youth were introduced to different communicative tools. These tools were used to address their problem and to plan a relevant activity/action. These were photography, storytelling, drama and advocacy. For instance, in the Photo workshop, the members took pictures to visualize their action plans, and in the Storytelling workshop, they produced stories they could use to educate the community.

In the last workshop, on Advocacy, the youth club members designed a strategy to promote the issues and opinions with which they wanted to address their chosen problem publicly to initiate change. This workshop especially included consideration and discussions on relevant stakeholders. Finally, the workshops were rounded off with a Most Significant Change evaluation, as a participatory way of monitoring and evaluating the changes experienced by the participants (Parks 2005: 22). The youth club members were asked to tell stories about the most significant change they had experienced in the course of the workshops.

Image 2. Action plan

After having identified problems and visions, the groups prepare their plans for action
Photo: Grauenkær Jensen, Grøndahl Hansen and Kromann-Larsen

In order to secure enough data on the processes and dynamics within the youth club, we supplemented the workshops with in-depth interviews, questionnaires and participatory evaluations. The workshops provide the bulk of our empirical data, and the statements used in this article are a direct result of them and the interviews conducted in connection with them. Thus, the findings in this article do not only refer to Mpemba youth club, but can be related to other youth clubs that would like to implement similar activities based on CFSC principles.

Theoretical approach

As mentioned, the data from the youth club indicate the types of communication and dynamics that have taken place during our workshop. In order to understand the potential that these type of clubs hold for empowering youth to become active participants in and drivers of social change processes, we analyse our data using the concept of community media. Community media encompass different theoretical contributions that explore the requisite for social change processes. We take our theoretical point of departure mainly in Colombian media and communication scholar Clemencia Rodriguez's thinking on citizens' media (Rodriguez 2001). This theory explores the processes through which a community media can be the locus of change processes in society. Furthermore, our theoretical approach is based on Paulo Freire's 'Education for Critical Consciousness' and 'Pedagogy of the Oppressed'. We apply this theory in order to analyse the communication processes that took place at the youth club during the CFSC-based activities. In the second part of the article, we analyse the youth club's potential for driving social change by seeing it as a social movement, using Brazilian Political Science Professor Leonardo Avritzer's and Columbian Social Scientist Arturo Escobar's theories. Finally, we try to identify the arena in which the youth club can partake, drawing upon the ideas on an 'African Civil Society' formulated by American Government Professors Stephen Orvis and Nelson M. Kasfir, as well as Kenyan Social Scientist and lawyer Wachira Maina.

Thus, this article does not only present an exploration of our initial limited intervention at the youth club in Mpemba. Rather, it offers an exploration of our empirical and theoretical findings, suggesting the potential for youth clubs in general to act as community media that constitute change agents in the fight against the HIV/AIDS epidemic.

The youth club as community media

Clemencia Rodriguez's idea is that through participation in community/alternative media, people "...*reshape their own identities, the identities of others, and their social environment, they produce power*" (Rodriguez 2001: 19). Adopting Belgian political theorist Chantal Mouffe's concept of citizenship as something that has to be constructed through daily political action (Rodriguez 2001: 19), Rodriguez considers community media as a way for people to enact this citizenship, thus citizens' media. Her theorization is based on personal experiences where she has seen *"... how dramatically pre-established cultural codes and traditional power relations were disrupted"* (Rodriguez 2001: 3). Community media is a possible platform for people to participate in and drive change processes.

Rodriguez summarizes her concept of citizen media in three points (Rodríguez, 2001: 20):

1. That a collectivity enacts its citizenship by actively intervening and transforming the established mediascape.
2. That these media contest social codes, legitimized identities, and institutionalized social relations.
3. That these communication practices empower the community involved, to the point where these transformations and changes are possible.

We use Rodriguez's three statements on citizens' media as structural elements for our article, redefining them to fit our study and the context of the youth club. Our redefinition is as follows:

1. How does the Mpemba Youth Club contribute to the localized mediascape?
2. Do the Mpemba Youth Club's activities and public dialogue contest established and legitimized social structures?
3. Does the Mpemba Youth Club mediate quotidian politics as a social movement to a degree that empowers the community of Mpemba and makes change possible?

The youth club's contribution to the localized mediascape

First, Rodriguez points out that citizens' media contribute with communication that changes the general communication flows of the mediascape. In this article, we primarily focus on how youth clubs influence the 'localized mediascape', which is the exchanges of meanings, information and initiatives in the community, which in effect shape a group identity.

In order to explore whether or not Mpemba Youth Club does in fact intervene with and transform the established localized mediascape, we draw upon British media scholar Chris Atton's thinking on 'alternative media'. Atton emphasizes community media's contribution of alternative content and new structures of access and participation to, in our case, the localized mediascape (Atton 2002). Rephrasing Rodriguez's first point, we ask how the activities of the youth club as a collectivity contribute to the localized mediascape with new issues and ideas as well as new structures of access to and participation in the production of meaning.

In the following, we will use the Mpemba Youth Club as an example and look at different statements from the workshops, which express an intention to create different activities that contribute to the localized mediascape. We assume that the activities of the Mpemba Youth Club are similar to those in other youth clubs, or at least that it would be possible for similar youth clubs to adopt these activities. Thus, our analysis of the Mpemba Youth Club's contribution to the localized mediascape indicates the potential that other youth clubs have.

The club members believe that they can contribute with something the community did not have previously: Information about the prevention and management of HIV/AIDS. As Steve Kudzala states in his fictional story from the storytelling workshop:

> People in this community are stopped from discriminating because they are given information by the people who know about AIDS; the community's dialogues, plays, poems and songs are part of getting information on what AIDS is, because they are disseminating information through these activities (Steve Kudzala, 18 years old)

In his understanding, the activities at the youth club provide a type of information that people in the community cannot get elsewhere. This contributes with alternative content and issues that the people in Mpemba did not know about before the youth club was established.

Not only the existence of the youth club ensures this contribution; the methods used in the workshops to discuss issues concerning HIV/AIDS also play an important role. Another club member, Yonam Mpanda, comments in the MSC evaluation on the most significant change he experienced:

> ...What I have learnt most is the importance of reflecting on all issues of HIV/AIDS. (...) What really made me realize this change is that problem tree (...) In terms of a youth club, it is important to us because we are equipped and this will help in disseminating the messages to the community. (Yonam Mpanda, 20 years old)

Based on the visualization in the problem tree, Yonam combines his knowledge in new ways and hereby considers the issues from new perspectives. In this way, the Problem Tree workshop contributes with alternatives to the exchanges of meaning concerning HIV/AIDS issues in the club discussions.

New communication tools such as photos, fictional stories and plays also make it possible for the youth club members to present their ideas and opinions to the community in an innovative way. The participants often expressed a belief that this would make people understand the issues better than if they were presented through other more traditional channels, such as written pamphlets and medical counselling.

> Photos can be used to show people with visual representations, the story being explained for easy understanding and appreciation. (Emmanuel, 27 years old)

If the photos and stories in fact make it easier for more people to understand the complex clinical information on HIV/AIDS, the use of these different communication tools will also provide the people of Mpemba with new structures of access to information on HIV/AIDS and the exchanges of meaning on these issues.

Furthermore, in an individual in-depth interview 22-year-old Francisco explains how the youth club takes its activities to the people of the community through community meetings. Most of the action plans also include a community meeting activity. They perform their plays and ask the audience their opinion. Thereby, they open up for discussion on issues concerning HIV/AIDS in their community, and offer the people of Mpemba an opportunity to contribute to the production of meaning assigned to HIV/AIDS issues.

With the different forms of communicative expressions, the youth club increases access to information about HIV/AIDS, and with their public activities

Image 3. Presentation of photo

Photo: Grauenkær Jensen, Grøndahl Hansen and Kromann-Larsen

also make it possible for people in Mpemba to participate in the production of this information.

Youth clubs contesting social structures

In light of this contribution to the localized mediascape, will the content of the youth club's public activities in fact contest established and legitimized social structures as Rodriguez suggests?

The communication must initiate a process of 'self discovery', whereby the social circumstances that define one's own social situation (or that of the community one belongs to) are explored and questioned. According to Paulo Freire, such an exploration will give the people involved in this process the power to redefine those very circumstances – and thus drive social change. This process is called "naming the world" (Freire 1974, 2005). This power lies within the (collective) "critical consciousness" that is an understanding of how different circumstances and inequalities work and are causally interrelated (Freire 1974: 39).

The HIV/AIDS epidemic in Malawi is driven by inequalities, especially by the social norms on male and female sexuality. Hence, the relationships between the genders create an unequal environment that puts everyone at risk (Lwanda 2004) (Arrehag 2006). Is there any potential for the youth club to identify these social inequalities, build up a critical consciousness, and take on a leading role for the people of Mpemba to name their world?

We look for an indication of this potential in the participants' discussions, and dialogue especially during the problem identification process and in their action plans.

Problem identification – social relationships and behaviour

At the initial workshops, the participants display a detailed and nuanced understanding of the inequalities that the HIV/AIDS epidemic creates. The members of the youth club are especially preoccupied with the social relationships that the epidemic creates, with AIDS-affected households being discriminated.

While the social situation of discrimination dominated the workshops, the participants' discussion during problem identification also indicates the possibility of addressing and contesting social structures. They especially identify social structures that work as drivers of the epidemic. These are mainly different types of social behaviour and social relationships, defined by uneven power relations.

One of the issues that recur several times during the workshops is the social behaviour by which young girls provide older man, sugar daddys, with sexual favours in exchange for gifts or cash. In a group discussion, Joana explores the circumstances that can lead a young girl into such a relationship:

> ... some girls, they prefer to have sugar daddies, because they want to have money and enjoy themselves, so they choose sugar daddies. Another answer I can give, poverty is also among people, some children (...) from very poor families (...) they tend to have sugar daddies and sugar mummies to stay in school. (Joana, 17 years old)

In collaboration with her friends, she identifies individual wishes to have fun as well as poverty as motivation for having sugar daddies. She does to some extent contest the legitimacy of the relationship by identifying it as a risk factor. However, she only identifies the individual motivation for entering the relationship and not the social structures that legitimize it. She does not reflect on the social roles of men and women, in which men dominate women and women are dependent on men, as a legitimizing factor for the relationship. In the discussion, only the individual behaviour of the girl and the man is contested – not the social structures that lead to the relationship.

The participants also identify risky social relationships, in which the unequal power distribution is more apparent. Different groups in society who exploit their authority for sexual domination are identified as special risk groups. One example is priests and witchdoctors. In a group discussion, two participants indirectly question the way priests and witchdoctors sometimes exploit their position in society to take advantage of women's often-vulnerable situation.

> Roderick, 20 years old: I said, coaxing them, that he is going to give them treatment, for example, the witch doctor, so that they should not pay, if they have less money, and he charged them a high price.(...)

> Joana, 17 years old: The witch doctors and pastors (...) ask women to sleep with them just because they want to satisfy their sexual desires.

The participants hold general contempt for powerful groups exploiting their position, but the discussion becomes one of individual moral values for the priests, witchdoctors and women involved. Neither the authority of the priest nor the vulnerable situation of women in society is questioned. None of these power relations is addressed in the participants' action plans, indicating that the activities in the workshops do not challenge these specific social roles and relations.

Reproducing social norms

Furthermore, the participants do not directly address and challenge norms. Rather, there are several examples of them reproducing norms that are problematic in relation to HIV/AIDS stigma and discrimination.

> When we young boys meet a girl of our age she accepts us and we innocently do not know what she has been doing in her past life. We end up being infected in the long run. (Roderick 20 years old)

Here Roderick states his opinion that PLWHA themselves are responsible, because he thinks that their behaviour is immoral. This is just one example of how the participants maintain their perceptions regarding women and sexuality; women who get HIV are promiscuous, and thus brought it on themselves.

In one of the groups' action plans on discrimination, the participants address attitudes and norms. However, these are identified with a lack of information rather than something that is socially constructed. They do not explore what these norms and attitudes entail further.

The problem identification during the initial workshops indicates that the Mpemba Youth Club's communication holds the potential to contest both the social structures of social behaviour and social relationships that drive the epidemic and the inequalities that the epidemic produces. However, the data also show that there is a risk that the youth club's activities can contribute to a reproduction of norms that might legitimize some of the relationships that the participants at the same time contest.

Youth clubs driving social change

Once the youth club members name their world they have increased their power, as they have redefined their world. But is this power enough for the youth club to actually play the role of change agent? Rodriguez points out how the communication processes have to empower participants in order for any transformation or change to occur. She finds that people enact their citizenship and produce power through *"quotidian politics – a politics which extends the terrain of political contestation to the everyday enactment of social practices..."* (McClure 1992, quoted in Rodriguez 2001: 21). Can youth clubs be the political subject that allows the members to enact their citizenship? In the language of CFSC, this enactment would, be called collective action.

In order to analyse whether the youth club can be a mediator for quotidian politics, we explore the club and its activities as a social movement. We find this concept relevant to use in our analysis, since social movements work at the level of everyday politics as opposed to the formal political level of parties and elections (Escobar 1992: 70). Social movements politicize everyday issues and take them out of the private sphere and into the public sphere. Thus, they collectively name the world and partake in the negotiation and reproduction of social structures. Leonardo Avritzer points out how this politicizing of daily issues of injustice is a form of collective action, which constructs a collective identity that can frame further action (Avritzer 2002: 44).

We analyse statements made by the participants on the activities they, as a youth club, can and intend to make in order to identify their collective identity. Furthermore, we analyse this identity's influence on their activities as collective actions of a social movement. The collective identity and the collective action will indicate whether the communicative dynamics in the club produce enough power for the club to drive social change processes.

Collective identity

During the workshops we found that the participants create a collective identity. By collective identity we mean a shared understanding of 'what we can and will do', a sort of common ground that specifies what "we will work for" (Melluci in Escobar 1992: 72). On several occasions, the participants express that there exists a kind of 'oneness' in the youth club, making it possible for them to work together. During the Most Significant Change evaluation, a group of the youth club members discusses the value of this oneness. 'Without unity we can't work'. Jon adds, 'We are going to contribute to other people, our community'. With this powerful unity, the youth club can help other people. The members gather around this common goal. However, their ability to help other people is based more on the fact that they are knowledgeable individuals than because they are a collective.

In a follow-up interview Joana says, *"We can help change some things"*, and gives the example that she herself can encourage someone to stay in school rather than looking for a sexual partner. Many of the statements on what the youth club can do have this focus; it concerns individual actions by the individual club member, not the club acting as a collective. This individual action is in most cases articulated as 'disseminating information about HIV/AIDS'. As they say, 'Spread the message – not the disease'. The youth club posses information that they can share with the community.

The way by which the youth club helps the community by providing information is created through politicizing situations which the members experience in their daily lives. When the participants reflect critically upon their daily encounters with friends and family who have been infected, they shape the situation as one of lack of information. They take a daily issue, for example 'Many friends and relatives are infected with HIV', and turn it into a political situation, one of 'the right to information'.

While the identity is one of 'I do' rather than 'We do', the members still find support in each other and confirm with each other that it is their duty to spread their knowledge. Furthermore, the participants stress the fact that they have a youth club that makes them knowledgeable and allows them to reach people. The participants express a common ground, which defines the members as not only being different from other people in the community, but also as being different from youth in general. They are different, because they are proactive and are doing something about the epidemic; they help people in their community.

Collective actions

The club members are knowledgeable individuals who educate and help their community. This collective identity defines the activities (collective action) the participants choose to undertake in their action plans. During the Photo workshop, Denison presents his group's photos and explains its action plan:

> Below our action plan is shown. It shows how with civic education about the impact of discrimination and its prevention we can achieve good health in the infected people. Frequent interaction and constant discussions (...) help ease problems of the mind and forge acceptance. (Denison, 21 years old)

The youth club members see themselves as a group of knowledgeable people who are obliged to share this knowledge with other people in the community. This collective identity results in many of the planned activities being centred on information, civic education and sensitizing campaigns. A common activity would be one in which the youth club would perform a community play and engage in dialogue with the spectators afterwards, giving information on HIV/AIDS and advice on how to avoid infection.

However, while the collective identity makes it possible for the participants to come up with a wide range of educational activities, the identity also limits their action. This aspect is evident in another group's presentation of their action plan on poverty. Jon presents the plan:

> Now our vision is that if there were something to preoccupy the people, like business, this could heavily reduce the incidence of AIDS (...) The livelihood of people does change if they are involved in income-generating activities, as we can see in this frame. (...) Doing topical communal plays can also assist in bringing change in terms of curbing discrimination, as shown in this frame. (Jon, 22 years old)

Focusing on the causal relation between poverty and the spread of HIV, the group identifies income-generating activities as something that would prevent, e.g., young women from prostituting themselves. However, this activity does not concord with their collective identity, and thus the activity the group comes up with is 'information through community plays'. Thus, even when the participants politicize the identified problem as one of lack of income, they choose to perform an informational activity, rather than conducting the income-generating activities first suggested.

Another aspect of the collective identity constructed in youth clubs, which also defines possible action, is the members' understanding of the arena in which the youth club can act, and their understanding of the role they can play in this arena. This will define whether the youth club will take its politicizing of everyday issues into the public sphere.

Image 4. Drama

The participants perform a drama on discrimination as part of a larger exhibition.
Photo: Grauenkær Jensen, Grøndahl Hansen and Kromann-Larsen

The arena

In the following, we identify the arena the youth club members consider themselves part of and where they find actors to interact with. Combined with their collective identity and collective actions (activities), we envisage what kind of role the youth club can play in society, and thus what the possibilities are for young people to actively partake in and drive social change processes through the youth club.

The participants identify an arena in which they themselves as a youth club can participate. That is, an arena of community meetings, demonstrations, rallies, etc. The stakeholders they find relevant to address when it comes to HIV/AIDS issues are chiefs and traditional authorities, the District Commissioner (DC), members of Parliament (MPs), ministers and government associations such as the church, educational institutions and the press. While the participants do not consider chiefs and traditional authorities as belonging to the same arena as the youth club, they are often included in the action plans. The youth club can relate to and consider interacting with the traditional authorities and the DC, but a step up the ladder, where ministers and MPs reside, the accessibility and transparency lessens.

The understanding that the youth club members express of the arena in which the youth club can play a part is similar to what Stephen Orvis terms African civil society, where a broad array of collective activity and associational life takes place (Orvis 2001:17). When discussing the constitution of African civil society, is it important not to restrict oneself to formal organizations. Family, tribe and ethnic divisions may also be loci of social and political change. In a context where state politics constrain formal association, informal groupings and gatherings such as funerals and weddings provide important occasions for political exchange and the reassertion of social and political identities (Kasfir 1998: 5 and Maina 1998: 144 in Howell & Pearce 2001: 185). Thus, the arena that the youth club members see as their own is the arena of civil society: An arena where their activities of community drama, storytelling and advocacy take place.

Considering the youth club's collective identity, collective action and arena, what exactly is the role the club can play in society?

The youth club's role in society

Emmanuel Chinzukira describes the role the participants see for the youth club, in his individual story:

> They give a civic education through drama with which they change this process of discrimination and help the community to unity and no discrimination and this leads to high development. (Emmanuel, 27 years old)

Here, Emmanuel indicates that the members of the youth club play a role in society by educating others. The youth club can create spaces of dialogue through their communicative actions, and engage community members in both dialogue and action. Furthermore, they show the community that it is possible to act, engage in decision-making and politicize daily issues.

However, the collective identity and understanding of the youth club's arena of action also allows for another role for the youth club – as a voice in the community. In the Advocacy workshop, the most common choice of activities the participants make is community meetings with plays, poems and songs, or rallies and demonstrations. However, this is not only connected to their collective identity of being knowledgeable people, who are obliged to share their knowledge; it is also connected to their understanding of the public arena they belong to. Most of the different activities include an idea of collective action at the public level, such as rallies and demonstrations. The participants place themselves in a central position where they express their opinions, and where they are heard in the arena of civil society. As they state, *"Community members have the influence and the youth have the power to change the problem"* (From one group's advocacy strategy). The participants believe that their dialogue can form part of a public dialogue through which a variety of actors want to contribute with their proposal on how to respond to the HIV/AIDS epidemic.

In the advocacy strategies, the participants often seek to target stakeholders of political, legislative or administrative power. The participants express an understanding of the tools they have access to as a youth club, which are similar to those of a social movement, that is, collective action at the public level in order to create public debate about an issue. They want to take active part in the issues concerning them and their society. Furthermore, one of the participants, Jon, emphasizes that the changes experienced by the members of the youth club will bring changes to the community as well:

> It will change in our clubs, it will bring change, and to the community also because we ourselves, we are the community, so it will bring change I can say.
> (Jon, 22 years old, in a Most Significant Change evaluation)

Thus, even though the participants might seem a bit sceptic when talking of being able to address issues in the sense of, e.g., laws and policies, they do at times express a belief that as a collective they have the opportunity, power and access to bring change to their communities. Moreover, and not least, that they have an obligation to themselves and to each other to enter the civil society arena and make their voices heard.

In conclusion

Our empirical material indicates that the Mpemba Youth Club does provide young people with the possibility to participate in and drive social change processes to some extent. The club provides an entry point for its members into an arena of informal association. Here the youth club becomes a civil society actor, which contributes with alternative meaning in the daily negotiation of social norms, beliefs and relations. Through the activities, such as community drama, rallies, etc., the young people of Mpemba are able to put issues on the agenda that otherwise are not raised. However, the extent to which the youth club will drive social change is limited by the fact that the communication in the youth club only partially challenges social norms and power relations. Furthermore, a collective identity is produced. However, this only allows the members to be informants, rather than citizens who actively shape their own environment. These findings indicate that youth clubs hold the potential to become locus points for reflection and discussion on local issues on HIV/AIDS, but their ability to be change agents and drive social change processes depends on the formation of a collective identity that allows for a wide range of activities.

Notes
1. This article is based on empirical data from our Master's thesis in Communication Studies, International Development Studies and cultural encounters, March 2008. http://hdl.handle.net/1800/3087
2. Comments and questions can be emailed to youthfightingaids@gmail.com
3. "CFSC can be defined as a process of public and private dialogue through which people themselves define who they are, what they need and how to get what they need in order to improve their own lives" (Parks 2005:3). CFSC is an approach to development communication in which the focus is on dialogue, participation and collective action by and for the community. The approach integrates a wide variety of theories and practices from development theory, communication theory, pedagogy, etc., and seeks to bridge the gap between Behaviour Change Communication and Participatory approaches saying that there is a reciprocal relationship between social changes and behaviour changes.

4. The LEFAM programme is funded by ADRA Denmark and utilizes a CFSC strategy encompassing both activities at local level and national media-driven activities.
5. The integrated model of CFSC is divided into four main levels: 1) Catalyst, 2) Community dialogue, 3) Collective action, and 4) Individual and social change.
    The catalyst initiates the process of the second 'level', the community dialogue that leads to the third 'level', collective action effecting individual and/or social change and lastly having societal impact.
6. The workshops sought to initiate community dialogue with the steps 'recognition of problem', 'clarification of perceptions', 'vision of the future', and to give the participants incentive to move into collective action with the steps of 'options for action' and 'action plan and consensus on action'.

References

Arrehag, Lisa et al. (2006) *The impact of HIV/AIDS on Livelihoods, Poverty and the Economy of Malawi*. Sida Studies 18.
Atton, Chris (2002) *Alternative Media*. Sage Publications Ltd.
Avritzer, Leonardo (2002) *Democracy and the Public Space in Latin America*. Princeton University Press.
Escobar Arturo (1992) *The Making of Social Movements in Latin America: Identity, Strategy and Democracy*. Westview Press.
Freire, Paulo (1974) *Pedagogy of the Oppressed*. The Seabury Press.
Freire, Paulo (2005) *Education for Critical Consciousness*. (First published in 1974). London: Continuum.
Howell, J. & Pearce, J. (2001) *Civil Society & Development – A Critical Exploration*. Lynne Rienner Publishers, Inc.
Kasfir, Nelson (ed.) (1998) *Civil Society & Democracy in Africa – Critical Perspectives*. Frank Cass & Co. Ltd.
Lwanda, John (2004) *Politics, Culture and Medicine in Malawi*. Kachere Series Zomba.
NAC Malawi (2007) *Report of the Malawi Triangulation Project: Synthesis of Data on Trends in the National and Local HIV Epidemic and the Reach and Intensity of Prevention Efforts*. January. Lilongwe, National AIDS Commission, WHO, University of California San Francisco, UNAIDS and United States Centers for Disease Control and Prevention.
Opubor, E. Alfred (1999) 'If Community Media is the Answer What is the Question?', in Gumuncio-Dagron, Alfonso & Tufte, Thomas (eds.) *Communication for Social Change Anthology: Historical and Contemporary Readings*. Communication for Social Change Consortium.
Orvis, Stephen (2001) 'Civil Society in Africa or African Civil Society?', *African and Asian Studies*, 36(2001)1[7]
Parks, W. Gray-Felder, D. Hunt, J. & Byrne, A. (2005) *Who Measures Change? An Introduction to Participatory Monitoring and Evaluation of Communication for Social Change*. Communication for Social Change Consortium.
Rodriguez, C. (2001) *Fissures in the Mediascape: An International Study of Citizens' Media*. Hampton Press.

From Voice to Participation?
Analysing Youth Agency in Letter Writing in Tanzania

Thomas Tufte, Aran Corrigan, Ylva Ekström, Minou Fuglesang & Datius Rweyemamu

Abstract

This article is about exploring forms of youth participation in processes of social change and good governance. While the thematic focus is on the practice of civil society driven media platforms, the core conceptual question is: to which degree can these media platforms actually articulate participatory governance? To which degree do they open discursive spaces that young people can engage in? The case we analyse is from Tanzania, where the NGO 'Femina HIP' has grown big and successful over the past decade. Femina HIP has developed a multi-pronged media platform used to both raise awareness and engage young people around a series of development questions, HIV/AIDS being one of the most prominent. Femina HIP is now producing two of Tanzania's largest print magazines. In this case, we analyse a large amount of letters that young Tanzanians have written to Femina HIP. We assess the degrees of participation expressed in the letters. As such, we inscribe this article both into the growing debate about the role of civil society driven media platforms in enhancing participatory governance. We also explore a particular evaluation tool to assess youth participation, which is the tool of letter analysis.

Over the past years, civil society throughout Africa has acquired important experience in the fight against HIV and AIDS. A particular characteristic of this longstanding struggle has been the development of media and communication technologies used actively for pro-social development. Big, sustainable and very visible media platforms have been developed, in some countries by NGOs, apparently giving these organizations political clout, visibility in the population and a gradually stronger role as change agents that can mobilize youth, advocate their causes and influence decision-makers and opinion leaders. Such civil-society-driven platforms have become central to the work of enhancing participatory governance.

In Tanzania, East Africa, the NGO Femina HIP (Health Information Project), established in 1999 as a media-focused NGO dealing with sexual and reproductive health and rights, has been engaged particularly with the problem of HIV and AIDS. The prevalence of HIV in Tanzania at the time was alarming, and it continues to be. Currently, the prevalence of HIV is estimated at 5.7% among 15- to 49-year-olds on the mainland, with the highest prevalence occurring among women in rural areas (THIS 2008). Young Tanzanians are among the most vulnerable, and HIV and AIDS thus represent a huge communication challenge in the country. In this context, Femina HIP is a relevant youth-oriented media-oriented NGO to explore.

Relevant questions raised by Femina HIP's work are:

- To what degree do platforms such as Femina HIP's media platforms *de facto* articulate participatory governance?

- To what degree do young people have a real opportunity and ability to engage in debate and dialogue in a mediated public sphere via such platforms?

- And to what degree does such participation influence policy formulation and implementation?

These core questions will be critically addressed in this chapter by assessing the possibilities and limitations for youth engagement in participatory governance via civil-society-driven media platforms.

NGOs, governance and potential youth agency

Over the past decade, African HIV/AIDS communication initiatives have evolved into strong NGO-driven media platforms, often constituting very visible parts of the public sphere. Thematically, they continue to play key roles in engaging public debate around health- and gender-related issues. They seem to have grown to such a magnitude and to hold such a strong position within the public sphere, that they are being approached by many others wishing to use them as carriers of local, national and global messages, and as vehicles for articulating public debate on a growing variety of development issues. Such issues include electoral education, environment and climate change, and sexual and reproductive health and rights.

Consequently, these civil-society-driven media platforms have developed into key actors in promoting public debate. Their ability to set agendas in the mediated public sphere and thereby to hold government accountable has undoubtedly grown. In the era of democracy and free and independent media, at least some of them are becoming increasingly powerful players, seemingly influential in two ways: upwards, by influencing policy development, policy dialogues and mediated conversation with opinion leaders, and downwards, by sharing knowledge and information, facilitating social networking, changing social norms and values, enhancing social mobilization, and providing space for citizens to voice their concerns and thus participate in the development process.

The core question in this chapter is to critically assess this second dimension – the link between NGOs and their constituency – their audience – particularly their relation with youth. Our case is the Tanzanian NGO Femina HIP. In the past decade, Femina HIP has grown to become one of the largest NGOs with regard to reaching young people and mediated visibility.

Femina HIP uses entertainment-education as its primary communication strategy to engage youth in specific Tanzanian development challenges, such as youth unemployment, HIV/AIDS, climate change and gender inequality. Today it is a multi-media initiative with the overall objective to build supportive environments in Tanzania, where two aims are pursued:

- Young people in their communities enjoy their right to access information and services and are empowered to make positive informed choices around sexuality and lead healthy lifestyles in order to reduce the negative impact of HIV/AIDS, and
- Communities exercise their right to express themselves, participate in public debate and engage in civil society. (Femina HIP Logical Framework, 2007)

Femina HIP's main media vehicle consists of two large print magazines. *Fema* (name changed from *Femina* in 2006) is the original Femina HIP product and flagship activity. It is a 64-page, full-colour magazine in English and Kiswahili distributed quarterly in 140,000 copies. The main target group is youth in secondary schools all over Tanzania. *Si Mchezo!* is a 32-page, bi-monthly, full-colour magazine in

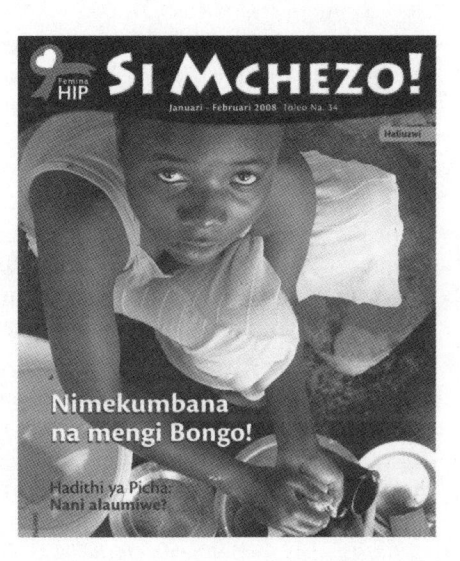

Source: Femina HIP

Kiswahili that started in 2003. Its target audience is rural, out-of-school, semi-literate youth aged 15-30 and their communities. It is published in 170,000 copies.

At the core of our inquiry lies this question: To what degree does the work of this particular civil-society-driven media platform *de facto* engage youth people in a development process, be it local, regional or national? There are two social processes of particular interest to us here: first, the process of young people accessing these civil-society-driven media platforms, and second, the societal outcomes and impact that access to and participation in these media platforms may have. This article will focus on the first aspect of exploring what this media access is doing to youth: Why and how do they become engaged with these media? What processes of empowerment and what feelings of ownership, leadership and commitment may emerge in young people with limited or no tradition of public representation and participation when they can suddenly write to a print magazine and see themselves in it?

The Tanzanian context

The opportunities for youth to engage in a development process are obviously inscribed into political, socio-economic and cultural contexts. The moment Tanzania is living today seems to mark a turning point in terms of these opportunities. However, they must be contextualized.

Tanzania is a huge country (945,000 km^2), with a population of 39 million, of which 80% live in rural areas. It is a country with a very young population (44% are under the age of 15). Thirty-one percent of the adult population is illiterate. It is one of the poorest countries in the world, ranked 159 on UNDP's Human Development Index (UNDP 2007).

Politically, Tanzania accepted a multi-party system in the early 1990s. After independence in 1961, Tanzania officially became a single-party state in 1965. This lasted for 30 years, with the first multiparty elections held in 1995. After severe economic crises in the 1970s and 1980s, in 1986 the state called on churches and NGOs to become involved in providing health and education services. This marked the beginning of an attempted state-controlled opening of public space to the civil society, resulting in a substantial increase in NGO and church activity within health and education. The number of registered organizations grew from 17 in 1978 to 813 in 1994. Today there are more than 8,000 NGOs registered, of which around 450 are estimated to be active (May and Magongo/CIS study 2005, in Corrigan 2006).

Despite the African and more specifically the Tanzanian move towards economic liberalization and electoral democracy in the 1990s, the government of Tanzania did not show any deep commitment to the process of democratization, maintaining a tight grip over the political sphere (Tripp 2000). Thus, the development of Tanzanian civil society in the 1990s took place within a very restrictive environment 'steeped in political culture and the legacy of the one-party state' (ibid). By

1995, although multi-party elections were introduced, the sphere of political debate remained limited. Effective political participation was hampered by 'a background of disengagement and disenchantment among the largely rural population' (Evans & Ngalwea 2003, in Corrigan 2006). Femina HIP emerged in this period.

Over the past decade, significant changes have been seen in Tanzania with regard to the nature and breadth of the public debate and the role of civil society and public participation herein. The relationship between government, civil society organizations and ordinary citizens' public participation seems to have become more dynamic and interactive. The nature of the policy dialogue and the public debate on policy development and on holding the government accountable seems to have reached an increased level of maturity over the past decade. Nevertheless, youth remain a very vulnerable group, whose predisposition to get involved is embedded in a history and legacy of limited participation in public debate, limited critique of government, and limited spaces to engage in debate and dialogue. It is in this context that Femina HIP emerges as an interesting mediated space.

Media development

Like the general international trend, Tanzanian society is becoming increasingly mediatized. The result is that politics, entertainment, news, fashion, civic education – and the general debate on manifold development challenges, ranging from the fight against HIV/AIDS to unemployment and climate change – are being mediated through the media. In this context, ordinary citizens both consume the media as well as engage actively in it by contributing opinions, voting, producing life stories and testimonials, etc.

Until the mid-1990s, Tanzania's media scene was small and largely state controlled. Following the democratic opening in the early 1990s and the multi-party election in 1995, the situation began to change, with a proliferation of radio and print. Although the growth of the broadcast media has been hindered by a lack of capital investment, dozens of private FM radio stations are on the air – most of them in urban areas.

Television was a latecomer: President Nyerere opposed it as a luxury that would widen the gap between rich and poor. State-run TV was not launched until 2001, several years after the first private station went on the air in 1994. Today, TV viewing is beginning to erode radio's traditional dominance, primarily in the urban areas.

As for information and communication technologies, the Internet has begun to take off – having grown in penetration from 40,000 Internet users in 2000 to 333,000 five years later (BBC WS Trust 2006: 44). Mobile phones have also exploded as an everyday commodity for a growing number of Tanzanians. In a country of 39 million, there are today 6.7 million mobile phones (CIA World Factbook).

NGO-Driven media platforms targeting youth

Within the context of the above-outlined development process, Femina HIP has become involved in emerging media opportunities, moving beyond its two key media vehicles, the print magazines Fema and SiMchezo. Today, Femina HIP pursues its objectives via the production, dissemination and active use of eight different types of communication activities, together creating a multimedia platform. The overall aim is to stimulate open talk, critical thinking and social change, and more specifically to 'foster healthy lifestyles and positive, responsible attitudes toward sexuality, HIV/AIDS and democratic culture' (Femina HIP 2007b). At the core of this multi-media health communication initiative are the two magazines, but the multimedia platform also includes a TV talk show, the co-production of a radio soap opera, an interactive website, and a network of Femina Clubs. Approximately 500 Clubs at secondary schools receive the print magazines, *Fema* in particular, and organize reading and the didactic use of these magazines at schools and in their neighbourhoods.

At the heart of all the activities is the "edutainment methodology" (often called entertainment-education, EE), which indicates an aim to entertain, and at the same time to educate audiences about certain essential topics. Edutainment can be defined as 'the use of entertainment as a communicative practice crafted to strategically communicate about development issues in a manner and with a purpose that can range from the more narrowly defined social marketing of individual behaviours to the liberating and citizen-driven articulation of social change agendas' (Tufte 2005b: 162).

A central aspect of Femina HIP's approach to the edutainment methodology is the "interactive participatory production process" (Fuglesang 2005: 5). One significant way in which the audience can participate is through writing letters, e-mails or sending text messages to Femina HIP, in the hope of being published in one of the magazines, being invited to participate in the talk show or getting a reply from the team. The ever-increasing amount of correspondence from readers that reaches Femina HIP is seen as a valuable source for scrutinizing whether the project actually lives up to its objectives, as well as a source for studying "audience involvement"[1] and project impact. Femina HIP has been part of the Tanzanian media landscape since 1999, and the audience letters dating back from that time offer an opportunity to analyse whether and in what way the audience discourse on issues relevant to Femina HIP – issues such as relationships, sexuality and HIV/AIDS – has changed over time.

How to assess audience involvement

Much of the early research on Entertainment-Education, conducted in the 1990s and even up into the new millennium, has focused on assessing *whether* a strategy had effects. Studies analysed the changes in audience members' knowledge, attitudes and behaviours, but did not look into *how* these changes took place. More recently, researchers interested in EE have begun to explore the process through which EE interventions have their 'effect', and in what ways audiences get involved in the programmes. "Audience involvement is the degree to which audience members engage in reflection upon, and parasocial interaction with, certain media programs, thus resulting in overt behavior change," writes Suruchi Sood (2002, p. 153). Although the focus is still primarily on emotional and psychological involvement, and not oriented towards social action, Sood's operationalization of audience involvement nevertheless represents an important opening towards the broad field of reception studies that grew out of British Cultural Studies in the 1980s.

Today, however, most EE research is still rooted in communication studies (including marketing and PR) and especially in exploring behaviour effects, drawing on social psychological theories. The epistemological aim of a growing corpus of more recent communication for development scholarship not only concerns individual behavioural change, but also speaks to human rights, citizenship and social justice agendas, thus digging deeper into the relation between communication and empowerment, communication and collective action, communication and the articulation of critical thinking, etc. The communication objective lies beyond individual behaviour change and rather in achieving changes of a structural and political nature in society. 'Communication for social change' thus poses new challenges to the history, trajectory and body of knowledge upon which most EE research rests, pushing the focus beyond 'effects' research and into a more political arena. Communication for social change is, ultimately, political communication.

Suruchi Sood (2002 p. 157) provides clear definitions of the most commonly analysed forms of audience involvement in her article "Audience Involvement and Entertainment-Education".

1. *Reflection* is "the degree to which audience members consider a media message and integrate it in their own life". Sood divides this into (a) *referential reflection*, "the degree to which audience individuals relate a media program to their personal experiences" by e.g. discussing it with others in terms of their own problems, and (b) *critical reflection*, "the degree to which audience members distance themselves from, and engage in, aesthetic construction of a media program" by e.g. reconstructing the programme or suggesting changes in it.

2. *Parasocial interaction* is divided into (a) *affectively oriented interaction*: "the degree to which audience members identify with characters or with other salient characteristics of a media program (for example, a place or community)," (b) *cognitively oriented interaction*: "the degree to which audience members pay careful attention to a media program/episode and think about its educational content once it is over," and (c) *behaviourally oriented interaction*: "the degree to which individuals talk to, or about,

media characters and rearrange their schedules to make time for exposure to a media program"

In addition to these levels of involvement, Sood also discusses three specific forms of *intermediate effects* that are often analysed in EE research. These are (1) an increase in *self-efficacy*, (2) an increase in *collective efficacy*, and (3) increased *interpersonal communication* among audience individuals:

1. *Self-efficacy* is a term used by social psychologist Albert Bandura and is defined as "people's beliefs about their capabilities to exercise control over events that affect their lives" (Sood 2002 p. 159). This concept draws attention to the importance of a person's cognitive reflections when evaluating a media message (Papa et al. 2000 p. 34), and according to Bandura, it should be studied in as situation-specific a manner as possible (Sood 2002 p. 159).

2. *Collective efficacy* is a relevant concept in many countries where EE interventions are implemented, as these cultures are often collective rather than individual. It is a system-level aspect of Bandura's social cognitive theory, and in his words it is defined as "people's beliefs in their joint capabilities to forge divergent self-interests into a shared agenda, to enlist supporters and resources for collective action, to devise effective strategies and to execute them successfully, and to withstand forcible opposition and discouraging setbacks." (Bandura 1995 in Sood 2002 p. 159).

3. Promoting *interpersonal communication* is believed to be an essential step for social change, and research on EE programmes has shown that EE implementations often lead to discussions about the programmes and their educational themes among peers and in their communities.

As is often done in EE effects research, Sood conducts a quantitative analysis of audience involvement in the radio soap opera *Tinka Tinka Sukh* in India, using these terms as pre-given categories. She suggests in the end that "sense-making and reception analysis techniques" could be utilized to take this analysis a step further. Interestingly enough for our study, she mentions that "[f]or example, qualitative textual analysis of letters by audience members can help in understanding audience involvement through the words of the audience themselves" (Sood 2002 p168). One problem with this quantitative approach, which we have brought forward elsewhere[2] (and which Sood acknowledges), is its total lack of cultural contextualization. Furthermore, her suggestion of using 'reception analysis techniques' does not change the epistemological aim of the study, but rather introduces new techniques to better understand how the communication intervention impacts on individual behaviour.

Despite the limitations identified in Sood's methodological proposal, it constitutes a useful first step in exploring audience involvement and 'intermediate effects'. For that purpose, the above conceptualization of audience involvement is relevant.

In addition to this, we find methodological inspiration in the article "Efficacy in Letter-Writing to an Entertainment-Education Radio Serial" by Sweety Law and Arvind Singhal (1999). The authors used a qualitative analysis of letters to *Tinka Tinka Sukh* in order to *inductively* discover what kinds and levels of audience involvement are taking place, instead of *deductively* searching for already defined types, and they found four types of efficacy effects – cognitive, affective, motivational and behavioural – and three aspects of efficacy – strength, magnitude and generality.

Measuring Societal Impact

Complementing the work to assess 'intermediate effects', which Sood's outline has helped us delineate, growing academic attention is being paid to developing monitoring and evaluation instruments that can assess the outcomes of communication for social change. An early piece by Figueroa et al. (2002) identified seven key indicators of social change. Within the logic of effects studies, the study developed a methodology to quantify the changes occurring, thus seeking to 'weigh' the change numerically. This is a difficult task, as the indicators are intended to capture social change processes. However, despite the limitations, we have also used these indicators in the present study. The seven social change indicators are: leadership, degree of equity of participation, information equity, collective self-efficacy, sense of ownership, social cohesion and social norms. These indicators have been incorporated into a coding scheme in which 11 indicators were thematized. The indicators of audience involvement and participation have thus been develop to capture both processes of individual reflection and interpersonal dialogue and processes contributing to societal change.

Research design

The overarching purpose of the present study is to critically assess Femina HIP's role in using EE to provide space and opportunity for Tanzanian youth to engage in public debate and action. This is done through an analysis of particular categories of reader letters to *Fema* and *Si Mchezo!* magazines. The specific questions guiding the analysis are:

- What are the most important *themes/topics discussed* by young letter writers to *Fema* and *Si Mchezo!* magazines over the years (1999-2007), and *what youth are writing?*

- What kinds of *audience involvement and citizen participation* are expressed in the letters of these youth?

- What does the analysis of the letters say about Femina HIP's ability to meet its *overall development objectives vis-à-vis youth in Tanzania?*

Femina HIP receives hundreds of letters and emails each month, which are filed into more than a dozen categories depending on their destination, purpose and content. The categories and filing system have evolved over time as the organization has grown and expanded in scope.

This study focuses on three categories of letters to each of the two magazines, Fema and Si Mchezo!: *Advice*; *Voices;* and *Letters from readers*. Each of these categories corresponds to an editorial section in the magazines where letters are printed and answered[3]. Though they vary in content and format, these letters have certain commonalities: they are all spontaneous in terms of content (although the editors encourage readers to write in) and it is logical to assume that the writer is hoping to see his/her letter published in the magazine. Of course, not all letters can be published, and in the present study we did not discriminate on the basis of whether a letter was published or not. However, Femina HIP does attempt to respond directly to non-published letters, to ensure that a dialogue is maintained. These categories of letters were also chosen because they were deemed to be some of the richest in terms of audience engagement, as they are generally written to seek or give advice, express opinions or share experiences.

The folders containing letters falling under the selected categories since the inception of Femina HIP in 1999 up until the end of 2007 were targeted here. However, we noted in the process that the file names and filing system have not been consistent over the years and that some letters were probably missing, especially from the early days of the project. The total number of letters that emerged in these categories was approximately 2,040[4].

To keep the study , it was considered necessary to use a limited number of categories. This may also have added some limitations, as other valuable letter categories were excluded in the process. One pertinent example is letters written from Fema Club members. Sometimes in the form of reports, other times in the form of letters discussing their latest activities, they regularly include photographs. In the future, it may be useful to compare these letters to the categories analysed here, especially in relation to the types of audience involvement demonstrated.

Results – quantitative analysis

The quantitative analysis highlighted the following points of interest:

- The majority of writers are male, and most of the photos were sent by males. This is evidence of greater male agency as well as perhaps a higher desire to participate or be seen in the public sphere. However, the fact that female writers show higher audience involvement is very significant.

- The average age of writers correlates closely to Femina HIP's core target group

- A large proportion of writers are students – the core target audience for Fema magazine
- In terms of geography, letters come from all over the country, not only the main cities
- The total number of letters is increasing over time as the magazines expand their reach
- Every third letter written to Fema was in English – this is undoubtedly linked to the high number of letters from students in secondary level who are schooled in English.
- Many letter writers used a formal language, which could also stem from the use of English or the fact that students are putting their formal letter-writing training into use.
- The themes and topics presented in the letters are highly relevant to Femina HIP's core strategic priorities. HIV/AIDS is the most common theme. Gender is, however, very uncommon.
- Almost 50% of the letters are advisory in nature, while a further 38% express opinions, demonstrating that readers are using the magazine to advise their peers on issues of importance and to share their views.

Results – qualitative analysis

One of the most striking elements of these letters from readers involved with Femina HIP is the confirmation that humans are basically social animals that, once inspired and engaged, strive to share, gather and organize themselves in groups – in this case Fema Clubs. The benefits of being in a group are many. Creating meaning, interpreting, learning and taking action is much easier. It is an empowering process for people to be part of a collective.

One category of letters expresses 'referential reflection' and 'parasocial relations', an engagement often starting at the individual level, showing that people are enthusiastically reading and getting involved in the material. Femina HIP's methodology of edutainment speaks to people, engages them and speaks to their emotions and experiences. It empowers and triggers the desire to share, discuss with others in the group, and makes their engagement a collective affair.

In Tanzania, readers are thankful. They are enthusiastic about getting Femina HIP products as they otherwise get nothing of the kind. It is *unique*, the first possibility for people to voice their views and express themselves, and it resonates very well with people's lives and with what they want. They want to be part of something and speak up; the potential is overwhelming. One of the reasons why so few voices are critical has to be discussed together with the overwhelming positive voices. This has to do with the polite Tanzanian mentality, especially

Reading SI MCHEZO together. *Source:* Femina HIP

when addressing the public sphere – there is virtually no political, music and art critique in Tanzania – people will not criticize you to your face. This again is a reflection of the former state-dominated, totalitarian society; the state was everything, and Nyerere the father and mind of the nation. Criticism has not been encouraged. Moreover, the free media are not well developed, particularly not for the rural areas. But things are changing and the large number of positive voices express a wish to participate, a wish to be heard, as well as the *seeds of a democratic voice and participation*. The fact that the critical voices are coming from Club members who are not in school and males should also be further explored in relation to the gender dimension, as should the focus and support of the Fema Clubs as a school phenomenon. Young people who are not in school are restless but very eager to be part of the Femina HIP initiative, and their participation in the Fema Clubs is more on their own initiative than on that of Femina HIP, which is interesting to note.

The analysis of category 2 and 3 letters is interesting, as it shows the general progression clearly. It takes some time before people get used to the style of communicating and internalize that way of communicating, but this is what happens after a while. A natural next step from there is to start sharing and talking to other people about the issues, and then wanting to get involved as peer educators, counsellors and in groups starting up Clubs. Those who are empowered to write letters also often assume the role as 'leader', getting clubs and other activities organized. Someone has to drive the process forward, and it is clear that leaders are often those who have come to feel strongly about the

Femina HIP mission and made it their own. Categories such as social efficacy, community dialogue and social connectedness are very similar, interdependent, and vital for social action.

The letters reveal that the *long-term, recurring nature of the Femina HIP media* is vital for creating a gradual process of engagement, resulting in groups and clubs that take on the agenda. It also underlines how important it is for Femina HIP to work with *community mobilization* and to help ensure that groups and clubs are set up, as these constitute a dynamic forum for learning, interpreting and taking action, not just as individuals but as a collective. Herein lies the challenge for communication for social change.

Overall conclusions
Summarizing the most important findings from the letter analysis

The core question driving this study has been: *How, and to what degree, are young people actually getting involved in civil-society-driven initiatives to curb some of Tanzania's most severe development challenges?* The simple finding that letters Femina HIP from young people are steadily increasing in number illustrates the growing eagerness among young Tanzanians to participate in the public sphere. That the letters originate from all the 21 regions of Tanzania plus Zanzibar, and to a large extent from small towns and villages, further shows that a media initiative like this is no longer a purely urban phenomenon (something development communication initiatives such as Femina HIP are often criticized for).

The results of this study indicate that Femina HIP has succeeded in its attempts to reach out to youth all over the country. A large proportion of the writers are between 15 and 24 years of age, and almost half of letter writers who indicate an occupation are students. These findings contribute to our positive assessment of the initiative's ability to reach out to its central target groups, and to manage to get them involved. However, a noteworthy and rather alarming result is that only one third of the letters in which gender is indicated are written by females. Thus, although gender issues have always been at the top of Femina HIP's educational agenda, and even though attempts have been made to involve and engage boys and girls equally, it is mainly male readers who taking advantage of the opportunity.

In relation to research question (1) – *What are the most important themes/ topics discussed by young letter writers to Fema (earlier Femina) and Si Mchezo magazines over the years (1999-2007), and what youth are writing?* – it is of great significance that the themes and topics reflected in the letters analysed here correspond very well with the educational themes of Femina HIP. This shows that the organization is managing to involve and engage its audience through its products. More than a quarter of the letters deal with 'HIV/AIDS', the most important educational theme of the magazines *Fema* and *Si Mchezo!*. 'Sex and sexuality', 'healthy lifestyles' and 'career/education' are other frequently discussed topics in the letters, and these topics are also within the focal area of the magazines. Themes such as 'youth involvement in society', 'livelihoods', 'democracy and accountability' and 'environment' are not as widely discussed – yet. This might be a sign that these topics still have not been picked up by the audience. As mentioned earlier, they have been included in the Femina HIP agenda quite recently, and the discourse around them is not as elaborated in the Tanzanian context at this point. Nevertheless, especially issues concerning livelihood and young people's involvement in society are of great importance as well as interest to youth in Tanzania, as shown in recent research (see, e.g., Helgesson 2006). But the findings may also indicate that young people in Tanzania have no other forum in which they can discuss HIV/AIDS, sex matters, and questions about healthy lifestyles openly. Maybe this is the area in which Femina HIP, after all, serves its most important purpose.

The letters are for the most part advisory and express opinions, which implies that the level of engagement is high. In order to answer research question (2) – *What kinds of audience involvement and citizen participation are expressed in the letters?* – all of the 638 sampled letters were coded for 11 types of "audience involvement and participation". The quantitative analysis shows that audience involvement is strong, especially when it comes to referential reflection, self-efficacy and collective efficacy. On the other hand, critical thinking and indications of involvement that can be characterized as "citizen participation" are not detected as frequently. This finding could be related to where Tanzania is in terms of its civil society development and its people's (lack of) participation in (participatory) governance. As briefly discussed in the introduction, the development of Tanzanian civil society has taken place within a very restrictive environment, coloured by a long history of a one-party system, whose culture still casts its shadows over the public sphere (see, e.g., Corrigan 2006). But, if we dig deeper into the letters in the qualitative analysis, it becomes evident that, however few they might be, those letter writers who do fall into the category of citizen participation in the public sphere do so with strong and engaged voices. They often refer to how they are committed to engaging their peers, classmates, students, club friends or the community in general in issues they feel urgently need to be discussed. These are important seeds of participation in an expanding civil society.

There is not only a lack of critical thinking, but also a lack of criticism of Femina HIP products. Only a few of the young writers express complaints about the magazines, whereas many praise Femina HIP (even when their main reason for writing may be another). As pointed out earlier, this may be related to the scarcity of such products on the still emerging Tanzanian media market. When delivered to secondary schools or youth centres around the country, *Fema* or *Si Mchezo!* represent extraordinarily "modern" and up-to-date products both in terms of quality and content, as compared to the ordinary school books or media material young people have access to. Furthermore, the lack of a critical voice also says something about young Tanzanians' relation to the public sphere, which results from the traditionally strict political culture. Such a political culture has also cast its shadows over the media market, where free, open and critical media are still rather undeveloped (see, e.g., Kilimwiko 2002; Hydén et al. 2002; Ekström 2009). Participatory media are not very widespread, particularly not in rural areas. But as other recent studies have shown, and as this analysis shows, things are changing, and the large number of voices that wish to be heard are, as we mentioned before, important seeds of a democratic voice and participation.

As regards research question (3) – *What does the analysis of the letters say about Femina HIP's ability to meet their overall development objectives vis-à-vis youth in Tanzania?* – many of the young Tanzanians quoted in the qualitative analysis section state that they do "enjoy their right to access information and services and are empowered to make positive informed choices around sexuality and lead healthy lifestyles in order to reduce the negative impact of HIV/AIDS." Many of the letters further show that the readers of *FEMA* and *Si Mchezo!* are inspired to take social action, individual as well as collective. Some letters are from writers interested in starting a FEMA club and others are written by a whole group, which in turn indicates that "[c]ommunities exercise their right to express themselves, participate in public debate & engage in civil society". This would probably become even clearer, however, if the club letters were included in an analysis as well.

A particular emphasis on gender

As it turned out, women were less visible in the present study: they tend to write fewer letters, and are much less likely to send photos with their letters. The number of letters from males reflects the societal trend towards greater male involvement. This may pose a challenge to Femina HIP's distribution systems (i.e., do they need to specifically target women?). Alternatively, it may not imply higher male readership, but rather that males have greater agency / wherewithal as regards sending a letter. The latter is most probably the case, and it correlates well with the "traditional" gender roles that largely still prevail in Tanzanian society, where, for instance, girls and women do not have the same access to public spaces as do men (see, e.g., Ntukula & Liljeström 2004; Rwebangira & Liljeström eds. 1998; Tumbo-Masabo & Liljeström eds.1994). But this is an alarming result, particularly when considered in relation to trends in the HIV pandemic, where young women are the most vulnerable group in contemporary Tanzania (THIS 2008). And it is perhaps a rather surprising result in a country where the women's movement has grown quite strong at least among educated women (Mbilinyi et al. 2003; Chachage & Mbilinyi 2003).

At the same time, it is important to note, as shown in both the quantitative and qualitative analysis, that more women than men show signs of audience involvement. However, they mainly tend to perform more emotional and psychologically reflective forms of involvement, such as 'referential reflection' and 'affective parasocial interaction'. When it comes to forms of involvement/participation more oriented towards the public sphere, such as 'interpersonal communication', 'social connectedness' and 'participation in the public sphere', the male writers are predominant, though only marginally. So, the "traditionally" gendered binary order still remains: female equals private and emotional issues, male equals public and intellectual issues.

Youth communicating for social change

The overarching purpose of the present study was to contribute to an assessment of Femina HIP's role in promoting social change among Tanzanian youth. The existence of a large and ever-increasing number of young letter writers who wish to make their voices heard is an indication of youth engagement. Femina HIP is contributing to the social change that is taking place in a country where the central topics on the agenda have been (and still are) surrounded by a culture of silence (see, e.g., Ntukula & Liljeström eds. 2004). The fact that not only young people but also teachers are writing to describe how they use Femina HIP products in their teaching job is a significant change, again indicating engagement in change processes, as we can see in the following quote:

> I am a teacher at Maranje primary school and a good reader of Femina since I was in secondary school. The magazines have helped me to change a lot and very time I read them I get stronger. They also help me to prepare my lectures by using some of the things written in the magazine such as lifeskills and counselling. (302)

This writer, like others in this study, shows signs of strong commitment to Femina HIP and its educational themes, and of wishing to spread the word in the society – a wish to contribute to social change. This quote, like other examples in the qualitative analysis, indicates that one letter often shows signs of a multitude of involvement and participation indicators. Audience involvement over time, however, is consistent with trends in the total number of letters received over time. An interesting question is why we are not seeing more fluctuation in terms of particular types of involvement over the years. The answer may be that Femina HIP still plays its greatest role in Tanzanian society in relation to the more psychological forms of audience involvement – leading more towards individual behavioural change. But if we dig deeper into the voices expressed in the letters in the qualitative analysis, we see clear signs of strong eagerness to participate in the public sphere, and a willingness to contribute to and a belief in collective social change.

One of the present study's important contributions has been to further develop existing methodology and methods for analysing audience involvement. Its aim has been to facilitate a methodological shift that corresponds to the theoretical move from BCC to CFSC within research and within the Femina HIP organization itself, and it has done so by combining indicators of audience involvement and participation that capture both processes of individual reflection and interpersonal dialogue, as well as processes that promote societal change.

By combining quantitative and qualitative methods of analysis, the present study has managed to get under the surface of the figures and numbers of the otherwise most commonly used quantitative analysis. By extensively quoting the words of people who write letters to Femina HIP, the study has given a voice to the growing group of young Tanzanians who are truly engaged in some of Tanzania's most critical development challenges. This is a group of young people who express their eagerness to speak out about the challenges in the public sphere, and their interest in and willingness to contribute to social change.

Notes

1. A term often used in measuring effectiveness of EE interventions. See e.g. Sood, Suruchi (2002) "Audience Involvement and Entertainment-Education" in *Communication Theory*, Vol. 12, issue 2 (page 153-172).
2. See, e.g., Tufte, Thomas (2003)
3. The editorial sections are as follows: Fema Dear Aunty / Uncle (advice); Fema Your voice (Sauti yangu); Fema letters from Readers (barua); Si Mchezo! Advice (Ushauri); Si Mchezo! My Voice (Sauti Yako); Si Mchezo! Letters from readers (barua).
4. About 100 emails were also found, but these were excluded as Femina HIP staff with responsibility for letters stated that they had only recently begun filing email correspondences.

References

Bandura, Albert (1995) 'Exercise of Personal and Collective Efficacy', in Bandura (ed.) *Self-Efficacy in Changing Societies*. New York: Cambridge University Press. Quoted in Sood, Suruchi (2002) 'Audience Involvement and Entertainment-Education', in *Communication Theory*, 12(2): 153-172).

Chachage & Mbilinyi (2003) *Against Neo-Liberalism. Gender, Democracy & Development*. TGNP / E&D Limited, Dar es Salaam.

Corrigan, Aran (2006) 'Are the Poverty Reduction Strategies Changing the Nature of State Civil Society Relations in Tanzania', Dublin City University. (MA Diss.)

Evans, Alison with Erasto Ngalwea (2003) 'Tanzania', in Booth, David (ed.) *Fighting Poverty in Africa. Are PRSPs Making a Difference?* London: Overseas Development Institute, pp 247-273.

Dallmer, Julia (2006) *Femina HIP Letter Analysis*. November 2005-January 2006.

Ekström, Ylva (forthcoming 2009) *We are like Chameleons. Popular Culture, Mediated Dreams and Navigation Between Different Modes of Femininity in Early 21st Century Dar es Salaam*. Uppsala: Uppsala University (Diss).

Femina HIP (undated) Unidentified statistics on letters 1999-2002.

Femina HIP (2006) *5-year Strategic Plan Document, 2006-2010 HIP Multimedia Initiative in Tanzania*.

Femina HIP (2007a) Logical Framework.

Femina HIP (2007b) Annual Report.

Figueroa, M.E., Kincaid, L., Rani, M., Lewis, G. (2002) 'Guidelines for the Measurement of Process and Outcome of Social Change Interventions', Baltimore, MD: CCP/JHU. Prepared for the Rockefeller Foundation.

Fuglesang, Minou (2005) 'SiMchezo! Magazine. Community Media Making a Difference', in Oscar Hemer & Thomas Tufte (2005) *Media and Glocal Change*. Gothenburg and Buenos Aires: Clacso and Nordicom.

Hydén, Göran et.al (2002) *Media and Democracy in Africa*. Uppsala: The Nordic Africa Institute.

Kilimwiko, Lawrence (2002) *The Fourth Estate in Tanzania*. Dar es Salaam: Colour Print.

Law, Sweety & Arvind Singhal (1999) 'Efficacy in Letter-Writing to an Entertainment-Education Radio Serial', *Gazette*, 61(5) Sage Publications, pp. 355-372.

May, Ann & Joanita Magongo (2005) 'NGOs in Development and Poverty Reduction, and Their Relationships with Donors and the State in Tanzania. Views from Civil Society'. Draft final report to the Centre for International Studies, Dublin City University. Tanzania: Research on Poverty Alleviation (REPOA).

Mbilinyi et al. (2003) *Activist Voices: Feminist Struggles for an Alternative World*. Dar es Salaam: TGNP / E&D Limited.

Ntukula & Liljeström (eds) (2004) *Umleavyo – The Dilemma of Parenting*. Uppsala: The Nordic Africa Institute.

Papa, Singhal, Law, Pant, Sood, Rogers, Shefner-Rogers (2000) 'Entertainment-Education and Social Change: An Analysis of Parasocial Interaction, Social Learning, Collective Efficacy, and Paradoxical Communication', *Journal of Communication*, 50(4): 31-55.

Rwebangira & Liljeström (eds. 1998) *Haraka, Haraka. Look before you leap: Youth at the Crossroad of Custom and Modernity*. Uppsala: The Nordic Africa Institute.

Sood, Suruchi (2002) 'Audience Involvement and Entertainment-Education', *Communication Theory*, 12(2): 153-172.

THIS (2008) Tanzania Health Indicator Survey.

Tripp, Aili Mari (2000) 'Political Reform in Tanzania: The Struggle for Associational Autonomy', *Comparative Politics* 32(2): 191-214.

Tufte, Thomas (2003) 'Soap Operas and Sense-Making: Mediations and Audience Ethnography', in Arvind Singhal, Michael Cody, Everett Rogers & Miguel Sabido (eds) *Entertainment-Education and Social Change. History, Research and Practice*. New Jersey: Lawrence Erlbaum Associates.

Tufte, Thomas (2005b) 'Entertainment-Education in Development Communication – Between Marketing Behaviours and Empowering People', in Oscar Hemer & Thomas Tufte (2005) *Media and Glocal Change. Rethinking Communication for Development*. Gothenburg: Nordicom

Tumbo-Masabo & Liljeström (eds) (1994) *Chelewa, Chelewa. The Dilemma of Teenage Girls*. Uppsala: The Nordic Africa Institute.

UNDP Human Development Report 2007. New York: UNDP.

"There Is No Permission to Love in Our Urfa"
Media, Youth Identities and Social Change in Southeast Turkey

Ece Algan

Abstract

Today media are central to young people's experience of modernity and identities everywhere in the world – not only those who are educated and live in the centers, but also those with little or no education who live in rural areas, ghettos, and the periphery. My research in Southeast Turkey illustrates how integral media are to the everyday lives of young people in Şanlıurfa. This research, however, does not necessarily suggest that the introduction of a new medium or programming content is drastically transforming their lives. Rather, as I show in this article, the media activities of the youth in Şanlıurfa are linked to much wider social change in Turkey, which we must understand in order to see the role media play in their lives, and their perceptions and experience of change. On the one hand, national, transnational and global media increase intergenerational tensions by pointing out the disparities that exist between the young people's realities in Southeast Turkey and those of other young people of the same generation living in the west of the country. On the other hand, local media and new communication technologies give them an opportunity to articulate youth identities shaped by and negotiated through both globally-induced socio-economic changes, as well as centuries-old patriarchal and tribal structures.

"We are not even allowed to love here. Please write what we are going through. Make our voices heard because we can't make them hear", cried Mehmet U, a 16 year-old Turkish boy in love with a girl whose father is marrying her off to her cousin. All the other young men who, along with Mehmut U and I, had gathered at a small neighborhood patisserie in one of the ghettos of Southeastern Turkish city of Şanlıurfa[1], nodded in agreement. Despite being devoted to ethnographic work, I have always been skeptical about ethnographers claiming to make people's voices heard, and I even questioned our ability to do so. I would have never thought I would be asked by my informants to do just that. However, as I engaged in researching local media consumption and production in Southeast Turkey, I was struck by how young people were using local radio and phones in order to bypass traditional and religious pressures that prevented them from dating and experiencing their gender identities and sexualities. What's more, they were able to hear each other's voices, share stories of resistance, and critique societal norms through their participation via call-in local radio stations. This article, based on the media ethnography I conducted among local media professionals and frequent media participants and users in Şanlıurfa, examines how young people utilize media in their everyday lives in order to make sense of the larger socio-cultural changes that are taking place in their city, in Turkey, and in the world. Today media are central to young people's experience of modernity and identities everywhere in the world – not only those who are educated and live in the centers, but also those with little or no education who live in rural areas, ghettos, and the periphery. My research in Southeast Turkey illustrates how integral media are to the everyday lives of young people in Şanlıurfa. This research, however, does not necessarily suggest that the introduction of a new medium or programming content is drastically transforming their lives. Rather, as I show in this article, the media activities of the youth in Şanlıurfa are linked to much wider social change in Turkey, which we must understand in order to see the role media play in their lives, and their perceptions and experience of change.

Rethinking the uneasy relationship between media and social change

As Debra Spitulnik (1993) insightfully observed, "Probably the most general – and most difficult – question about the place of mass media in modern societies is their implications for fundamental and irreversible social and cultural change" (p. 307). From the early media effects tradition to later models that acknowledge media's indirect effects, mass communication scholars have been eager to find causal relationship between media and how we are influenced by it. Even though Daniel Lerner's (1958) classic *Passing of Traditional Society*, which illustrated that modern media can modernize traditional societies, has been highly criticized, we can still find unproblematized, easy equations between media and social change in communication studies, especially in the communication for development field – for instance the assertion that the entertainment-education media will foster social change (Singhal 2007, p. 266).[2] However, rather than predicting long-term social change instigated via media as a result of short-term campaigns or programming, I agree with Stig Hjarvard's (2008) suggestion that "the task before us is instead to try to gain an understanding of the ways in which social institutions and cultural processes have changed character, function and structure in response to the omnipresence of media" (pp. 105-106).

Tackling the relationship between media and social change, therefore, requires us to take a broader approach. We need to consider media's role in shifting identity politics and media's ability to facilitate interactions among communities, nations, societies, and regions to map social and cultural dynamics in question. Such an approach should neither equate the term social change with development nor see media simply as agents through which the change occurs. As Tufte (2008) has argued, the drivers of today's change processes emerge as a result of global processes, such as transnational advocacy networks, which emphasize issues of citizenship and bottom-up globalization practices (p. 36). Moreover, Hemer & Tufte (2005) remind us that development is no longer a process reserved for 'developing countries,' and that Pieterse's (2001) critical globalist concept of "world development" indicates a paradigm shift in the field of 'communication for development and social change.' We must account for the power geometry in current development, change, and cultural globalization processes (Gumucio-Dagron and Tufte 2006).

Therefore, following Featherstone and Lash (1995) and other globalization scholars, in this article I use the term *social change* to mean not the development of societies but rather a sociocultural process that emerges "as the global begins to replace the nation-state as the decisive framework for social life" (p. 2). As Ekecrantz (2007) argues, "Globalization forces us not only to focus more on *transnational* phenomena in general, but also to highlight *social change and difference,* which are almost unprecedented in pace and scope and directly and indirectly caused by globalization processes" (p. 171). Scholars have increasingly taken a trans-societal perspective on social change, seeing it as taking place not through national institutions but as a result of global forces and global cultural flows, including media (Appadurai 1990; Friedman 1995; Pieterse 2001; Robertson 1995). Springing from this approach, we often see an emphasis on new media's role in aiding global processes of socioeconomic change, as in the examples of NGO activities and larger global social movements, being highlighted as great examples of the global bypassing national institutions.

Transnational media, such as satellite television and other forms of new media, indeed allow people to experience their identities in many more levels than it was possible before. As Straubhaar (2008) states, "these layers of identity are articulated with a variety of media, such as television and the Internet, but not in a simple sense of being primarily influenced by media" (p. 11). However, today older forms of media, such as local television and radio, can also weaken the stronghold of national institutions as the main framework through which we imagine our identities, because these media allow people more easily to articulate their identities in ways that are familiar, acceptable and accessible in their community. Therefore, conducting media ethnographies can help us understand how media facilitate what Tufte (2008) calls the *new patterns of identification* on multiple levels at the same time – such as the local, national, regional, and global.

Even though this research approaches social change from a trans-societal perspective with an emphasis on the role of global cultural forces, it aims neither to replicate "those global media studies, where globalization was used as a starting point, as a key theoretical concept, and a key conclusion" (Rantanen 2008, p. 34), nor to understate change, as Straubhaar (2008) believes some globalization hypotheses do. Instead, this study focuses on the local both in terms of people and their media experiences while underlining the importance of connecting media use in its geographic and historical specificity in order to understand the transformation of everyday realities and lives in that particular locale.

Conducting media ethnography in Şanlıurfa

As young people turn to media to make sense of larger socio-cultural change and negotiate their place in the world, they seek and create ways of expressing themselves, using media in unique ways that shed light on struggles, changing realities, and larger economic, political and social structures that shape everyday life and identities. An ethnographic approach, which allows us to situate media as an intricate part of these dynamics but not an ultimate determinant of them, can uncover the dialectical relationship between global, national and local forces at play (Algan 2009 and 2003a). As Spitulnik (1993) argues,

> Although anthropologists have just begun to look at the various political, social, cultural, and linguistic dimensions of mass media, they have in some way already bypassed many of the debates within media studies. Perhaps this is because they implicitly theorize media processes, products, and uses as complex parts of social reality, and expect to locate media power and value in more a diffuse, rather than direct and causal, sense. (p. 307)

Therefore, media ethnography emerges as the best methodological approach to deconstruct and make sense out of some of the complex relationship between social change and globalization. This study uses it to examine how youth in Şanlıurfa experience their agency and articulate their identities, which are increasingly influenced and reshaped by global cultural values and national media's glocalized interpretations of those lifestyles.

This essay draws from the media ethnography I conducted in the city of Şanlıurfa using a multi-sited research approach that moved "out from the single sites and local situations of conventional ethnographic research designs to examine the circulation of cultural meanings, objects, and identities in diffuse time-space" (Marcus 1995/1998: 79). I traveled to Şanlıurfa three times with the goal of understanding the role of local media in people's lives and the impact of global, national and local forces on their interpretation and use of media:

Young women are learning to make crafts in Yakubiye ÇATOM (Multi-purpose Community Center) *Photo:* Ece Algan

twice during 2001, spending a total of three months, and once in the summer of 2007, spending five weeks there. I conducted formal in-depth interviews with local media owners, managers and DJs; and both formal and informal in-depth interviews and participant observation with many young men and women whom I met at Harran University, internet cafes, shops and other public places. I also recorded several days of radio programming to observe audience interaction on local radio and conducted in-depth and focus group interviews with young women who attended the Multi Purpose Community Center (ÇATOM) in Yakubiye (one of Şanlıurfa's ghettos), which provides training programs for women and young girls in literacy, health and family planning, maternal and child health, nutrition, home economy and income-generating activities.[3]

Between rural and urban: Şanlıurfa

The city of Şanlıurfa, which is inhabited mostly by people of Kurdish and Arabic descent, is located 30 miles from the Syrian border in the least developed (according to the standard socio-economic signs of development) Southeastern Anatolian region of Turkey. The city, which has a population of around half a million, has undergone very rapid growth and urbanization just in the last two decades due to the Turkey's integration into the global economy and government development projects. Therefore, despite my initial expectations of finding a small, ancient city in the rural Southeast with little or no connection to the rest of the world, Şanlıurfa turned out to be a city with modern, concrete apartment buildings and schools, several nice parks that families enjoy on the weekends, many small businesses, a busy downtown with several state and municipal buildings, restaurants, internet cafes and both modern and traditional shopping areas. A couple of new neighborhoods reminded me of those in İstanbul. A local pharmacist pointed to a modern street in one of those neighborhoods with five-to-six-story apartment buildings and neon lights coming from shops on the lower levels. "If you had come ten years ago, you would have found empty fields in place of these neighborhoods and half the population we have right now", he told me. Even in the squatter home (gecekondu) neighborhoods such as Yakubiye and Eyübiye, shabby houses were transformed into more stable concrete buildings, were given title deeds as well as schools, water and electricity, and were integrated into the city. The modern white buildings of Harran University, built in 1992, reached out from the outskirts of Şanlıurfa's southern edge toward the vast yellow fields of Harran. New apartment buildings were being built, and so was the tallest building in the city, which is a hotel with approximately 500 beds. Since the arrest of Abdullah Öcalan, the leader of the separatist Kurdish Worker's Party (PKK), both domestic and foreign tourists had begun to visit the city again, although the increase was small compared to two decades ago when there was no armed conflict between the military and PKK militants.

In Şanlıurfa, development was apparent in many ways. For instance, during my stay I never witnessed a water service stoppage or serious power blackout (except an hour-and-a-half blackout when it snowed). The people I talked to admitted that less than a decade ago they had many infrastructural problems, such as a lack of reliable running water. The increase in local capital was obvious in the recent construction of many modern department stores, apartment buildings, shops and supermarkets, which were very popular, especially among women. Every man carried a cellular phone attached to his belt, and internet cafes were full of young men enjoying computers. In addition to the impact that the nationwide economic change caused in Şanlıurfa, the Southeast Anatolia Project (its Turkish acronym is 'GAP'), a state development project, also contributed to drastic changes, not only in Şanlıurfa's economy and urban infrastructure, but also in its socio-cultural characteristics. By bringing irrigation agriculture to the plains south of the city, the GAP project increased agricultural production and profit, initiated industrial development, and caused people to relocate due to increased opportunities and the construction of a series of dams. As a result, this ancient city received a large number of immigrants from the many rural villages and towns of the region and expanded to accommodate two brand new upscale neighborhoods – which housed expensive furniture, appliance and electronic stores, among other businesses – in addition to many new ghettos.

I was quite impressed by the city I saw and openly expressed my impressions to the people of Şanlıurfa whenever they asked my opinion of it. Soon I realized, however, that almost every young person I encountered did not share the same feelings, even though they were pleased to hear that I thought very highly of Şanlıurfa. One of the DJs I met, DJ Mahmut, who works for Güneydoğu Radyo ve Televizyon, echoed many others when he said that:

> Şanlıurfa seems developed to you, but it's only an appearance. The important thing is the change in the mindset [which is lacking here]. For instance, there are many girls I know but I can't hang out with them freely. However, they still think I have many girlfriends. I'd like to take my sister to a movie or café, but I cannot. They would think she is my lover. (DJ Mahmut, personal interview, February 16, 2001)

Despite the new and modern neighborhoods, public spaces such as parks, internet cafes and fast food restaurants, and better educational opportunities, young people felt they could not utilize Şanlıurfa's places freely. On the contrary, they felt trapped in the mindset of a city they did not see as the modern urban place outsiders like me saw. I kept hearing from them: "We have no social life here;" "We can't be free like you are in the west [of Turkey];" "You don't know Şanlıurfa's traditions"; and "There is a tribal system here." The more time I spent in the city talking with them about their experiences, the more I saw life in Şanlıurfa through their eyes. I saw the role local radio and phones played in young people's struggle to have a "social life." The government policies on the ethnic conflict in the region, rural to urban immigration prompted by the conflict, and the GAP project and its introduction of irrigation agriculture in the province all have impacted the cityscape in many different ways, but these changes left the problems of the youth either unanswered or worsened. Moreover, a number of forces changed the city's small but progressive urban character, including the increasing power of the local government with its reactionary, conservative and religious agenda; disparity in wealth; the increasing power of landlords gained through irrigation agriculture; and martial law that was in effect on and off until 2000.

Today Şanlıurfa is inhabited mainly by two different social groups and an expanding youth population. On the one hand, there are the new immigrants who struggle to adapt to modern life in the city while maintaining their rural lifestyle and religious traditions. On the other, the city has a rooted, secular, urban population, which is relatively wealthy and educated. As a result, the young men and women of Şanlıurfa, especially those who are relatively new to the city and live on its fringes, strive to experience modern ways of living in this urban environment and to interact freely with each other – despite the restrictions of traditions deeply rooted in the tribal and feudal social structure of the region, which have existed for centuries.[4] As Bülent Okur, a journalist who ran the Doğan News Agency in Şanlıurfa during my research there, explained the social and cultural change that took place before and after the 1980s:

> It was a wealthy urban society back then. Villagers lived in the villages and the urban lived in the city. There used to be costume balls, 7-8 movie theaters and other places that families can go together. Families used to go to the movies together. Throughout the last 25 years, this urban structure has deteriorated. I think it is mostly due to the immigration from the villages. The villagers could not become

> urbanized, but the urban became rural. We can add the powerful reign of the Virtue Party [the conservative, religious party that governs the municipality] to that, and the closure of the movie theaters one by one. There is now one movie theater that university students go to. There are no restaurants that families can go. There are some café houses that students go to, but since they are under the control of the "Virtuous" gentlemen, they serve no alcohol. So, the social life has suffocated. (Bülent Okur, personal interview, February 17, 2001)

The Şanlıurfa municipality was run in 2001 by the religious and conservative Virtue (Fazilet) Party members, and since then it has been run by the equally conservative AKP Party[5]. Another local journalist, Özcan Güneş, owner and editor-in-chief of Şanlıurfa Radyo Televizyon (ŞRT), was in agreement with Mr. Okur and many others about how Islamic revivalism began in Şanlıurfa and how religion was used against the uprising of PKK (Kurdish Workers Party):

> The government officials who were assigned to this region, especially in the 1980s, used religion to fight against terror. In the other provinces, such as Diyarbakır, this didn't work much. In Urfa, there was not much terror, there has never been much, either. However, the weapon that the government used is now directed to itself. Its regime is in danger. On the one hand religiosity, and on the other hand feudal structure took the social life backward to a degree that almost destroyed it... (Ö. Güneş, personal interview, February 21, 2001)

When the PKK gained power, support, and visibility as a Marxist organization and workers' party in the region, the state and governments of the time followed a policy that aimed to counteract their leftist ideology with religious and rightist ideologies, support for nationalist youth groups, and funding for religious schools, organizations and leaders. The fear of communism during the cold war era contributed to the Turkish military and state's drastic measures nationwide, and their reactionary but flawed policies not only resulted in military coups but also in a deepened conflict between secularists and Islamists that empowered the religious parties and local governments. The increasing power of local religious leaders and political authorities, which have adopted the Islamist discourse and ideology, created numerous constraints on several aspects of social life in Şanlıurfa, especially women's participation in the public sphere. Establishments that serve alcoholic drinks as well as restaurants and movie theaters where both women and men could go were closed as a result of the social pressure that growing religious sentiment caused. In addition, participating in those spaces was not a routine part of the daily lives of the new residents of the city who migrated from the rural areas. Thus, those urban spaces increasingly vanished from the new landscape of the city. Today, women in the city of Şanlıurfa – even though they worked in the fields along with their husbands prior to settling in the city – are discouraged from working in businesses, especially restaurants, cafes and other shops, where they can be exposed to many people. Very few young women work in their fathers' businesses. I saw no women working for the local media stations during my research.

In many other cities in Turkey, it is common for women who migrated from rural areas to the city to adopt the headscarf and long trench coats to be able to mediate between private and public spaces (İlyasoğlu 1998) and between traditional and modern (Macleod 1991). Even though the new urban style of veiling and conservative clothing are also embraced by women in Şanlıurfa, it does not provide free access to the city, because the unequal male-female relations in the private sphere are perpetuated through religion, traditions, tribal and patriarchal culture. Since they no longer live in a small town or village among families that belong to the same tribe and have close kinship ties with each other, women are expected to stay at home and not leave without a male chaperon or older women's supervision – like a mother or mother-in-law – and appropriately modest clothing and headscarf. Religion is heavily used to enforce these patriarchal practices. For instance, some of the young girls I met at the ÇATOM told me that it is a sin for a woman to walk alone on the streets without a chaperone and that they would burn in hell if they did so.

Şanlıurfa's semi-feudal tribal structure, which is the strongest in the region, perpetuates a centuries-old tradition of loyalty to a prominent family, landlord and/or tribal head. This structure mandates that marriages occur within the extended family in order to strengthen it and thus, the tribe. While marriages are common between families of the same tribe, most marriages occur between the children of two brothers within the same family, and marriages between the families of different tribes are very rare. This structure not only minimizes the input of the young in choosing their spouses but also prohibits dating and relationships for both men and women and severely punishes people suspected of having such a relationship, sometimes even leading to their murder in the name of tradition and family honor. As a result, almost everyone ends up in an arranged marriage with a cousin or relative with whom they grew up and have no romantic feelings toward. This is a key part of the social context in which the young people of Şanlıurfa turn to local media.

Turkish media as a marker of difference

The Turkish media environment underwent a significant transformation in the 1990s, which deepened the intergenerational conflict between the youth and their families. The Turkish state monopoly in radio and television broadcasting was broken as a result of media liberalization, globalization, and the infiltration of satellite and other new communication technologies. Within less than a year Turkish broadcasting changed from a couple of state-owned-and-controlled radio and TV broadcast channels (TRT) to 16 national commercial TV networks and almost 2000 local radio stations nationwide. Commercial TV and radio channels quickly began broadcasting programs that mimicked their Western counterparts, which gained immediate popularity with Turkish audiences tired of the formal, elitist and old-fashioned state broadcasting. These new channels, especially radio stations, offered a special emphasis on audience participation and attracted many listeners with their live interactive broadcasting style in which the audience was able to participate by sending messages via fax, telephone, mail and e-mail to express their appreciation for the new programming and voice their opinions on current political and social issues. This media environment created a new democratic forum for many Turks, especially those living in urban centers, to freely challenge the hegemony of state authority and the official ideology, at least during the first half of the 1990s (Algan 2003b).

While audience interaction and communication with radio stations slowed down during the second half of the 1990s, the popularity of these radio channels continued and the number of both local and national channels increased. Networks broadcasting from urban centers, especially İstanbul,[6] reached most of the country and illustrated realities of life and new trends from the nation's urban center of İstanbul. TV dramas modeled after telenovelas and comedies modeled after American sitcoms depicted mostly urban Turkish people living in their beautifully decorated apartments, wearing fashionable clothing, working in nice offices, leading modern lives just like their global counterparts. The transition from a highly didactic, controlled, and technically humble state broadcasting system to a commercial one led young people living in the geographical periphery of Southeast Turkey to see the disparity between their own realities and those in the western part of the country. In some of the new sitcoms and TV series, for instance, mothers worked in office jobs alongside men and they made important decisions regarding family and finances; teenagers used personal computers, freely dated, threw birthday parties and attended school dances; and unmarried female university students traveled freely and even got pregnant without being rejected by their families and friends.

In Southeast Turkey, however, most young girls are not allowed to go to school for more than a few years, if at all, and most boys only attend elementary school. Not only do young people lack any social space to experience their gender identities and sexualities as they can now see represented from İstanbul, but they are also expected to obey traditional ways regarding their education, work, and marriage. In this context, since their launch in the mid-1990s, local commercial radio channels in Şanlıurfa have functioned as a vitally important site for young people – who can now see the extent of the disparity between their lives and those in the west – to vocalize their dissatisfaction with the status quo and traditions. Young people call in to discuss arranged marriage practices, bride price, *berdel* – the cross-marriage of male and female children of two families – and other traditions that prioritize marriage among relatives, as well as restrictions on women's education. In addition, local radio has functioned as a social space for them to experience various aspects of their youth identities by sharing cultural works they create, such as songs and poems, and by pursuing romantic relationships via sending songs and messages to each other (Algan 2005).

Love Line: radio and the politics of love

Dating over the radio gained publicity and popularity soon after the first commercial radio station of Şanlıurfa, GAP FM, began broadcasting in 1993. The radio's manager, Tezel, founded a fan club called *Love Line* (Sevgi Hattı Fan Klubü), where members read their love poems, requested songs, and presented their views about love-related topics on the air over two hours on Saturdays and Sundays. She charged 500 TL (around $10 at the time) as a membership fee, which was actually a donation for Mehmet Saçlı Elementary School. In return she sent listeners a membership card, which provided discounts for certain shops. She had over one thousand members consisting of not only the young people of Şanlıurfa but also people of different ages and backgrounds from other provinces, such as Siirt and Ordu, and even from across the border in Syria. Tezel remembers that a teenage girl who was not allowed by her father to become a member – because he thought that she was trying to become a prostitute – brought him to the station to prove him wrong. This club and program were so popular that one of my informants said the entire city tuned in to the show and that "you couldn't see any open TV sets during the time the show was on" (a fan of the show, personal interview, February 21, 2001).

When two young people who came to register for the fan club met at the radio station, fell in love, and carried a romantic relationship via GAP FM, the station's popularity soared. After many months of messages and song exchanges, these two people, who were known on the radio by the code names Red Microbe and Bahar, decided to get married. When Bahar's father refused to permit it, Red Microbe did what is common in the region despite its occasional fatal ending: he kidnapped her with her permission. What was unusual was that he called the radio at every stage of the kidnapping. Tezel said that the station had to change its regular programming so she could learn what was happening and let the listeners know. When Red Microbe and Bahar realized the strong support they were getting from the people of Şanlıurfa, they decided to take refuge at the radio station. When Bahar's father heard where they were, he invaded the radio station with his relatives. Via radio, Tezel was able to summon not only the police but also a big crowd who came to rescue the lovers. With the community's support behind them, Red Microbe and Bahar were able to get married.

While the story of Red Microbe and Bahar is not a common one, this program, *Love Line*, was influential for providing young people the "social life" they wanted to have by creating a vibrant youth community and allowing young people to pursue romantic relationships. Through song requests, poems and messages they express feelings for their love interests over the radio. However, not every radio-mediated relationship or innocent song request ends happily. Consider the case of Hacer, who did not even have a romantic affair on the radio, though she actively participated on the air, her story is widely known in Şanlıurfa and it stokes fear among many who try to subvert Şanlıurfa's strict norms on relationships. Wanting to experience love freely like others seemed to do on the radio, and to live a life like the independent and rich women on TV, Hacer ran away from home, but she was found by the police and returned to her family (Faraç 1998, p. 26). According to them, her honor had been damaged. The family murdered her, and she became a victim of honor killings.[7]

Most young girls I talked to were afraid of sending songs to someone toward whom they had romantic feelings, out of fear of being recognized and labeled a bad girl. One of Tezel's short radio plays, which became very popular and was repeatedly requested by listeners, depicts girls' fear of sending songs over the radio. The play was called *Dedo Aşki* (which means Dedo's love or a young man's love) and depicted two lovers trying to communicate secretly through radio and telephones. From memory, Tezel told me listeners' favorite lines of the play:

Dedo: Girl, I sent a song for you last night, didn't you listen?

Hatice: How could I miss?

Dedo: Then, why didn't you respond?

Hatice: How could I? What if my brother finds out? I was afraid he would kill us both. (from Tezel's radio play, *Dedo Aşki*)

Despite possible consequences, secret romantic love expressed through song requests and telephones is common. There are a few stories like Red Microbe and

I was DJ Murat Büyükler's guest for his program, Sugar Microphone, at Radyo Rempo in Şanlıurfa.

Bahar's, but most romantic relationships pursued over the radio end either because the fathers do not allow marriage or the couples decide to break up themselves. Social custom constricts possibility. As one of my informants explains,

> Urfa's traditions, customs and manners are very different. Our east is not like the west. For instance in the west[8], two people can get married as they like if they love each other or they can live together. However, it's not like that here. There is no permission to love in our Urfa. You can't even talk to a girl. She cannot come near me and talk to me. Why can't she? Because if relatives or neighbors see her, they either badmouth her or gossip about her. So, it's shameful here [for a girl to talk to a man]. (Mehmet U, personal interview, February 22, 2001)

Hacer wanting to live a life like girls on TV and Mehmet U's belief about how lovers can live together without marriage in the west of Turkey suggest that the new commercial TV channels have shaped young people's imagination about life in İstanbul and other cities. What is significant in Mehmet U's assessment is his generalization of small number of people's experiences in big cities as the common practice of relationships in the west of Turkey. It reflects the fact that the new commercial TV channels had created edgy programming with lots of intricate love and crime stories and upper class lifestyles mimicking American TV series as a way to appeal to audiences tired of TRT's depiction of respectful, "civilized", nuclear families. This began to change, however, in the early 2000s, when new dramas appeared that depicted average, traditional Turkish families and dealt realistically with their struggles negotiating traditional and modern. Once networks realized how this programming boosted ratings throughout Turkey, especially in rural areas, they even began introducing storylines that depicted some of the realities in the east. This introduced a different set of image into the nation's collective imaginary.

Courting via SMS messages and reflecting on local radio and social change

When I returned to Şanlıurfa in the summer of 2007, my interactions with young people showed that even though many seemed to have a more nuanced understanding of the disparity between their lives in Southeast Turkey and those in the west, they still longed for a social space of their own and continued to utilize new technologies to create and maintain that space. Since 2003, they had been deprived of the opportunity to call-in and be on air to directly voice their opinions or share their songs, poems and messages. Local radio was struggling economically, and Şanlıurfa's station owners and managers met and made a decision to only allow messages and song requests through SMS (Short Message Service) text messaging. Operating costs had risen due to the strict enforcement of royalty payments for songs broadcast, but they learned from radio stations outside the region how lucrative SMS could be.

In the summer of 2007, young people were still actively sending their messages and song requests for their love interests through text messages via cell phones. At first I was concerned that women would not be able to interact as much, but I immediately found out that there were not many women left in the city without cell phones: when men began obtaining newer cell phones, they gave their old ones to their sisters and daughters. When I did my fieldwork in 2001, women were accessing the stations using their home phones, which restricted their participation in the evenings. In 2001, they did not have any cell phones but every man carried one, and they functioned as must-have status symbols of manhood. In 2007, lack of access to a mobile phone was not an issue for women, but rather having enough money to afford making phone calls and sending SMS messages was. DJs voiced young women's complaints about their love interests not sending enough minutes to them as a gift and how infrequently, for that reason, they were able to send SMS messages to the radio stations.

Another frequent listener complaint regarded DJs not reading their SMS or shortening them and changing the meaning of the messages as a result. DJs read the messages after each song they played and frequently apologized if they had a hard time reading the message or if the message arrived partially. Fully aware of their long-ago established matchmaker and facilitator roles on air (Algan 2005), they were very respectful of the messages and quite diligent about reading them. Most messages were song requests for their love interests, but some were direct messages that voiced relationship disappointments and problems. Dissatisfaction with their lives and the status quo, desires to leave Şanlıurfa for a better life elsewhere, and feelings of loneliness were other topics that often surfaced. The main difference I observed between participating via call-ins and SMS messaging was the curtailment of interaction with the DJs and the sharing of their cultural production through poems, songs, etc. Up until 2003, DJs frequently ran call-in shows and games encouraging discussions on topics that mattered to the young people of Şanlıurfa. Even though such programming does not exist anymore, young people still use the radio to pursue their romantic relationships despite the local radio stations' restricting all communication to SMS messages.

Due to the existing patriarchal and tribal structures, radio continues to constitute the safest haven for young people to do what they believe their generation should do and pursue love. By doing so, they are part of more widespread phenomena. As Edmunds & Turner (2005) argued in their article on global generations and social change, "the forces commonly associated with globalization are also forces that increase intergenerational tensions within nations and intra-generational affinities between nations, thereby contributing to the new (global) generation becoming activated against its predecessor's passivity" (p. 572). Interactions via local radio in Southeast Turkey have illustrated the ways in which young people are active in matters that pertain to their own lives. Instead of obeying their parents, they choose to engage in romantic relationships over the radio with the hope of ending up in a marriage based on love instead of one arranged by family.

The variety of media channels and programming young people have access to – from national television and its mix of domestic, foreign and glocal programming, to transnational programming like the Kurdish and Arabic language channels consumed via satellite – allow them to see who they are and how they fit into their own community, Turkey, the, region and the broader world. On the one hand, national, transnational and global media increase intergenerational tensions by pointing out the disparities that exist between their realities in Southeast Turkey and those of other young people of the same generation living in the west of the country. On the other hand, local media and new communication technologies give them an opportunity to articulate youth identities shaped by and negotiated through both globally-induced socio-economic changes, as well as centuries-old patriarchal and tribal structures.

As this study shows, media alone do not instigate social change but they can be instrumental in giving people an avenue to articulate their unique realities and multiple identities and to express what kind of social change they strive for. In Şanlıurfa, social change has been taking place as a result of various local and national institutions and state development projects attempting to integrate Turkey into the global economy. Young people's lives are affected by these initiatives both in rural and urban areas. They find themselves deprived of education due to existing patriarchal and tribal structures, but still expected to compete in a new capitalist economy that they are not equipped even to understand. They are more aware of their identity differences with the west and strive to lessen them by dressing, acting and behaving like the teenagers in İstanbul. Local radio makes it easier for them to experience their gender identities and sexualities, and to pursue romantic relationships because it allows them to date without any face-to-face encounters and thus, to obey the local traditions and Islamic restrictions on pre-marital relationships. Media ethnography is an excellent method to grasp these realities and contribute to a more comprehensive and nuanced look at media's place and role in social change more generally. Ethnographies can also be instrumental in cautioning us against the sweeping claims of grand narratives regarding the power of media as the main agents of social change.

Notes

1. The title 'Şanlı' (meaning *Glorious*) was given to the city by Atatürk to honor its residents for their courageous defense of the city during Turkey's War of Independence. Even though Şanlıurfa is the city's official name, residents often use its original short name, Urfa.
2. According to Adams (2006), recent work that aims to re-evaluate media's role in social change increasingly emphasizes how entertainment-education remains a top-down project and the long-term effects of such projects are weak with their success being dependent on the local infrastructure to support such changes.
3. For more on the ÇATOM activities and their influence on women in the region, see Fazlıoğlu (2003) and Harris & Atalan (2003).

4. For more on the struggles of young people, especially women, against strict traditions, see Faraç (1998), and for the impact of the GAP development project on the people of Şanlıurfa, see Elmas (2004) and Faraç (2001).
5. After the closure of the Virtue Party in August 2001 due to their active and positive stance on the wearing of headscarves in government buildings and state institutions, the party members founded AKP and continue to retain their power in the province.
6. İstanbul has always determined the cultural agenda in Turkey. The country's print media, music and film industries have always been centered in İstanbul, a city not only located in the northwest or European side of Turkey, but which also mimics and appropriates culture from the West. After the 1990s, when the state monopoly in broadcasting was broken, İstanbul also commanded the broadcasting industry with many new commercial broadcast networks airing throughout Anatolia, the Asian part of Turkey.
7. Honor killings or custom murders are the names given to the murder of a woman by the male members of her family as a result of a family judgment that she damaged the honor of the family. Honor killings are common in Southeast Turkey and until recently used to be treated as low-level felonies by the courts. Custom and tradition are taken into consideration by the courts as circumstantial evidence supporting a lighter sentence for the person chosen to carry out the killing. A new bill passed in April 2003 prohibited any decrease in sentences for honor killings, however such murders still continue and sometimes girls are forced to commit suicide. The main reasons for honor killings are "the involvement of a girl in an affair with a man despite parental disapproval, bearing an illegitimate child, leaving her husband and escaping with another man, becoming pregnant outside marriage, being a prostitute, etc." (Women 2000, p. 449). However, a simple conversation between an unmarried woman and a man can be considered an affair and an act that damages the woman's virtue and thus, the family honor as well.
8. Many young people I talked to compared the west and the east based on their understanding or sometimes direct experience with life in the western part of Turkey. First, I thought they referred to the Western countries, but my questions confirmed that they only referred to the western part of Turkey, especially İstanbul, whose social life is widely depicted in domestic soap operas and dramas that are popular nationwide.

References

Adams, D.M. (2006) 'Media and Development in the Middle East', *Transformation* 23(3): 170-186.
Algan, E. (2003a) 'The Problem of Textuality in Ethnographic Audience Research: Lessons learned in Southeast Turkey', in M. Kraidy & P. Murphy (eds) *Global Media Studies: Ethnographic Perspectives*. New York: Routledge, pp. 23-39.
Algan, E. (2003b) 'Privatization of Media in Turkey and the Question of Media Hegemony in the Era of Globalization', in L. Artz & Y.R. Kamalipour (eds) *The Globalization of Corporate Media Hegemony*. New York: SUNY Press, pp. 169-192.
Algan, E. (2005) 'The Role of Turkish Local Radio in the Construction of a Youth Community', *The Radio Journal: International Studies in Broadcast & Audio Media* 3(2): 75-92.
Algan, E. (2009) 'What of Ethnography?', *Television and New Media* 10(1): 7-9.
Appadurai, A. (1990) 'Disjuncture and Difference in the Global Cultural Economy', *Theory, Culture & Society* 7(2-3): 295-310.
Edmunds, J. & Turner, B.S. (2005) 'Global Generations: Social Change in the Twentieth Century', *The British Journal of Sociology* 56(4): 559-577.
Ekecrantz, J. (2007) 'Media and Communication Studies Going Global', *Nordicom Review. Jubilee Issue*: 169-181.
Elmas, G. (2004) 'Women, Urbanization and Regional Development in Southeast Anatolia: A Case Study for Turkey', *Turkish Studies* 5(3): 1-24.
Faraç, M. (1998) *Töre kıskacında kadın*. İstanbul: Çağdaş Yayınları.
Faraç, M. (2001) *Suyu arayan toprak: Harran ve Fırat'ın bin yıllık dramı*. İstanbul: Ozan Yayıncılık.

Fazlıoğlu, A. (2003) ÇATOM: A Model for Empowering Women in Southeastern Anatolia. *Kadin/ Woman 2000* 3(1): 43-63.
Featherstone, M. & Lash, S. (1995) 'Globalization, Modernity and the Spatialization of Social Theory: An Introduction', in M. Featherstone, S. Lash & R. Robertson (eds.) *Global Modernities* (pp. 1-24) Thousand Oaks, CA: Sage.
Friedman, J. (1995) 'Global System, Globalization and the Parameters of Modernity', in M. Featherstone, S. Lash & R. Robertson (eds.) *Global Modernities* (pp. 69-90). Thousand Oaks, CA: Sage.
Gumucio-Dagron, A. & Tufte, T. (2006) *Communication for Social Change Anthology: Historical and Contemporary Readings*. New Jersey: The Communication for Social Change Consortium.
Harris, L.M. & Atalan, N. (2003) 'Developing Women's Spaces: Evaluation of the Importance of Sex-segregated Spaces for Gender and Development Goals in Southeastern Turkey', *Kadin/ Woman 2000* 3(2): 17-46.
Hemer, O. & Tufte, T. (eds) (2005) *Media and Glocal Change. Rethinking Communication for Development*. Göteborg: Nordicom, and Buenos Aires: CLACSO.
Hjarvard, S. (2008) 'The Mediatization of Society: A Theory of the Media as Agents of Social and Cultural Change', *Nordicom Review* 29 (2): 105-134.
İlyasoglu, A. (1998) 'Islamist Women in Turkey: Their Identity and Self-image', in Z. Arat (ed.) *Deconstructing Images of "the Turkish woman"* (pp. 241-61) NY: St. Martin's Press.
Lerner, D. (1958) *Passing of Traditional Society: Modernizing the Middle East*. Glencoe, IL: Free Press.
Macleod, A.E. (1991) *Accommodating Protest: Working Women, the New Veiling, and Change in Cairo*. NY: Columbia University Press.
Marcus, G.E. (1998) 'Ethnography in/of the World System: The Emergence of Multi-sited Ethnography', in G.E. Marcus, *Ethnography through Thick and Thin*. Princeton, NJ: Princeton University Press. (Reprinted from (1995), *Annual Review of Anthropology* 24: 95-117.
Pieterse, J.N. (2001) *Development Theory. Deconstructions/Reconstructions*. Thousand Oaks, CA: Sage.
Rantanen, T. (2008) 'From International Communication to Global Media Studies. What Next?', *Nordicom Review* 29(2): 35-39.
Robertson, R. (1995) 'Glocalization: Time-space and Homogeneity-heterogeneity', in M. Featherstone, S. Lash & R. Robertson (eds.) *Global Modernities* (pp. 25-44). Thousand Oaks, CA: Sage.
Singhal, A. (2007) 'Popular Media and Social Change: Lessons from Peru, Mexico, and South Africa', *Brown Journal of World Affairs* 13(2): 259-269.
Spitulnik, D. (1993) 'Anthropology and Mass Media', *Annual Review of Anthropology* 22: 293-315.
Straubhaar, J.D. (2008) 'Global, Hybrid or Multiple? Cultural Identities in the Age of Satellite TV and the Internet', *Nordicom Review* 29(2): 11-29.
Tufte, T. (2008) 'Exploring Cultural Globalization: New Forms of Experience and Citizen-driven Change Processes', *Nordicom Review* 29(2): 35-39.
Women 2000: An Investigation into the Status of Women's Rights in the former Soviet Union and Central and South-Eastern Europe (2000) Vienna: The International Helsinki Federation for Human Rights (IHF).

Youth as Subjects – of Content, Programs, Projects and Regulations

Media Portrayals of Youth Involvement in Social Change
The Roles of Agency, Praxis, and Conflict Resolution Processes in TV Programs

Peter Lemish & Elke Schlote

Abstract

This study on media portrayals of youth involvement in social change sought to assess the nature of such portrayals in television programs produced for the youth audience. For this purpose, we assembled a corpus of quality TV productions directed at youth in which a social problem or conflict is presented and actors apply various tactics through a series of actions with anticipated and unanticipated consequences. Drawing on edu-tainment and conflict resolution frameworks as well as on the work of Paulo Freire and scriptwriting manuals, we show in in-depth media analyses of selected fiction and non-fiction segments how individual youth agents are portrayed dealing with these social situations and what kinds of portrayals are more likely to support learning about social change processes.

> *We find out whether someone is a deep citizen not merely by examining their judicial status, but also by examining what it is that they are doing.*
> (Clarke 1996: 122)

Among the many prescriptive calls for citizen involvement in civil society, we are told that "strong" or "deep" democracy requires active citizen involvement (Barber 1984; Clarke 1996; Dewey 1916); that youth should be educated for active participation in civic life (e.g. Dewey 1916; Freire 1970, 1973; Shor and Freire 1987); and that teens can use a wide variety of strategies to advance social change in their everyday lives (e.g. Alson and Burnett 2003; Halpin 2004; Hoose 2002; Goodman 2003; Lewis, Espeland and Pernu 1998). From the empirical side, investigating how youth actually engage in social change and/or how they learn to do so involves examining the resources of information and learning processes available to them.

Given that consumption of media, and television programs in particular, are among the chief components of young peoples' life-worlds, worldwide (Lemish, D. 2007), and that they may be a rich resource for learning about social change, the study reported here of media portrayals of youth involvement in social change sought to assess the nature of such portrayals in television programs produced for the youth audience. Media portrayals were of interest because they exist at the nexus of social change endeavors, which involves by necessity dynamic individual-society interactions: A social problem or conflict is presented, be it in a micro-social situation (e.g. in interpersonal relations or in their family) or in relation to macro-social problems (e.g. in confronting poverty, inter-ethnic conflict, global warming) and actors apply various tactics through a series of actions with anticipated and unanticipated consequences that contribute to social change.[1] Further, some texts grant us access to characters' thinking in defining the problems, their feelings about events as they take place, reasons for selecting and planning tactics, assessments of their own and others actions/reactions, and so forth. Indeed, "edu-tainment" studies (Singhal and Rogers 1999; Singhal, Cody, Rogers and Sabido 2004) have found that media portrayals are opportunities for young viewers' to learn about social phenomena and issues, as well as models of proactive behavior. We would like to claim that complex life-processes, too, may be learned from these texts, though an understanding of the nature of all such learning must be advanced through reception studies.

Taking this to the production side, from the author or scriptwriter's perspective, the challenge is to create a story linking characters' thoughts, feelings, and values with actions, interactions, consequences, through successive cycles, so that the audience has access to a story that is interesting and insightful about how, in our case, young people are involved in constructing social life (e.g. Rosenthal 1995) and in advancing social change. Indeed, the quality of character portrayal and plot represent the scriptwriters' and directors' understandings of how social life is produced and changed. Hence, the study presented here focused on one important aspect of the social change puzzle: The TV resources available to youth that they, their parents, as well as educators in formal and informal settings could access to enrich their understanding of the nature of involvement in social change, be it in their own micro-social world or as participants in broader, collective macro-social change efforts.

We do not assume that there is a direct, causal relationship between media consumption and youth-viewer involvement in social change. Indeed, it may well be the case that the subtlety and complexity of social change processes found to be present in the texts investigated require use of critical media literacy skills[2] and viewing guided by a more experienced co-viewer who understands the nature of inter-relationship between individuals and social change. Furthermore, while acknowledging that, ultimately, collective efforts should aim to advance structural transformation, we posit that social change also requires the intimate involvement and drive of individual agents. Hence, we claim that study of media portrayals of youth involved in social change may be a rich resource included in social change education oriented to assisting youth become attuned and inspired to become active participants in social life and social change.

Research process

The study reported here is part of a more extensive research project investigating the roles of conflict resolution processes in television texts for children and youth (Lemish 2007, 2008; Lemish and Schlote in-progress).[3] The textual analyses reported in this chapter drew upon a pre-existent corpus of children's TV programs selected from the archives of the past six Prix Jeunesse (PJ) International Festivals (1996-2006).[4] This corpus consists of 46 texts [non-fiction (36) as well as fiction, and docu-dramas (8), along with a few news programs (4).[5] Guided by our focus in the case study of media portrayals of youth involved in advancing social change developed for this chapter, we found 14 films for analysis that met the following criterion:[6] An individual or group of tweens, teenagers, or young adults were portrayed advancing a social change effort in micro-settings (e.g. in inter-personal relations, in their family, or at school) or in macro-settings (e.g. society-wide social and political change). While small in number, this select corpus is meritorious because of the wide range of countries and social change efforts represented as well as differences in scriptwriters' understandings.[7]

1. The primary question addressed in the research reported in this article asked: What is the nature of media portrayals of youth involvement in social change? The following secondary questions assisted us to answer this question:

2. How are the inter-linking processes agency, praxis, and conflict resolution shown to be involved in advancing social change, and how do they structure the films?

3. What is the quality of the main characters' (scriptwriters') understandings of these processes?

In terms of potential viewer learning about social change from these films: Would it be possible to infer these processes from the structure of the plot and/or the main characters' thoughts, experiences, and actions?

The qualitative analysis of these films conducted in this study sought to illuminate and analyze the "process" dimensions of everyday social life which is one of the key goals of qualitative research studies (Lindlof and Taylor 2002). To do so, we analyzed each of the films using three process constructs postulated (see next section) as necessarily involved in individual's involvement in social change. For example, use of conflict resolution as a theoretical construct enabled us to analyze the conflict at the core of the change effort; different participant stances as they developed through the text; as well as different resolution phases in terms of their duration, the tactics planned and applied, and consequences.

Theoretical constructs

Our review of the literature did not reveal deep analyses of media portrayals of children or youth involvement in social change. Furthermore, juxtaposed to a rich literature prescribing how to write television or films scripts (e.g. Aronson 2000; Cowgill 1999; Dancyger and Rush 2007; Field 1994; Rosenthal 1995; Thomas 1999), systematic analyses and theories of "screenwork" is just now emerging as an academic domain (MacDonald 2008).

In search of constructs, strategies, and assumptions that could assist us in analysis of media texts linked to advancing social change, we turned to a specific proactive research paradigm, edu-tainment – a communication strategy to induce behavioral and social change (Singhal et al. 2004). According to this paradigm, a media message can be purposely designed and implemented "to both entertain and educate, in order to increase audience knowledge about an educational issue, create favorable attitudes, and change overt behavior." (2004: 5) To do so, typical storylines of popular TV and radio formats are enriched with pro-social messages and model characters so that viewers live vicariously through social experiences involving, for example, HIV/AIDS, gender inequality, or illiteracy (e.g. Singhal and Rogers 1999; Sood et al. 2004; Tufte 2003).

One of the key theoretical foundations of edu-tainment is US social psychologist Bandura's re-visited approach to assessing viewer learning from social models (e.g. Bandura 2004; Bandura 2001: 126). Bandura claimed that symbolic communication of knowledge, values, new behaviors, and the modeling of positive and negative outcomes of this behavior can initiate individual psychosocial changes and increase the awareness of social-change topics in communities or societal groups. From the media side, two main issues determine the success of such an endeavor: The modeling of characters and the plot (Bandura 2004: 81ff). While research of the reception of pro-social messages and audience involvement with the characters, for example, are the key interests pursued to date through the edu-tainment paradigm (e.g. Sood et al. 2004), to the best of our knowledge, viewer learning of *processes*, such as presented here, have not been advanced.[8]

Just as the processes of agency, praxis, and conflict resolution are essential in advancing social change in everyday life, these three processes are or should be used in structuring media portrayals of social change efforts. While these processes function in an interwoven manner, we present them separately in order to understand their conceptual foundations and key characteristics. This is followed by presentation of the results of applying these analytical concepts to selected TV programs that portray youth advancing social change.

Agency

Agency, or the practice of acting in social life, is the necessary and sufficient condition for social change; be it the actions of an individual, group, or movement. The formal act of agency, the "taking a stand", is simultaneously a public declaration of the existence of a conflict or problem and initiation of a process whose purpose is to seek its resolution. This starting point leads, cyclically, to responses by others and further agentive actions that have outcomes and consequences, possibly inducing changes in attitudes, understandings, decisions, and even social structures.

Yet, actions are not a *creatio ex nihilo*, rather they are expressions of internal, private, "backstage" processes taking place behind the "frontstage" in the self's production of participation in everyday life (Goffman 1959). Study of these backstage processes, the groundwater of the phenomenology of agency (Bayne 2008; Borshuk 2004), draws upon investigations of how individuals and groups produce participation in everyday life. Such studies attend, for example, to how social life and contextuality are defined; the social production of emotion and knowledge; planning, execution, and assessment of tactics employed; the roles of conversational exchanges and other forms of relational interaction; and the motivations driving activism.[9] Accordingly, access via scripts to the "backstage" of social change-oriented actions enables us to understand their meaning for the characters, and vis-a-vis the edu-tainment paradigm, for example, could be an important contribution towards understanding how viewers' learn about how social change is performed in everyday life.

Bandura's social cognitive theory, too, addresses this philosophical concept (Bandura 2001, Bandura 2006): "To be an agent is to influence intentionally one's functioning and life circumstances. [...] Effecting social change requires perseverant, collective action in common cause." (Bandura 2006: 3, 29) Developing confidence in one's own or joint efficacy (i.e., assurances that a single person or a group can accomplish a task) to bring about changes is a core component of this conception of agency.[10] According to this theory, individual and collective efficacy expectations are good predictors of the efforts people will expend and their persistence when confronted with difficulties. Thus, developing individual and collective efficacy is important for pursuing social change endeavors, especially "as adolescents expand the nature and scope of their activities into the larger social community." (Bandura 2006: 6). This pro-social model claims that personal and collective efficacy can be developed – among others – through vicarious experiences (e.g. through the modeling of behavior observed in the media) as well as through performance accomplishments (Bandura 2001; Bandura 2004).

However, as posited initially, we do not have evidence for the claim that vicarious media-based experiences will lead necessarily to direct involvement in social change endeavors. Rather, we view these texts as resources which when discussed in an informed, critical manner can lead to greater understanding and, perhaps, desire to become involved in social life and change. Thus, in terms of *deep* democracy, enabling young viewers the opportunity to view models of peers engaging in social change, individually and in groups, and granting access to agents' thinking, emotions, tactical planning in advance of their actions can make significant contributions to modeling and learning about proactive involvement in civic life. Following Brazilian educator Paulo Freire, this interactive, reflection-action process is referred to as "praxis".

Praxis

Praxis is defined, for our purposes, as actions conducted through understanding and moral judgment.[11] Such an approach to the phenomenology of agency requires that we engage, continually, with our immediate world. Freire's understandings grew from his extensive experience and reflection about the nature of praxis as well as its development with youth and adults in educational and social settings.[12] In building upon his work, we understand that conscious development of *praxis*, as may be advanced through media texts (and especially television series), can achieve two manifest aims: conscientization and empowerment.

This Freirian approach to praxis involves the following activities:

- Problematizing, or questioning one's perceptions of social reality in order to identify essential relations, problems, and conflicts affecting one's own and other persons' lives.

- Probing for and developing a deep understanding of social life that enables one to contextualize and relate actions and processes to patterns in historical and contemporary social life. The aim in doing so is to understand the underlying structures that created and sustain problems and conflicts, such as power relations, organizational structures and strategies as well as ideological interests and hegemonic mechanisms.

- Reflecting and making judgments related to questions of a moral nature, such as, is this situation humane? Are human rights violated? Who is able to participate in social life and what is the nature of their participation?

- Posing action options, selecting tactics, planning implementation, guiding action, and assessing consequences.

Overall, this Freirian-based conceptualization of praxis provides us with a holistic view of the phenomenology of agency, constructs that can be applied in analysis of media portrayals of youth involved in social change, and questions, such as: How does a situation perceived by others to be normal come to be seen as problematic by the social actor? What understandings are applied in this process or develop through praxis? What action and tactics are developed in order to intervene with the problem? How does the actor respond to reactions provoked by initial and follow-up actions? What is the relationship between aims and assessments of what was achieved? What meanings and significance are assigned such a process?

Conflict resolution (CR)

Conflict, or the existence of differences of opinion, values, interests, or desires held by individuals, groups, or nations – is a precondition for the advancement of social change efforts, since conflict must exist in actual social reality as well as in perceived, existential reality (e.g. Vago 1996).[13] That is, engagement in praxis by an individual or group can lead to the realization that action, agency, must be initiated to confront a social problem or perceived conflict that may well lead to change, or, minimally, have more positive consequences. Given this realization, the pragmatic question – how to advance such an effort? – can be addressed by individuals' engagement in CR as an initial process that will assist them to both understand as well as to define action options.[14]

Each society develops modes of managing conflicts. Some permit the use of violence, verbal as well as physical; other societies socialize and permit only the use of a wide array of non-violent tactics and processes; while still other societies set out processes that only in extreme cases permit the use of violence (e.g. Augsburger 1992; Fay 2006). CR, then, is the general social science term for this management process. Interestingly, empirical studies of social change have not involved CR theory or paradigms; and, vice versa; hence, warranting the following brief overview of key principles and concepts applied in this study.

Conventional CR theories portray a linear process consisting of three stages: emergence of the conflict, confrontation, negotiation and signing of a resolution agreement. Alternatively, the Cyclical Model of Conflict Resolution (Lemish 2007; see Picture 1) functions on significantly different assumptions from the conventional, linear model: First, the model assumes that CR is a dynamic, complex process. Second, the model includes two additional phases – implementation of agreement and reconciliation. And, accordingly, it accounts for the frequent need for renegotiation and adaptations of social life due to the consequences of moving forward with the resolution process. And, hence, the fundamental principle of the model – namely the *cyclical* nature of the CR process – claims that as long as the core reasons for the conflict continue to fester, they will erupt in any phase until a satisfactory manner of managing them is achieved and maintained.[15]

Practically, there are four key dimensions involved in successful management of the CR process, dimensions that we submit should be included in media portrayals of such processes (Lemish 2007):

- The core dimensions of the conflict need to be clearly understood by the parties;
- There needs to be a humane, fair presentation of opposing sides' points of view;

- All five phases of the full conflict resolution process should be attended to, or included contextually;
- There should be a creative exploration of a wide range of resolution options.

Picture 1. The cyclical model of conflict resolution

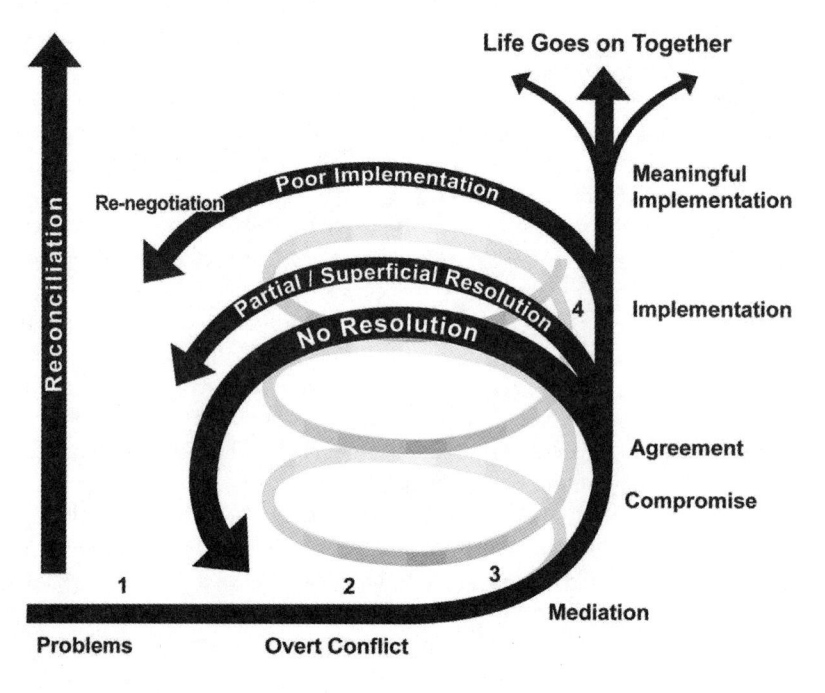

Source: Lemish 2007: 219.

Dramas and docu-dramas, as well as some non-fiction TV programs, are particularly well-suited to enable young viewers to understand the lived-experience of managing the conflict resolution process. According to literary theory, conflict is a central characteristic of plot structure in fiction: "Action in drama depends upon conflict, which is defined as the opposition of persons or forces, the struggle in a plot which grows out of the interaction of opposing ideas, interests or wills. Conflict is the essence of storytelling, it is the starting point of all drama" (Cowgill 1999: 80); and docu-drama (Rosenthal 1995). Thomas (1999: 86) presented a view of drama that combines agency, praxis, and CR: "Conflict must be more than an intellectual abstraction. It must be concrete and have a human face. In other words, it must involve the characters themselves. This kind of conflict stems from concrete conditions in the given circumstances."

Applying the dominant literary perspective that sees conflict in utilitarian terms (i.e., conflict creates the tension necessary for audience expectation and enjoyment), Cowgill (1999: 83) presented an adversarial, linear CR approach: "To be effective in plot construction, conflict needs to rise in waves. Along the way, there may be temporary solutions or ceasefires, but they shouldn't last. Short term solutions delay the audience's arrival at the moment of final confrontation with the antagonist ... and the release of tension with the resolution."[16] In contrast, the Cyclical CR Model is closer to "alternative approaches" to structuring scripts (e.g. Aronson 2000; Dancyger and Rush 2007). It allows for non-linearity and indeed calls for continuation of the storyline into the consequences of living with agreement implementation and reconciliation phases; or, alternatively, in-depth probing of conflict cycles that are the result of failures to deal with the essence of a conflict or poor implementation of negotiated agreements. Our in-depth film analyses presented in the following findings section demonstrate these principles.

Findings

The three processes postulated – agency, praxis, and CR – were present and used to structure nearly all media portrayals of youth involvement in social change in the select corpus. All 14 programs analyzed in this study feature active teen agents' involvement in social change, since this was a necessary condition for selection of the program for analysis (see Appendix 1 for a short description of the films). While elements of CR were present in all these programs, the 14 films were nearly evenly split between multiple and single-phase programs (e.g. latter probed in-depth the consequences of violent confrontation, mediation, or agreement implementation processes). Four single-phase films did not present the issues involved in the conflict, rather the conflict situation was simply assumed (as in living with the consequences of life during a war). In terms of praxis, all five non-fiction programs in our corpus reported on group actions with very little accounting for how individuals came to participate in these activities. In contrast, most of the main characters in fiction and docu-drama scripts (7 out of 9) shared their feelings, thoughts, and planning of tactics throughout different CR phases.

Overall, we found a spectrum that spans, on one end, "well-developed" texts with rich accounts of the three processes and their inter-relationship and, at the opposite end, "under-developed" scripts and characters.[17] In order to support and demonstrate this primary finding, we present our analysis of media portrayals and changes sought in five of these 14 programs.

Well-developed accounts[18]

The criteria for a well-developed script required evidence of strong agency and praxis (as a process and/or outcome), and maximal use of social science-based

CR paradigm to portray the production of social change. Five films met these criteria in sufficient proportion, from very rich to somewhat fully developed accounts of youth involvement in social change.

People Power II (Philippines, PJ 2002), the strongest example of a well-developed script, opens with a scene filmed moments before realization of the movement's social change aim: thousands await the exit of deposed/resigned Philippine President Estrada from the state residence. The teen presenters state the purpose of the program: To recall how youth-led actions led to the president's departure (see Picture 2).

The chronological portrayal of these events includes four key CR components: A continual reminder of the essence of the conflict – the alleged corruption of the president – functions as a main structural vector throughout the program; fair presentation of the contending parties' points of view; multiple phases of the Cyclical Model of CR is another main script vector; and, use of key CR skills: cooperation, creativity, commitment, rule of law, and direct, inter-personal and mass media communication.

Picture 2. The teen presenters – Screenshot from *People Power II*

© Prix Jeunesse International

The praxis process driving these efforts threads it way throughout the entire text, including problematizing and judgment of the social-political-economic system based upon understanding the extensive system of corruption that infiltrates and drives the hegemonic order. This is reiterated in the film's final statement, when an interviewee asked: "Will our success really lead to the end of corruption? No, apparently there will be a need for People Power III." Hence, the underlying message transmitted in their retracing the steps of People Power II movement seems to be: We believe that the process we advanced, like the goal we achieved, strengthens the democratic nature of our society, but the process must continue because the deeper social problem, the authentic conflict, corruption, continues to dominate Philippine society.

Furthermore, this program is the best evidence in the corpus of a central hypothesis of the Cyclical CR Model: namely, conflicts will continue to exist until the parties implement mechanisms that manage or control the causes of corruption. Applying the model, we can distinguish between the macro and micro-CR cycles used to structure the script. The *macro*-cycle is found in the Filipinos' overall framing of this as People Power II and postulation in the program's final sentences that there is likely to be People Power III, since the source of conflict – corruption – remains. The *micro*-cycle structures the film's chronology and includes nearly all phases and, in particular, multiple cycles of confrontation and implementation (e.g. raising and verifying the charge of corruption; use of multiple, legal confrontation mechanisms such as mass protest and petitioning political leaders to advance arbitration mechanisms including an impeachment trial in the country's senate; return to mass protest when the senate reached a stalemate; and delay of celebrations until full implementation of Estrada's resignation before declaring success). One phase not present – reconciliation – cannot be included, logically, since there is recognition that social change efforts must continue given continued existence of corruption in Philippine society.

In the film *Strong Language* (Great Britain, PJ 2000), from the series *Off Limits*, Zoe, a deaf teen, has to deal with identity issues and conflicts with her non-deaf classmates, parents, and teachers. The script demonstrates the evolution and inter-relationship of agency, praxis and CR processes in sharing Zoe's thoughts, feelings, and actions.

The core conflict is the lack of tolerance for deaf persons by hearing society, and as predicted by the cyclical model it reappears through various resolution efforts. Initially, the conflict is manifest through misunderstandings as well as her hearing classmates' mockery and derision. Her teacher exhibits a lack of understanding about her learning difficulties in a mainstream classroom. Even her hearing parents criticize her for not getting along at school. Zoe is frustrated in her attempts to deal with their inability to accept her, blames herself, and feels rejected and alone.

One key transition in the script occurs when Zoe decides to seek the comfort of more tolerant persons. In CR terms, instead of negotiation, Zoe declared a unilateral disengagement in response to an angry confrontation with her parents by announcing her decision to stay with her sister who is hearing but fluent in sign-language as she has a hearing-impaired little son. In attempting to understand her action options, Zoe consults with a hearing-impaired friend, Ben, about how he handles things at their school. Ben shares with her the concept of "deaf pride" and directs her to the possibility of collective agency: "When deaf hearts beat together they can move mountains." Zoe's statement – "when will it ever change?" – indicates that she has yet to recognize her own responsibility for her situation and agency to advance resolution options.

As an intern at a magazine, Zoe is assigned to work with Mark, a deaf graphic artist. Mark tells her how he manages his job and confirms that she is not alone in facing intolerant situations, as he faces them daily as a black and deaf person. He demonstrates use of a common conflict deflection tactic, humor, when a staff member jokes about their use of sign language and teaches her to use specially designed equipment for the hearing impaired. Zoe returns to her work space and proudly uses her hearing assisted telephone to call Ben – an act of independence and solidarity.

Another key transition point involves Zoe's advancing praxis through an action decision in which she will problematize her situation for hearing others. This occurs when Zoe decides that her media project will be to produce a film and a leaflet about her own and others' experiences with deafness, entitled *This is how I see it*. This becomes a collective social change effort when Ben and Mark surprise her by distributing copies of her leaflet to her classmates.

At first, Zoe does not feel a sense of agency in a world of hearing people, and is lost in her inner and exterior conflicts. In Ben and Mark, she finds friends and models of persons in a similar situation who are applying successful strategies for dealing with conflicts with intolerant hearing persons. Ben points out collective action ('deaf pride') as one solution, and Mark demonstrates how a deaf person can be self-confident and successful in his job. The script shows problematizing and evolving perceptions of Zoe's situation; the understandings she achieves of her own capabilities and identity; how her questioning, willingness to confront difficulties, learning to shift the problem from herself to others, and openness to receive assistance from more experienced deaf persons lead her to advance what we come to see is the beginning of a social change initiative – which also demonstrates how youth-made media develop: the making of a video about her experiences and mass distribution of a glossy pamphlet documenting her difficulties with classmates. While structural transformation has not occurred, and indeed not envisioned, this program could provide viewers with several important insights: The transition of a teen from passive to active agent of change that involves agency, praxis and CR; and the significant contribution of support by others when advancing a social change effort.

Under-developed texts[19]

This category includes texts which, on the one hand, portray agency and involvement in social change, some in very significant ways; yet, on the other hand, we found that either praxis and/or CR processes were under-developed in each of these scripts. Our brief presentation highlights both aspects.

A program from *With No ID* (Colombia, PJ 2004), a news magazine for youth, reported on a local peer mediation scheme initiated by pupils to reduce violence rampant in their school. The episode recalls how volunteer candidates were elected to be "heart councilors"; the training they received in various phases of the CR process; and skills they learned in order to manage the mediation process, such as listening to both sides, defining the conflict, raising and discussing resolution options, drawing up an agreement, and advancing symbolic reconciliation by having the opposing parties shake hands. Examples of successful mediation process are recalled and reconstructed.

This program is both realistic and allegorical. In both cases, accounting for context and praxis would have enriched the text. At the micro-social level, we are left to speculate about the nature of the experience, learning, and meaning for heart councilors, the school as a collective entity, as well as for pupils whose conflicts were mediated by the councilors. At the macro-social level, viewers are left to reflect on the obvious allegorical nature of the report, which could be a form of problematizing their macro-socio-political situation: If this can be accomplished in San Jose High School in Bogotá, why can't it take place throughout the country?

In contrast, the overt aim of an episode of *School for Human Rights* (Colombia, PJ 2004) was to advance viewers' praxis by problematizing the assumed-to-be-normal, violent nature of Colombian society. Yet, it did so with limited agency and under-developed discussion of the CR process in Colombia. This film presents the discussion by a group of Bogotá teens gathered in a TV studio to discuss the question "Are Colombians violent by nature?" In praxis-like manner, the investigation recorded involved viewing and discussing three films that present interviews with residents who retell the history of their village and recall their own experiences. Violence dominates the history of two villages, but a third – with a similar agricultural and economic basis to the other two – has managed to keep violence out of their community. The comparison of the histories of these villages leads participants to speculate that while Colombians are not violent by nature, in some cases they have allowed fear of military operations and drug-related affairs to dominate their lives, "so that we are violent when violence affects us." However, the dominant reactions were doubt, confusion, and desire to continue such investigations. Our recommendation would be to have included in the praxis process a broader contextualization that would also include investigation of not just the violent versus a-violent dichotomy, but rather evidence towards the full CR process in Colombia.

We conclude these brief analyses with evidence from a full-length documentary, *Little Peace of Mine* (Israel, PJ 2006). Nadav, a 13-year-old Israeli, seeks to establish a children's peace movement – 'Peace for the Future', whose goal is to bring the peace between Israelis and Palestinians that adults failed to achieve. The film presents segments that document Nadav's efforts over the space of a year to advance the "movement", and begins with his problematizing the situation, following a suicide bomb attack on a bus. Nadav and his friends advance their peace initiative by proclaiming their aim – "to recruit thousands of Israelis and Palestinians" – at a peace rally, publicizing their intentions on a contemporary affairs program, and soliciting assistance from Israeli politicians in recruiting Palestinian children.

Picture 3. Mai and Nadav engage in a discussion over politics – Screenshot from *Little Peace of Mine*

© Prix Jeunesse International

The conflicts and difficulties that emerge in advancing this initiative surprise and "paralyze" Nadav. Yet, these micro-conflicts are understandable because they reproduce extant conflicts between Israelis and Palestinians as well as within the Israeli community. Nadav's situation occurs, we submit, because his actions are unaccompanied by praxis and understanding CR processes. For example, two conflicting approaches are used when Nadav and his compatriots meet with six Palestinian youth: The Israelis want to meet the Palestinians on the human level, while the Palestinians want to talk about oppression (i.e., politics). Thus, Mai (14), a Palestinian, introduces herself by sharing photos documenting what happens to Palestinians at Israeli roadblocks when coming to Jerusalem to attend their meetings. Later, in a segment from Nadav's self-recorded video diary, he reflects on the impact of the "shocking" details shared by Mai and shares his newfound empathy with the Palestinian experience: "Today I realized what it means to be a Palestinian. Now I can understand their anger, their frustration. To be honest, if I was a Palestinian maybe I'd be throwing stones, out of frustration, helplessness. That's how I'd feel if I was Palestinian." Yet, had Nadav undertaken praxis and CR-guided preparations, he would have investigated and begun to understand how Palestinians view and experience the conflict. Had he done so, perhaps he would not have been surprised by learning about the roadblocks, which are iconic for Palestinians, and questioned why he had not learned about this important Israeli policy from mainstream media or in school?

Later Mai and Nadav engage in heated political discussions that reproduce familiar arguments used by leaders from both sides. Immediately after, an inner group conflict erupts between Nadav and his Israeli peace compatriots, who argue from the naive, mythic view of peace: "you get too deep into politics, talking about bombs and terrorists" ... "you should talk about ways to achieve peace. You should talk about the movement..." Perhaps Nadav does not respond to their claims, because he does not understand the process he initiated? Actually, there was no "next time," because other events – the opposition to the Wall Israel was building, continued terrorist attacks, and other obligations – left only Nadav and Mai to meet, which they did on a number of occasions, as friends.

As an agent of social change, Nadav demonstrates many characteristics of the activist-leader ethos (e.g. passion, leadership, infallible optimism, and recognition of the first steps needed to advance social change). However, under-developed praxis limited his genuinely sincere efforts (e.g. his lack of understanding about the realities of the lives of the Palestinians; failure to question the roles of the Israeli government and military; limited understanding of CR, inter-group processes, and his friends' needs). Yet, meeting Mai enabled him to begin to understand his partner's perspective on the conflict, so that further reflection and investigation might have enabled him to attain a deeper understanding of the nature of the conflict, the persons involved, as well as where to intervene in order to advance both CR and change processes.

A critical discussion by students viewing such a film who understand the three processes analyzed in this article might argue that consciously pursuing praxis might have led Nadav, first, to question his fragmented, ideological understanding;[20] second, to engage in critical reflection that might have led him to re-directing change efforts to confront the school curricula, media, and other multiple manifestations of militarism that infuse Israeli culture;[21] and, third, to abandon the juxtaposition of war versus peace, in favor of the CR paradigm as a way to understand and work within the complex process of managing deeply held differences of opinion and interests.

Discussion

Two of the main issues underlying the focused study reported here are concerned with the nature of scriptwriters' understanding of social change and potential viewer learning about social processes and social change from the programs analyzed.

Scriptwriters

Based on this limited sample, these scriptwriters' interest in social change seemed to differ by genre: Youth were portrayed acting on macro-social issues in micro-social settings in all the fiction programs (e.g. child rights, deafness, healthy eating, CR, and one docu-drama – a girl's rights to education). In contrast, three non-fiction programs and three (of four) docu-dramas portrayed youth acting to advance change within a war context; more specifically, five took place during the confrontation phase. This war-orientation and locus within one CR phase is similar to the adult news format. Yet, three non-fiction, multi-phase programs – *People Power II, Fatma,* and *With No ID* – are evidence that other topics and formats are possible; a matter worth investigating in the full research study.

In answer to our primary research question, our analyses of the 14 program corpus found that the social processes of agency, praxis, and conflict resolution were among the primary structures used by scriptwriters in their portrayal of social change. An interesting question in this regard is how scriptwriters understand such structures? This is a matter of utmost importance, indeed one of our central tasks in working with producers in our full action-research study.

In regard to scriptwriter portrayal of social change-oriented agency, characters take their stand and initiate social change in micro- and macro-situations. Some start off initiating change in their everyday lives, linked to macro-social issues (*My life as a Popat, With no ID*). Other characters start with macro-issues and experience individual growth (e.g. *Little Peace of Mine*). Some characters grow during these processes (four out of the ten individual characters, e.g. Zoe from *Off Limits: Strong Language,* Nadav from *Little Peace of Mine*), while other characters do not change. Furthermore, character portrayal is constructed in different ways; be it through sharing the main characters' views, reflections, feelings, and tactics (praxis) that develop in approaching the conflict (e.g. in the fictional film *Hungry* or the series *Sweet World,* in the docu-drama *Fatma,* or in the documentary *School for Human Rights*) and/or be via CR (e.g. *Off Limits: Strong Language, My life as a Popat, People Power II, With No ID*). None, fully met all of the criteria for presenting social processes that we established for a well-developed script.

Finally, only the "well-developed" programs approached use of all four, basic characteristics of the CR process. Hence, in half of these programs, viewers would have to infer the nature of the conflict and/or be very familiar with the context in order to understand the core conflict and the parties' differing positions. In this regard, the distinction between the cyclical and linear CR models is useful. In the five well-developed programs and one fiction program, *My life as a Popat,* the Cyclical CR Model is used to structure the script and there is clarity about the nature of the conflict, the parties differing positions, as well as richer accounts of the CR process. In contrast, when the conventional three-stage, linear model is applied, similar to Field's "character arc", (see footnote 16) the conflict is less clearly defined, differing positions are not always clear, the resolution process is abbreviated or is a located in one phase. While this may serve the needs for creating drama, we submit that it may limit viewers' learning about social issues and processes, including CR. On the other hand, in all fairness, understanding – indeed even perceiving – the three processes in the well-developed programs (e.g. *People Power II* or *My life as a Popat*) would require previous experience learning about these processes, as might be obtained in a media literacy program, or viewing guided by an older co-viewer capable of pointing out these structures.

All in all, the media portrayals could be richer and more balanced in terms of both the issues addressed as well as more inclusion of the three processes: Either, we gain insight into the praxis of the main character as a social agent involved in CR without seeing the CR phases, contextualization, variety of options of the CR process (e.g. *Little Peace of Mine*, *Devils of the Magosa Tree*); or, CR is presented in a rich manner but the main character remains one-dimensional (e.g. *My life as a Popat, Sweet World, Fatma, U: South Africa*).

Edu-tainment

Generally, in relation to the edu-tainment perspective and the two key edu-tainment learning domains – character portrayal and plot – we found that the three processes infuse and drive plot and character structures in the well-developed programs so that viewers might well learn from, as well as enjoy, vicariously, the nature of the lived-experience of involvement in social change. More specifically, what might viewers learn from the character's experiences? Here, fictional programs seem to have an advantage, because they portray praxis; the inner, *backstage* world of the character's feelings, insights, and tactics that guide the character's actions. Following Bandura's (2004) re-visited assessment of differential learning from modeling by characters, it would be useful to distinguish between positive, negative, and transitional models. Bandura found that viewers seem to be attracted to, draw inspiration from, and to identify with transformative models similar to them and their own life circumstances, especially when the characters succeed in bettering their lives. In our study, four of the ten programs featuring a teenage "individual agent" portrayed transitional characters alongside "good" characters.[22] In this regard we suspect that one advantage of a series versus single programs is that viewer learning – including understanding processes – will be reinforced as the series unfolds.

As the research proceeds, we feel that developing a fuller corpus, audience studies, and interviews with scriptwriters should enable us to probe the postulates, findings, and questions raised in this focused study that will enable us to illuminate what teenagers actually learn about agency, praxis and conflict resolution, in short about social change, from these TV portrayals.

Final word about agency

The importance of agency advanced through praxis as well as CR should not be taken for granted or underestimated: Taking a stand and advancing agency involves transcendence; that is, the use of free will to choose to act in order to advance change, often when others accept situations as unproblematic or they are unwilling to act to confront problems in everyday social life. According to Jean-Paul Sartre (1946), such transcendence is the key to *humanitas*, to being an authentic human being. "Man is nothing else but what he makes of himself" (1946: 349), "…there is no reality except in action." (1946: 358), "When we say that man chooses himself, we do mean that every one of us must choose himself; but by that we also mean that in choosing for himself he chooses for all men." (1946: 350) Paulo Freire shared a similar sentiment: "Humans … are beings of 'praxis:' of action and of reflection. Humans find themselves marked by the results of their own actions in their relations with the world, and through action in it. By acting they transform; by transforming they create a reality which conditions their manner of acting." (Freire 1982: 102) Thus, in terms of *deep* democracy, enabling young viewers the opportunity to view models of peers engaging in social change and granting access to their thinking, emotions, tactical planning, as well as their actions, may well have significant implications for advancing their own understanding, and perhaps ignite or advance interest in their own pro-active involvement in civic life.

> She doesn't want to play all the time, she wants to talk. So do you mind if we miss the language game? Because if not, she'll leave the Movement. She doesn't want just to make chocolate balls.
>
> Nadav speaking to his Israeli compatriot, Shai, in *Little Peace of Mine*

Notes

1. The term "social change" is used here in a non-normative manner to refer to changes, ultimatively, of social structures via alternative institutional functioning and practices advanced by individuals participating, usually in collective actions. Accordingly, developing individuals' awareness, attitudes, knowledge, and understandings is a necessary but insufficient condition for social change, in and of itself.
2. See Lemish, D. (2007), Chapter 6, for a review of media literacy approaches.
3. The goal of this action research project is to offer recommendations to producers of media for children who seek to address and to enable viewers to understand complex social processes, such as conflict resolution. To do so, we are engaged in four projects: 1) Text analyses in four

Acknowledgements

The authors thank Dafna Lemish and the volume's editors for their very useful feedback on earlier versions of this article; and Maya Götz, head of the Prix Jeunesse International Festival and of Internationales Zentralinstitut für das Jugend- und Bildungsfernsehen beim Bayerischen Rundfunk (IZI), for support of this project.

genres: fiction, docu-drama, non-fiction, and news; 2) Producer's studies; 3) Cross-cultural reception studies; and 4) Prix Jeunesse suitcase workshops conducted with producers, to date in 9 countries.

4. Meeting biannually for over 40 years, the Prix Jeunesse International Festival has been a venue to explore and to celebrate the highest quality TV programs aimed for viewing by 2- to 15+ year-olds.
5. The core of the corpus used in this study consists of selected non-fiction films that portray conflict resolution processes. As a pilot, fiction and docu-dramas were added using a random sample technique in which every fourth film was examined for the presence of conflict resolution. Neither agency nor praxis were criteria applied in compiling this initial corpus.
6. See Appendix 1 for production details and analyses of each film presented.
7. Countries represented in select corpus of this study: Colombia (2), Egypt, Great Britain (2), The Netherlands, Iran, Israel, Jordan, Macedonia, Norway-South Africa, Palestinian Authority, Philippines, Sri Lanka.
8. If so, what remains an open question is how to structure plots and character behaviors in order to advance learning about social processes in a media text? Reception studies that we are undertaking in our full action-research project could clarify how youth viewers understand the social change processes portrayed in these texts. Again, our caveat limits the claims to be made of our analysis to assessments of resources available to youth and their educators.
9. See, for example, Adler, Adler and Fontana (1987); Bayne (2008); de Certeau (1984); Garfinkel (1967); Goffman (1959, 1967); Heller (1984).
10. "Human competency requires not only skills, but also self-belief in one's capabilities to use those skills well. Modeling influences must, therefore, be designed to build self-efficacy as well as to convey knowledge and rules of behavior." (Bandura 2001: 144)
11. The discussion of praxis builds upon the writings of Au (2007), Bernstein (1971); Fay (1977); Freire (1970, 1973, 1985); Lemish (1997, 2003); Shor (1980); Shor and Freire (1987).
12. See, for example, Freire (1970, 1973, 1985); Shor and Freire (1987).
13. See Vago's specific discussion of the role of conflict in social change (1996: 19-25), as well as his review of how various social change theories conceptualize conflict.
14. Alson and Burnett (2003) as well as Folger, Poole and Stutman (2005) come closest to discussing the involvement of CR in micro-social situations though these are generally prescriptive monographs that include anecdotal discussions of the involvement of CR processes in the everyday life situations of individuals, groups or organizations, several of which could be considered social change endeavors. For additional prescriptive proposals related to CR that could be applied to social change situations, see for example, Bartos and Wehr (2002); Hammerich (2002); Mayer (2000).
15. See Lemish (2007) for extended presentation of the Cyclical CR Model as well as analyses of television programs for youth in which both the "linear" and the "cyclical" approaches are implemented as script structures.
16. This depiction of how conflict is an essential part of plot structure is similar to the "character arc" prescribed by Syd Field (1994) in a manual considered to be influential among Hollywood screenwriters.
17. Analyses of two of the 14 films were categorized as "indirect" accounts of youth involvement in social change: *The Basket* and *The Long Road Home*. They are not included in this presentation as doing so would require extended discussion of how allegorical texts can be involved in presenting social problems and change processes.
18. Five films out of our 14 film corpus: *People Power II* and an episode of *Our Neighborhood* (not presented here) are collective social change efforts; whereas, in *Hungry, Fatma,* and *Off Limits: Strong Language* individuals model strategies that can help advance social change. See Lemish (2007) for detailed analysis of *People Power II* and *Fatma*.
19. Seven films out of the 14 film corpus: *With No ID, School for Human Rights, Little Peace of Mine, Devils of the Magosa Tree, My Life as a Popat, Sweet World, U: South Africa*.
20. See Freire (1970), chapter 2.

21. See Lemish (2003) for the analysis of banking education in the civic education of Israelis; and Lemish (1997) for analysis of attempts to advance Freirian critical education in the midst of this process through use of film with Israeli youth.
22. "Transitional"/"good" characters: Nadav/Mai from *Little Peace of Mine*, Charlot/Maaike from *Hungry*, Beni/Karmen from *Our Neighborhood* , Zoe/Mark, Ben from *Off Limit: Strong Language*.

References

Adler, P.A., Adler, P. & Fontana, A. (1987) 'Everyday Life Sociology', *Annual Review of Sociology* 13: 217-235.

Alson, S. & Burnett, G. (2003) *Peace in Everyday Relationships*. Alameda, CA: Hunter House.

Aronson, L. (2000) *Scriptwriting Updated: New and Conventional Ways of Writing for the Screen*. New York, NY: Allen and Unwin.

Au, W. (2007) 'Epistemology of the Oppressed: The Dialectics of Paulo Freire's Theory of Knowledge', *Journal for Critical Education Policy Studies* 5(2). http://www.jceps.com/index.php?pageID=article&articleID=100

Augsburger, D. (1992) *Conflict Mediation Across Cultures*. Louisville, KY: Westminster Knox.

Bandura, A. (2001) 'Social Cognitive Theory of Mass Communication', in Bryant, J. & Zillman, D. (eds.) *Media Effects: Advances in Theory and Research*. 2nd ed. Hillsdale, NJ: Erlbaum.

Bandura, A. (2004) 'Social Cognitive Theory for Personal and Social Change by Enabling Media', in Singhal, A. et al. (eds.) *Entertainment-education and Social Change*. Mahwah, NJ: Lawrence Erlbaum.

Bandura, A. (2006) 'Adolescent Development from an Agentic Perspective', in Pajares, F. & Urdan, T. (eds.) *Self-efficacy Beliefs of Adolescents*. Greenwich, CT: Information Age.

Barber, B. (1984) *Strong Democracy: Participatory Politics for a New Age*. Berkeley, CA: University of California Press.

Bartos, O. & Wehr, P. (2002) *Using Conflict Theory*. Cambridge: Cambridge University Press.

Bayne, T. (2008) 'The Phenomenology of Agency', *Philosophical Compass* 3(1): 182-202.

Bernstein, R. (1971) *Praxis and Action: Contemporary Philosophies of Human Activity*. Philadelphia, PA: University of Pennsylvania Press.

Borshuk, C. (2004) 'An Interpretative Investigation into Motivations for Outgroup Activism', *The Qualitative Report* 9(2): 300-319.

Clarke, P.B. (1996) *Deep Citizenship*. London: Pluto.

Cowgill, L.J. (1999) *Secrets of Screenplay Structure: How to Recognize and Emulate the Structural Frameworks of Great Films*. New York, NY: Watson-Guptill.

Dancyger, K. & Rush, J. (2007) *Alternative Scriptwriting: Successfully Breaking the Rules*. Boston, MA: Focal.

De Certeau, M. (1984) *The Practice of Everyday life*. Transl. by S. Rendall. Berkeley, Los Angeles, CA: University of California Press.

Dewey, J. (1916) *Democracy and Education*. New York, NY: Macmillan.

Fay, B. (1977) 'How People Change Themselves: The Relationship between Critical Theory and its Audience', in Ball, T. (ed.) *Political Theory and Praxis: New Perspectives*. Minneapolis, Minn.: University of Minnesota Press.

Field, S. (1994) *Screenplay: The Foundations of Screenwriting*. New York, NY: Dell.

Folger, J., Poole, M., & Stutman, R. (2005) *Working through Conflict: Strategies for Relationships, Groups, and Organizations*. 5th ed. Boston; MA: Pearson, Allyn and Bacon.

Freire, P. (1970) *Pedagogy of the Oppressed*. New York, NY: Continuum.

Freire, P. (1973) *Education for Critical Consciousness*. New York, NY: Continuum.

Freire, P. (1985) *The Politics of Education*. South Hadley, MA: Bergin and Garvey.

Fry, D. (2006) The Human Potential for Peace: An Anthropological Challenge to Assumptions about war and violence. Oxford: Oxford University Press.

Garfinkel, H. (1967) *Studies in Ethnomethodology*. Englewood Cliffs, NJ: Prentice-Hall.
Goffman, E. (1959) *The Presentation of Self in Everyday Life*. New York, NY: Bantam-Doubleday.
Goffman, E. (1967) *Interaction Ritual*. New York, NY: Doubleday Anchor.
Goodman, S. (2003) *Teaching Youth Media: A Critical Guide to Literacy, Video Production and Social Change*. New York, NY: Teachers College.
Halpin, M. (2004) *It's Your World – If You don't Like It, Change It: Activism for Teenagers*. New York, NY: Simon Pulse.
Hammerich, E. (2002) *Meeting Conflicts Mindfully*. Dharmasala, Copenhagen: Tibetian Centre for Conflict Resolution and Danish Centre for Conflict Resolution.
Heller, A. (1984) *Everyday Life*. London: Routledge and Kegan Paul.
Hoose, P. (1999, 2002) *It's Our World, Too! Young People Who are Making a Difference: How they Do it and How You Can, Too!* New York, NY: Farrar, Straus and Giroux.
Hunt, D. & Sullivan, R. (1974) *Between Psychology and Education*. Hinsdale, Ill.: Dryden.
Lemish, D. (2007) *Children and Television: A Global Perspective*. Malden, MA: Blackwell.
Lemish, P. (1997) 'Exposing Indifference: Applying Films in Praxis Pedagogy with Teenagers in a Conflicted Society', *Radical Teacher* 50: 17-22.
Lemish, P. (2003) 'Civic and Citizenship Education in Israel', *Cambridge Review of Education* 33(1): 53-72.
Lemish, P. (2007) 'Developing Children's Understanding of Conflict Resolution Through Television', in Lemish, D. and Götz, M. (eds.) *Children and Media in Times of War and Conflict*. Cresskill, NJ: Hampton.
Lemish, P. & Schlote, E. (in progress) *Role of Children and Youth Television Programs in Developing an Understanding of Conflict Resolution*. Action-research Projected Conducted with the Support of IZI, Bavarian Broadcasting Corporation.
Lewis, B., Espeland, P., & Pernu, C. (1998) *The Kid's Guide to Social Action*. Minneapolis, MN: Free Spirit.
Lindlof, T.R. & Taylor, B.C. (2002) *Qualitative Communication Research Methods*. 2nd ed. Thousand Oaks, CA: Sage.
MacDonald, I. (2008) Re-thinking the Screenplay. Call for papers. www.leeds.ac.uk/ics (accessed 17 May 2008).
Mayer, B. (2000) *The Dynamics of Conflict Resolution: A Practioner's Guide to Clear Thinking*. San Francisco, CA: Jossey-Bass.
Rosenthal, A. (1995) *Writing Docu-drama: Dramatizing Reality for Film and TV*. Boston, MA: Focal.
Sartre, J.-P. (1946, 1956) 'Existentialism is a Humanism', in Kaufman, W. (ed.) *Existentialism from Dostoyevsky to Sartre*. New York, NY World.
Shor, I. & Freire, P. (1987) *A Pedagogy for Liberation*. South Hadley, MA: Bergin and Garvey.
Singhal, A. & Rogers, E.M. (1999) *Entertainment-education: A Communication Strategy for Social Change*. Mahwah, NJ: Lawrence Erlbaum.
Singhal, A., Cody, M.J., Rogers, E.M. & Sabido, M. (eds.) (2004) *Entertainment-Education and Social Change: History, Research, and Practice*. Mahwah, NJ: Lawrence Erlbaum.
Sood, S., Menard, T. & Witte, K. (2004) 'The Theory behind Entertainment-Education', in Singhal, A. et al. (eds.) *Entertainment-education and Social Change*. Mahwah, NJ: Lawrence Erlbaum.
Thomas, J. (1999) *Script Analysis for Actors, Directors, and Designers*. Boston, MA: Focal.
Tufte, T. (2003) 'Entertainment in HIV/AIDS Communication: Beyond Marketing, Towards Empowerment', in Feilitzen, C. v. & Carlsson, U. (eds.) *Promote or Protect? Perspectives on Media Literacy and Media Regulations*. Göteborg University: Nordicom.
Vago, S. (1996) *Social Change*. 3rd ed. Upper Saddle River, NJ: Prentice Hall.

Appendix: Corpus of media portrayals youth involved in social change in TV programs for children (PJ – Prix Jeunesse International)

	Program title Director, Production Co.	Country Year	Genre Audience Age Duration	Agency Individual/Group	Conflict Phases Single / Multiple	Conflict presented Both sides views	Praxis
1	*The Long Road to School* A. Abu Asi; Jordan Radio & TV Corp.	Jordan PJ 2004	Docu-drama 7-11 15 min.	Individual	Confrontation	No No	Allegory: Sarah [Palestinians] averts Israeli roadblocks preventing her from performing school concert (surviving).
2	*Devils of the Magosa Tree* A. Abeynayake; Cineli	Sri Lanka PJ 2000	Docu-drama 11-15 24 min.	Individual	Confronation	No No	Jajathu, a war orphan, demonstrates that survival, too, can advance social change.
3	*Fatma* H. Mady; Egyptian radio & TV Union	Egypt PJ 2006	Docu-drama 7-11 15 min.	Individual	Multiple	Yes Yes	Fatma demands-achieves permission from father to attend school; struggles to implement agreement.
4	*Hungry* A. van Duren; VPRO Television	Netherlands PJ 1998	Fiction 7-12 15 min.	Individual	Multiple	Yes Yes	Maaike uses rights view to oppose autocratic uncle; serves as model for cousin, Charlot.
5	*Little Peace of Mine* E. Avneri; Eden Productions	Israel PJ 2006	Non-Fiction 12-15 56 min.	Individual > Group	Confrontation (Multiple)	Yes Yes	Nadav initiates & assesses actions to establish peace movement; is educated to activism & conflict by Mai.
6	*Off Limits: ep. Strong Language* C. Ware; Resource Base Production	Great Britain PJ 2000	Fiction 6-15 30 min.	Individual	Multiple	Yes Yes	Zoe learns to be independent & to educate her school peers about being deaf.
7	*Our Neighborhood: ep. Dime's Party* D. Kasapi; Common Ground Productions	Macedonia PJ 2000	Fiction 7-12 25 min.	Individual	Multiple	Yes Yes	Attempts by Albanian father to prevent son from attending multi-ethnic party are opposed successfully.
8	*People Power II : Ruled by Kids!* M. Mosura & D.-T. Tolentino; Probe Productions	Philippines PJ 2002	Non-fiction 11-15 20 min.	Group	Multiple	Yes Yes	Reconstructs successful deposition of Philippine president, and youth role in movement.
9	*My Life as a Popat: ep. Health is Wealth* B. Richards; Feelgood Fiction	Great Britain PJ 2006	Fiction 8-12 22 min.	Individual	Multiple	Yes Yes	Anand obtains trial period to convince family to eat a healthy diet & has difficulty implementing agreement
10	*School for Human Rights* C. Garcia; Cituma, Ocho y medios comunicaciones	Colombia PJ 2004	Non-fiction 12-15 25 min.	Group	Confrontation	Yes Yes	Investigation: Are Colombians violent by nature? Participants share views in the discussions.
11	*The Basket* L. Sayegh, G. Khlifeh; Al-Quds Educational TV	Palestine PJ 2006	Docu-drama 7-11 14 min.	Individual	Confrontation	No No	Allegory; Sarah [Palestinians] "speaks" through music & helps her brother emerge from trauma.
12	*The Sweet World: ep. Scent of Rice* B. Baghaie; IRIB TV Channel One	Iran PJ 2000	Fiction 11-15 19 min.	Individual	Multiple	Yes Yes	Shirin writes in her diary about using CR to resolve her parents' relationship problems.
13	*U – South Africa* K. Fürst; NRK	Norway & South Africa PJ 1996	Non-fiction 12-17 30 min.	Individual	Implementation	Yes Yes	Young adults discuss changes & difficulties in adjusting to the New South Africa.
14	*With No Id-magazine* M. Baquero; Sin Cédula	Colombia PJ 2004	Non-fiction 9-13 8 min.	Group	Mediation	–	Pupils (& staff) establish peer mediation program in Bogotá school.

Contesting Norms on China's Internet?
The Party-state, Youth, and Social Change

Johan Lagerkvist

Abstract

Young citizens' creativity, innovation and experimentation with self-expression and identity is making huge strides in China, a country that according to many observers has the world's most sophisticated Internet censorship regime. How is this possible? Are all the human resources devoted to maintaining and instilling censorship among young bloggers and journalists ineffective? And are young Chinese users undermining the central government's legitimacy by their online behavior, or, are they largely supportive of government policy, as witnessed in the aftermath of the riots in Tibet's capital Lhasa in March 2008?

This chapter addresses these questions and attempts to shed new light to understand the above paradox. It is argued that this paradox can be explained by on the one hand the continuous drive for searching and performing both personal and political identities online among various youth groups, while on the other hand many Internet users still wish the party-state to control the Internet. It is also argued that coexistence and contestation of norms do not stop ongoing social change among China's youth and teenagers, but that state policies toward the Internet slow it down.

The Chinese people seem to be way ahead of Americans in living a digital life[1]

China's Internet and research questions

As the above statement, given by the American media giant InterActiveCorp (IAC)'s Chairman and CEO Barry Diller when he cited a recent study speaking to students at Peking University shows, Chinese have not just overtaken Americans in sheer numbers of Internet users. Young Chinese are even becoming more apt than US teenagers at experimenting and using the Internet in new ways. Looking at Chinese youth behavior and speech acts online, is like having a pigeon hole through which not only a picture of the future global Internet takes form, but also a more pluralized China of tomorrow emerges. This observation, however, presents researchers with a paradox: citizen creativity, innovation and experimentation with self-expression and identity is making huge strides in an authoritarian country often said to perform the "most sophisticated Internet censorship regime in the world" (Zittrain and Edelman 2005), maintaining "the great firewall of China" by way of its multi-billion dollar "Golden Shield project". How is this possible? Is the technological great firewall a misleading metaphor (Tsui 2008), and all the human resources devoted to maintaining and instilling censorship among young bloggers and journalists ineffective, only seemingly presenting us with the above paradox? Are, for example, young Chinese users undermining the central government's legitimacy by their online behavior, or, are they largely supportive of government policy, as witnessed in the aftermath of the riots in Tibet's capital Lhasa in March 2008?

This chapter attempts to address and understand this paradox. The focus is on the formation and contestation of legal norms regarding managing, influencing and controlling online public opinion especially in relation to the vibrant Chinese blogosphere, populated and operated predominantly by young Chinese. Thereby, a better understanding of the context of various contested norms may be achieved. According to the China Internet Network Information Center (CNNIC), as of January 2009, the Chinese networks that are currently accessing the global Internet are hosts to 2.878 million web sites and 298 million users.[2] As of July 2009, China's Internet had increased to 338 million users.[3] In fact, it was already in July 2008 that China overtook the United States as the country with the biggest Internet population in the world, having as many as 162 million blogs on Chinese networks. This, however, does not mean that 162 million people actually write blogs every day. One person may have many blogs, some of which are not active. What is clear though, is that the Chinese blogosphere has grown tremendously since China's first blogging service started in 2002. The number of Internet users under the age of 30 has reached 204 million, accounting for as much as 68.4 percent of all Internet users in China. A significant comparison shows that "netizens" above the age of fifty only amount to 5.7 percent of China's Internet population.[4] As these staggering numbers make clear, Internet use in China is very much a youth phenomenon. And it is dynamic too: thirty-three percent of these young Chinese, mainly urban male professionals, regularly update their blogs within six months.[5]

The social and normative context of the Chinese blogosphere

It is important to understand that the formation of norms in society is shaped differently in democracies than in authoritarian ruled countries, as the existing popular norms are oftentimes more easily engineered in the latter. But without a spark of underlying support, compliance and implementation of rules may get seriously hampered – also in an authoritarian setting. The social and

Youth using the Internet in the Xuhui city, district of Shanghai. *Photo:* Johan Lagerkvist

normative context in which the legal measures and political provisions, issued by the central government, regulate and control the Internet industry in China are what determines behavior on the Internet and in the Chinese blogosphere. These measures are never issued in a social vacuum as there always are societal norms which the legal norms will compete with or complement in one way or another. Legal provisions cannot be expected to have any sustainable effect, if they do not correspond to these existing norms. It is the overlapping sphere where agencies of the state, youth and business on the normative level partake in shaping public opinion vis-à-vis rules and regulations targeting an Internet industry that invariably produces content deemed either "unhealthy" by the authorities *and* society, or perfectly "normal" or "modern" by groups in society, especially teenagers or people between the age of twenty and thirty.

In the overall context of challenges for implementing internet regulations, especially on the regional and local levels, it is important to note how provisions targeting behavior that compound activity in the online virtual world with presence in the physical world have been most effective. This is evidenced by the fact that Internet café regulations are among the few laws that have been most efficiently implemented of any Chinese rules and regulations in recent years. At least in the bigger cities, the laws targeting net cafés are exceptions to conventional wisdom about problems of law implementation in China (Lagerkvist 2008). In the case of the Internet café industry, the implementation of one specific regulation, following a tragic fire in an Internet café in May 2002, proved to be fairly easy since one very strong driving force for harsher regulation came from the parents of children spending much time in the net cafés. Thus the net café regulations, particularly the one implemented after the arson corresponded well with "Main Street" and majority views on the matter. Not much protest from either owners of net cafés or Chinese youth followed the implementation, as the pretext for the overhaul of the industry structure and squeezing out many independent operators out of the market was ostensibly about non-partisan security issues.

Internet café in the Xuhui city, district of Shanghai. *Photo:* Johan Lagerkvist

The Chinese blogosphere and the emergence of young citizen journalism

Is the Chinese blogosphere representative of Chinese society at large? Not for the time being, as the typical Internet user in China is most likely a young student, or a young man holding a job as a teacher or a white-collar worker with a high income. Thus, the content of their blogging activities is related to the lifestyle and worldview of these particular users (Hsu and Lin 2008).

The content found in the blogosphere of the People's Republic of China at large, is certainly an avant-garde representation of the enormous social changes related to identity and world outlook underway in Chinese society. As Internet applications and activities are considered cool by China's youth, many young people feel that they must relate to what's happening online (Fallows 2008). In China, it was the young journalist Mu Zimei's blog and the online cultural debates that centered on celebrity bloggers Mu Zimei in 2004 and sister Fu Rong in 2005 that made blogging popular among the urban young, as well as a focal point for the party-state's regulatory agencies set to weed out "unhealthy content" on the Internet (Farrer 2005). If the blogosphere started out as an arena for exploring and discussing identity, it has increasingly diversified into an effective platform from where demands of accountability from power holders are made. There have been numerous recent demonstrations of the emerging power of the Internet, ranging from exposés of corruption to a web campaign that led to the freeing of hundreds of children and mentally handicapped men who had been kidnapped and forced to work as slaves in brick kilns to the relocation of a chemical plant away from the port city of Xiamen. The *fenqing*, so called "angry youth" users also reacted strongly to the case of "the Beijing boy", a high-school student who, as shown on a video-clip on YouTube in March 2007, abused his elderly teacher badly in his school in the Haidian district of Beijing.[6]

Increasingly, though few in relative numbers compared to bloggers writing about entertainment, sports and celebrities, rights-conscious political bloggers demand accountability of power holders on behalf of non-Internet users as they want more space for individual freedom. These politically inclined young Chinese bloggers, however, would seldom use or borrow terms from Western liberalism to advance their interests or the cause of the disenfranchised in Chinese society. This fact notwithstanding, the mentality which permeates many bloggers' writing amounts to a belief in individualism. Many seem to believe, or want to believe, that armed with a laptop and broadband access you can change society, China and the world on your own. Paradoxically, at the same time these young individualists of the "me"-generation, many of them growing up without siblings due to China's one-child policy, only exert concrete influence on society and have tangible political effects on rights development or a foreign policy issue when they act in concert together with other bloggers for a cause, about an issue that stirs emotions and sentiments among a collective of people.

One illustrative case was the nationalistic anti-CNN movement that swept China after CNN's "slanderous and false reporting" about China's crackdown on Tibetan protests in Lhasa in March 2008 aggrieved many Chinese. But it was mainly the young that rallied and organized street protests and set up nationalistic websites such as "Anti-CNN" on China's Internet networks. According to some observers of the Chinese blogosphere, there is also among Chinese bloggers a tendency to disregard traditional culture and beliefs.[7] Thus the political belief in collectivism in Chinese society, either originating from the Chinese version of communism in the 1950s or 1960s, or the Confucian principles of collectivism and hierarchy preceding Mao Zedong is out of fashion among the young bloggers, who paradoxically also functions as a well-knit community nevertheless, especially when what is perceived as slights against China provokes nationalistic sentiments.

According to some researchers the Chinese state increasingly loses its ability to influence young Chinese people's minds (Marolt 2008). While this may be true for a long-term perspective, this observation is not an entirely accurate description of the contemporary scene. In several annual studies conducted by the Chinese Academy of Social Sciences it is evident how both users and non-users strongly believe that the Internet should be heavily regulated, with a particular strong increase in 2006 (Guo 2007). According to the survey, women are more prone to agree that control of the Internet is necessary, while there is no significant difference between different age groups. As many as 83.5 percent of informants in a 2007 study by the Chinese Academy of Social Sciences were of the opinion that Internet management and control was "very necessary" or "necessary" (Guo 2007: 10). As many as 44 percent agreed though that political content should be controlled: a significant increase from the mere 5 percent who thought so in 2005. And 30 percent of respondents believed that online chatting in chat forums should be controlled. The reason for this is probably due to many negative reports about Internet fraud, addiction to online gaming, and "disorder in the cyber world", which according to Chinese officials is due to the anonymity of blogs (Li 2007). Thus, it is obvious that government efforts to reign in what they see as a disorderly and disruptive online world do not ring hollow in the ears of Chinese Internet users.

Regarding the issue of censorship in China's blogosphere; while outright political censorship from the authorities, such as closing down a blog or deleting posts are rare on a large scale, is unlikely to be as ubiquitous as one is often led to believe by Western media reports,[8] self-control and self-censorship exist to a degree. The predominant reason for this is probably the adaptive behavior of users, who may use outspoken political language, but with caution for using the names of top politicians or heavy direct criticism of the Communist Party in order to avoid being censored. Thus, there is a form of self-censorship appropriated by bloggers who have to shift to other tactics to get their message across. Young people in the blogosphere who, for example, want to address social and political ills often take the opportunity presented by big social and media events such as the cover-up by state authorities during the SARS health crises of 2003,[9] the use of child labor in brick-kiln in Shaanxi province in 2007 (French 2007), and the deadly scandal with melamine contaminated milk in 2008. Amid all the grief and criticism, many Internet users made satirical jokes about both Chinese officials and state-owned businesses. These well-known cases and events are welcome opportunities to criticize social phenomena and officialdom, as the huge numbers of other *fenqing* users give each individual some sense of protection. It should be mentioned that the term angry youth often refer to young nationalists who more than young rights activists have the leeway to use overt ideological language or strong political rhetoric. In general, young Internet commentators' verbal actions directed at corrupt local officials and businesses, indirectly point to underlying criticism of the political system and its institutions.

On the user side, it is possible to differentiate three kinds of self-censorship on China's Internet. As this is a process of socialization into established practices which takes time and is the result of negotiation between different norms in society, it can be expected that teenagers are less aware of sociopolitical boundaries than people in their twenties and thirties are. Nevertheless, I believe the following distinction hold also for most young people. The first kind exhibits a conscious, resigned acceptance, as occasionally seen when young employees in the Chinese Internet industry say that because they don't want to get shut down, they shut down anything that could be offensive on their website. The second sort of self-censorship is full compliance and conscious acceptance of the status quo as exemplified by the manager of web portal Sina's local Shanghai branch: "Actually, we work very, very closely with the government, the propaganda department…we are not allowed to have our own correspondents; we are dependent on the government for news. It is a good way – saves cost also."[10] The third kind is the most interesting because it is quite complex: it is permeated with irony, and ambivalence that occasionally looks like resistance. Nonetheless, there is a contradiction to this approach – a contradiction between bloggers feeling like 'loners fighting battles on their own' while they still have appeal and impact by using coded and ironic language, being sarcastic etc. This can be illustrated by the blog of China's perhaps most influential intellectual blogger, the 41 year old Wang Xiaofeng, who is quite young for being a Chinese intellectual having considerable impact. His blog is called "Bu xu lianxiang", literally meaning, "You must not associate (this) with thinking."

In the same vein, Chinese intellectuals have mocked mainstream media tendencies and media organizations like China Central Television (CCTV) with "Anti-CCTV" and "Anti-wave" features on the web, but without being openly hostile or appearing critical against the existing political order and media system in place. One may wonder though what influence you have on politics if you are only very subtle. The party-state definitely influences, through ideotainment, i.e. the intermeshing of high-tech images and designs with subtle, and at times overt, ideological constructs, symbols, and nationalistically inclined messages of persuasion (Lagerkvist 2008: 123). But can ironic bloggers be influential, except when a media storm breaks out, caused by, for example, a food scandal?

Thus, it seems like the Chinese blogosphere is changing politics by way of shunning conspicuous political rhetoric and instead becomes a platform for concrete advocacy on social issues and social activism. While it is true that the majority of bloggers are not social activists, or that Internet users generally devote their time online to chatting and playing games, news of political scandals broken first on the Internet has meant that the Chinese blogosphere increasingly is turning into the main vehicle for Chinese citizens to demand accountability from corrupt, unfair and law-breaking authorities. This is not surprising as offline journalism and the court system have been dependent and controlled by the authorities according to proven and effective methods for decades.

The increasingly important interaction between young blogging and citizen journalists is a new and very important trend, which needs to be studied closer in the immediate future. One example is the twenty-eight year old former vegetable seller Zhou Shugang who became famous all over China with his blog *Zhou Shuguang's Golden Age*, when he made known the situation of the countryside losers sitting in the media shadow of China's economic miracle. At the height of its fame, Zhou, who proudly called himself Zola, had 20,000 readers per day. And in line with the original French literary writer and social activist bearing the name, he wanted to both accuse the authorities and inspire some of the country's 70 million other bloggers to join him. He traveled around China addressing social and political problems left unreported by traditional media, armed only with a USB-stick, a digital camera, a mobile phone and an email-address. Zhou also wanted to educate other young followers interested in setting up their own blogs, posting, taking digital photos and videos, using instant-messaging tools and websites like Flickr, Twitter and Skype (Elegant 2008).

Alongside the tremendous growth of the Chinese Internet and blogosphere, there are the party-state's various bureaucratic entities, which enforce the regulations that effectively serve to halt the ever-expanding space of online free speech. In accordance with the stated needs of the party-state to uphold social and political stability, the police across the country periodically react and crack down on any content created that is perceived to undermine the ruling Communist Party's hold on power. But proactive ideas and measures are also tried out in order to fall in line with China's President Hu Jintao's exhortation at a Politburo study meeting in January 2007 that the government should use advanced technologies to better guide public opinion on the Internet.[11] Thus, it comes as no surprise that provincial police units in the last two years have resorted to new tactics to influence public opinion in online forums, such as bulletin board systems (BBS), by way of using low-paid staff to counter "negative" opinions criticizing the state, the Communist Party or the police. Employed by the provincial governments of Jiangsu and Hunan provinces, these young propaganda recruits have been called *wu mao dang*, or "the 50 cent Party" as they besides their monthly wages are given 50 Chinese fen in payment for each "positive" counter-posting the make in an online forum. According to some estimates, though unconfirmed and hard to believe, these paid commentators amount to as many as 280,000 people nationwide. As China's Internet population is so dominated by youth, it follows naturally that the 50-cent Party members must be young and use youthful language when correcting or guiding their peers. These tactics were first tried out by Nanjing University officials, who in 2005 recruited a team of students who supervised their fellows as "web commentators" (Bandurski 2008). Taken together, these efforts by provincial governments to reign in online behavior and speech, which are deemed risky for political stability, echo the exhortations made by the central leadership under President Hu Jintao.

It is commonplace to argue that the continued hold on power by the communist party is dependent on economic growth and development (Fewsmith 1997: 478; Zhao 2001: 441). The implicit argument is that increased levels of welfare and decreasing levels of poverty "buy" trust and acquiescence from the public into tacit acceptance of the status quo. Along the lines of economic logic, there are those who argue that with an increase in post-materialist values, critical new and young generations of citizens will emerge as a mass phenomenon (Wang 2005: 156). In China, however, the regime-enhancing effect of economic development still dominates the regime-eroding effect.

Wang Zhengxu has ruled out arguments that persuasive propaganda, or whatever is left of strategies to convince people through news media, has any part in the regime-enhancing effect, and argues that achieving those aims will become even harder in the future. With a long time perspective there are indications that this forecast is feasible. First, time is likely to be on the side of young Internet users. Second, the Chinese government is moving away from the propaganda model, and the Party's dominant role is increasingly difficult to uphold (Lynch 1999, Latham 2000: 654 and Lee 1990: 3). Trying to measure effects of mass media propaganda, in its totality, however, is an extremely difficult task (Elllul 1965: 265). Therefore, it is too early to reject the role of propaganda, asserting that only economic growth generates political legitimacy. Although observers see the older propaganda model as losing its validity, this perspective neglects the emergence of a new framework of propaganda and information dissemination (Lagerkvist 2006; Brady 2007). Indeed, it makes little sense to seek the factors for democratic "delay" in rapid economic growth only. Despite the enormous growth of the Internet in China and the rise of alternative television programming, talk radio, and a growing plethora of popular magazines and newsweeklies, most ordinary citizens and journalists, including young Internet users, still conform to the hegemonic position and line of the Communist Party and government policies.

For the Leninist party-state, the most problematic phase for implementing Internet regulations is when the legal ideals of the law meet the normative realities of society. It is when the normative content from the policy-making top meets the undercurrent of existing norms in society that tensions are at their highest in the implementation process. For the legal milieu of China, it must also be added that although the personal freedom to cultivate one's own opinion and norms has increased significantly since the beginning of the 1990s, in the post-Mao era, political constraints and systemic conditions characterize China today. The party-state, given its control of the news media, still manages a hegemonic discourse on political change. Legal legitimacy is always dependent on the mainstream norm tacitly or actively supporting a law.

In the light of this dependency, have there then been any critical frictions between the "young" blogosphere and the "old" party-state bureaucracy and state-controlled media, i.e. when the normative content in the regulations targeting the Chinese blogosphere formulated from above met the undercurrent of existing norms in Chinese society? The answer is yes, as frictions have occurred both concerning proposals to outlaw anonymous blogging using pseudonyms, and several cases where young bloggers have cornered authorities and state media about false reporting. The Internet Society of China (ISC), which is an organization under the Ministry of Information Industry has long been pushing the envelope to make anonymous blogging illegal (MacCartney).[12] But ever since their zealous mission to control blogging got known, there was a huge outcry from Internet users about concerns of privacy and individual integrity. Thus, ISC had to back down and re-designed the law proposal into a "self-discipline code for blog services". The Secretary General of ISC, Huang Chengqing, had to state that "conditions are not yet mature for implementing real-name registration as we lack reliable technology for privacy protection and identity verification."[13]

One of the most highlighted cases in recent years concerned the initial cover-up of the reasons behind the death of a 16-year old school girl in Wengan County in Guizhou Province in July 2008 (Fewsmith 2008). The obvious reason for the

Chinese Party-State's worry is that comments from an army of sometimes unidentified bloggers, chat room postings, and sms-writing influence both domestic and foreign policy and has since 2001 been functioning as a sort of "popular tribunal" directed against social and political ills, contributing to the rise of online public opinion in China (Lagerkvist 2005). Part of the worries of China's communist party leaders is Chinese popular nationalism that is very strong among China's youth. The nationalist views among an increasingly well-educated and well-traveled young citizenry were especially evident in the anti-Japanese rallies in Shanghai and Beijing in 2005, which were organized by young students, the abovementioned "angry youth", using texting and chat room postings to mobilize. Xenophobic campaigning was also visible in the venting of anger by many young Chinese who angrily posted comments on the Internet about the social unrest in the Tibet Autonomous Region (TAR) in March 2008. Being able to watch, listen, and read only snippets of information about the killings and street protests in Lhasa in state controlled media, they verbally attacked the Dalai Lama, Tibetan separatists in exile, and a western world "afraid of China's rise."

Thus, in line with my discussion on norms in this article, it is reasonable to argue that the normative ideals, i.e. the party-state norm, in the legal drafts to ban anonymous blogging was complemented by another powerful norm in society, the "parental norm" of many non-Internet users. These two norms contested with what can be termed "the youth and subaltern norm (Lagerkvist 2008b)",[14] represented by individuals in the blogosphere wanting to protect both personal integrity online and seek redress to injustices in the physical world. Throughout China's fairly short Internet history, with commercial year zero beginning only in 1994, the sheer force of the more powerful norms has marginalized these weaker norms. I would argue that the Party-State's use of moral arguments of cultural regulation has in many cases created an opportunity for bureaucratic agencies to regulate Internet businesses in line with their own political objectives of political stability and economic interests. In other words, the moral concerns, effectively advanced by policy-maker's statements or Chinese intellectuals in traditional mass media, have many times served as an effective disguise for political interests and ideological concerns of the Chinese Communist Party. Therefore, an understanding of how mainstream norms in Chinese society interact with the rationale behind the governments policies in the age of globalization yields significant insights about the legitimacy of laws directed at the Internet industry in general, foreign invested or not, mass media organizations and private blogs. Moreover, big international Internet companies like Google, Yahoo and Microsoft also play a role in creating a normative understanding in society and legal legitimacy for Internet café regulations in China.[15] By not standing up for principles *not* to censor their customers, web logs, websites, or chat room postings, they make it easier for the government to mold public opinion in favor of establishing a controlled, "harmonious", and "healthy" Internet. This also shows how skilful the Chinese party-state has been in controlling and co-opting different parts of Chinese society in accordance with their interests to contain the dynamic Internet culture of China's youth. But this is proving to become exceedingly more difficult. The reason for that is an increasingly expanding young Chinese blogosphere in which people like the blogger Zola, and other young citizen journalists like him dig much deeper into social issues which expose an underlying problematique which leads to new popular awareness and probably, in the long run, less trust of the people in power.

The staying power of the communist party-state in the Internet age

When observing the growth of Internet use in dictatorships or in countries with authoritarian political systems, there was for a long time consensus among observers. The Internet and related communications technologies would surely become the nemesis of autocratic political practices around the world: technological determinism was during the 1990s the ruling paradigm.[16] Instead, in the first decade of the 21st century, countries like Saudi-Arabia, Singapore and China have proven these determinist observers wrong.

Notwithstanding the rise of a middle-class, and social protests among disenfranchised groups, such as students, peasants, and young migrant workers, surveys have shown that interpersonal trust, as well as trust in party and state institutions, is high in China despite the ban on independent social organizations and the existing undemocratic political system (Chan and Nesbitt-Larking 1995: 306; Chen, Zhong, and Hillard 1997: 60; *World Values Survey* 2000). The Chinese regime's ability to rehabilitate its legitimacy from the ebb point of the 1989 crushing of the Tiananmen square student and workers movement has puzzled many scholars. The authoritarian political system has proven "resilient" in upholding a political status quo, when general theories of authoritarian regimes, along with empirical impressions of the situation in China, might lead one to expect low levels of perceived legitimacy (Nathan 2003: 14). Observers point to restored legitimacy, such as high economic growth and the disappearance of socialist ideology, but fail to recognize the importance of nationalism as a crucial ideological component and re-engineered propaganda techniques designed to maintain legitimacy for the ruling Chinese Communist Party.

To understand China's authoritarian resilience in the context of rapid market reform, exponential growth of Internet use, and alternative information, I would argue that there is a need to appreciate the continued importance of both institutional legacies and gradual adaptation to socioeconomic realities. The corporatist model has been put into use to explain many aspects of the state – society relationship in China (Unger and Chan 1995: 29). It has been argued, though, that the Chinese state is more ambitious ideologically than many other corporatist authoritarian states (Yang 2004: 6). It is precisely this ambition and the use of a pragmatist-nationalist ideological framework, together with high-speed economic growth, that is the major reason why the Chinese party-state is able to maintain its grip over politics and the media system – and also many young middleclass people. It remains to be seen if the party-state will also be able to win over the hearts and minds of the increasingly individualistic Internet-savvy teenagers and young people of China in the future, as the country continues to open up to outside influences and global media flows.

One question of importance for future development and attempts at moral and cultural regulation by the Party-State is what happens when the first cohort of China's blogger generation grows up and becomes parents. Will perhaps cultural regulation of the Internet and blogs come more natural for them at that stage? It has been claimed that while external forces change Chinese culture fundamentally, earlier values do not disappear, as they shape the possible responses to incoming influence (Weller 1999: 138). The classical corporatist state recognizes the existence of independent societal interests; it merely wishes to manage the aggregation and articulation of these interests. In sharp contrast, though, the current ideology of the Communist Party entails no less than the monopolization of the articulation of societal interests. Therefore, the hegemonic position occupied by the Party in Chinese politics remains largely uncontested offline. There is more contestation between the party-state norm and the youth and subaltern norm online. As of yet though, the party-state still "holds the line" in the online world. A description of the institutional arrangements alone, however, is not enough to explain the ways that political and public discourse are shaped in order to defend the status quo of the political system.

It is important to distinguish between specific and diffuse regime support. Specific support has to do with how happy individuals are with concrete government policies. Diffuse support has to do with overall citizen satisfaction of their existing system of governance (Dimitrov 2008). Current research shows that while the Chinese are dissatisfied with the specific actions of local officials, there is still widespread diffuse support for the regime and the central leadership in Beijing. The poor have less social and political capital and thus often resort to violent protests in the countryside. Interestingly, it may therefore be probable to assume that the forces for change of the political status quo grow stronger in middle-poor and semi-educated areas rather than rich areas with higher living standards and relatively more freedom. Due to the arrival of new technology and commercial media, especially the young in poor areas know how much better their lives could be. Quite often, these discontent people vent their pent-up anger against local corrupt power holders. Many so called mass incidents in recent years, sparked by maltreatment of individual peasants, school girls, or migrant workers have involved tens of thousands of demonstrators. Many of these angry demonstrators do not always know the circumstances of a particular case, but they may use it as an opportunity to protest against the government since they are deeply frustrated by political mismanagement in the countryside (Fewsmith 2008). Young migrant workers have been apt at using their online communication skills for setting up blogs outlining motives and progress of workers strikes. One case concerned a huge strike involving 16,000 workers at a plant in Shenzhen in 2005.[17] Jack Linchuan Qiu has observed that these "information-have-less" have a significant potential to act as agents of social change as they are increasingly using low cost information and communication technology (2009: 13).

The winners on economic reform, on the other hand, are quite content with the status quo, while the ones who have lost out are starting to fight for their rights to equal opportunity – although – still inside the current political arrangements, not wanting regime change. But given a serious recession in China or even worse environmental degradation than what is currently experienced, demands for a more thorough overhaul of the system of governance may also emerge, as was reflected by the Tiananmen student demonstrations of 1989 which were brutally crushed by the People's Liberation Army taking orders from the Communist Party.

For many years local corruption, illegal taxes, land confiscation, and mistreatment of peasants and migrant workers have led to strikes, sit-ins and social unrest in the Chinese countryside and provincial cities. People have traveled to Beijing from the provinces to petition the central government about ongoing abuse in the provinces. If these grievances are not handled well, the hidden anger may be directed toward central leaders, who in recent years have taken more responsibility for overall social reform in the countryside. Still, this reform agenda is one reason explaining why the central government enjoys legitimacy despite the persisting democratic deficit in China.

It is, however, also important to note that increasing political participation in politics may come in ways acceptable to, and strategically allowed or initiated by, the Communist Party. For example; peasant demonstrations in the countryside, as well as young migrant worker protests and nationalistic student rallies in urban areas that are *not* brutally put down, can be seen as adaptations to changing economic and political realities. It can be viewed as introducing a safety valve to reduce pressure on the Party. These social protests are allowed as long as they remain within certain boundaries. Although it can be argued that the party-state dictates where lines are drawn, it is nevertheless the case that the realm of freedom has expanded as a result of ongoing social processes within these boundaries (Oi 2004: 274). In this sense, stability, continuity of control, and gradual change are achieved and tolerated by the party-state, while the citizenry has been allowed more public space than ever before to air its grievances through traditional media and on the Internet. And China's youth, in different forms, is a strong driving force; as either rich urban nationalists protesting against Japan and the west, or poor migrant workers and peasants protesting against local corrupt cadres in the countryside.

Conclusion

For the Chinese government, it is quite likely that a severe economic or social crisis in society may affect the balance of control in a negative way. Change is likely to come also when the Internet in China goes from being a preoccupation for elites to become a significant grassroots phenomenon for discontent groups like peasants and migrant workers. The current state of widespread social acceptance for Internet control may disappear and the state's costs for coercive control skyrocket to unacceptable levels for moderate officials and liberal reformists in the Party. Thus, the contestation of norms in the blogosphere and on the Internet has deep implications for how society and politics will be organized in a future China. Many cases in recent years show how grassroots' voices in the blogosphere and on bulletin board systems have revealed misconduct of local government officials and that these voices are increasingly transferred via the mass media having an impact on decision makers in Beijing seeking to expose improper behavior of local government. This phenomenon, however, must be balanced against the fact that that bureaucratic agencies like the Internet Society of China, the police force, and the propaganda units of the Communist Party are increasingly using methods to influence public opinion useful to reach their immediate objectives of social and political stability.

The contestation between different norms and interests in Chinese society is clearly visible in the wrangling over legal provisions and ideological tactics to control opinion and expression on China's Internet and in the blogosphere. Online freedom of expression is generally greater than in offline media outlets and the physical world. But – it is under pressure from the party-state norm that the youth and subaltern norm imports a regime of self-censorship that co-exists with young citizens activity and young journalist-bloggers exposing corruption and abuse of power in both cities and in rural areas. The paradox of a pluralizing and creative online world and youthful blogosphere existing with quite effective censorship policies and mechanisms and Internet regulations in the People's Republic of China can on the one hand be explained by the continuous drive for searching and performing both personal and political identities online among various youth groups: urban nationalistic elites, pleasure seeking hedonists, or disenfranchised rural teenagers. On the other hand, while many Internet users may want to address socio-political and foreign policy issues, they also believe, or are led by the Party-State to believe, that the Internet should also be controlled. It is reasonable to believe that this paradox and coexistence and contestation of norms do not stop ongoing social change among China's youth and teenagers, but the policies in place and the rationale behind it do, to some extent, slow it down.

Notes

1. IAC Chairman and CEO Barry Diller speaking to more than 350 Chinese students at Peking University, "America's Emobyte Deficit', The Economist, 27 November 2007, http://www.economist.com/daily/columns/businessview/displaystory.cfm?story_id=10201521, last accessed 2009-04-14
2. See Statistical Survey Report on the Internet Development in China, *China Internet Network Information Center* (CNNIC), January 2009. http://www.cnnic.cn/uploadfiles/pdf/2009/3/23/153540.pdf, last accessed 2009-04-14.
3. http://www.cnnic.com/html/Dir/2009/07/15/5637.htm, last accessed 2009-08-03.

4. Ibid.
5. Ibid.
6. The young blogger "Eric_z" argued in his blog that the incident "made all Chinese and China's educational system lose face", see http://blog.sina.com.cn/s/blog_4b6b012101000a7j.html, last accessed 2009-04-14.
7. Personal conversation with Hong Kong blogger and translator Roland Soong in Hong Kong, June 14 2008.
8. Some reports making headlines in Western media concerned when Microsoft's blogging service deleted some clients posting deemed to offensive to Chinese authorities. See "Microsoft Censors Its Blog Tool", available online "Microsoft Censors Its Blog Tool", available online available online, www.rsf.org/article.php3?id_article=14069, 2005, last accessed 2009-04-14.
9. SARS is the abbreviation for "Severe Acute Respiratory Syndrome." It is a respiratory disease in humans which is caused by the SARS coronavirus. It's first major epidemic outbreak occurred in China, between November 2002 and July 2003, with 8,096 known cases of the disease, and 774 deaths", see the World Health Organization's (WHO) summary, http://www.who.int/csr/sars/country/table2004_04_21/en/index.html, last accessed 2009-04-14.
10. Interview with manager of the private web portal Sina, interview in Shanghai, October 2003.
11. See "Hu urges better management of the Internet", *China Daily*, http://www.chinadaily.com.cn/china/2007-01/25/content_792065.htm, last accessed 2008-10-16.
12. See also "Oversight vs Privacy", *China Daily*, p.4, December 1, 2006.
13. "China's main blog service providers subscribe to self-discipline code", August 22, 2007, http://english.people.com.cn/90001/90778/6245199.html, last accessed 2009-04-14.
14. These subaltern voices who, in the debate on closing down many privately owned Internet cafés during 2002, argued on behalf of less powerful interests like small scale operators, low income groups unable to access the Internet from their homes, or Chinese youths in general. This weaker norm I call "the youth and subaltern norm" to be contrasted against the parental norm and the party-state norm.
15. See "Net giants lashed over the Great Firewall of China", *South China Morning Post*, October 6, 2006.
16. See for example "A declaration of independence in cyberspace" by John Perry Barlow, available at homes.eff.org/~barlow/Declaration-Final.html, last accessed 2009-04-14, and statement made by former US president Bill Clinton, arguing that China's leaders would not be able to control the Internet, available online, www.usembassy-china.org.cn/press/release/2000/clinton38.html, last accessed 2009-04-14.
17. See "Thanks everyone: will found a trade union in July", ("Xiexie dajia guanxin: jiang zai 7 yue chengli gonghui"), http://unidenppl.blogcn.com/index.shtml, last accessed 2008-10-16.

References

Bandurski, D. (2008) 'China's Guerilla War for the Web', *The Far Eastern Economic Review*, July 2008, http://www.feer.com/essays/2008/august/chinas-guerrilla-war-for-the-web?

Brady, A-M. (2008) *Marketing Dictatorship: Propaganda and Thought Work in Contemporary China*, Lanham, MD: Rowman and Littlefield.

Chan, A.L. & Nesbitt-Larking, P. (1995) 'Critical Citizenship and Civil Society in Contemporary China', *Canadian Journal of Political Science*, 28(1995)2: 293-309.

Chen, J., Zhong, Y., Hillard, J.W. (1997) 'The Level and Sources of Popular Support for China's Current Political Regime', *Communist and Post-Communist Studies*, 30(1997)1: 45-64.

'China's Main Blog Service Providers Subscribe to Self-discipline Code', August 22, 2007, http://english.people.com.cn/90001/90778/6245199.html.

Dimitrov, M. (2008) 'The Resilient Authoritarians', *Current History* 107: 24-29, January.

Elegant, S. (2008) 'The Hazards of Citizen Journalism in China', *Time*, January 24 http://www.time.com/time/world/article/0,8599,1820345,00.html.

Ellul, J. (1965) *Propaganda: The Formation of Men's Attitudes*. New York: Alfred A. Knopf.

Fallows, D. (2008) 'Most Chinese Say they Approve of Government Control', China and the Internet: Myths and Realities, 6th annual Chinese Internet Research Conference June 13-14, 2008, Hong Kong (paper).

Farrer, J. (2005) 'Interpreting the 'Mu Zimei Phenomenon': Chinese Sexual Politics in the Internet Age', Conference Presentation, at the International Conference of Asia Scholars (ICAS 4), Shanghai.

Fewsmith, J. (1997) 'Reaction, Resurgence, and Succession: Chinese Politics since Tiananmen', in MacFarquhar, R. (ed.) *The Politics of China: The Eras of Mao and Deng*, 2nd ed., Cambridge: Cambridge University Press.

French, H. (2007) 'Ideals and Reality Conflict on Chinese Child Labor', *The International Herald Tribune*, June 18, 2007, http://www.iht.com/articles/2007/06/18/news/china.php?page=1, last accessed 2008-10-16.

Guo L. (2007) '*Surveying Internet Usage and its Impact in Seven Chinese Cities*', Chinese Academy of Social Sciences.

Hsu, C-H. & Jia L. (2008) 'What Chinese Bloggers Blog – Examining China's top 100 weblogs', paper presented at *China and the Internet: Myths and Realities*, 6th annual Chinese Internet Research Conference, June 13-14, 2008, Hong Kong (paper).

Lagerkvist, J. (2005) 'The Rise of Online Public Opinion in China', *China: An International Journal*, 3(2005)1: 119-30, March.

Lagerkvist, J. (2006) 'In the Crossfire of Demands: Chinese News Portals between Propaganda and the Public', in Thomas, S. & Damm, J. (eds.) *Chinese Cyberspaces: Technological Changes and Political Effects*. London: Routledge.

Lagerkvist, J. (2008a) 'Internet Ideotainment in the PRC: National Responses to Cultural Globalization', *Journal of Contemporary China*, 17(2008)54: 121-40.

Lagerkvist, J. (2008b) 'Norms and the Legitimacy of Law in China: the Case of 'Black Internet Cafés', 'China and the Internet: Myths and Realities', Sixth annual Chinese Internet Research Conference, June 13-14, 2008, Hong Kong (paper).

Latham, K. (2000) 'Nothing But the Truth: News Media, Power and Nothing But the Truth: News Media, Power and Hegemony in South China', *China Quarterly*, 163: 633-654, September.

Lee, C.C. (1990) 'Massmedia: of China, About China', in Lee, C.C. (ed.) *Voices of China. The Interplay of Politics and Journalism in China*. New York: Guilford Press.Li Q. (2007) 'Chinese weblogs thriving', http://www.chinadaily.com.cn/china/2007-01/11/content_781602.htm

Lynch, D. (1999) *After the Propaganda State: Media, Politics, and 'Thought Work' in Reformed China*. Stanford: Stanford University Press.

Macartney, J. (2007) 'China Moves to Ban AnonymoUs Online Posts', *The Times*, 6 July, http://timesonline.co.uk/tol/news/world/asia/article2037158, last accessed 2008-10-16.

Marolt, P. (2008) 'Crossing the River by Groping for Stones: From Free Expression to Shared Meanings to Collective Political Action in China's Blogosphere', China and the Internet: Myths and Realities, 6th annual Chinese Internet Research Conference, June 13-14, 2008, Hong Kong (paper).

Nathan, A.J. (2003) 'China's Changing of the Guard. Authoritarian Resilience', *Journal of Democracy*, 14(1): 6-17, January.

Oi, J.C. (2004) 'Realms of Freedom in Post-Mao China', in Kirby, W.C. (ed.) *Realms of Freedom in Modern China*. Stanford: Stanford University Press.

Qiu, J.L. (2009) *Working Class Network Society: Communications Technology and the Information Have-Less in Urban China*. Cambridge: The MIT Press.

Tsui, L. (2008) 'The Great Firewall as Iron Curtain 2.0: The Implications of China's Internet Most Dominant Metaphor for U.S. Foreign Policy', 'China and the Internet: Myths and Realities', 6th annual Chinese Internet Research Conference, June 13-14, 2008, Hong Kong (paper).

Unger, J. & Chan, A. (1995) 'China, Corporatism and the East Asian Model', *Australian Journal of Chinese Affairs*, 32: 29-53, January.

Wang, Z. (2005) 'Before the Emergence of Critical Citizens: Economic Development and Political Trust in China', *International Review of Sociology*, 15(1)March: 155-171.

Weller, R.P. (1999) *Alternate Civilities: Democracy and Culture in China Democracy and Culture in China and Taiwan*. Boulder: Westview Press.

World Values Survey 2000, www.worldvaluessurvey.org,15.10.2006.

Yang Da-hua, D. (2004) 'Civil Society as an Analytic Lens for Contemporary China', *China: An International Journal*, 1: 1-27, March.

Zhao, D. (2001) 'China's Prolonged Stability and Political Future: Same Political System, Different Policies and Methods', *Journal of Contemporary China*, 10(28): 427-444.

Zittrain, J. & Edelman B. (2008) 'Empirical Analysis of Internet Filtering in China', Berkman Center for Internet & Society, Harvard Law School, http://cyber.law.harvard.edu/filtering/china/, 08.10.2008.

Critical Voices
Student Activism, Communication and Social Change in Zimbabwe

Nkosi Martin Ndlela

Abstract

Throughout the post-independence history of Zimbabwe, student activism has played a crucial and yet ambivalent role in the struggle for democracy – ambivalent in the sense that the early years of independence were marked by student subservience to a political establishment committing grave human rights abuses on its political opponents. The political establishment co-opted young people into its political realm, and they became its vanguards. The consciousness of students was, however, not to be suppressed forever as evidenced by the resurgence of a strong student movement actively seeking to influence political change in the country. This article examines the role of the student movement in the struggles for democracy in Zimbabwe and their creative utilization of available communication spaces in a context in which the government is actively seeking to silence dissenting voices.

The dominant perspective of the youth in Africa has been that of youth facing a dire situation marred by the now stereotypical African woes, presented by the bleak pictures of war, poverty, crisis, crime and violence. These pictures are reinforced in the international media and through academic works. In the words of Abbink (2004: 1), youth in Africa "are facing tremendous odds and do not seem to have the future in their own hands". The causes of these odds are many, ranging from exponential population increases and fierce competition for resources to nepotism, stalled development and generally malfunctioning or failing states. These factors have led to a relative decline in the well-being and social advancement of young people in Africa. It has been noted in the media that youth in Africa in general face massive unemployment, exclusion, poverty and health pandemics like HIV/AIDS, and are generally marginalized in state policies. Transformations in family and social structures have also led to a large proportion of youth having no well-defined place in society and being vulnerable and dependent, especially in urban conditions (Abbink 2004). African youth are thus vulnerable to recruitment into illegal activities such as crime and insurgency. The vulnerability of African youth has created stereotypical perceptions, collaborated by research findings of NGOs, social analysts and governments (UNICEF, 2006, UN World Youth Report 2005, 2007). According to the World Youth Report (2005), young people constitute the most criminally active segment of the population. While this view is understandable, this article avoids positing youths as passive and consistently a problem, instead focusing on their active role in changing their world against tremendous odds.

While not denying the limited possibilities available to youth in Africa, in the words of Abbink (2004) it would be a mistake to deny African youth intentionality of action and agency, as has often happened in African discourse. This perspective takes the view that "youth are neither universally manipulated nor passive actors in a world designed by others but individuals who are trying to chart their own course" (Abbink 2004). The agency approach demands the use of communication media. Through the media, be it mainstream or alternative, modern or traditional, youth can articulate their voices. In this article contribution to social change by the youth is conceptualized as a variety of communication initiatives and actions that set social transformations in motion.

Focusing mainly on the Zimbabwe National Students Union (ZINASU), an umbrella student organization incorporating student unions from different universities and colleges in the country, this article examines the role of communication in the student struggles for democracy and human rights in Zimbabwe. The union indirectly represents approximately 260,000[1] students in more than 43 tertiary institutions. ZINASU's stated goals are to create a platform for students in the fight for good governance, human rights and empowerment of underprivileged youths. ZINASU perceive itself as a 'catalyst for social change' in society and a vanguard of the youth in Zimbabwe. It is aware that, given its involvement in issues of national importance such as democracy, human rights and development, "students are a prime target of state brutality and oppressive tactics and strategies"[2].

Political context – entrapped youths

This article proceeds from a presumption that the majority of problems faced by youth in Zimbabwe have a political dimension and their responses to them have political implications. The political context creates the foundation and framework through which young people can participate in social change. It also set parameters in their communication abilities. In order to understand the role of the student movement in social change, one needs to understand the political ramifications in the country. A political contextualization is therefore prudent at this stage as it governs the communicative spaces available to youth.

By their sheer numbers, mobility, energy, availability and eagerness to be recruited into some projects, youth in Zimbabwe have played a pivotal role in both pre-colonial and post-colonial history. It is on this basis that different political movements often seek to establish a solid youth base in their quest to achieve political power in the country. Youths have been mobilized to support political agendas in a carefully calculated move to exploit their social, political and economic vulnerabilities. Since its independence in 1980, Zimbabwe has been dominated by the ruling party ZANU PF (Zimbabwe African National Union – Patriotic Front) under the leadership of President Robert Mugabe, while opposition parties like the PF ZAPU (the Zimbabwe African People's Union – Patriotic Front), the Zimbabwe Unity Movement (ZUM), and recently the Movement for Democratic Change (MDC) have at different times contested the political space. Even though Zimbabwe has held regular multiparty elections every five years, the dominance of ZANU PF and the extent of marginalization of the opposition have led to some theorists describing Zimbabwe as a *de facto* one-party state (Nkiwane 1998, Sithole and Makumbe 1997).

ZANU PF remained virtually unchallenged in the political arena until the formation of the MDC in 1999, drawing its support from various groups in civil society, and supported by Western countries, such as the UK and the US. MDC created a formidable opposition to Mugabe's rule. With a general disillusionment in the country and popular anger over government policies in the midst of economic and political crisis, MDC presented the populace with a political alternative. The emergence of MDC precipitated violent contestation for political spaces, with the ruling party eager to preserve the status quo. This violent contestation was notable during the 2000 Parliamentary election, the 2002 Presidential election and the 2005 Parliamentary election in. The elections were held within a polarized platform.

Youths found themselves entrapped in the polarized political campaign agendas of the two contending parties. ZANU PF based its political campaigns on the country's liberation war against colonialism and Western imperialism, and introduced controversial seizures of land owned by white commercial farmers, for distribution to landless blacks. It branded its campaign as the country's *Third Chimurenga*[3] – a struggle to defend national sovereignty against imperial forces epitomized by the UK and its Western allies. The anti-imperial revolution therefore implied that those opposed to ZANU PF were imperial puppets and hence counter-revolutionary. This strategy was not new, but rather a revitalization of the strategy used during the liberation war and in the post-independence era, prescribing complete allegiance by youth and women's organizations. As noted by Zeilig (2008: 216), ZANU PF's prescription for the student movement was very clear: students were to play an obedient role in the coming struggles, "being part of the revolutionary movement you are to…be directed by it" and there was no space for an independent line (quoting Cefkin, 1975: 149). The post-colonial hegemonic processes by the ruling ZANU PF continued with this strategy and aimed at complete emasculation of the independency of student unions. This hegemony sought to close avenues of youth organization and hence their abilities to communicate outside the dominant frames built by the post-colonial government. Part of the ruling ZANU PF's hegemonic agenda after independence was to perpetuate itself through reconstitution of vital social organizations representing workers, youth, women and war veterans. The reconstitution occurred through formal and informal channels, which ultimately achieved similar goals. Through formal means like governmental projects such as general livelihood enhancement projects, skills enhancement centres or national services developed under the auspices government departments responsible for youth affairs, or through informal recruitment measures run by the ruling party, young people found themselves entrapped. Youths not aligned with the ruling party were systematically marginalized.

Through an elaborate patronage system, youth groups were enticed or coerced into partnership with the ruling party and helped the party in its consolidation over the political spaces in the country. The state department for youth affairs, which in essence drives political party activities, took over the youth organizations under the ambit of the ZANU PF Youth League. Through programs like the National Service Youth Training Programme and National Youth Service (2001), the youth were appropriated to serve the party. Youth Brigades, or Green Bombers (name derived from the green military uniforms), have been central to the ZANU PF government, by campaigning for the ruling party, perpetrating violent acts on opposition supporters politicizing the electorate, ensuring that party cadres and supporters are well catered to in times of drought and enforcing government policies. During the chronic food shortages in 2002 and 2003, the youth brigade ensured that shop owners did not charge prices over those set by the government, controlled food and fuel queues, arrested people found in possession of scarce commodities, in some cases prevented opposition supporters from getting food aid, and generally contained the increasingly restive population. As noted by Obed Madondo, *AfricaFiles*' Zimbabwe Editor, since 2001 "these domestic forces have proved so threatening that the youth militia has become the government's tool of choice for subduing any form of dissent."[4] In return, the youth militia has immunity from prosecution, and its members are favoured for jobs in the civil service.

While the government proclamation on youth policy[5] is that youth national service is generally empowering to youths in that it increases their political consciousness – a politically conscious youth willing to participate in national building efforts – in effect it has been a disempowering policy designed to precipitate a culture of obedience amongst youth, with youths themselves having little input in decision-making. The policy gave youth limited room for political participation, that is, through the ruling party structures and the government it controls.

As a result, looking at the early years of independence and the heyday of the ZANU PF Youth League, youth as an independent force disappeared entirely from the political scenes. As noted by Zimunya (2007), the student unions went into dormancy soon after independence. The student unions, largely part of the ruling ZANU PF's youth wing and allies of the government, partially suffered from such an alliance (Zimunya 2007). The political consciousness of the students suffered from this alliance as they remained silent against human rights abuses in the early 1980s when government forces violently cracked down on political dissent in the southern regions. The youth remained silent on the critical issues surrounding the violation of civil liberties, freedom of expression and political pluralism. All these issues had direct bearing on the lives of young people. Former student activists from the southern region have explained this "unusual silence" from students on the basis of ethnicity (interviews 06.06.08; 06.05.08). The majority of the students at the University of Zimbabwe were Shona speaking (a dominant group in the ruling party/government), and part of the ruling party's youth wing, and could therefore afford to turn a blind eye on the atrocities committed by their party on the opposition party PF ZAPU, then dominated by the minority Ndebele people from western Zimbabwe.

Anchored on a different platform, the MDC has positioned itself as movement seeking democratic change in Zimbabwe. It claims that it is fighting for democratic reforms that will eventually guarantee fundamental human rights and hence development. The party's policy documents state that "MDC's vision is of a nation that includes informed, responsible, creative and participating young people, who are fully developed mentally, spiritually, socially and physically, and who contribute to the economic prosperity of the country."[6] The MDC draws its strength from a coalition of civic society organizations, including the student movement, which played a pivotal role in the formation of the MDC (Zeilig 2008, Zimunya 2007). This was a culmination of several years of student opposition and was critical of government policies and mismanagement. As early as 1988 students took to the streets, protesting high-level corruption in government, mismanagement and increasing economic hardship. The historic anti-corruption demonstration by students in September 1988 led to the formation of a commission of inquiry and the subsequent resignation of prominent ministers. The students had finally managed to stand independently and voice critical concern against the government on a wide range of issues. University students became a source of inspiration for other youths because their concern was not only student or campus- related grievances but a direct confrontation of the declining social and legal rights. They demanded protection of human rights, and democratic reforms. In the absence of a vibrant opposition, university students filled the void and claimed to be the 'voice of the voiceless', 'revolutionary intellectuals'. This fight for democracy set the student movement on a collision course with a party that had always regarded students as its own. By usurping a role as the opposition, student activism, although somewhat elitist, undoubtedly ushered in a new era of resistance in civil society, more particularly the labour movement. The alliance with the labour movement was not only due to a confluence of economic and political interests; the students unions were led by working-class children, who felt excluded by a political elite who under the guise of youth empowerment were offering their own children lucrative scholarships abroad.

ZINASU activities intensified in the late 1990s when a broad-based pro-democracy movement emerged as a multitude of non-governmental organizations and labour unions, student organizations and religious organizations formed alliances to confront the ruling party. The shrinking economic conditions forced students into alliances with workers' union, which has always been better organized, independent and national in scope compared to youth organizations. ZINASU joined forces with pro-democracy movements. The student organizations played a pivotal role in the formation of the MDC in 1999 and eventually became an important ally. Alliance with the MDC was inevitable, given the historical linkages between the students and the workers' union (the backbone behind the MDC). It is therefore not incidental that the opposition party and its allies in civil society have in their top leadership a number of young people, most of whom have been involved in student activism. After the 2000 parliamentary election, the MDC ushered into Parliament some of the youngest parliamentarians Zimbabwe had ever seen: Tafadzwa Musekiwa (24), Learnmore Jongwe (26) and Job Sikhala (28). Former student leaders like Tendai Biti, Nelson Chamisa, Arthur Mutambara, Job Sikhala, Munyaradzi Gwisai and Brian Kagoro have in various capacities and affiliations been central in the pro-democracy struggles. Active youth participation in the MDC and its NGO allies serves as a counterbalance to the ZANU PF. As noted by Madondo (see Note 2), "a strong youth presence in the MDC did not just provide a counterbalance to the ZANU PF Youth League but also meant the beginning of the end of the ruling party's stranglehold on Zimbabwean youth." Through forging alliances with different sectors of the civil society, student organizations have emerged as influential actors reshaping power formations and social relations in the country.

This article thus posits that a discussion of a ZINASU's communication initiatives cannot be divorced from Zimbabwe's polarized politics represented by ZANU PF and the MDC. These organizations define the operational parameters and communicative abilities of the student movement in Zimbabwe.

Mainstream media and the exclusion of critical voices

ZINASU is one of the youth organizations contributing to the struggles for democracy and social change in Zimbabwe. In order to carry on with its communication goals, ZINASU (like any other organization) is dependent on access to and utilization of the existing media and other means of communication. To reach its interest groups, such as university and college students, the public, government officials, and local and international NGOs, ZINASU needs access to the type of media best suited for target groups. Much of the information the target groups receive and act upon comes to them through various types of media and communication platforms.

Researchers in Western democracies often talk about the 'mediatization' of the political process because of the centrality of the media in modern politics, and argue that few would deny that "the media are politics, and politics are the media" (McNair 2000). In the Zimbabwean context, one would have to be cautious about mass-mediated politics. The media in Zimbabwe have been overwhelmingly dominated by the government. Through a series of media laws and extralegal actions media spaces have shrunk greatly, thus limiting the range of views that can be disseminated through them and also reducing the numbers of potential media users. It is not that Zimbabwe cannot afford a plural and diverse modern media; it is rather a planned deficiency. Stiff (2000) has noted that it is axiomatic of Marxism, fascism and other forms of centrally-controlled government that if you want to control the people, you first must gain control of all means of public communication and propaganda. Since independence, the ZANU PF government has sought overall control of all means of public communication, ranging from modern mass media to face-to-face public communication such as public rallies.

Within a month of coming into power in April 1980, the new post-independence government completely took over the broadcasting services, reorganized them and staffed them with personnel drawn from the ruling party. Four months later the government bought out the South African Press Association (SAPA) shareholding in the country's news agency, the Zimbabwe Inter-Africa News Agency (ZIANA). A few months later the government bought the entire 45.24% shareholding from the Argus-controlled Zimbabwe Printing and Publishing Co. Government shares were to be vested on a public trust, Zimbabwe Mass Media Trust. Within two years the government had taken over the entire mass media in the country – comprising broadcasting, newspapers, magazines and the news agency. This was also complimented by control of the Ministry of Information. Since then the government has had control over the mainstream media in Zimbabwe – controlling the main daily and weekly newspapers as well the only broadcasting institution, the Zimbabwe Broadcasting Corporation. Government-controlled media are thus the largest and the most dominant media in the country. With this control over the mainstream media, the government has been able to shut out dissenting views while ensuring that only voices that are sympathetic to ruling party policies find their way into the media. Organizations critical of the government have limited or no access to government-controlled media. ZINASU is one such organization whose access to the government-controlled media has been severely restricted. As noted by ZINASU's Information and Publicity Secretary, Blessing Vava:

> The media in Zimbabwe is very polarised and the state owned media are partisan and very hostile to organisations perceived to be anti government. ZINASU is perceived to be a threat to the government of Zimbabwe. It is only the privately owned media which gives ZINASU considerable and unbiased coverage (e-mail interview, 22.10.08).

It is evident from the above that access to mainstream media is severely restricted for all organizations critical of the ruling party, since their views have to go through filters in government-controlled media or be channelled through alternative channels. ZINASU thus feels that its voice is excluded in the mainstream media and hence cannot use the medium to communicate with its constituencies and the general public.

The independent media provides alternative spaces for critical voices in the democratic struggles in Zimbabwe. Independent newspapers, which include *The Daily News*, *The Financial Gazette*, *The Zimbabwe Independent*, *The Standard*, *The Daily Mirror*, *The Sunday Mirror* and several monthly magazines, have been platforms for critical voices. Vava (ibid.) acknowledges that "the independent media is very accessible; however the only challenge is that newspapers are out of reach to many students and Zimbabweans in general as they are expensive." Access to independent media is thus not guaranteed due to their limited operational environment. The independent press is so curtailed that it has been virtually impossible to successfully run an independent daily newspaper. Even though it remains legal to start a newspaper, extralegal and legal actions have been employed in order to strain the economic resources of these independent players. In 2003 the government shut down the largest independent daily, the *Daily News*, as well as three other independent newspapers. The closure of the *Daily News* further narrowed the democratic spaces. The government has thus deliberately sought to shrink communicative spaces that might be accessed by its critics. Communication spaces in the independent media are narrowed by the fact that independent newspapers have a limited circulation.

ZINASU's communication alternatives

The continued suppression of freedom of expression and the lack of diversity in the Zimbabwean media landscape compels people to explore other avenues of communication. Given the media restrictions and limited access to the mainstream media, critical voices like ZINASU are compelled to use alternative forms of communication, the independent press and word of mouth. For the majority of pro-democracy activists and non-governmental organizations, the alternative media are the most plausible and effective communication channels given the government's control of the mainstream media. According ZINASU, the organization has turned to alternative media sympathetic to social movements. It has also resorted to technology-aided communications. Internet technology provided opportunities for alternative communication spaces. It offered individuals, organizations and non-governmental organizations opportunities for networking and collaboration with the international community, thereby subverting official communication gatekeeping structures. The technology altered the ways people and pro-democracy movements came together and communicated. Asked how ZINASU would describe its usage of new information and communication technologies in its communication efforts, Vava commented as follows:

> Our usage of the new information and communication technologies has been very wonderful and has significantly improved of late, as we have managed to establish a website which is upgraded regularly, we have also managed to come up with a students and media mailing list as a way of communicating with our constituencies and the relevant partners. The greatest challenge we have is that internet access in Zimbabwe is very expensive especially to the students (e-mail interview 22.10.08).

Developments in new information and communication technologies in Zimbabwe have provided ZINASU and other pro-democracy movements with unique opportunities to expand their communication horizons. Creative use of new technologies, particularly the Internet, allows ZINASU to bypass the restrictive media environment and communicate its messages to local and international interest groups. Through its website www.zinasu.org, news updates, news alerts, press releases and reports are disseminated locally and globally, raising awareness of not only the plight of students but also the state of democratization in the country. The message has also been distributed through websites hosted by other local NGOs such as www.kubatana.net (an NGO alliance project), www.crisiszimbabwe.org (coalition of NGOs working on the Zimbabwean crisis), and other externally run websites such as www.nearinternational.org (A international network for education and academic rights) and www.saih.no (Norwegian Students' and Academics' International Assistance Fund). Even though there is a dearth of new communication technologies in the country to warrant effective utilization of information technologies, Internet penetration at universities and colleges is good enough to reach opinion leaders and other NGOs thereby setting in motion social change processes.

The Internet creates linkages with international NGOs and Zimbabweans in the Diaspora. One way of challenging the hegemony in the mainstream media has been the establishment of numerous news and information websites not directly linked to traditional media houses.[7] The news sites hosted in foreign domains, far from the clutches of repressive media laws, seem keen to provide alternative communicative spaces for the people in Zimbabwe. The opportunities for alternative avenues of communication brought by the Internet have boosted ZINASU's communication abilities. They have given credence to Castells' (1999: 1) contention that Internet technology does not in itself determine social process, but has become "a mediating factor in the complex matrix of interaction between social structures, social actors and their socially constructed tools." The Internet's role in defining present and future social processes is that, among other things, it offers immense opportunities for connecting and networking dispersed population segments as well as social movements and voluntary organizations. The Internet has also emerged as a facilitative tool for mediating the Zimbabwean crisis by allowing a variety of discursive spaces, including online discussion boards. The social effect of virtual networks created by the Internet is that they have generated alternative ways of knowing, opportunities for participation and spaces of expression in an environment less controlled by government. The Internet thus provides an alternative medium for freedom of expression and activist publications on a range of issues that normally would not be published in the state-controlled media, or even in the limited space offered by the independent newspapers.

The communication range for ZINASU thus includes alternative radio stations hosted in foreign countries and broadcast both via the Internet and on short wave or AM. Radio stations, *SW Radio Africa*, the *Voice of America's Studio 7*, and the *Voice of the People (Radio VOP)* offer time for pro-democracy movements and seek to highlight the democratic struggles in Zimbabwe. The radio stations target the grassroots population in Zimbabwe, who can tune in at particular times via short wave or AM. The radio stations use all the three main languages, English, Shona and Ndebele. *SW Radio Africa* claims to be the voice of the voiceless, giving its audience opportunities to call in and air their first-hand experiences of the situation in Zimbabwe. Students have participated in call-in programmes, airing their version of events in the country. *SW Radio Africa* also allows readers of its news site opportunities to participate through discussion forums. The radio stations remain a rare independent voice in a country where there is a monopoly on the airwaves. A Google search for ZINASU on www.swradioafrica.com on 21 August 2008 gave 130 hits covering news releases and news stories. If one includes radio interviews, ZINASU's critical voices are clearly visible. This indicates ZINASU's concerted efforts to make its voice heard.

The government, eager to exercise its control and hegemony on all communicative spaces, has described these alternative radio stations as irresponsible media working with the enemies of the state. The government claims that foreign interests are using the media to effect a regime change in the country. Radio stations have attracted the wrath of the government as they pose a real threat to information dissemination in the country via radio. The radio stations can be accessed by anyone with a radio, thus making them the only alternative broadcasting media, in an environment characterized by government monopoly. Aided by China, the government secured equipment that has been used intermittently for jamming outside broadcasts from *SW Radio Africa* and the *Voice of America's Studio 7*.[8]

News websites also offer alternative communication channels for ZINASU. One way of challenging the homogeneity and hegemony in the mainstream media has been the establishment of news and information sites not linked to traditional media houses in Zimbabwe. The past few years have seen the establishment of news sites and other computer mediated communications, providing alternative communicative spaces for the people of Zimbabwe and the international community. The news sites hosted in foreign countries and run by former Zimbabwean journalists, far from the clutches of repressive media laws, seem to be interested in generating public discourse on the socio-political problems facing Zimbabwe. The public discussion generated in these news sites is unparalleled in the mainstream media in Zimbabwe. They provide a reader-response mechanism to news articles, commentaries, discussions and entertainment. Almost all the news sites describe and perceive themselves as alternative spaces of communication and information for Zimbabweans. For example, the sites www.newzimbabwe.com, www.zwnews.com, www.zimonline.co.za and www.thezimbabwetimes.com offer links to pro-democracy social movements. ZINASU is a visible organization on these websites. A Google search for ZINASU on www.zimbabwesituation.com gives 421 hits and 28 hits on www.newzimbabwe.com.[9] ZINASU's voices are well represented on the news sites as news stories and commentaries, and in discussion forums. Online newspapers have thus increased the visibility of ZINASU as a main player within the pro-democracy movement.

While the news websites have so far operated freely outside the realm of Zimbabwean law, a number of legal and extralegal measures have been taken to cut off the supply of stories from Zimbabwe. The Access to Information and Protection of Privacy Act prohibits individuals from supplying journalistic works without a government journalism licence. As the local reporting environment has become difficult, a number of journalists and activists like ZINASU have been feeding their reports into the international media. Another law, the Interception of Communications Act,[10] came into effect August 2007 and aims at the censorship of e-mail and Internet communications. Internet Services Providers are required by law to acquire systems that are technically capable to intercept communications. The Act also made provisions for the setting up of communication monitoring centres. The project hit a snag, however, due to the overwhelming task awaiting the monitors as well as the high costs of Internet spying equipment, which the ISP cannot afford. For pro-democracy movements, the Act is yet another attempt to close loopholes in the already oppressive communication environment.[11]

Word of mouth: meetings and public rallies

Another form of communication which ZINASU has used is word of mouth. The dissemination of information through word-of-mouth communication should not be underestimated in Zimbabwe, where it is still the most effective medium of communication. Given that the majority of the population (64%) live in rural areas outside the reach of modern media (including radio to a certain extent), oral communication is of fundamental importance.[12] Commenting on the use of traditional systems, Wilson (1987:89) argues that "these traditional systems are also trusted and the majority of the people seem to believe in what comes out of them and usually use them and supplement them with whatever additional information may filter through opinion leaders about events elsewhere." Despite the government's overwhelming control of the media, ZINASU has effectively managed to mobilize its supporters to meetings and demonstrations, and has participated in rallies organized by other allies through the word of mouth and other alternative forms. ZINASU has extensively used oral communication to mobilize students in different universities and colleges, and also used this method in its voter registration campaign (ZINASU 2007). The ZINASU strategy was based on the premise that "students command respect and influence in their local constituencies" (ZINASU 2007: 8). The activities of the youth organizations described above underscore the usefulness of traditional communication systems in the mobilization of people at the grassroots level. In the words of ZINASU's Information and Publicity Secretary, Blessing Vava, to a certain extent:

> The use of oral communication has been effective as a means of communicating with the students, in the sense that as the students' leadership we constantly hold general meetings in tertiary institutions around the country and this has been working well. The union has also devised other communication strategies in the form of public meetings which we conduct on a monthly basis (e-mail interview 22.10.08)

This strategy is also augmented by a newsletter, *The Student*, which is published monthly and distributed to university and college campuses.

The alternative communication forms mentioned above, however, have not been completely free from government interference. The government has tried on several occasions to manipulate and restrict word-of-mouth communication. The provisions of the Public Order and Security Act regulate the conduct at meetings and rallies. They also regulate speeches likely to endanger public peace or harm the reputation of the President. Police are empowered to call off meetings or rallies. Student leaders have sometimes been arrested and detained for holding 'illegal meetings' with fellow students. For example, in September 2006, more than 50 student leaders were arrested while conducting a ZINASU general council meeting in the town of Mutare. Seven were detained in Harare prior the meeting[13]; the police alleged that their conduct was likely to lead to a breach of peace. Arrests are often made as pre-emptive measures designed to disrupt ZINASU's capacity to mobilize students for demonstrations.

Demonstrations: "By any means necessary"

Interviews with former student leaders and student activists[14] in Zimbabwe highlight the centrality of demonstrations as the preferred route for expressing discontentment, be it about food in the dining halls, student grants and loans, or social matters. The strength of the student union is therefore measured by its ability to host successful demonstrations. Demonstration is one of the most effective advocacy and communication tools used by students to express displeasure at government policies. The success of demonstrations depends on the numbers participants and the coverage they get from the media. In a scenario in which the majority of students live on campus, demonstrations have been relatively easy to organize without any reliance on modern media. Posters and meetings have been the most preferred communication channels in the organization of demonstrations. Depending on the issue at hand, student advocacy often begins with low-intensity activities such as letters to the university authorities and government officials, demanding an immediate response within a given deadline. Printed t-shirts, stickers and badges with slogans, and posters often mark the medium-intensity levels which invariably lead to a strike or demonstration. Students often take their demonstrations to the city centre or government offices, where visibility is often higher than on university or college campuses. Disrupting traffic, singing and sometimes smashing police cars have become major characteristics of student demonstrations. Through this, students have been able to increase media visibility. Asked why students often resort to demonstration and whether this method is at all effective, ZINASU's Information and Publicity Secretary, Blessing Vava, argues that:

> Demonstrations have a greater effect and impact in sending a message to a greater number of people. It is another way of exercising our freedom of expression. Demonstration is one of the routes we use in trying to get attention from the relevant authorities because dialogue seems to be failing and the strategy seems to be working. For example, it was only after students demonstrated at parliament on the 14th of October 2008 that parliament had to focus its attention to the students' grievances. Parliament also extended their invitation to the ZINASU leadership to discuss the issues the students had tabled to the house, and this comes as a victory to us (e-mail interview, 22.10.08).

Predictably, authorities in Zimbabwe have been hostile to student demonstrations, whether peaceful or violent. Several measures have been employed by the government to curtail the impact of student demonstrations. Attempts have been made to weaken student leadership through pre-emptive arrests, detention and outright dismissal of 'troublesome' leaders from universities and colleges. For example, the University of Zimbabwe Amendment Act of 1990 granted more power to the state and university authorities to easily dismiss students behind violent demonstrations or withdraw government grants from student activists. Anti-riot police or military police have also been regularly deployed to deal with demonstrating students. Often, the presence of anti-riot police has led to violent confrontation and even destruction of property. With the slogan "By any means necessary", students have fought running battles with the police.

The near total absence of communicative spaces or forums for peaceful participation for young people leaves violence as a primary means of expression. Violence is one of the most utilized forms of expression by youth in political engagements. Violence – perpetrating it or being its victim – has become the means of expression in any political engagement in Zimbabwe. For a meaningful understanding of violence as a means of communication and the youth's role in it, one must consider the historical background as outlined in the context above.

The deficit of modern communication means has meant that expressions are vented through anger. This has given the government justification for branding demonstrators as mere 'hooligans', thus reducing the significance and impact of their actions. This also justifies brutal police actions, arrests and harassment of participants and their leaders. However, not everyone can be duped by this propaganda. As noted by the Student Solidarity Trust in relation to the demonstrations at the University of Zimbabwe on the night of 14 October 2004, "the targeted beatings and detention of these student leaders are symptomatic of the injustice that is prevailing across the board in the country, and exemplifies what they wanted to fight against"[15]

Another government ploy to reduce the significance of student demonstrations is to place a blockade on state media coverage or reduce the numbers of participants. Large student demonstrations have passed unnoticed as state media merely ignores them. As noted by pressure group Sokwanele in June 2005, one such demonstration comprised 2,000 students from Bulawayo Polytechnic who took part in a peaceful demonstration that was sparked by student discontent caused by repeated delays by the college authorities in paying out student loans[16]. The protest went unnoticed in the mainstream media.

Other methods used to suppress demonstrations include the general ban on rallies and demonstrations. Provisions of the Public Order and Security Act (POSA) and its predecessor the Law and Order (Maintenance) Act gives local police the power to ban demonstrations and public meetings. Demonstrators are forced to apply for permission, which in most cases is denied, thus making any demonstrations thereafter illegal.

Another strategy by the government has been to demobilize the student unions by shutting down the universities, arresting student leaders and evicting students from the halls of residence. For example, following the disturbances on 3 and 7 July 2007 sparked by an increase in fees, the government closed down the institution on 9 July and gave students only 30 minutes to vacate the campus. Riot police were again used to evict students from their halls of residence. The university cited destruction of property as the primary reason for closure, whilst ZINASU believes that "the move by the University was a political strategy to demobilize the students, who are a vital constituency to pro-democracy forces in Zimbabwe" (ZINASU 2007).

Despite these legal and extralegal measures, student demonstrations have persevered. Sokwanele has observes that:

> Traditionally, the world around, student activists have been at the forefront of those protesting human rights abuses and demanding democratic change. Zimbabwe's dictator has not been slow to appreciate this potential threat to his continued hold on power, and he has used great cunning as well as brutal force to undermine the natural leadership emerging from Zimbabwe's tertiary institutions of learning.[17]

Conclusion

The discussion above has highlighted ZINASU's active role in the Zimbabwean political processes. Students, through organizations like ZINASU, have managed to consolidate themselves into formidable student movements, voicing critical concern about the regime of Robert Mugabe. They have done so against insurmountable obstacles and have thereby given weight to Nyamnjoh's (2005) claim that however repressive a government is and however profound the spiral of silence induced by standardized global media menus is, few people are ever completely mystified or wholly duped. In other words, there is always room – sometimes through radical or alternative media. The youth's contribution to social change in Zimbabwe has been recognized internationally, with ZINASU winning the 2003 student prize awarded by ISFiT (Institutional Student Festival in Trondheim, Norway) in recognition of their engagement in democracy and human rights.

Notes

1. ZINASU General Council consists of student union presidents from all the tertiary institutions in the country. However, this does not mean that all students in these institutions are members of ZINASU. The number of students registered in tertiary institutions has declined over the past eight years.
2. http://www.zinasu.org/reports/Report%20on%20uz%20evictions.pdf (accessed 2 June 2008).
3. Chimurenga is a Shona word for 'struggle', and has been used to denote the struggles against colonialism. The first Chimurenga denote the 1896-1897 African insurrection against British colonial rule. The Second Chimurenga denotes the War of liberation from colonial settler rule (1966-1980).
4. Madondo, O. The problem of youth in Mugabe's Zimbabwe, in Africa Files available at http://www.africafiles.org/article.asp?ID=6498 (accessed 15.05.2008).
5. http://www.mydgec.gov.zw/nys.htm (Ministry of Youth Development and Employment Creation).
6. http://www.kubatana.net/docs/polpar/mdc_policies_natl_integration_0802.pdf (accessed 31/05/08).
7. News sites include: www.newzimbabwe.com, www.thezimbabwetimes.com, www.zimonline.co.za, www.zimdaily.com, www.thezimbabwean.com, www.swradioafrica.com, www.zimbabwesituation.com, etc.
8. See, for example, http://www.kubatana.net/html/archive/inftec/070807swradio.asp?spec_code=060426commdex&sector=INFTEC&year=0&range_start=1&intMainYear=0&intTodayYear=2008.
9. Searched 21 August 2008.
10. See gazette bill at http://www.kubatana.net/docs/legisl/icb_060526.pdf
11. See, for example, responses to the Act from the Media Institute of Southern Africa, The Zimbabwe Union of Journalists, at http://www.kubatana.net/html/archive/archspecialentry_index.asp?spec_code=060426commdex&sector=INFTEC.
12. See the survey conducted by the Zimbabwe All Media Products Survey at http://www.zarf.co.zw/.
13. http://www.swradioafrica.com/news11.09.06/zinasu110906.htm.
14. A total of six interviews were carried out with former student leaders and student activists. Interviews were conducted mostly by telephone and e-mail.
15. http://www.nearinternational.org/campaigns/zimbabwe/education_in_crisis/localvoices_studentsolidaritytruststatement21oct2004_d8840b.php (accessed 2 June 2008).

16. http://www.sokwanele.com/articles/sokwanele/dissentingvoices_29july2005.html (accessed 2 June 2008).
17. http://www.sokwanele.com/articles/sokwanele/dissentingvoices_29july2005.html (accessed 2 June 2008).

References

Abbink, J. (2004) 'Being Young in Africa: The Politics of Despair and Renewal', in Abbink, J. (2004) *Vanguard or Vandals: Youth, Politics, and Conflict in Africa*. Leiden: Brill.

Castells, M. (1999) 'The Social Implications of Information and Communication Technologies', in UNESCO (ed.) *World Social Science Report*. New York: UNESCO

Kagoro, B. (2003) 'The Opposition and Civil Society', in Cornwell, R. (2003) *Zimbabwe's Turmoil. Problems and Prospects*. Monograph no. 87, September 2003. Tshwane, South Africa; Institute for Security Studies.

Madondo, O. (not dated) *The Problem of Youth in Mugabe's Zimbabwe*, africafiles.org.

McIntyre, A. (2003) 'Rights, Root Causes and Recruitment. The Youth Factor in Africa's Armed Conflicts', *African Security Review* 12(2003)2.

McNair, B. (2000) *Journalism and Democracy: An Evaluation of the Political Public Sphere*. London: Routledge.

Nkiwane, T. (1998) 'Opposition Politics in Zimbabwe', in Olukoshi, A. (ed.) *The Politics of Opposition in Contemporary Africa*. Uppsala: The Nordic Africa Institute.

Saunders, R. (2000) *Never the Same Again: Zimbabwe's Growth Towards Democracy 1980-2000*. Harare: Edwina Spicer.

Stiff, P. (2000) *Cry Zimbabwe. Independence-Twenty Years On*. Alberton, RSA: Galago Publishing.

UNICEF (2006) *World Report on Violence against Children*, http://www.unviolencestudy.org/

Wilson, D. (1987) 'Traditional Systems of Communication in Modern African Development: An Analytical Viewpoint', *Africa Media Review* 1(1987)2, African Council on Communication Education.

Zeilig, L. (2008) 'Student Politics and Activism in Zimbabwe: The Frustrated Transition', *Journal of Asian and African Studies*, 43(2008)2.

Zimunya, I. (2007) *Claiming Our Future: A Focus on the Students Movement in Zimbabwe*. Harare.

ZINASU (2007) *It's Politics, Stupid*. A Report on the Mass Eviction of Resident Students at the University of Zimbabwe, July 2007.

Ethical Challenges in U.S. Youth Radio Training Programs

Robert Huesca

Abstract

Throughout the 1990s, youth radio training programs in the United States grew enormously, but research on them has been virtually non-existent. This study examined four, long-running youth radio training programs and found that they frequently face situations of emotional stress and conflict that create ethical challenges for adult leaders. Neither the media literacy scholarship, nor the youth radio training literature has identified ethical challenges as a salient issue in youth media programs. This study suggests that this is an overlooked area that requires active reflection and practical strategies for facing this common occurrence.

Beginning in the early 1990s, radio training projects began emerging throughout the United States that were aimed at teaching youth (ages 15-early 20s) the basics of audio production. These "youth radio" training programs mushroomed to about 50 different places across the country due to the availability of grants from individuals, foundations, and state agencies with a variety of agendas. Despite more than a decade of experience, youth radio training programs have received journalistic attention, but very little scholarly analysis (Featherstone 1998; Graber 2001; Kelliher 2003; Wagg 2004). In response to this situation, the author launched a broad research project in the summer of 2006 to explore four, well-established, yet structurally diverse youth radio training programs in the United States.

In-depth interviews conducted with youth participants at these four sites explored the programs' practices and impacts. Interviews asked participants to speak generally about their involvement with the programs before requesting them to identify a single, memorable, concrete experience for an in-depth discussion. The analysis of interview transcripts revealed multiple themes illuminating the relationships between program structure, organization, activity, and impact on participants. But one unanticipated theme arising from the data concerned ethical issues, problems, and challenges resulting from youth experiences.

The emergence of ethical issues in the data raises questions that go to the very heart of youth radio training programs and must be addressed by scholars and adult leaders in this field. That is, youth radio training programs claim a central objective of including youth voices and perspectives in the media environment that has excluded them for years. Often these programs are driven by social justice agendas and lead to youth engagement with topics aimed at social and political transformation.

Nevertheless, in the process of recording and presenting youth perspectives publicly, these programs apparently have subjected participants to risk, discomfort, and harm. A small, but significant, percentage of participants (about one-third), described experiences that they classified as embarrassing, uncomfortable, or otherwise problematic in the course of producing and airing audio projects. Interviewees described personal difficulties including tension and conflict among family and friends, exposure to negative judgments by others, or permanent records of expressions that they judged in hindsight as being ill-advised or contrary to their contemporary points of view and opinions. The purpose of this chapter is to describe and analyze these ethical issues in a way that will raise awareness of, provoke thought about, and document responses to the challenges faced by youth media scholars and practitioners in various contexts.

This chapter will first provide a general portrait of the four youth radio training programs in terms of their structures, objectives, activities, and participants, and the research methods used to examine them. Next it will review selected youth media scholarship, with emphasis on studies focused specifically on radio. A focused discussion of ethical considerations and theories, along with models for decision making will follow. This discussion of ethical considerations will act as the primary theoretical framework used in analyzing the experiences of youth participants. The remainder of the chapter will present the findings, discussion, and conclusion of this research project.

The research setting and methods

An overview of the four youth radio training programs examined in this project is necessary to understand the context in which practitioners operated and in which ethical tensions arose. Each location was visited for a period of two weeks per program in the summer 2006 in the following, chronological order: Radio Rookies in New York, Blunt Youth Radio in Portland, Maine, Radio Arte in Chicago, and Youth Radio Berkeley. Conceptually, the four programs were selected because of their diversity in terms of formal structures and program goals. The objective of the research design was to focus on maximally different programs in order to tap the widest range possible of approaches to training and experiences of participants.

Structural diversity included the formal, organizational designs of programs. Two of the programs (Blunt Youth Radio and Youth Radio Berkeley) were independent, non-profit organizations with affiliations with broadcast stations. Blunt Youth Radio functioned independently, but was given a weekly program slot on WMPG-FM, a community radio station. Similarly, Youth Radio Berkeley operated independently, but maintained ties with a well-established community broadcaster (KPFA-FM), a commercial station (KCBS-AM), and a national distribution network (National Public Radio). The other two youth radio programs operated as parts of larger organizations, which provided them with direction and resources. For example, Radio Rookies is a project of a large station, New York's WNYC-AM and FM, while Radio Arte is an initiative of the Mexican Fine Arts Center Museum in Chicago. Another structural difference regarded youth access to the programs themselves, which ranged from an open door policy at Blunt to a highly competitive application and interview at Radio Arte. Finally, the four programs differed widely in terms of their financial and personnel resources, from the relative affluence of Youth Radio Berkeley at one end (more than 30 full-time staffers with a multi-million dollar capital campaign in progress) to financially struggling Blunt Youth Radio on the other (three paid part-time leaders).

Despite the formal structural diversity, all of the youth radio training programs shared the overall objective of responding to the near absence of youth perspectives, opinions, and voices in their respective media environments. Providing tools and platforms for youth expression was seen as a way of empowering participants by giving them direct access to communication media. The circulation of youth perspectives was also seen as a way of counteracting negative stereotypes and breaking down social barriers experienced by youths of different class, ethnic, and gender backgrounds. Finally, the objective of giving voice to youths was viewed as serving the public interest by providing fresh perspectives on multiple issues to audiences across formats. The programs responded to this general objective by training youth to create audio productions ranging from personal diaries to disinterested news features.

Even though the general objectives and production ends were similar across programs, the means of implementation varied widely from those that focused mostly on the communication process involving participants to others devoted to perfecting the audio product for distribution. Programs that emphasized communication processes adopted activities concerned mostly with youth development. Programs that focused more intently on professionally sounding audio worthy of being broadcast on public and commercial radio stations and networks incorporated more tasks aimed at perfecting reporting, writing, and producing skills. Although all of the programs attended to both elements, they differed in the proportion of attention to process and product with Blunt Youth Radio and Radio Arte being more process focused, and Youth Radio Berkeley and Radio Rookies being more product oriented. Youth Radio Berkeley and Radio Rookies incorporated lengthy lessons on technical proficiencies, for example, and carved out substantial periods of classroom and one-on-one instruction. In contrast,

Blunt Youth Radio cycled trainees through hands-on work stations on an irregular basis, encouraging students to develop their skills by putting them into practice in a range of radio activities. Radio Arte occupied a middle space, with ample classroom equipment and training for a lengthy period of time, combined with almost immediate access of novices to a broadcast station.

The characteristics of the participants in this study reflected the recruitment processes, program objectives, and demographic qualities of the various locations of the training programs. Blunt attracted a fairly homogeneous group (in terms of race and class) of high school aged participants despite its broad recruitment efforts and low barrier entree to the program. The largely white, middle class group reflected the ethnic and class make up of the home base city of Portland. Likewise, Radio Arte in Chicago attracted a virtually exclusively Latino, working class population given its location in Chicago's largely Mexican American, Pilsen neighborhood. Furthermore, its recruitment via its low-powered broadcast signal as well as via Spanish-language television in the city ensured a large Mexican and Mexican American group who were bilingual and monolingual Spanish speakers. Despite this seeming homogeneity, Radio Arte's participants differed in terms of their migration timelines, which resulted in different levels of involvement with the radio station. That is, the training included separate English and Spanish-language programs, with the former attracting second and third-generation Latinos and the latter bringing recent, first-generation participants. The greatest difference between these two groups was the stronger level of commitment of the recent immigrants, who used the training program as a socializing and networking vehicle, in addition to its function as a communication project. Finally, Youth Radio Berkeley and Radio Rookies both targeted underresourced schools and neighborhoods, which resulted in a pronounced working class and ethnic minority presence in the programs. Each station also desired a diverse mix among their youth participants and actively sought out white, middle class participants, as well. This resulted in striking contrasts, such as functionally illiterate individuals working alongside college-bound students.

The method of data collection in this study was in-depth interviews mostly with youth radio participants, though one or two adult leaders were interviewed at all sites, as well. A total of 55 interviews were conducted, tape recorded, and transcribed. Pseudonyms are used for all participants. Interviews were guided by the Sense-Making methodology, a communication-based approach that places the experiences, thoughts, and feelings of the interviewee at the center of the questions (Dervin 2002). Questions derived from the Sense-Making approach ask respondents to identify and discuss concrete, lived experiences, rather than to respond to externally identified topics. The ethical difficulties arising in the data, therefore, emerged from the lived experiences of the participants, not from an explicit interview question focusing on the topic of media ethics.

The interview data generated in this study were examined in light of theoretical contributions by scholars of youth media production. The unexpected emergence of ethical issues was further analyzed with respect to basic theories of media ethics.

Thinking about youth media and ethics

Because so little research had been done on the rapidly growing youth radio training programs in the United States, this study began as a mostly descriptive project with only the most general theoretical questions driving it. As such, it relied primarily on U.S. based youth media and media literacy scholarship, though it did branch out to include applicable European studies, as well. Data collection and analysis revealed that the training issues faced in a developed nation often mirrored the problems and challenges of similar activities in the context of development communication projects, but space limitations preclude a review of that literature. Nevertheless, the ethical challenges under review here should be read with an eye toward enriching understandings of the issues faced in global youth media in developing nations, as well.

Scholarship of youth media production

Scholarship of youth media literacy and media education is quite robust, yet scant attention has been given to creative, production activities; radio production has been the subject of even fewer studies (Buckingham 2003; Tyner 2007). A comprehensive survey commissioned by the British government in 2004, for example, indicated that "radio *production* by youth is an extremely under-researched area" (Buckingham n.d.: 30, author's emphasis). Instead, the media literacy research has dealt with either normative, theoretical questions or zeroed in on issues of access and impact.

Scholarship of the creative activities of youth media programs typically has focused attention on three areas: 1. goals, objectives, and rationales of the programs; 2. topics and content of actual productions; and 3. impacts of the programs on youth participants. Virtually none of this research addresses ethical questions directly.

Researchers of youth media production have identified goals, objectives, and rationales for these projects that split into two directions that are often embraced simultaneously by training programs. On the one hand, programs focus on youth development by adopting goals as specific as diversion from drugs and underage sex (Thomas 2007) to more abstract objectives of "empowerment" and the discovery of voice (Berson 2001; Wagg 2004; Whitney 2007). At the same time, youth media training programs embrace a goal of contributing to the public sphere by addressing the absence of young people as content producers in the communication environment (Berson 2001; Goodman 2003; Richman 2002).

Nearly all scholars and practitioners have approached these dual goals, objectives, and rationales as coexisting in a benign, unproblematic relationship. An exception has been noted at Youth Radio Berkeley, however, where students and staff members have documented instances where contributing to the public sphere with "high-impact" productions occasionally has threatened the well-being of youth media makers (Soep 2007). She correctly generalizes that community-based training programs will routinely need to deal with "challenges when it comes to reconciling youth development goals with professional principles and social justice work" (Soep 2007: 105-106).

Indeed, much of the source of the conflict between these dual goals is fueled by the topics and content that youth generate in their productions. Scholars have documented a wide variety of topics that are approached by young producers, "ranging from the sweet stuff of teenage dreams to memories of growing up and everything in between" (Thomas 2007: 33). Despite this diversity, however, youth media productions tend to cluster around themes of sex, drugs, and identity issues, and often they are expressed in language that is crude, vulgar, or offensive (Dauncey & Hare 1999; Glevarec 2005; Wagg 2004). These high salience issues are inherently risky topics as they expose intimate thoughts and vulnerable behaviors to a wide, public audience.

Negotiating risky topics is complicated by the nature of the impact that these activities have on participants. Some scholars who have examined youth development impacts such as identity transformation, empowerment, or learning new skills have noted that these gains are intertwined and even dependent upon the public and intimate nature of expression afforded by media production (Dauncey & Hare 1999; Glevarec 2005; Wagg 2004). For example, interviews with Canadian youth radio producers found that participant empowerment occurred most intensely with the production of audio features and diaries (Wagg 2004). Moreover, the youth interviewed in this research said that a large part of their personal gains were dependent upon the circulation of audio pieces to a broadcast audience. Other scholars have similarly documented that positive impacts of media participation on youth depend upon creating products in an authentic voice (Kearney 2006; Mayer 2003; Whitney 2007), and circulating those products to a broad, public audience (Dauncey & Hare 1999; Glevarec 2005). The propensity for youth media producers to encounter risky situations, compounded by the importance of public and intimate communications as an avenue for achieving youth development goals, mandates scholars and practitioners to attend to the ethics of negotiating complex circumstances.

Ethical principles and practices

Scholars of media ethics tend to come out of a journalism background and share twin concerns of theoretical and philosophical premises on the one hand, and practical applications on the other (Christians, Fackler & Rotzoll 1998; Lambeth 1992). This approach to ethical difficulties is particularly well suited to youth media training programs as they also share twin concerns of achieving theoretical aims (youth development and enriched public discourse) and creating concrete products.

Theoretical orientations to ethical decision making range from universal to contingent perspectives (Christians, Fackler & Rotzoll 1995; Couldry 2006; Land 2006). Universal ethics are often traced back to the work of Kant (1964) whose "categorical imperatives" functioned as transcendent principles, such as "do no harm", which constituted obligations and duties for decision makers. This school of "deontological ethics" stands in contrast to teleological and situational approaches, such as utilitarian philosophies that focus on end points and outcomes as providing guidance for decision making (e.g. Mill 1861). Situational philosophers rightly point out that deontological approaches fail to acknowledge that universal principles frequently contradict one another, and they provide no direction in determining when and why one universal principle should trump another (Land 2006). A flaw in the situational approach, however, regards the inability to predict with certainty either positive or negative outcomes of specific decisions, uncertainty that is heightened by the variable nature of communication.

Despite the shortcomings of the various philosophical approaches, media scholars have used them as starting points leading to pragmatic models for decision making. Models and procedures for decision-making attempt to delineate steps for practitioners to follow when facing dilemmas in their work (Christians, Fackler & Rotzoll 1995; Lambeth 1992; Land 2006). These models vary in slight details, but they all recommend a process that approaches difficult situations by determining the facts and context underlying the case, identifying the philosophical principles that are in play, noting the values that relate to the principles, and establishing the stakeholders who are affected. Moving through these various steps will clarify and delineate competing principles and values as they relate to facts and stakeholders.

Drawing on the work of various media ethics scholars, Land (2006) identified five broad principles to include in a decision-making model, and two of them correspond closely to the conflicts identified in the youth media practices reviewed above. The first principle, "humanness", directs practitioners to "do no harm" and to perhaps "render aid" to stakeholders in a situation. The second principle, "stewardship", speaks to duty to provide content that serves the public interest by contributing discourse that enriches and expands the communication environment. Both principles are relevant to youth media practitioners examined in this study.

The contributions of media ethics scholars combined with the research of youth media production leads to the following questions:

- Do structural factors such as operational independence and availability of resources affect ethical decision-making and outcomes?

- Do means of implementation – process versus product emphases – change the approaches and outcomes of ethically challenging situations?

- Do particular production activities – personal diaries versus disinterested news features – lead to or result in ethical difficulties?

- When approaching ethical challenges in their work, do youth radio training practitioners implicitly or explicitly draw on frames of reference either implicitly or explicitly that either affirm, contradict, modify, or extend theoretical and practical approaches present in the communication research?

Findings

About one-third of all interviews identified conflicts, stresses, or other difficulties that raised ethical challenges for youth radio training programs. An examination of the context surrounding ethical situations is crucial for making sense of their development, resolution, and eventual outcomes.

Situations

Although one-third of participants in this study identified experiences that constituted ethical challenges, most of them occurred in just two locations: Radio Rookies in New York and Youth Radio Berkeley. Structurally, these two programs were distinctive for their relative emphasis on final audio products that were polished and engaging for a broad audience. They also spent significantly larger amounts of time working with youth on identifying topics and developing them in-depth through reporting and writing activities. Furthermore, adult trainers at Radio Rookies and Youth Radio Berkeley encouraged participants to explore issues with which they felt passionate, personal connections. In contrast, broadcast program topics at Blunt and Radio Arte were more oriented toward public affairs and social problems external to participating youth.

Indeed, ethical difficulties often arose because youth pursued topics close to their lives such as problems, difficulties, or experiences that they were confronting. For example, ethical difficulties in this study resulted from introspective reporting activities focusing on sexual identity, obesity, teen pregnancy, suicide, and broken homes. These sorts of topics are often emotionally charged, at times marked by conflict, and sometimes in violation of social norms, which makes them inherently vulnerable items to be pursuing for a broadcast audience. A young woman who wanted to use the audio feature to explore her own romantic "obsession" with a girl at her high school felt she needed to tell her father about it because of the negative impact the obsession had on her grades and family interactions:

> The hard part was interviewing people, even close ones, especially about my personal story. Like I had to interview my father. That was very difficult. I was like, "I don't want to tell my dad." But that was very important to me because I was sharing a big part of my life that I kept like secret from him. And I was telling him I was bisexual, and I was scared that he might see me differently and stuff. (Cuevas 2006)

This experience was tightly intertwined with the participant's individual development involving a close circle of family and friends. But revealing information about one's intimate life can also have repercussions outside of the boundaries of family and friends. Depending on the material in the audio feature, individuals could receive unwanted attention from school officials, law enforcement, or employers. Youths often expressed awareness of these repercussions only after producing the materials, and sometimes years after their completion:

> The first line in [my] commentary, and I don't think I'm ever going to forget it, was "The last thing on my mind when I go to sleep is suicide, and the first thing I think about when I awake is homicide." The most surprising thing was probably that it was broadcast. That was like the craziest thing. (Metz 2006)

The appraisal of this "surprising" decision was made several years after the original broadcast, but a few youth expressed awareness during their training that "you don't want to overshare things too personal for the air" (Moss 2006).

The emergence of ethical challenges resulting from the pursuit of highly personal topics might lead one to recommend avoiding such territory in order to prevent harming young producers. Such a step would go against the participatory nature of most youth radio training programs (since young people are typically involved in selecting their topics), but more importantly, it would undermine the success of the projects. Youth participants noted repeatedly that they had considered dropping out of the training programs because of the demand on their time and energy. The single most important factor that they identified as helping to sustain their commitment to the program was the high salience of the topics that they were able to explore in their work:

> The work does feel overwhelming. And so unless you have that story that you really need to tell, that's the only thing that can get you through the overwhelming work. Unless you have the drive to tell that story, that's the only thing that can get you through it. (Riddah 2006)

In addition to highly personal themes leading to ethical challenges, reporting practices sometimes led to strained relationships and conflictive interactions. Many of the participants interviewed in this study said that they approached friends and family as a part of their reporting duties, and those interactions brought them into stressful, sometimes combative situations:

> I was interviewing my dad and I was like, you know, I have to start asking him the real questions. "Dad, why do you make fun of me?" And the real questions got the real responses. And so of course the difficulty was interviewing my dad and so just admitting that you're a reporter and you walk outside with this microphone takes a lot of courage. (Riddah 2006)

In addition to interpersonal, family dynamics creating stress in interviews, sometimes the topics took producers into legal shadows that created fear within both families and external sources of information.

One youth producer, for example, described first-hand the immigrant experience of her family, which at the time of the reporting, had not completed the legal processes of becoming permanent residents:

> Pretty much like no one wanted me to do the story. Everybody was saying you know, even the lawyer was like, you want to wait until you get your permanent residence before you go on the air and talk about this. I was nervous about it. My uncle, he didn't want to do the interview, he didn't want me to do the story at all. So here I was doing a story and trying to get them to be interviewed and he was not having it at all. (Vickers 2006)

Outside of formal interviews, most of the teens recorded ambient sound and informal gatherings, which sometimes inadvertently captured slices of domestic life that family members insisted remain private. These situations created dilemmas and even conflicts for the participants who had been taught some fundamental principles of journalism and who now expressed a sense of importance and even duty to maintain captured audio in the story:

> I kind of knew my sister felt that having certain clothes made her less of a person. She said this one sentence like, she feels embarrassed that she doesn't have these clothes, and it's not like a one day thing. She has to go to school 10 months out of the year. So she feels this every day. She said something like, don't say that, don't say that, like you're embarrassing me, but I had to keep that in [the audio piece]. So that was hard. (Sollers 2006)

These kinds of situations presented difficulties that even seasoned professionals would find complex in terms of negotiating a satisfactory decision that balanced responsibility to the humaneness of the source with the duty of public service reporting.

On still other occasions, some youth reporters learned information in the process of information gathering that led to potential conflicts with their families. For example, one participant conducted a series of interviews surrounding his battle with cancer that had been successfully waged some years earlier. In the process of gathering information for the story, he learned that the stresses of his childhood disease nearly led to the breakup of his parents' marriage, a detail that he revealed, but only after some consternation.

Aside from the types of topics or relational conflicts that led to difficult situations, the broadcast nature of the programs raised ethical difficulties, as well. Even though youth participants faced difficulties and challenges during the reporting, writing, and editing phases of their work, the pressures and anxieties increased exponentially as their work came closer to being broadcast:

> I think the biggest effect was the night before my story was going to air. I told [the adult leader] Priya, "I don't want to put this on the air. I can't put myself on the air like this." (Riddah 2006)

In rare cases, youth participants noted that they actively avoided sharing the time and day of broadcasts with family members in order to avoid hurt feelings and conflicts.

Part of the anxiety stemming from the broadcast nature of their work was related to the permanence of the medium and the impact it had on teens looking back on their work. Several students noted that they were embarrassed about both the content and technical quality of work they had done in the initial phases of their involvement in the programs:

> It's also been very interesting for me, getting older and looking back at things that I have put out there in the past. There's things that I wrote about when I was 16 and I'm like I would never say that now, and I don't believe that any more. But now in this day and age, it doesn't just go into the ether. That will be there for the rest of your life when somebody looks you up, and so that was of particular concern when I wrote a commentary about experiencing like really severe depression. (Buentello 2006)

The consequences of youth productions and ethical decision making, therefore, are much higher for digital recordings than they were in the broadcast era.

Negotiations

The ways that ethical challenges were confronted included multiple approaches, but the various training programs consistently placed the objective of youth development over program production. Interviewees repeatedly noted that adult trainers emphasized that content control and final decisions were always in the hands of producers. But the adults did not merely toss the ethical ball back to the court of youth producers. They spent a significant amount of time dialoguing with the participants regarding various aspects of the situation.

Sometimes the adult advisors listed the facts surrounding the situations such as the players, the actions, the context, and the outcomes of specific topics. They also provided guidance and assistance in fact-checking both details, such as dates and places, as well as general assertions and conclusions inasmuch as that was possible. This exercise helped to provide clarity that led to sound decision-making:

> The people from the radio station they're like real understanding. They let me make complete decision, but they did kind of advise me. So they would tell me like, you know this is something that really happened during your disease. It would make for a good story if you would mention it because it just makes for a thicker plot. So I mean they kind of like told me the facts and like they tried to do everything to make me feel comfortable. (Escobar 2006)

The adult trainers also brainstormed options and possible responses that youth producers might pursue in facing ethical difficulties, including narrative and editing techniques that would address potential harm:

> They were like, you know, we could make it like, like we don't want to expose it completely. They said, we'll take less and less of it out because the, that specific piece was like really long, so they said, we'll take less and less of it out, we'll try to smoothen it out a bit so we won't make it look that bad. So I mean, they were just really helpful overall. (Escobar 2006)

Likewise, the adult trainers spent time thinking through potential positive and negative outcomes from the options that might be pursued in the production and broadcast of an audio feature. This was especially true in cases involving the law, such as the legal status of an immigrant and her family:

> Like I said, Radio Rookies has been very protective of me. We wasn't even sure when we started the story whether it was going to be a story. At first she [the adult leader] wasn't even sure if it could get aired when we first started interviewing people because you know... we wanted to make sure we understood what was legal, for nothing to happen to me. So that sort of took the pressure off too, to ask questions. (Vickers 2006)

Despite the efforts to project outcomes, some youth actively avoided thinking about the potential impacts of their work once it circulated in the public arena. This "denial", according to one youth participant, helped to produce the most "honest output for a really big audience" (Buentello 2006).

Sometimes adult leaders merely slowed down the process of decision-making to give youth ample time to process all of the factors at play in a situation. At Youth Radio Berkeley, for example, one commentary on a personal bout with severe depression was delayed for almost four years from inception to broadcast.

Although adult trainers played a pivotal role in helping youth negotiate complex situations and decisions, peer interactions also played a significant part in the various youth radio programs. Students listened to one another as they pitched story ideas and narrative directions, providing suggestions for paths to explore and interviews to conduct. They also provided a listening ear to students who were struggling, sometimes anguishing, over a perceived consequence related to an interview or a revelation. One producer was stressing over an upcoming interview where she intended to confess to her sister that she had lied to her about school activities:

> I don't know why I was so scared. You know, Chico, my other radio friend, he was like "It's a white lie, it's not that bad. When you tell her, she's not going to be mad." I'm like, "No, you're just saying that to make me happy." Well he was right. (Cuevas 2006)

Peer interactions often functioned to center youth participants who lacked the depth of experience needed to make sober, realistic appraisals of likely consequences. And because of the tight social connection with one another, youth-to-youth feedback reflected a credibility that adults simply could not achieve. This authenticity in providing advice complemented adult interventions in a way that helped assess situations and guide responses to them.

Consequences

Although the stresses and discomforts identified by youth participants were at times acute, all of the interviewees in this study reported satisfactory outcomes from their experiences. The uncertainty of anticipating fruitful outcomes, however, heightens the difficulties in making ethically responsible decisions.

Even though the situations noted above created discomfort, pressure, or embarrassment for youth producers, the ability to control the content of a personal issue seemed to justify these difficulties. The processes of autonomy in production seemed to go a long way to address personal struggles faced by youth:

> For me to structure my story and tell this complicated story was so profound. It had such a huge meaning to me that I'm telling my complex story and I have control of how it's told, and when it's told, and why it's told. (Riddah 2006)

Similarly, having the opportunity to vocalize thoughts and emotions that had been internalized seemed to function therapeutically for participants in a way that justified the difficult situations that youth experienced:

> After I wrote it, I didn't think it was going to bother me, like emotionally, I was kind of sad after I read it, but actually it felt like something was different. It felt like I kind of got something off my shoulders, like I needed to express that. And it made it feel better because you are saying it out loud instead of saying it just to yourself. (Moss 2006)

Some of the very practices and processes that led to problematic situations seemed to ameliorate them, as well. A good example of this concerns the public service nature of the programs. Many youth participants noted that the conflicts and stresses that they experienced were mitigated once the impact on the public was demonstrated to them. Most of the youth in this study – whether or not they identified an ethical dilemma – linked successes of the program to the social impact of their efforts.

This was especially true for participants who had struggled with a personal, ethical conflict:

> The thing that really changed my view on it was when I played the clip of my uncle, and I could see people's reaction to the story, and everybody asking all these

questions and having complete concern for somebody that they don't even know. So that was when I was like "OK, yeah, I really want to go on with the story. I think that maybe even if it touches one person, it sounds corny, but you know, like it would be worth it. (Vickers 2006)

Sometimes ethically challenging situations involved a period of discomfort for participants that was deemed worthwhile, but only after the audio project was completed and circulated to the public. Participants noted that in the process of working on their projects, the appreciation of the outcome was impossible to anticipate:

It's really tricky. You don't see the positive effect of this until the story airs on the radio. That's when everything kicks in. When you turn on that radio station, and right after hearing the journalist say, "dad dada dada da", you hear, "Hi, my name is Elie", that's when all your hard work kicks in. (Riddah 2006)

Participants noted that in the process of completing audio features, many youth were unable to see the end point that would justify the difficulties, challenges, and commitments experienced in these programs.

Discussion

The literature review indicating a lack of attention to youth media production activities, especially in the area of radio, has been expanded by this study in a way that demonstrates the utility of this sort of research. The preceding accounts of conflicts and stresses illustrate the inherent complexities of youth media training programs that defy simple recipes or calculations regarding ethical decision making.

All of the programs examined in this study, for example, embraced the dual goals of contributing to the public interest and cultivating the well-being of participants. Achieving both of these aims frequently resulted in situations that created ethical dilemmas for practitioners. Likewise, the focus on autobiographical stories that contributed so strongly to youth involvement were the very types of productions that led to emotional vulnerability and familial disagreements. As long as youth radio training programs pursue the dual goals of making strong public communications and cultivating youth well-being, they will continue to confront ethical challenges on a regular basis.

This study revealed, however, that not all programs are destined to deal with regularly recurring ethical difficulties. The youth radio training programs with stronger "product" orientations tended to generate more ethically challenging situations than did the programs that were more "process" focused. Radio Rookies and Youth Radio Berkeley directed its students to produce audio features and commentaries that went into greater depth, substance, and detail than did the programs at Blunt and Radio Arte. By directing students to make larger time and energy commitments to their audio productions, Radio Rookies and Youth Radio encouraged students to focus on issues with which they had a personal claim.

While focusing on topics with high personal salience was very practical in ensuring sustained youth involvement with the production, this step also led to increased producer vulnerability in the process. It would be a mistake to conclude from this that training programs should avoid "product" focused goals.

Instead, this finding should alert youth training personnel that high impact, in-depth audio features with which producers have a strong personal tie are more likely to lead to situations demanding sensitive ethical decision making.

Finally, the findings of this study demonstrated that youth radio trainers responded to challenges by adopting a hybrid approach to ethical difficulties. That is, they seemed to adopt both a universalist and a situational orientation toward ethical decision-making by on the one hand granting primacy to youth development outcomes over communication product goals (universalist), while on the other hand helping youth participants think through the potential consequences and outcomes of their decisions (situational). Likewise, adult leaders seemed to adopt some of the values and procedures described by scholars, such as helping youth producers establish facts, consider narrative and editing techniques, and evaluate information and communication options that were available to them. Nevertheless, this study offers no evidence that youth radio trainers operate in a systematic manner when dealing with various situations. If this study has one lasting contribution to make, therefore, it is the suggestion that formal attention to media ethics would be a practical and frequently used investment for professionals interested in youth media production programs.

References

Berson, G. (2001) 'Forward', in Graber, D. (ed.) *Let a Thousand Voices Speak: A Guide to Youth Radio Programs in the United States and Hints for Starting Your Own*. San Francisco: National Federation of Community Broadcasters.

Buckingham, D. (n.d.) *The Media Literacy of Children and Young People: A Review of the Research Literature on Behalf of Ofcom*. London: Center for the Study of Children.

Buckingham, D. (2003) Media Education: Literacy, Learning, and Contemporary Culture. Cambridge, UK: Polity Press.

Buentello, Maritza. [pseud.] (2006) Interview by author. Tape recording. Berkeley, CA, July 31.

Christians, C.G., Fackler, M., & Rotzoll, K.B. (1998) *Media Ethics: Cases & Moral Reasoning* (5th ed.). New York: Longman.

Couldry, N. (2006) *Listening Beyond the Echoes: Media, Ethics, and Agency in an Uncertain World*. Boulder, CO: Paradigm Publishers.

Cuevas, Sandra. [pseud.] (2006) Interview by author. Tape recording. New York, NY, June 16.

Dauncey, H., & Hare, G. (1999) 'French Youth Talk Radio: The Free Market and Free Speech', *Media, Culture & Society* 21(1): 93-108.

Dervin, B. (2002) *Sense-Making Methodology Reader*. Cresskill, NJ: Hampton Press.

Escobar, Edward. [pseud.] (2006) Interview by author. Tape recording. New York, NY, June 15.

Featherstone, L. (1998) 'Making Waves', Columbia Journalism Review September/October: 18.

Glevarec, H. (2005) 'Youth Radio as "Social Object": The Social Meaning of "Free Radio" Shows for Young People in France', *Media, Culture & Society* 27(3): 333-351.

Goodman, S. (2003) *Teaching Youth Media: A Critical Guide to Literacy, Video Production, & Social Change.* New York: Teachers College Press.

Graber, D. (2001) *Let a Thousand Voices Speak: A Guide to Youth Radio Programs in the United States and Hints for Starting Your Own.* San Francisco: National Federation of Communication Broadcasters.

Kant, I. (1964) *Groundwork of the Metaphysics of Morals.* New York: Harper Torchbooks.

Kearney, M.C. (2006) *Girls Make Media.* New York: Routledge.

Kelliher, L. (2003) 'Low Power, High Intensity', *Columbia Journalism Review* September/October: 31-33.

Lambeth, E.B. (1992) *Committed Journalism: An Ethic for the Profession* (2nd ed). Blomington, IN: Indiana University Press.

Land, M. (2006) 'Mass Media Ethics and the Point-of-decision pyramid', in Land, M. & Hornaday B. W. (eds.) *Contemporary Media Ethics.* Spokane. WA: Marquette Books.

Mayer, V. (2003) *Producing Dreams, Consuming Youth: Mexican Americans and Mass Media.* New Brunswick, NJ: Rutgers University Press.

Metz, Terrence. [pseud.] (2006) Interview by author. Tape recording. Berkeley, CA, July 31.

Mill, J.S. (1861) *Utilitarianism.* London: J.M. Dent.

Moss, Carla. [pseud.] (2006) Interview by author. Tape recording. Berkeley, CA, August 2.

O'Neill, O. (1996) *Towards Justice and Virtue: A Constructive Account of Practical Reasoning.* Cambridge: Cambridge University Press.

Richman, J. (2002) Finding the Truth in the Words, Sighs and Silences. http://www.npr.org/templates/story/story.php?storyId=881837. Accessed June 28, 2005.

Riddah, Elie. [pseud.] (2006) Interview by author. Tape recording. New York, NY, June 14.

Soep, E. (2007) 'Jumping for Joy, Wracking Our Brains, Searching Our Souls: Youth Media and Its Digital Contradictions', *Youth Media Reporter: The Professional Journal of the Youth Media Field* 1(special features): 102-109.

Sollers, Jessica. [pseud.] (2006) Interview by author. Tape recording. New York, NY, June 19.

Thomas, M. (2007) 'Girls Write Now: A Showcase of Intergenerational Learning', *Youth Media Reporter: The Professional Journal of the Youth Media Field* 1(3): 32-34.

Tyner, K. (2007) 'Youth Media at the Threshold: A Research Based Field-Building Agenda', *Youth Media Reporter: The Professional Journal of the Youth Media Field* 1(special features): 110-119.

Vickers, Kate. [pseud.] (2006) Interview by author. Tape recording. New York, NY, June 16.

Wagg, H. (2004) 'Empowering Youth with Radio Power: "Anything Goes" on CKUT Campus-Community Radio', *Journal of Radio Studies* 11: 268-276.

Whitney, E. (2007) 'Finding Youth Voice in Print Media: The Power of Zines in a Digital Age', *Youth Media Reporter: The Professional Journal of the Youth Media Field* 1(3): 35-37.

Youth in Processes: Participatory Production

Participatory Communication Processes as Infusions of Innovation
The Case of 'Scenarios from Africa'[1]

Karen Greiner

Abstract

Based on field research conducted in Senegal, this chapter describes how 'Scenarios from Africa', an HIV/AIDS communication process has generated extensive youth engagement – 105,000 participants in 10 years – and has expanded the role of young people from recipient or target of informational campaigns to agents and creators of health communication content. I examine how the Scenarios from Africa script writing contest serves as a mechanism for catalyzing and channeling the ideas of creative young people, resulting in a culturally situated "infusion" of innovative ideas. My analysis stems from field notes, transcripts of interviews with contest participants, the "Scenarios from Africa" founders, Senegalese contest organizers, and a thorough review of actual and archival "Scenarios from Africa" written and audio-visual materials. The aim of this chapter is to contribute to our understanding of how participatory communication processes can generate engaging health communication content by tapping into the innovative ideas of young people.

> *The task of an organizer is to set up structures so people can participate.*
> (Mike Prokash, United for a Fair Economy)[2]

Walking through the halls of Galee Nanon Diral, a community center in the outskirts of Dakar, one can see a variety of HIV/AIDS prevention messages targeting young people – the community center's main draw. One framed poster sponsored by the Senegalese Minister of Health reads: "Being faithful: a measure of security." Another poster, sponsored by the U.S. Agency for International Development, shows a young man jogging by a scantily clad woman, who is beckoning him to approach. "Abstaining until marriage: It's my way to say no to ISTs, HIV and AIDS", the text reads. Arriving at the end of one hallway one then comes across an unframed Scenarios from Africa poster. The poster features the names of the winners of the 2005 Scenarios from Africa script writing contest. The names of several local teenagers have been highlighted: these are the 2005 grand prize winners who prepared their entries with the help of Galee Nanon Diral staff. On the bottom of the Scenarios poster, in large block letters, are the words: "Congratulations to the winners!" The contrast between the posters produced by government agencies (whether Senegalese or U.S.) and Scenarios from Africa reflects a difference in how communication about HIV/AIDS is approached by each entity. The government produced posters are message driven: fidelity and marriage are the chosen themes and young people are the target. The sponsors of the posters are well marked, and yet it remains unclear how the content and design of the messages were developed or chosen. The Scenarios from Africa poster lists the names of young people who submitted prize-winning original scripts about HIV/AIDS and provides a website address to view the films created from the scripts. From the Scenarios poster we gather that films about HIV/AIDS have been produced using as content the ideas submitted by young Africans across the continent. Here young people are *producers* of content, and the young participants, and the result of their talent, are the focus of the poster.

The centerpiece of the Scenarios from Africa approach to communication is the contest, a popular mechanism for inviting young people to be innovators and agents of change in their own communities. In *What Pragmatism Means*,

Aida Sene, Fatimata Ba, Aminata Ba, Kadi Diaw, Maguette Lo and Oulmata Sy, Scenarios Contestants and 2005 TV5 Grand Prize Winners at the Galee Nanon Diral community center in Yeumbeul (outskirts of Dakar).
Photo: Karen Greiner

William James suggests that "there can be no difference anywhere that doesn't make a difference elsewhere" (379). In this essay, I argue that the "Scenarios from Africa approach" to HIV/AIDS communication, and in particular the use of the contest mechanism, is different in several important ways from traditional "message driven", diffusion/dissemination approaches that promote behavior change at the individual level. However, rather than presenting a binary, "either or" argument, I hope to illustrate how the Scenarios from Africa approach to communication can supplement what I am calling traditional, message driven approaches to HIV/AIDS prevention. With 22 million people living with HIV in Sub-Saharan Africa (UNAIDS, 2007), it is clear that carefully crafted messages are still necessary to help raise awareness about modes of HIV transmission and means of prevention. Yet in addition to developing informational messages of prevention, it is important that "target populations" also have opportunities to participate in meaningful ways in interventions developed for their benefit. The Scenarios from Africa approach to HIV/AIDS communication goes beyond "messaging" by inviting extensive participation in the creation and dissemination of culturally appropriate content about HIV/AIDS. The Scenarios from Africa approach, I contend, offers a model (rather than a recipe), of how to create mechanisms for young people to become active producers, rather than mere beneficiaries, of HIV/AIDS communication interventions. By creating a structure people can participate in, the Scenarios from Africa process offers a community based activity in which the "community" shifts from setting/target to agent/resource (McLeroy et al. 2003: 529).

Theoretically, I position the highly participatory and invitational[3] nature of the Scenarios from Africa approach as an inversion of the classic "diffusion of innovations" model developed by Everett Rogers, and many other scholars[4] (See Rogers 2003; Coleman et al. 1966; Deutschmann & Danielson 1960; Deutschmann & Fals Borda 1962; Katz 1961, 1962, 1999; Valente 1995). This theoretical perspective will be developed in conversation with the narratives of several Scenarios contestants, many of whom have gone on to participate in other aspects of the Scenarios process. Based on the quantity and quality of youth participation in the Scenarios process, I am calling the Scenarios process a mechanism for eliciting and channeling an "infusion of innovation" from young people.

In the sections that follow, I provide background on the history and people behind Scenarios from Africa and elaborate on what I am calling the Scenarios from Africa approach to HIV/AIDS communication. Further, I clarify my use of key terms like "participation" and "infusions of innovation" while theorizing how the Scenarios approach differs from other communication interventions, and – to paraphrase Gregory Bateson – in what ways these are "differences which make a difference" (318).

My analysis is based on archival research, interviews with the founders of Scenarios, and five weeks of field work in Senegal during which I engaged in direct observation and conducted interviews with more than two dozen individuals involved with the Scenarios process, including several contest participants.

Background on Scenarios from Africa

Scenarios from Africa is a communication process[5] that involves a contest for African youth under the age of 25 who are invited to submit scripts about issues of HIV/AIDS based on their understanding of the epidemic in their own communities. Contestant scripts are evaluated by national and international juries comprised of a wide variety of individuals including people living with HIV/AIDS (PLWHA), HIV/AIDS specialists, educators, former contest winners, and representatives from non-governmental organizations (NGOs) working primarily, but not exclusively, in HIV/AIDS prevention, testing and stigma reduction[6]. Contest winners' original ideas are turned into short films by renowned African directors and after being dubbed into several African languages[7], are distribute free of charge to broadcasters, government health agencies, educational institutions and non-governmental organizations across the continent. To date, there have been five completed "editions" of the Scenarios contest held in Africa (1997, 2000, 2002 & 2005). Now held in 35 African countries,[8] the contest has grown steadily since its inception in 1997, reaching more than 105,000 young people by then end of the fourth edition in 2005.

Since 1997, 31 Scenarios films, varying in length from 2 to 15 minutes, have been produced based on winning contest ideas (Global Dialogues 2007: 3). As of February, 2008, 90,000 copies of the films have been distributed VHS cassettes, CD-Roms, or DVDs to community based organization and government agencies

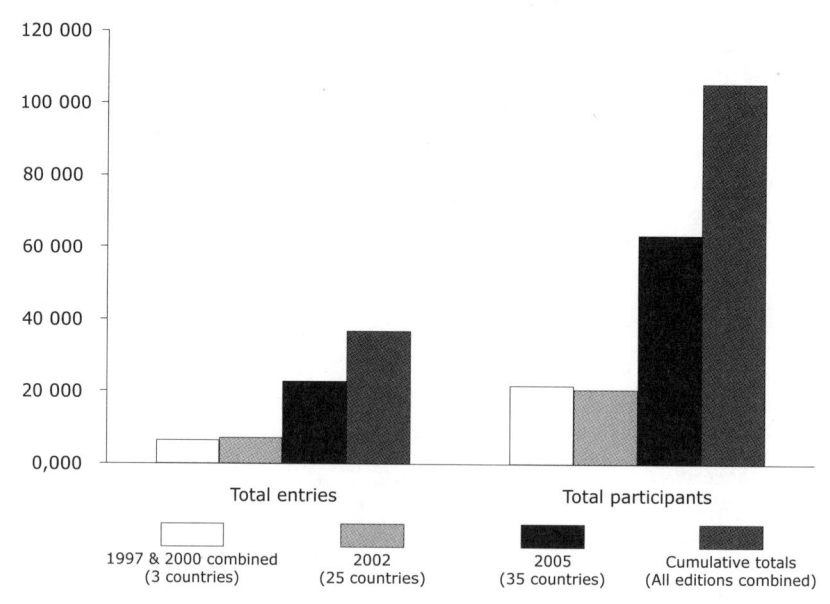

Figure 1. Youth participation in Scenarios Contests, 1997-2005

Source: *Global Dialogues*, SFA 2005 final report.

in Africa as well as to the European headquarters of corporations with offices in Africa[9]. The most recent final report issued by Global Dialogues confirms that Scenarios films have been broadcast on 100 television stations in 35 countries of sub-Saharan Africa, as well as on local stations serving immigrant African populations in Europe and the United States. (Global Dialogues 2007: 3).

The entire Scenarios from Africa process (contest, jury, film production and distribution) is implemented by hundreds of non-governmental organizations (NGOs) and community based organizations (CBOs) across sub-saharan Africa. The process is co-coordinated by Global Dialogues, a British charitable organization founded by Kate Winskell and Daniel Enger in 1996, and was first inspired by "3000 scenarios against a virus",[10] a scriptwriting contest held in France in 1992 (Winskell & Enger 2007: 6). Global Dialogues has been responsible for securing the financing which supports the bulk of the activities implemented "in the field" by local organizations (dissemination and collection of contest materials, organization of writing mentorship programs, etc.). Scenarios from Africa has been supported financially since 1997 by a variety of organizations[11], the most long-standing and consistent contributors including: Comic Relief (UK), the UK Department for International Development, the UK National Lottery's Charity Board, the Pfizer Foundation, and the United Nations Population Fund (UNFPA) (Winskell & Enger 2007: 6). The Scenarios process also includes a research component: the National Institutes of Health is currently[12] funding a systematic analysis of a sample of the 22,000 stories submitted during the 2005 contest cycle with the aim of gaining insight into young people's representations of HIV/AIDS and to compare the representations of young people from different African countries with contrasting epidemiological profiles (CRISP database 2008)[13].

In their comprehensive article on Scenarios from Africa, Scenarios founders Kate Winskell and Daniel Enger describe Scenarios process as being comprised of "three basic steps": 1) the contest, 2) selection and analysis of the scripts, and 3) production and distribution of the films created from the winning script ideas (2005: 3). The conceptual model of the Scenarios process offered by Winskell and Enger lists two primary goals: reduced transmission of HIV and reduced stigma for people living with HIV/AIDS (2005: 4). These primary goals notwithstanding, Winskell and Enger describe the Scenarios process as one with several additional intended outcomes, including increasing dialogue and reflection (2005: 4) and putting young people "in a position such that society in general becomes the beneficiary of their knowledge, creativity, and energy"" (Winskell & Enger 2005: 12). In her article on participatory communication, Cecilia Peruzzo notes that one of the most important yet oft overlooked means for fostering community involvement is as simple as the creation of multiple avenues and channels (1996: 175). What Scenarios from Africa has done since 1997, via the contest mechanism, has been centered around the creation of channels to elicit youth participation in the HIV/AIDS communication process.

The Scenarios contest, they write: "is designed to help break the silence around HIV and to generate dialogue and debate between young people themselves, as well as between young people and a range of other interlocutors in their communities" (Global Dialogues 2005c: 2). Scenarios co-founder Daniel Enger offered this comment on the intentions of Scenarios organizers:

> Some people argue that the contest should be seized as an opportunity to teach young people key information of the day. I increasingly realize that the contest is ideally a moment for young people to explore, learn and express themselves on their own terms, and for the massive and diverse Scenarios contest team to listen to the young participants and to learn from them. The focus is on learning, not teaching – a mindset that might not come naturally to many who occupy leadership positions in education, health, the media and government.[14]

The Scenarios founders describe dialogue as "guiding philosophical principle, a *modus operandi*, and a primary outcome" of their activities (Winskell & Enger 2005: 7). A post-contest survey conducted in 2005 with more than 300 contest participants in three countries[15] reflected that:

- 82.32% of survey participants had spoken about HIV/AIDS with others while creating their contest entries;
- Those who had discussed HIV/AIDS with others during the contest had spoken on average with 5.86 different people about the epidemic;
- 61.09% of all survey participants said they had discussed HIV/AIDS with a certain person(s) for the first time in their lives as they prepared their entries;
- 52.06% of the survey participants said that, while creating their contest entries, they sought information at a local HIV/AIDS resource center; and
- 82.59% of respondents reported having read documents on HIV/AIDS to learn more about the epidemic as they prepared their contest entries.

(Global Dialogues 2005a: 9-10, 2005c: 2).

This essay draws seeks to give texture to these statistics by calling upon the voices of contest participants in Senegal, a country with 10 years of experience hosting Scenarios contests. The reflections of participants of several editions of the contest in Senegal will help illustrate their involvement with the Scenarios process, which will provide insight on the myriad ways in which the Scenarios approach creates opportunities for participation and dialogue for and among young people.

In this next section, I provide a glimpse of what forms "participation" in the Scenarios process can take. I refrain from major commentary on the narratives, preferring to leave them intact by withholding analysis until the end of the last interview.

Participant voices

The first contest participant[16] I interviewed was Diarra Diakhaté, who was 17 and a junior in high school when he entered the first edition of the Scenarios from Africa Contest (then called 'Scenarios from the Sahel') in 1997. His entry was chosen by an international jury as one of 13 to be turned into films by reknown African Directors. His ideas were used as the basis for the film "Just Once"[17] (Pour Une Fois), directed by Idrissa Ouédraogo,

> I got the entry form at ACI (African Consultants International, a non-governmental organization in Dakar). Actually, I got two entry forms, because I had many ideas. Like many people my age, I thought: It's a contest, so of course I want to participate. But I didn't think about winning – I just wanted to participate and I wanted to submit comic strips as my entry. I drew a story about a man whose wife has HIV, and the man wants to have sex with his wife, but he doesn't have condoms and he say "I don't care", he still wants to have sex – but the woman insists that he needs to wear a condom so he won't get HIV. But the husband can't find condoms anywhere – everywhere is sold out. When he finally gets back to his house he realizes that all along the wife had condoms but she wanted to see if he was determined enough to do what was necessary to get the condom – and of course, he is upset that all along she had a condom but in the end they wind up in bed together.

I asked Diarra why he decided to draw a story about an HIV positive woman with an HIV negative husband. He replied:

> At the time I was writing the script – there was still very little information available about this topic – everyone was talking about prevention – how to avoid transmission – I wanted to go a little farther and talk about people who are already living with HIV – to talk about issues affecting this group of people.

Diarra now works in the document center at Africa Consultants International. His duties include the dissemination of educational materials, including Scenarios Films, to other NGOs and government agencies throughout Senegal. According to Diarra, the Scenarios Films are frequently requested. "Since the films are free, they are very easy to distribute – I often slip them in with other materials that people ask for. But the fact that they are free might also mean that people don't take care of them as they would if they had paid for them."

When I asked him what final comments he had about his participation in the Scenarios process, Diarra said that what he most enjoyed about participating was "the spirit of competition and a sense of curiosity it inspires." With a sly smile, he added: "But I would like to see the age limit increased so that 'old guys' like me could still compete." Although he can no longer win prizes, Diarra accepted the invitation of the Scenarios team in Senegal to continue participating in the contest as a jury member.

The grand prize winners[18] of the 2005 Scenarios from Africa contest was a team of 16 young people from Yembeuil, on the outskirts of Dakar. At the time of their contest participation, several of the team members were working as outreach workers at health center in the Galee Nanon Diral community center. In December 2008, I interviewed six of the sixteen team members, who jointly related the process of their participation in the contest:

> The Scenarios coordinator Gabriel Diouf called the center (Galee Nanon Diral) and told us that a contest was starting. We went to meet him to get the contest entry forms and information about the contest. We decided to meet every Saturday for one hour to share information and work on our script. When we would then go home, and we would all think some more and then when we would get together we would share more ideas. Seinabou Diop, the supervisor of the health program (at Galee), was very supportive in helping us and providing information. For our contest entry, we didn't just submit a script; we also submitted a poem and some songs.
>
> In our story, we talk about a small business owner, who instead of worrying about making money, really cares about the well-being of his employees. One of his employees gets diagnosed with HIV and he hears her crying, so he comes to ask her what's wrong – and he comes and sees her crying, and he sees that she is holding a paper that has a positive test for HIV…and the boss consoles her and tells the woman that he wants her to take some time off and he tells her he will support her. The thing to retain from our story is that it is important to help people who are living with the virus and that even if people have HIV they can still work. In our story we are trying to talk about the discrimination and stigmatization of people living with HIV. A lot of our ideas for the script came from things we would hear in the news, and also things we hear about AIDS in the neighborhood.

When I asked for any final comments about the contest, one young woman responded: "In the neighborhood we also hear people say that AIDS doesn't exist. If we had to write another script we should probably talk about the importance of testing."

Three years after winning the contest, many of the original team members are still doing outreach work at the Galee Nanon Diral health center, including the six young women I interviewed. The women lead twice-weekly "conversation clubs" about HIV/AIDS and sexual/reproductive health with groups of teenagers aged 13-16.

I met another contest participant, Lamine Sagna, one sunny afternoon in mid-December at the Alliance Francaise in Dakar. I was introduced to Lamine by Gabriel Diouf, the national coordinator of Scenarios in Senegal. Lamine described his participation in the two contests, which began in 2000:

> I first participated in the contest when it was still called "Scenarios from the Sahel." One of the friends of my older brothers came to talk to me about participating in the contest. He was volunteering with an HIV outreach organization, and he knew

that I love literature, and that I love writing, and so he told me about the contest. I already had some stories I was working with before hearing about the contest. For that entry I adapted what I was writing to talk about HIV. I wrote about a young football (soccer) player who contracts HIV and loses his career. I tried to portray the cruel character of the epidemic at that time. After the contest, I started volunteering at the organization with my brother's friend. During the sessions we held for other young people I got a lot of ideas for other stories. In 2003 I entered the contest again and wrote a love story, about a businessman who falls in love with a girl who is HIV positive. She is afraid to tell him at first but then she finally does and they eventually get married and adopt a baby. The second time I entered the contest it was a lot easier because I had a much more information because of my volunteer work.

At the end of the interview I asked Lamine what comments or suggestions he had regarding the Scenarios process. His response came quickly: "I think all of the contestant's scripts should be published. There are a lot of scripts that can't be made into films", he said, "but that doesn't mean that they aren't all good stories."

When I left Lamine, Gabriel Diouf was just pulling up a chair to his table. "I'm going to ask Lamine to help us organize this years contest", he announced. I later learned that Lamine had agreed. For his continued participation, this time as team member, he would be receiving a small budget for materials and transportation.

Another look at participation

Direct participation has been heralded as a necessary correction to models of development and communication that view change and innovation as always emanating from the core (or the global North) out to a periphery (or global South). Rural sociologist Robert Chambers has dedicated his professional career to promoting increased participation of local communities in development efforts. In his book *Whose Reality Counts? Putting the First Last,* Chambers describes the objective of development as "well being for all" and argues that a key component in achieving well being is participation (9). Sustainable development approaches, he writes, should include: "facilitating participation, with approaches which are bottom up with processes of learning, rather than top-down with blue prints" (11).

Brazilian educator Paulo Freire's designation for the "top-down" approach in his field was the term "the banking method" of instruction. The banking method limits the role of the "recipient" to that of a passive storage receptacle while the teacher's task is to "'fill' the students with the contents of his narration" (1993: 71). Participatory approaches attempt to reverse the top-down, core-periphery flow of information and innovation. And yet, as many have acknowledged, not all forms of participation are necessarily liberating. Take, for example, the common practice in business of inviting employees to a meeting at which management presents new ideas and asks for employee "participation", which invariable takes the form of rubber-stamping what has already been decided upon. In other words, power dynamics in the workplace, as in international development, often do not allow for genuine participation.

Chambers concedes that the popularity of participatory approaches have created a "fad", which has led to occasions when participation is "co-opted and contorted" by donors who in some cases "demand" an inclusive approach. Uma Kothari, a contributor to the book *Participation: The New Tyranny?*, echoes Chambers warning by suggesting that participatory approaches in international development settings are often used as a means of control. She writes:

> Those people who have the greatest reason to challenge and confront power relations and structures are brought, or even bought, through the promise of development assistance, into the development process in ways that disempower them to change the prevailing hierarchies and inequalities in society...(2001: 143).

For Kothari, participation can become a form of "inclusionary control" which only serves to induce conformity (2001: 143).

The young people I interviewed were (and are) eagerly and voluntarily involved in the fight against HIV/AIDS. Their engagement exceeds, and in some cases, precedes, their direct participation as contestants in Scenarios from Africa. The invitational nature of the Scenarios process made it possible – and attractive – for these motivated youngsters to put their creative talents to use in the creation of culturally appropriate and youth-friendly HIV/AIDS communication content. The contest mechanism is not used to convoke or persuade young people to participate: it merely creates the *potential* for participation. The success or failure of the contest (and the subsequent films) begins with Scenarios' young participants. The porous nature of the Scenarios process allows for participation to continue beyond the life cycle of one contest. I use to term "porous" to convey the idea of a process with multiple and continuous entry points and opportunities for involvement.

Interviews with the Scenarios founders and a review of their annual reports reveal that Diarra, Lamine and the team from Galee Nanon Diral are not the only contest participants who have made "multiple entries" into the Scenarios process. Ten years after submitting a script for the 1997 contest, participant Olga Ouédraogo took the initiative to create audio versions of several stories which were previously only available in visual formats.[19] A 2002 contest participant, Sandra Nsambi Nzali of the Democratic Republic of Congo, helped disseminate information about the Scenarios contest when she was invited to speak on the radio in Belgium.[20] In 2007, the Scenarios team in Burkina Faso received 3 different scenarios from a young man from the Comoro Islands living in Egypt. He told the Scenarios team that he had heard about the contest through Radio

France International (RFI), and that he intended to mobilize his Egyptian friends to take part.[21] Several people living with HIV/AIDS serving as Scenarios mentors in Burkina Faso bravely volunteered to appear as actors in a Scenarios film about living with HIV.[22] The depth and breadth of participation catalyzed by the Scenarios process reflect the variety of interests, skills and talents, which young Africans can put into action when provided an outlet.

Global dialogues co-founder Daniel Enger describes the unanticipated and unplanned benefits of the participants' contributions to the Scenarios process as being a product of trust. For Enger, trust means "having faith in everyday people's capacity to take a process (contest) and a tool (films) and run with them in a direction you might never have thought of – or perhaps even agree with."[23]

Two models of communication

Everett Rogers defines the diffusion of innovations as the "process in which an innovation is communicated through certain channels over time among the members of a social system (2003: 5). Typically, diffusion interventions involve an effort to promote the adoption of an idea, technology or practice, which is perceived as new by the target community. In many cases, those promoting adoption of an innovation are the creators/marketers of the innovation, or government agencies. Examples of diffusion interventions include the Egyptian government's oral rehydration therapy (ORT) campaign aimed at reducing infant mortality from diarrhea-related dehydration (Rogers 2003: 380; see also Abdulla 2003), and the successful promotion by a local community association of solar energy in rural areas of the Dominican Republic (Rogers 2003: 31; see also Lesnick 2000). Generally speaking, diffusion interventions are perceived by the change agents who promote them as attempts to spread the adoption of ideas, technologies or practices which are deemed socially beneficial by the change agents. In some cases, diffusion techniques are employed by corporations attempting to gain a market advantage over competitors, as occurred when the makers of VHS version of the VCR recorder triumphed over its BETA competitor (Rogers 351). The purpose of diffusion campaigns is to persuade targeted groups (citizens, consumers, etc.) to adopt the innovation promoted by change agents.

The Scenarios from Africa approach to communication inverts this process in several ways. The term "infusions of innovation" is used to describe the Scenarios process because 1) the directionality of communication is inverted (coming in instead of going out), and 2) the locus of innovation is inverted (created by the community rather than the change agent). The contest mechanism invites and channels "infusion", thousands of entries submitted by over 105,000 participants, of creative ideas "innovation". The difference in these two processes, in very simplified form, can be visually depicted in this way:

Figure 2. Two models of communication

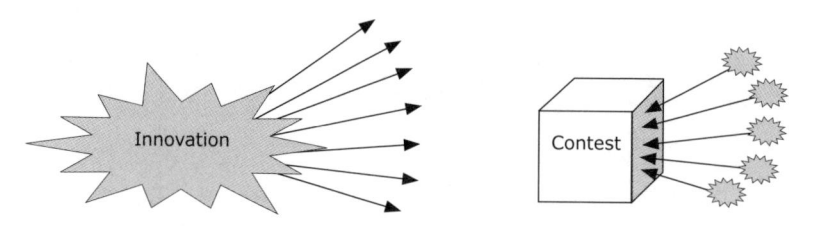

Diffusion model: Change agents promote diffuse innovation to community

Infusion model: Change agents create mechanisms to channel community innovation

The innovativeness of the contest participants is most apparent in the films created from their scripts. The storylines reflect the humor, compassion, perceptiveness and ingenuity of the young people who generated the content of the films. Contestants like Diarra, with his comic strip entries and the team from Yembeuil, with their poetry and songs, pushed the boundaries of what formats script ideas could take. The term "infusions of innovation" aims to capture both the quantity and quality of youth participation in the Scenarios process. Youth participation ranged from contestant, to juror, to contest organizer, to actor, to audio producer and voice actor. Each of the contest participants I interviewed continued or began HIV/AIDS outreach work after the contest cycle was over. Although the number of participants interviewed is small, their stories provide a textured look at youth participation in the Scenarios process within and beyond the contest cycle. Evaluations of the Scenario process provide many more testimonies of young people – contestants, mentors and organizers alike – describing their pride and satisfaction at being able to contribute to the fight against HIV/AIDS in their communities (See Gannon 2001, 2003; Global Dialogues 2005a, 2005b, 2005c, 2005d; and Hounnou, 2005).

Conclusion

Several representatives of the local organizations who lend their energy and talent to help organize the Scenarios in Senegal stated that one of the most valuable lessons from their experience was how much there was to be learned from young people.[24] The Scenarios process provides the opportunity for young people to be innovative and to contribute to their communities in meaningful ways and provides their elders with an opportunity to experience them as such. In her joint article with Daniel Enger, Kate Winskell echoes this observation. She writes:

> Without doubt, young people are key beneficiaries of the *Scenarios* process. However, that process also serves to put young people in a position such that society

in general becomes the beneficiary of their knowledge, creativity, and energy (Winskell & Enger 2005: 12).

The question of assessing the importance and relevance of extensive and varied youth participation returns us to the matter of trust. A willingness to adopt or adapt the Scenarios approach to communication requires trust in the enthusiasm, capacity and creativity of young people. When adult organizers are ready to relinquish strict control of social change interventions and begin creating mechanisms that invite meaningful youth participation, an infusion of innovations just might follow.

Notes

1. I would like to thank Kate Winskell and Daniel Enger of Global Dialogues, Gabriel Diouf of Scenarios Senegal and Gary Engelberg and the entire staff of Africa Consultants International for their incredible generosity and support before, during and after my fieldwork in Senegal. I am also indebted to Arvind Singhal for his unflagging support and mentorship.
2. Cited in Boyd, 2002: 252 and personal interview with A. Boyd, August, 2008.
3. My use of the term "invitational" is influenced by the writing of rhetoricians Karen Foss and Cindy Griffen. (See Foss & Griffin 1995).
4. Diffusion of innovations research has a long and rich history. For in-depth bibliographies and summaries of diffusion of innovations research see Haider, M. & Kreps, G. L. (2004); Hornik (2004); and Rogers, Singhal & Quinlan (2008).
5. I use the term "process" rather than project for several reasons: 1) Scenarios founders Kate Winskell and Daniel Enger give preference to this term (See Winskell & Enger, 2005); 2) the effort and participation involved with Scenarios contest implementation, jury sessions, film production and distribution far exceed the scope of a traditional time-bound project ; and 3) the Scenarios process is deliberately decentralized in nature, with many collaborators but no central project office or exclusive project staff (beyond the Scenarios founders, who dedicate what available time they have to assist the Scenarios process).
6. Several organizations assisting with the implementation of the contest and/or using the product of the contest (the films) are not directly involved with HIV/AIDS work but rather address the needs of populations that can be affected: street children, sex workers, young people, immigrant laborers, etc.
7. The films are currently in sixteen languages: 1) a "Sahel" version, with Dioula, Hausa, Moorè, Pulaar, Wolof (+ English, French, Portuguese), 2) "West African Coastal" version, with Fon, Igbo, Mina, Twi, Yoruba (+ English, French, Portuguese) and 3) "Great Lakes" version, with Kinyarwanda, Lingala, Swahili (+ English, French, Portuguese, with plans to add two additional East/South African languages). Source: Global Dialogues (2007). Report on the production, dubbing, distribution and use of the *Scenarios* films, Ouagadougou, Burkina Faso: unpublished report.
8. The contest is strongest in 16 "core countries" (up from 8 in 2002): Benin, Kenya, Namibia, Swaziland, Burkina Faso, Madagascar, Niger, Tanzania, Cape Verde, Mali, Nigeria, Togo, Guinea-Bissau, Mozambique, Senegal, Zambia (Global Dialogues, 2005: 6).
9. Personal correspondence with Daniel Enger, February 4, 2008.
10. The contest, originally titled: *3000 Scenarios Contre un Virus*, was sponsored by CRIPS (Centres régionaux d'information et de prévention du sida – CRIPS), Medecins sans Frontiers (Doctors without Borders) and AESSA (Association des enseignants sida de l'hôpital Saint-Antoine). See http://gateway.nlm.nih.gov/MeetingAbstracts/ma?f=102209193.html
11. Other donors and sponsors include: United Nations Population Fund (UNFPA), UK Department for International Development (DFID),the Futures Group International (Mali), PLAN International

(Senegal), Peace Corps/USAID (USA) and the World Health Organization, Swatch (Switzerland), Rainbow of California (USA), CRIPS, Newcastle Sporting Club (UK), the Edward Thompson Group (UK), PLAN/Burkina Faso, Groupe Accor, Air France, DHL International, Radio France Internationale (RFI), TV5Monde and Africa Consultants International (Winskell & Enger, 1999: 12; personal interviews with K. Winsell and D. Enger, Nov., 2007).
12. Project dates: September, 2007-August, 2009.
13. This grant was mentioned in a personal interview with Kate Winkell, November, 2007. See: http://crisp.cit.nih.gov/crisp/CRISP_.getdoc?textkey=7338270&p_grant_num=1R03HD054323-01A1&p_query=&ticket=73726401&p_audit_session_id=357038922&p_keywords=
14. Personal correspondence with Daniel Enger, February 22, 2008.
15. Countries where youth were surveyed: Burkina Faso, Senegal and Togo. N=339, average age of the survey respondents = 17.49 years; 52.21% female. Global Dialogues (2005), Scenarios from Africa Final Report, Appendix 9: Post-contest survey of participants: 1-2.
16. Contest winners names were provided to me by Scenarios team members. I was unable to access the names of participants who were not awarded prizes because all scripts had been collected and sent to Atlanta Georgia for narrative analysis.
17. There are 28 films from the first 3 editions of the Scenarios contest are available for online viewing at: http://www.globaldialogues.org/Films.htm
18. In each participating country, "national winners" are selected by a local jury and then advance to the international round where a second jury assesses their entry. In 2005 there were 30 international winners. The grand prize is awarded to the most highly rated contest among the international winners.
19. As related in an interview with Global Dialogues co-founder Daniel Enger November 25, 2008.
20. Personal correspondence with Daniel Enger, February 4, 2008.
21. Ibid.
22. As related in an interview with Global Dialogues co-founder Daniel Enger November 25, 2008.
23. Personal correspondence with Daniel Enger, February 22, 2008.
24. This comment was made by several interviewees, including Engelberg, Diouf, Konate and Digne, December, 2007.

References

Abdulla, R. (2003) 'Entertainment-education in the Middle East: Lessons from the Egyptian Orgal Rehydration Therapy Campaign', in Singhal, A.; Cody, M.; Rogers, E.; & Sabido, M.: Entertainment-education Worldwide: History, Research, and Practice. Mahwah, N.J.: Lawrence Erlbaum Associates.

Bateson, G. (2000) *Steps to an Ecology of Mind*. Chicago: Chicago University Press.

Boyd, A. (2002) Irony, Meme Warfare, and the Extreme Costume Ball, in Shepard, B., & Hayduk, R. (eds.) *From ACT UP to the WTO: Urban Protest and Community Building in the Era of Globalization*. New York: Verso.

Chambers, R. (1999) *Whose Reality Counts? Putting the First Last*. London: Intermediate Technology Publications.

Coleman, J.S., Katz, E., & Menzel, H. (1966) *Medical Innovation: Diffusion of a Medical Drug among Doctors*. Indianapolis, Bobbs-Merrill.

CRISP Database entry for NIH grant # 1R03HD054323-01A1, *HIV/AIDS through the Eyes of Young Africans: An Analysis of Fictional Narratives*. Primary Investigator: K. Winskell.

Deutschmann, P.J., & Danielson, W.A. (1960) Diffusion of Knowledge of the Major News Story, *Journalism Quarterly* 37, 345-355.

Deutschmann, P.J., & Fals Borda, O. (1962) *Communication and Adoption Patterns in an Andean Village*. San José, Costa Rica: Programa Interamericano de Informacíon Popular.

Freire, P. (1993) *Pedagogy of the Oppressed*. 30th Anniversary ed. New York: Continuum, 1993.

Foss, S., & Griffin, C. (1995) 'Beyond Persuasion: A Proposal for an Invitational Rhetoric.', *Communication Monographs* 62: 2-18.
Gannon, S. (2001) *An External Evaluation of the Scenarios from the Sahel Contest in Senegal*. Dakar: Global Dialogues.
Gannon, S. (2003) *Evaluation of Usage and Impact of the Scenarios Films in Senegal*. Dakar: Global Dialogues.
Global Dialogues(2005a) Scenarios from Africa 2005 final report. Ouagadougou, Burkina Faso: Unpublished report.
Global Dialogues(2005b) Scenarios from Africa 2005 final report: Appendix 7: Evaluation of contest by team members. Ouagadougou: Unpublished report.
Global Dialogues(2005c) Scenarios from Africa 2005 final report: Appendix 9: Post-contest survey of participants. Ouagadougou: Unpublished report.
Global Dialogues(2005d) Scenarios from Africa 2005 final report: Appendix 10: Evaluation of selection process by jurors. Ouagadougou: Unpublished report.
Global Dialogues (2007) Report on the Production, Dubbing, Distribution and Use of the Scenarios films: October 2004 to January 2007. Ouagadougou: Unpublished report.
Haider, M. & Kreps, G.L. (2004) 'Forty Years of Diffusion of Innovations: Utility and Value in Public Health', *Journal of Health Communication,* 9(1), 3-11.
Hornik, R. (2004) Some Reflections on Diffusion Theory and the Role of Everett Rogers. *Journal of Health Communication* 9, 143-148.
Hounnou, P.V. (2005) *Evaluation of Scenarios from Africa in Burkina Faso: Critical Analysis of the Process to Data and Suggestions for Improvements*. Ouagadougou: Global Dialogues.
James, W. (1991) *Pragmatism*. Amherst, NY: Prometheus Books.
Jayle D., Ugidos A., Poutier A., Boujenah J., Guilbert M., Roux P., Poirot J. (1994) *A Creative Competition: '3000 Film Scenarios against a Virus,* International AIDS Conference Abstract (no. PD0031) Retrieved on February 1, 2007 from http://www.aegis.com/conferences/iac/1994/PD0031.html.
Katz, E. (1961) 'The Social Itinerary of Social Change: Two Studies on the Diffusion of Innovation', in Schramm, W. (ed.) *Studies of Innovation and of Communication to the Public*. Stanford, CA: Stanford University Institute for Communication Research.
Katz, E. (1962) 'Notes on the Adoption of Diffusion Research', *Sociological Inquiry* 32: 3-9.
Katz, E. (1999) 'Theorizing Diffusion: Tarde and Sorokin Revisited', *The Annals* 566: 144-155.
Kothari, U. (2001) 'Power, Knowledge and Social Control in Pariticipatory Development', in Cook, B. & Kothari, U. (eds.) *Participation: The New Tyranny?* London: Zed Books.
Lesnick, P. (2000) *Technology Transfer in the Dominican Republic: A Case Study of the Diffusion of Photovoltaics*. Union Institute, Cincinnait, Ohio. (Ph.D. diss.)
McLeroy, K., Norton, B., Kegler, M., Burdine, J. & Sumaya, C. (2003) 'Community Based Interventions', *American Journal of Public Health* 93(4): 529-533.
Peruzzo, C.M. (1996) 'Participation in Community Communication', in Servaes, J.; Jacobson, T., & White, S. (eds.) *Participatory Communication for Social Change*. New Delhi: Sage Publications.
Rogers, E. (2003) *Diffusion of Innovations*. 5th ed. New York: Free Press.
Rogers, E. Sinhgal, A., & Quinlan, M. (2008) 'Diffusion of Innovations', in Salwen, M. & Stacks, D. (eds.) *An Integrated Approach to Communication Theory and Research*. Lawrence Erlbaum.
Ryan, B., & Gross, N. (1943) 'The Diffusion of Hybrid Seed Corn in Two Iowa Communities', *Rural Sociology* 8: 15-24.
Servaes, J., Jacobson, T., & White, S. (eds.) (1996) *Participatory Communication for Social Change*. New Delhi: Sage Publications.
Valente, T.W. (1995) *Network Models of the Diffusion of Innovations*. Creskill, NJ: Hampton Press.
Winskell, K., & Enger, D. (1999) Scenarios from the Sahel: Working in Partnership to Stop AIDS. Replication guide commissioned by the United Nations Development Programme HIV and Development Programme. Retrieved on 05.10.07 from www.undp.org/hiv/publications/sahel.doc
Winskell, K., & Enger, D. (2005) 'Young Voices Travel Far: A Case Study of Scenarios from Africa', in Hemer, O. & Tufte, T. (eds) *Media & Glocal Change: Rethinking Communication for Development*. Göteborg: Nordicom/Clacso, pp. 403-416.

Winskell, K. & Enger, D. (2007) 'A Special Kind of Aura', Community Capacity, Empowerment and Symbolic Capital in an HIV/AIDS Communication Process in Africa. Unpublished manuscript.

Interview Schedule

Kate Winskell Co-Founder, Global Dialogues, Atlanta, GA: November 24-25, 2007
Daniel Enger, Co-Founder, Global Dialogues, Atlanta, GA: November 24-25, 2007
Gabriel Diaga Diouf, Scenarios from Africa National Coordinator, Representative (Kolda & Dakar Region) Africa Consultants International (ACI), Dakar: November 30 & December 31, Kolda: December 3, 13, 14, Mbour: December, 24, 2007.
Fatimata Ba, Aida Sene, Aminata Ba, Kadi Diaw, Oulmata Sy, Maguette Lo, Scenarios Contestant and 2005 TV5 Grand Prize Winners, Yeumbeul: December 1, 2007
Daour Wade, Africa Consultants International (ACI), Dakar: December 1, 2007
Cheikh Ndongo Fall (Thiés Region) Africa Consultants International (ACI), Dakar: December 1 & December 4, 2007
Diarra Diakhata, Scenarios Contestant, December 3, 2007
Alpha Ibrahimia Ndiaye, President and Adama Watt, Mamadou Ndiaye, Massata Ndoye, Aboudou Aziz Ndiaye, Representatives, Association Nationale pour le Bien-etre de la Population (ANBEP), Pikine: December 6, 2007.
El Hadj Malick Seck, Assistant Peace Corps Director (APCD), Health Sector, United States Peace Corps, December 7, 2007
Mamadou Ba, Director, Avenir de l'Enfant, Rufisque: December 10, 2007
Abdoulaye Konaté, Representative (Kaolack Region) Africa Consultants International (ACI), Dakar: December 10, 2007
Moustapha Dieng (Ziguinchor Region) Africa Consultants International (ACI), Dakar: December 13, 2007
Lama Ba, Program Officer, Deutsche Gesellschaft für Technische Zusammenarbeit (GTZ), Ziguinchor, December 13, 2007.
Sadick Sall, Program Officer, Project d'Appui á l'Enseignement Moyen (PAEM), Kolda: December 14, 2007.
Gary Engelberg, Director, Africa Consultants International, December 3, 10 & 31, 2007.
Oumar Pam, President, Regional Union of Popular Theater and Music, and Regional Coordinator of the Association of Traditional Communicators, Kolda: December 14, 2007.
Assane Ndione, Representative, CISERM/Bandia, Ziguinchor: December 24, 2007.
Madame Ngom, Representative, RASFEMS, Dakar: December 26, 2007.
Lamine Sagna, Scenarios Contestant and two-time National Winner, Dakar: December 26, 2007
Michel Digne, Co-founder, Institut pour le Developpement Local, Dakar: December 26, 2007.
Simon Pierre Sagna, Program Officer, SIDA Service, Dakar: December 27, 2007.
Moctar Fall, Representative, Fédération des Reseaux d'Information, Education and Communication (FRIEC) de Pikine, Pikine: December 28, 2007.

Views in Progress, Views in Process
A Participatory Video Experience with Young People in a Space of Borderlands

Ana Zanotti

Abstract

This is the tale of a group of 50 teens and youngsters – aged 14 to 21 – coming from economically poor environments, in the borderland province of Misiones in northeast Argentina.

This is the narration of a story of empowerment.

From target group to producers, during the greater part of 2006 they gathered around the participatory video programme "One Minute for My Rights", designed by UNICEF Argentina and KINE Cultural and Educational Foundation, and deeply related to their status as holders of rights.

I intend to go over some significant sequences of the process, a gradually growing itinerary that entailed five months of intense involvement, meeting weekly in two workshop groups that took place in two distinct environments of intercultural Misiones, aiming at our final objective: to build up ten one-minute video pieces that would speak about how young people deal with identity matters and how they perceive themselves as valuable subjects in their own communities.

A starting point for this narration stems from my personal experiential convergence between social anthropology and audiovisual production. First, as a member of the video department in a teleducative public institution in the Argentine province of Misiones addressing major educational background difficulties; and more recently as an independent documentary filmmaker, though always on the basis of a strict command over the audiovisual process itself.

When at the end of 2005 an invitation came from Alina Frapiccini[1] to join the provincial chapter of the "One Minute for My Rights"[2] programme – as Misiones was about to step into UNICEF national scheme – I gave this request a great deal of thought, as it would be an utterly new challenge to shift from my usual role of director to the horizontal one of facilitator during an extensive, intensive, collaborative process of audiovisual construction involving the participation of a full party of adolescents and youngsters as target group. The result was a "kaleidoscopic" participatory experience in Shirley White's conception (White 2003: 8), changing colour and shape according to who is handling it. This article intends to guide the reader through some of its moments, all of them valuable footsteps in understanding that there is perhaps no better secret to "success" than an open, considerate attitude towards the people we come into contact with.

The year is 2006; the beginning of 2006. For the second time, a participatory video experience involving young people and their rights is about to start in several Argentine provinces. This narration of empowerment takes place in Misiones, a north-eastern borderland territory between Paraguay and Brazil.

Argentina has traditionally been considered a "rich" country within the South-American context, but it became extremely vulnerable to changes in the international economy during the past 25 years – particularly during the nineties and the beginning of this millennium, with its drastic burden of unemployment and social exclusion.

The neoliberal economical model firmly spread and established itself during the last decade of the twentieth century, almost threatened to death public education, health and culture – a sound pride in the past – as most public functions and corporations were placed in private hands and a wide opening onto the international market led to a new social model, leaving vast portions of its civil society practically at their own risk, dramatically thrown into the uncertain realm of the informal market.

UNICEF (Argentina) and KINE Cultural and Educational Foundation, an Argentine NGO institution, started a programme called "One Minute for My Rights" [Un Minuto por mis Derechos] in 2005 to address these difficulties in the field of childhood and youth. It recalls its origin in the *OneMinutesJr* international collaboration established in November 2002 by the European Cultural Foundation, UNICEF and the Sandberg Institute. *OneMinutesJr* are 60 seconds of video made by young people who produce their own messages, thus expressing themselves and learning valuable media skills in the process.

The Argentine version of this sociocultural intervention defines it as:

> ...audiovisual production workshops in community centres, schools, clubs and churches, in which children and young people share spaces for dialogue about their aspirations, realities and problems, reflecting about them as subjects with rights. (...) They make their voices heard; they take a hard look at the world that surrounds them and look for ways to transform it. (KINE 2006)

The following year the programme broadened its scope to further economically depressed regions, Misiones being one of the provinces to host it.

Before moving on to narrate some particulars of the experience itself, it would be useful to point out some of the programme's basic lines in order to allow sustainability and continuity of its achievements:

- audiovisual workshops motivate the cooperation of social subjects – at the public, private and community levels – towards the supportive building of a fairer society, growing social and economical inclusion as well as giving way to collective creative thought;
- training new young filmmakers- in both social and technical skills – opens up capabilities and aptitudes to reflect on the overall community life;
- culture – the short films produced and disseminated – encourages citizenship, reinforces local identities and self-worth, and contributes to narrowing the effects of prejudice and stigma among peoples.

The first task was to call on a team of two facilitators in each province,

> ....local professionals with a background in audiovisual language and experience working with children and young people (...) integrating teams of local professionals with varied backgrounds, all related to communication, education and culture. (KINE 2006)

who would be helped by one or two assistants.

All the facilitators attended a one-week training course in Buenos Aires before actually starting their work, with the intention of getting to know each other and to share visions concerning their fields of practice and knowledge, as well as their concerns and expectations. As some facilitators were in the programme for the second year, their input was particularly valuable to the newcomers, even though it is likely that none of the shared experiences would exactly match the incoming participatory situations. Some specific contents were also provided by external experienced professionals on human rights issues, mobilization skills and audiovisual animation techniques.

The facilitators would then assume the responsibility to locally select the host partner institutions as well as the locations where two weekly workshops would be held, each involving no more than 25 young participants (ages 14-21).

Facilitators were allowed ample freedom – within the general lines set up by the programme – to make decisions on both matters, provided they would deal with youngsters from unsafe socioeconomic backgrounds.

The overall purpose of the programme was *to develop five-month "hands on" training workshops on filmmaking to build up a fertile process of reflection on youth rights, while steadily progressing towards a final aim: creating ten one-minute video pieces telling how young people deal with identity matters and how they perceive themselves as subjects of rights and respect in their own communities.*

Our working group consisted of a teacher and journalist (Mirian), a social communication student (Lara) and myself. Our joint input, coming from varied backgrounds, would represent a balanced blend of communication, education, art and culture during the activities.

The province of Misiones is the north-easternmost borderland in Argentina, a narrow land spreading between the national territories of Paraguay and southern Brazil, forming with them a shared cultural region of close bonds built throughout their common histories.

> Borders are unique (...) because they are major laboratories of direct integration between populations with physical and geographical contact. And this is so because it is at the borders where actual contact develops among concrete people and not amid abstract regulations. (Abinzano 1998, my translation)

Throughout its history, this regional territory has been the common ground for a shared experience. The chronological chain of socio-cultural patterns that stretches from an ancient extensive aboriginal settlement in pre-colonial times, followed by the burden of centuries of European conquest, regionally represented in the Jesuit Missions, after which Misiones can clearly trace its current denomination, to an uneasy coexistence during the 19th century, until times of war and battle gave birth to the three nation-states, drawing lines where there had always been continuity.

> The region appears as a succession of superimposed layers concerning systems of activity and ways of dealing with land and the use of space (...), a common history, a shared ecosystem, similar productive, environmental, agrarian dilemmas; similar relative marginality. (Abinzano 1998, my translation)

In addition to this, the 20th century was a time of intense overseas migration into the whole region – German, Polish, Ukrainian, Scandinavian, Russian, Italian, Japanese and other nationalities driven by war and poverty conditions – so the social and cultural landscape outlines a peculiar space of borderlands, with the print of cross-cultural encounters deeply rooted in everyday life.

Thus, the concept of "region" is entirely significant for portraying this space: one that *contains* borders instead of being restrained because of them.

As a result of these merged settings, life evolves in a continuous scenery of interculturality.

> Through interculturality we will understand the symmetrical dialogue and relationship among persons, practices, beliefs, languages, products, societies and social processes, all of them inserted in differential cultural traditions. (Reguillo 2002: 5, my translation)

The borderlands allow a fluency of dynamic dialogue and debate – not always fully recognized or accepted; perhaps not even politically "correct"; a precarious balance, an obstinate will to pursue the need of being, feeling and doing things one's "own" way.

> Turbulence (...) allows nominating the unnamed: anxiety, uncertainty, vague uneasiness, deafening and chaotic noise coming from a world undergoing reconfiguration processes (...) How would we place the question about interculturality without relating it to this ambiance of dissolutions, of rupture, of implosions? How would we think about the urgent challenges by which communication should enhance dialogue and meeting spaces among the different? (Reguillo 2002: 1,4, my translation)

The question of language – essential to culture, essential to identity – is immediately related to proximity across borders. The confrontation of official languages – Spanish and Portuguese in the region, both languages of the conquerors – with the diversity of "lesser" varieties being widely used and produced in the borderland spaces adds up another turn to the reflection on interculturality – that of the issue of power as it is daily exerted within people's lives.

> Validity and prestige in speech do not depend on grammar, but on power relations. (...) Speech can be either valid, in force, acceptable, legitimate, or else excluded, unacceptable, insignificant, illegitimate, according to the options adopted by those in power. And these options crystallize in linguistic policies (...) Democratic linguistic policies presuppose an ethics of clearly exposing the game regulations and centralizing decisions around tolerance of differences. (Camblong et al. 1996: 4,5, my translation)

Language lives and functions in human interaction. Thus, dialogue should stand the ideal framework to allow new meanings, new words, new worlds, to appear – as both communication scholars Camblong (Arg.) and Reguillo (Mex.) suggest – through the encounter of all voices in open, respectful, creative conversation.

This was also our intention as facilitators at the "One Minute for My Rights" programme in Misiones.

In order to mirror this cultural background, the following were the locations chosen for the two workshops:

- *El Soberbio*, a small rural town bordering Brazil, with strong influences from its neighbour's culture and language. A privileged natural environment with very little presence of national institutions, undergoing a fluent unstructured migration process across the bordering Uruguay River.
- *Villa Cabello*, a suburban citadel in the peripheries of Posadas – the provincial capital, neighbouring Paraguay – containing a third of Misiones' population, around a million people. Posadas is presently highly affected by the Yacyreta dam, a huge binational hydroelectric project on the Parana

River, forcing massive relocation of coastal dwellers into a series of densely populated uniform citadels.

Every Wednesday we would drive to El Soberbio, 250 km north of Posadas, and every Saturday we would gather in Villa Cabello to progress on the workshop activities. The different backgrounds of both locations would allow us parallel input concerning similarities and differences so each process could serve as interesting feedback to the other.

Once we decided upon the locations, we agreed to choose two public secondary schools as the physical premises of our weekly gatherings, though the participants would not necessarily be their students. The provincial Ministry of Education willingly accepted our offer and – in the case of El Soberbio – collaborated, providing fuel for the twenty trips.

As for the technology involved, KINE lent us a digital handycam for shooting footage. The chosen schools were to provide computers with basic processing resources for the audiovisual exercises, while their directors were to allow all participants – even those who may not be their students – to use their ICT labs. Not at all an easy task to accomplish.

Maximo, the school director in El Soberbio, was very enthusiastic about the new prospects, as small, remote places are hardly ever well positioned in the official educational agenda for innovative initiatives. They rely mainly on their representatives' commitment and skills to negotiate properly outside the local level. So we were truly welcome at their school, the only public secondary level school in town.

In Villa Cabello the situation was quite different. The chosen school would only let us access their premises through another institution – the Centre of Youth Activities, CAJ with its Spanish initials – developing their activities on Saturdays, when there were no formal school activities.

Andy, the CAJ coordinator in Villa Cabello, was the equivalent to Maximo in El Soberbio. A passionate, energetic organizer, he became our key partner in creating and sustaining a proper open atmosphere as well as a reliable environment for the complex process to develop jointly.

Knowledge – content, the "world" – is apprehended in the relationship with the other, as Paulo Freire coherently advocates throughout his vast educational theory and practice. He has a clear awareness that it is a political intention; education in itself entails a political procedure and purpose. He speaks extensively about critical perception of reality, the unveiling process of "reading" in order to acquire conscientization, and therefore allow transformation, the "re-writing" of the world.

It is very interesting to follow the second literary thread (Freire 1994), in which he relives his Pedagogy of the Oppressed while fervently supporting the need to add "hope" – a dream – in the struggle to remake the world.

> In our making and remaking of ourselves in the process of making history – as subjects and objects, persons, becoming beings of insertion in the world and not of

pure adaptation to the world – we should end by having the dream, too, a mover of history. There is no change without dream, as there is no dream without hope. (…) History does not become immobilized, does not die. On the contrary it goes on. The understanding of history as opportunity and not determinism, would be unintelligible without the dream. (Freire: Chapter 3, 1994)

The question of the horizontal and the vertical is also raised. Authoritarism is "learnt" during actual experiences in our everyday life, circumstances we need to recognize, reveal and re-learn through horizontal participation in a genuine dialogue established respectfully with the other.

Here is one of the tasks of democratic popular education, of a pedagogy of hope: that of enabling the popular classes to develop their language (...) their own language which – emerging from and returning upon their reality – sketches out the conjectures, the designs, the anticipations of their new world. Here is one of the central questions of popular education -that of language as a route to the invention of citizenship. (Freire: Chapter 1, 1994)

And in the purpose of making up this citizenship, there are also new contents that certainly have to be conveyed, precise knowledge coming from specific fields or disciplines that the educator needs to embrace as an awakening vertical responsibility, though giving way to everyone's tempo and pace. The great difference with what he calls "banking" education is that the process should depart from what everyone *is* and *knows*.

The educator needs to know that his or her "here" and "now" are nearly always the educands' "there" and "then". Even though the educator's dream is not only to render his or her "here-and-now" accessible to educands, but to get beyond their own "here-and-now" with them, or to understand and rejoice that educands have got beyond their "here" so that this dream is realized, she or he must begin with the educands' "here", and not with her or his own. At the very least, the educator must keep account of the existence of his or her educands' "here" and respect it. Let me put it this way: you never get there by starting from there, you get there by starting from some here. This means, ultimately that the educator must not be ignorant of, underestimate, or reject any of the "knowledge of living experience" with which educands come. (Freire: Chapter 2, 1994)

Freire's contribution to participatory education and communication is so immense that pointing out just a handful of his conceptual guiding principles means opening up a mindful way to approximate, get together and steadily start to reflect and take action.

This is what we basically tried to do during this way to empowerment – work on hoping, dreaming, having a dialogue, caring for the word and the world of the other, dealing with the meaningful vertical and the encouraging horizontal as our approach procedures.

So there we were, in front of us a full itinerary of 40 gathering sessions – twenty for each workshop – each one four hours long, during which we would engage in this challenging, provocative new task.

We had many things working in our favour – working freedom, a significant job ahead, an enthusiastic facilitating team, some local institutional collaboration – and one major drawback – the need to wrap up the complex process in five months, with the essential requirement of having eight to ten videominutes ready for a local screening the sixth month, and a national screening the seventh month, after the programme's start.

The programme's concise time schedule made it particularly difficult to carry out a suitable call to "fill the vacancies" assigned to each workshop, mainly in El Soberbio, where we had been allocated fuel resources strictly for the twenty sessions. Therefore we could not conduct this important part of the process ourselves and had to rely on the representatives of the partner institutions to conduct the actual callings. In Villa Cabello this was easily solved, as the CAJ centres already develop their social intervention in socio-economically affected environments. We ended up with a large group of kids, all of them teens and youngsters from the surrounding peripheral citadels, or "barrios", in Posadas. But in El Soberbio we had to campaign – face-to-face and over local radio – in order to reach more kids besides those attending the secondary school itself. After the first month the group was finally formed, including a couple of teens from the rural surroundings.

Some descriptive facts about the youngsters:

Participants by age group and sex, 2006

El Soberbio

Age Groups	Boys	Girls	Total
14-16	4	3	7
17-18	1	5	6
19-21	3	0	3
Total	8	8	16

Villa Cabello

Age Groups	Boys	Girls	Total
14-16	4	0	4
17-18	6	4	10
19-21	5	5	10
Total	15	9	24

Considering their *ages* in both workshops, the majority of the participants (40%) belonged to the 17-18 age group, that is to say, in the average last years of the secondary school. In El Soberbio, the group was much younger (81.3% gathering the two younger age groups as shown in the table above) than in Villa Cabello (83.3% gathering the two older age groups as also shown in the table above).

Regarding their *educational situation* as a whole, almost all participants were in the formal education system. In El Soberbio all participants (100%) were regularly attending the secondary school. In Villa Cabello, two-thirds (16 participants) were secondary level students, while approximately one-third (7 participants) were starting superior studies at the free public university, and only one boy was a dropout from the formal education system.

| El Soberbio | Villa Cabello |

As for their general *cross-cultural profile*, there are some peculiar facts in each of the workshop groups:

- In El Soberbio, besides speaking standard Spanish, almost all of them spoke fluent Portuguese except for Pedro, a young boy from the Mbya Guarani aboriginal ethnic group, whose mother tongue was Mbya, and found it quite hard to express himself in fluent standard Spanish. Considering their family origin, more than half the participants had European origin, mainly German.

- In Villa Cabello, 16 participants (66%) were related to a remote Spanish origin, and some were also connected to the Paraguayan nationality. Seven (29%) had European ancestors, and one, Japanese parents. Almost everyone exclusively spoke Spanish fluently. Very few could understand some Guarani, and one spoke some Japanese.

Taking into account their *place of residence*, four participants (25%) in El Soberbio lived in the countryside and one in a nearby aboriginal community. In Villa Cabello, they were all urban or suburban residents, with the particularity that two-thirds had endured a forced relocation scheme with their families due to the recent filling of the Yacyreta dam. This fact would probably entail an identity question, as was later expressed in one of the ten films.

Basically, there were three axes to entwine during the sessions, fully coincident with the general aims of the project:

a. the question of the perception of human rights,

b. the learning of audiovisual tools, and

c. the developing of creative communication bonds among a newly formed group of people having to accomplish a joint creative task together.

In a way, these three broad lines could be largely related to the conceptual categories structuring US participatory communication scholar Shirley White's collected essays on participation and development, in which she groups them into the following three large chapters: the art of activation, the art of technique, and the art of building community (White 1999).

It would be useful to illustrate these three axes with actual narrations from a situational perspective, in order to grasp the progressive building up of power resulting from this participatory approach. *"Empowerment implies a change in power relations"*, White categorically states (1999: 54), thus identifying the heart of the question, as it is in this gradual shift that genuine empowerment slowly starts to arise.

Initially, when choosing school premises as workshop locations, we knew we ran the potential risk of allowing the rigidity these formal institutional spaces are generally associated with to "permeate" this open, innovative, communicative experience. So from the very beginning we took good care of depriving them of their usual marks. For this sake, each place was constantly transformed, re-signified, in order that activities could flow with spontaneity and freedom. The library in Villa Cabello, or the computer lab in El Soberbio, would alternatively turn into a courtyard, a cafeteria, a cinema, a classroom, a shooting set or an editing room, according to the activities performed.

During every workshop, we would basically engage in getting to know each other's world through activities we intentionally devised to install creative proximity, using playtime as the starting point for ice-breaking as well as for generating an emotional connection among everyone, which was essential for supporting the full process to come.

It was interesting to see that the physical warm-up moments proved to be good ways to bridge age divides, both among themselves – a teen of 14 differs quite a bit from a 21-year-old – and between them and ourselves as the adults. Games allowed these barriers to be openly crossed while laughing and enjoying, while playing around with movements, paces and rhythms, while explicitly perceiving the space around us with each of our five senses, and the like. It was then quite simple to create a relaxed atmosphere to make the confrontation of ideas, the fruitful encounter of worlds, easy.

Narration 1. The Major (El Soberbio – 3rd session)

We started that session by talking openly about daily experiences that bring about discomfort or anger. The first month's sessions were mostly to inaugurate dialogue as the gate to common agreements. Among the arising situations, Damian came to passionately address the lack of a decent urban place where youngsters could gather, play sports, have fun; and not only youngsters but the community as a whole. This theme was immediately appropriated by everyone. They started to talk about the "Poli", a community multi-purpose building started some thirty years ago but still unfinished. They related it directly to the indifference of local authorities – personified in the local mayor – to community issues. And as El Soberbio is a very small town, they provided all sort of anecdotes and tales to back up their words.

We then suggested that they dramatize in groups some of the highlighted distressing situations. One of the groups swiftly selected the one that Damian exposed, actually asking him to play the main character, the mayor of their small town.

The role-playing sequence was just breathtaking. Every popular cliché associated with the generalized contempt and distrust towards politicians and the public sphere in our country could be clearly perceived here. The created situation portrayed a schoolteacher with a couple of students visiting the mayor in order to get his signature on a "contract" to finish building the Poli premises before a regional inter-school sport meeting later in the year. Damian, as "the mayor", intentionally disregarded the visitors' request, making jokes, paying attention to his assistant offering him something to drink, and explicitly ignoring them to answer a sudden incoming mobile phone call from a friend inviting him to a party; in the end he simply left the contract to be signed by his assistant, thus eluding his civic responsibilities concerning the community's welfare.

The scene was very successful. The rest of the participants initially laughed when they recognized something they knew a great deal about, but when we gathered afterwards to talk about the dramatizations it was clear that they had all felt the breaching of an essential right there. We talked about how it is sometimes necessary to make visible what is usually perceived as "natural" in order to start to take action.

For us facilitators, as representatives of the adult world, it clearly showed how early – and deeply – antidemocratic norms may become accepted and internalized. And when they chose the themes of the final films the following month, this situation was entered in the videominute called "Poliiii".

In this respect, Colombian communicator Martín-Barbero's words (2000) are truly eloquent when he analyses how young people today are exposed to a double educational system – the traditional one implying schools, teachers and books, and the communicative ecosystem, made up of bits and pieces of information generated and spread from the audiovisual media as well as from the digital technologies. This environment pervades daily life today, and exerts its powerful influence over almost every phase of experience. Thus education expanded education – should aim at building up young citizens who can learn to read every fragment of the world with a critical, questioning mind, disassembling the usual inertia that usually finds suitability in wealth and resignation in poverty. In his – and our – view, there is no need for a saviour in society; only for a sociability in which to live, negotiate and respect all the regulations of the citizen game, no matter how large or small they are.

Images and sounds were to be our new tools of empowerment. Therefore, throughout every session we organized activities dealing with them, even explicitly or as a complement to some other content. That is to say, if we were going to talk about rights, or about everyday life, or about social and cultural contexts, we always chose to introduce audiovisual input – excerpts of well-known features or documentary films, for instance – to allocate audiovisual tools a central position in the empowering process.

So around the end of the second month, it was necessary to start learning the basics of reading and writing the audiovisual language, a somehow vertical transmission as there was also a precise technical terminology (shots, angles, positions, movements and the like) to be grasped. We decided to design a horizontal activity before actually engaging in the conceptualization issues. The idea was to again reinforce their emotional bond, which by this time was becoming very strong.

Narration 2. The Little Window (Villa Cabello – 7th session)

Lara, one of the facilitators, came up with an ingenious game. In turns, two groups were to enact two everyday situations: a dog-walker taking a group of dogs for a walk, and an architect building a house. When the first group started their performance, they would be suddenly "frozen" in a position – a "frame" – and the participants from the other group would explore the scene. We provided them with pieces of cardboard with a small window cut out, with which they observed the whole group or just a part of it, focussed on a particular detail, and so on. Then, they shifted positions.

The purpose was to experience that we can – and actually do – select only a part of the world in front of us; that it is our ideas, intentions and background that guide our viewpoints, making us include or exclude particular portions of the real.

Behind this simple activity and reflection was a central understanding: that technology is by no means neutral, and neither are its languages or uses. Quite the opposite. The language of images and sounds activates a thorough cognitive process based on the conjunction of intimate subjective meanings together with rigorous hegemonic frameworks, thus reinforcing its intrinsic ideological nature. Again meeting Paulo Freire's conception (1994), the act of reading and writing the world – the audiovisual language world for us – precisely exemplifies the political nature of educational practice.

To close this brief kaleidoscopic overview of our empowerment process, there is a further activity that allowed us to gain deeper insight into these adolescents and youngsters. In committing themselves to the task of gaining control over technology for the first time, they generously opened their world of dreams to all of us, their fellow workshop mates.

Narration 3. Identity (El Soberbio – Villa Cabello – 10th session)

This activity had a multilayer intention: on the one hand, an individual commitment to storytelling, as everyone would prepare a short personal statement to be shared with all participants in the workshop; and on the other hand, a technical involvement as they were also to operate a domestic camcorder, filming their fellow mates' statements; and still a third one, encouraging a flow of synergy and empathy to ascertain true solidarity during these "contributions" of naked feelings to the open group.

The first shooting was planned as an almost "raw" situation, as we gave no specific technical instructions for audiovisual capturing, such as shots, framing and the like. We just wanted the kids to introduce and share their personal input and/or backgrounds concerning their own expectations and self-explanations. Later we would revise the footage collectively, producing a joint comment on the audiovisual material.

The following is a selection of some of their statements.

Fernando

If somebody asks me about myself, I can say a few things, for instance that my name is Fernando, that I am 19... I worry too much about some things. I feel... I have the crazy idea of changing the world, something typical of my age. Well, I feel I came to this world to fulfil a mission. I still don't quite know what I am doing here.

Joel

Hi, I am Luis Joel. They call me Polo Kleins, but I like to be called Joel. I am 17. ... I like to dance. I also like to fight. I like girls very much, obviously... Not that I ever fell in love... but there are many girls I like in my neighbourhood. ... The fruit I like best is the apple...! (suddenly taking a shiny apple out of his pocket). It's my favourite.

Aimara (through Lara, her sister)

Lara: And we are the little Schwieter siblings... I am Lara and she is...
Aimara: ...Aimara.
Lara: She does not like to talk very much, so I will talk instead...

Belen

Hello, my name is Maria Belen. I participate as a volunteer at an institution working with situations related to sexual health; I like this job so much, it fills my soul. I am a very friendly person, though I also enjoy being alone. But not feeling lonely, as this is one of my biggest fears.

Camila

Hi. My name is Camila, I am 17. I live in El Soberbio. Actually, I live in two places, here and in the countryside where my family lives... I like feeling I'm a part of all this beauty, though at the same time it's a whole mess, on account of all the troubles we have over here. .. What else...? Yes! I am also the "queen of smells"... of essences... (everybody laughs, as Camila has just been crowned national beauty queen of a local agricultural production)... And that's it. Cut!

Pedro

Well, I am an aboriginal boy, coming from Jejy, a community nearby El Soberbio, Misiones. Well, I'm studying now and I like to be with the other kids here in town, and with the other kids there in my village as well. And I like to take part in our work, and also in the activities from school, to show the kids at school an image of my community, telling them what the community is, and that our cultures are different.

Yesica

Hi, I'm Yesica. Who am I? A huge question. I define myself as one decade and eight years, as a hidden dream, as the wind... that flies softly... in search of its own destiny. I'm a sister, I'm a friend, I'm a daughter. Am I happy? Yes, I am; with my friends, at school, doing what I like to do. I always think of me as a stain that should not disappear because it dreams and lives. I'm like a war, a challenge, always questioning and searching for her real self. This is me.

Whether told by themselves (*"Hi. I am..."*, as most started) or through the words of others (*"She is..."*, as Lara says); whether highly exposed (*"This is me"*, Yesica utters defiantly) or simply melting into a broader identity (Pedro never tells us his name; only his community belonging), this crucial issue of self-perceived identity inspires, activates, mobilizes. A simple shooting session could turn into a bridge to the world of the other, guided by the words of the other.

And this is plainly the cognitive strategy used during the progressing exercises, the reflective ones as well as the audiovisual ones. What we did was give way to the concealed, and make it emerge as valuable input for group activity. Focusing on participation, the ten storylines were then collectively agreed on and developed, their scripts were written, their sequences were preproduced and shot, and one month later, they were edited and shared with their closer community. Afterwards, UNICEF and KINE would organize a nationwide screening and facilitate further television broadcasting in order to allow these views an expanded outreach.

The "One Minute for My Rights" programme had also designed an overall evaluation scheme parallel with the first official screening of the produced video pieces at a major cinema in Buenos Aires, the national capital city. All participants in Argentina were expected to attend a two-day gathering there, during which they would all meet each other and follow a designed assessment schedule. To ensure everyone's participation, the programme provided accommodation and eating facilities in Buenos Aires, while the trip expenses were expected to be covered by the local government level. Unfortunately, the provincial authorities in Misiones failed to provide this support, due mainly to the fact that a political ballot process was taking place precisely during that particular time, thus arousing real disappointment and despair on the part of the youngsters.

This was the only actual, major drawback that we – the kids and the facilitators – had to encounter during the process, and even though we tried to do whatever we thought might be helpful to overcome it, we were not able to find another suitable way to cover the travelling costs.

Nevertheless, this sad situation did not represent a serious interference with everything that had already developed among the youths during the workshops, as most of them still maintain a close relationship today, while a handful – three from Villa Cabello and one from El Soberbio – managed to get together the following year and shoot a couple of short documentary video stories about their communities' grassroots difficulties.

These small experiential stories about our participatory process only intend to illustrate our approach as catalysts and facilitators of it. They obviously do not account for everything that occurred. Putting into words what we so intensely went through will never do justice to the actual interweaving developed there. But I hope it can provide at least an approximate feeling of the way things went on during our two workshops within the "One Minute for My Rights" proposal[3].

Bringing together experience with already quoted theoretical lines, the process provided a chance to assemble *dialogue* with *cultural diversity*; the first as an open way to approach each pursued goal as the process evolved and the second as the wealthy settings allowing the youngsters to identify the contextual conditions playing a favourable role in the unfolding of the programme.

And even though this social development programme is essentially a top-down proposition (product-oriented, rigorous time constraints, among other features already mentioned), its methodology involves a participatory approach allowing self-respect and promoting mutual understanding. As everyone is equally engaged in such a complex process as movie-making, the feeling that joint, organized collaboration can lead to a worthy outcome can be fully experienced.

As for the use of *audiovisual tools* – though this somehow may not seem central in these narrated sequences – they added up strongly to this sequence of empowerment, setting in motion the participatory chain of choices, decisions and actions allowing the actual making of the films.

Ten powerful short films that spoke about the youths' rights to open access to education, to live in a well cared-for environment, to avoid young girls' pregnancy, to stop young girls' prostitution, to live under a safe roof, to grow deep roots with people and places, to find an understanding family background, to be considered equals, to be listened to.

Moreover, all participants were able to sense that they have a voice and a view, and that they have a real value – and what is perhaps most significant, the possibility of understanding that we may learn from certainties, but we can definitely learn a great deal from difficulties and doubts. From life itself, in progressive process.

Notes
1. Project Director at the KINE Foundation, a cultural and educational NGO selected by UNICEF Argentina to conduct its nationwide programme "One Minute for My Rights".
2. The experience also provides the contextual and methodological basis for my project work (PW) to complete my Master-level degree on "Communication for Development" at Malmö University (Sweden). For my PW, I am producing both a written and an audiovisual document on this participatory research experience, as I also managed to keep a full record of the whole process in digital video.

All the pictures are stills captured from the video recordings made during the development of the participatory process itself.

3. All the Argentine videominutes can be accessed and viewed at the KINE home page (http://www.1minutoxmisderechos.org.ar/). The ten films we produced at El Soberbio and Villa Cabello (Misiones, 2006) can also be accessed and/or downloaded at: www.misiones.gov.ar/infomisiones/4PRO/minuto/index.htm

Bibliography

Abinzano Roberto (1998) *Globalizacion, Regiones y Fronteras*. [Globalization, regions and borders.] Debate document N° 27, MOST, UNESCO, http://www.unesco.org/most/abinzano.htm

Camblong, Ana; Skupien, Ines; Lirussi, Marta; Daviña, Liliana y Santander, Carmen (1996) *Consideraciones generales acerca de la situacion linguistica en la Provincia de Misiones*. [General considerations on the linguistic situation within the province of misiones.] Facultad de Humanidades y Ciencias Sociales, Universidad Nacional de Misiones – UnaM, Argentina.

Freire, Paulo (1994) *Pedagogy of Hope. Reliving Pedagogy of the Oppressed*. New York: Continuum, http://www.universidadabierta.edu.mx/Biblio/F/FreirePaulo_PedagogyOfHope.txt

KINE Foundation (2006) *Aumentar las Miradas es Aumentar el Mundo*. [Enhancing sights is enhancing the world.] UN-Habitat Best Practices Database. http://staging.unchs.org/bestpractices/2006/mainview.asp?BPID=664

Martín-Barbero, Jesus (2002) 'Jovenes: Comunicacion e Identidad' [Youth, communication and identity.] *Pensar Iberoamerica – Revista de Cultura*, Número 0, http://www.comminit.com/en/node/149764, http://www.oei.es/pensariberoamerica/ric00a03.htm

Reguillo, Rossana (2002) *Pensar en el mundo en y desde America Latina. Desafio intercultural y politicas de representacion*. [Thinking about the world in and from Latin America. Intercultural challenge and policies of representation.] IAMCR, Barcelona, http://www.portalcomunicacion.com/catunesco/esp/3/down/reguillo/reg.pdf

White, Shirley A. (1999) *The Art of Facilitating Participation*. Cornell University: Sage Publications Pvt. Ltd.

White, Shirley A. (2003) *Participatory Video. Images that Transform and Empower*. Sage Publications Pvt. Ltd.

Learning to Change the World Right Here
Youth, Educommunication and Social Change in Rio de Janeiro, Brazil

Claudius Ceccon*

Abstract

The Profile of Brazilian Youth, a national study conducted by Abramo and Branco (2005), showed that 84% of Brazilian youths believe they could change the world, but only 2% of them are involved in actions to cope with the social problems they identify, such as violence, misery, unemployment, drug abuse. They are not aware that their spontaneous interventions in the field of communication and culture are antidotes for these situations. One of the research conclusions is that "youngsters, in order to contribute to change, must be supported". The present article will discuss the work that CECIP, *Center for the Creation of Popular Image*, has been doing with Brazilian youths in projects that deal with media education and young people's perceptions of themselves as citizens with the power to express their own ideas, and act in a cooperative way to make innovations and transform society.

We will start by giving some background data on being young in Brazil. We will then deal with the basic principles of our actions with youths and how we began to work with them. We will provide examples of supporting youths as social actors and a critical reflection on the social changes these examples indicate.

Being young in Brazil

Brazil's foreign image is young: a country with 8,000 km of sunny beaches, inhabited by smiling people, where carnival, bossa nova and the art of football reign. In the last census (2005), 19% of the Brazilian population[1] – 35.1 million people – were between 15 and 24 years old. Brazil has become more inclusive in the past three decades: in 1970, only 32% of the homes had water services, 26% had refrigerators, less than 5% had telephones. In 2006, water services raised to 83.2%, 89% have refrigerators in their homes, and 74% can communicate by their own telephones. Thirty years ago, no one had computers, and now 22.1%

of the population – which means more than 40 million people – have entered the digital era (IBGE- Censo 1970, Censo 2000, PNAD 2006).

In spite of these positive statistics, most of these boys and girls are poor: 42% belong to families with a income of less than US$ 300, and 31% live in families with a income between US$ 300 and US$ 700. These youngsters' teachers earn a monthly salary of around US$ 400 for 40-hour work weeks. Poverty means more than having very little money. Lack of money limits the range of one's choices, including access to cultural and leisure spaces. Accordingly to the Abramo and Branco study, 36% of youth have never gone to a music show, 39% have never entered a cinema, and 62% have never seen a play at a theater. It is no surprise that 52% don't know the location of a library, but it is almost incredible that in a country that has five times been the world champion, 54% have never seen a football game in a stadium and 72% have never practiced any sport.

At the end of the 20th century, Brazil finally succeeded in enrolling 97% of the children in elementary school (1st to 8th grade), as a result of a governmental effort to open new places in schools for secondary students. Nevertheless, at the beginning of this new century, only 17% of 18-year-olds and 35% of 25-year-olds had concluded high school. Only 1.2% of youths between 18 and 24 get to go to university (IBGE, Censo demográfico 2000, cf. Madeira 2007).

In 2006, more than half (53.12%) of youths between 15 and 24 years – 18.45 million – did not attend school (IBGE, PNAD 2006). Of those who did attend for at least 6 years, 70% cannot read and interpret complex texts (MEC-INEP 2007).

More than 60% of the students who were interviewed for the "Profile of Brazilian Youth" survey considered their school incapable of dealing with contemporary questions, 72% thought that the school was uninterested in their problems, and according to 76%, the schools simply do not understand youngsters (Abramo and Branco). Even so, 57% of the high school youths interviewed like their schools, probably because that's where they socialize, exchange ideas, have common experiences and make friendships that may last all their lives. The school is fine, but the school contents are not: they are meaningless. This explains the subversion of the power relationship with teachers, who, in large numbers, declare themselves incapable of getting the students to listen during classes (Abramovay 2006). The so-called indiscipline is a reaction to school violence: absence of meaning, absence of dialogue, absence of skills essential to learning, such as self-mastery, cooperation, and systems thinking (Senge 2001).

The struggle for survival sees 78% of youths linked to the work market. They are working, unemployed, or looking for work. When they do find a job, it is usually a dreadful one, with low a salary (64% earn US$ 350 a month or less) and a heavy workload (up to 44 weekly hours). Eight million youths (17%) are not studying, working, or looking for a job (Brazilian Institute for Geography and Statistics IBGE 2005 and Camarano 2006).

Being a country of contrasts, there are also positive signs: Brazilian youths – even the poorest – are more and more transitioning from being consumers of culture to producers of culture, and from being passive receivers of communication to active and creative communicators. As Tommasi (2007) puts it: "It's interesting to consider the spaces for self-expression created by juvenile groups as public spaces that reinvent the ways of political intervention. There are youths that present their questions through music, dance, graffiti, painting walls, radical sports, fanzines (magazines for young people), poetry, blogs and alternative media." The youngsters face great challenges that demand all their creativity. In spite of all the difficulties, almost 80% of the youth interviewed in the above-mentioned survey declared they saw more positive than negative aspects of being young.

When the boys and girls who are now 15 to 24 years of age reach their sixties, they will be living in a better Brazil, one they helped to make. In his book "A brief history of the Future", Jacques Attali (2008) sees Brazil, with 210 million inhabitants in 2025, as the world's fourth economic power, behind US, China, India and ahead of Japan.

It looks like a mirage. Will the present pace of economic growth be enough? Since the middle of the 90s, a slow but steady improvement in our social and economic indicators placed Brazil in the High Human Development group, with 0.8, even if the gap between the rich and the poor persists. The gap is so big that even with investing comparatively little in the social agenda, in the past decade, around eight million people rose above the poverty line thanks to government social measures.

Young people have been playing a protagonist role throughout our country's history. They fought the military dictatorship that lasted 21 years (1964-1985), actively participated in the national mobilization to elect the National Assembly and have the 1988 Constitution that restored democracy, and took to the streets to force a corrupt president to resign (President Collor, 1990-1992).

Today, young people's political participation is much more pervasive than in the past, creating new ways to occupy spaces and communicate their aspirations. CECIP is learning from them, helping, on a small scale, to empower them by improving their ability to communicate.

An NGO hand in hand with youth

CECIP is an autonomous, not-for-profit, civil society organization, founded in 1986 by a group of friends, all renowned professionals in their respective areas. The main concern of this group was with basic citizenship rights as later expressed in the 1988 Constitution. How can these rights be made common knowledge? Brazilians discuss football with such passion because they know the rules. Couldn't the same apply to the basic rights every citizen should demand?

CECIP's mission was defined as helping to design public policies for human rights in economic, social, cultural and environmental areas. CECIP specialized itself in the creation of educational toolkits. The next step was to complement these educational materials by organizing training workshops and seminars ad-

> **What is CECIP**
>
> Founded in 1986, CECIP, the Center for the Creation of Popular Image, is an autonomous non-profit civil society organization that seeks to democratize the access by all layers of Brazilian Society to quality information on their basic rights, thus fostering a conscientious, active and participative citizenry.
>
> CECIP's actions are directed at social actors, such as teachers, school administrators, students and health, human rights and environmental workers and promoters.
>
> CECIP's mission is to contribute to the definition of public policies that promote human rights in all their aspects – economic, social, cultural, political and environmental
>
> **Partners**
>
> CECIP got a start in 1986 with a grant from NOVIB, a Dutch Agency, for basic professional video equipment. Later in that year, a grant from Brot fur die Welt supported the project that enabled CECIP to produce videos with inhabitants of Rio's poor periphery neighborhoods. In the 22 years that followed, CECIP projects were supported by a wide variety of foreign agencies, institutes and foundations, such as Christian Aid, Cafod, CCFD, WCC, Diakonia, Heinrich Böll, Bernard van Leer, Ford, McArthur, and W.K. Kellogg. CECIP has also developed projects with the support of multilateral agencies, such as WHO, Unicef, Unesco, ILO, Unifem, UNDP, UNAIDS, OAS and the European Union. On the national scene, CECIP has been carrying out projects with Brazilian Government ministries (Education, Health, Justice, Work and Employment, Environment and Culture) and agencies, on federal, state and municipal (local) levels, as well as with Brazilian institutes and foundations. CECIP is affiliated with ABONG, the Brazilian Association of NGOs, of which it was one of the founders. It is registered in the CNAS, the National Council of Social Service, at the federal as well as municipal level; it is registered in the Municipal Council for Children and Adolescents' Rights and received the title of Public Utility Institution, granted by the Ministry of Justice.

dressed to youngsters, teachers, school leaders and other social agents. At the same time, we have been training these actors in how to use the new information and communication technologies to create their own products.

From the beginning, young people have been one of CECIP's main concerns. In recent years, CECIP has become increasingly involved in projects with adolescents and youths, using ICT, Information and Communication Technologies, as part of its methodology. This choice was not only the result of a theoretical reflection about new media and the way new generations have access to it, but the natural consequence of a work in progress. Working with youngsters, from 14 up to around 20, was a development of the experience inherent in one of CECIP's main concerns: the empowerment of youths, enabling them to be full citizens, with rights and duties, capable of perceiving how their decisions and actions can benefit the community and contribute to building a more just, fair and happy society.

Our experience with young people, accumulated over the years, provides the inspiration to meet new challenges. Every new project demands a great deal of creativity, but some principles are reaffirmed by successful practices and the good results obtained:

Education and Communication are two sides of the same coin: we define ourselves as educommunicators. This neologism means that we don't differentiate, in our practice, between the areas of education and communication. That seems a platitude, but the reality is that communicators and educators behave like two different tribes that have difficulties talking to each other. Educommunication is concerned with providing information with transparent honesty, economy, clarity and factual, historical or scientific precision, no matter what subject is being dealt with. Educommunication is concerned also with the praxis of the people that receive the content, with what they will be able to do with the knowledge or tools acquired. It is concerned with not only information, but also with learning, with capacity building, with awareness raising, and with the actions that result from this process of empowering people to change their realities.

Dialogue is the foundation of change: we use a participatory methodology, the central part of which is dialogue. Listening to the other, to a different, divergent opinion must be learned. Learning to listen is linked to learning to speak, to organizing one's own ideas and being able to express them clearly and fluently. Our inspiration is the Brazilian educator Paulo Freire, who started in the 60s what was considered a revolution in literacy education. The essence of Freire's method, as it came to be known worldwide, was dialogue. As Freire expressed in Pedagogy of the Oppressed[2]: *Instead of teaching, listen. Instead of being a professor who knows everything, be a facilitator who can help people express themselves; instead of offering a ready-made package to be imposed, build a common knowledge base; instead of learning for the sake of it, understand that the real purpose of learning is to transform the world.* To Freire, *learning to read* meant *to understand* the world – that is, to have access to the treasures of all literature, all the knowledge produced so far in written form. And *learning to write* was understood as being empowered *to change* the world – to change by imprinting your own experience, by expressing your personal opinion, by making your point of view count. Once your word is communicated, the world is no longer the same as it was a moment before; your action has already changed it.

Our way of working with youngsters on a new project, a script, a campaign or any product that has to be created, starts by listening to them. We stimulate a brainstorm based on their legitimate interests, instead of bringing our points of view on how they *should* deal with it. This learning process has no traditional classes, no teacher delivering his or her wisdom to a passive audience. The knowledge is created collectively – it is a common achievement, built up thanks to the contribution of all participants, in a sometimes hectic, but always fun and productive environment. Of course there is a professional who has more experience and possibly knows more, yet he or she does not act hierarchically, but instead participates on equal terms in the discussions, providing help when requested by the group. At the end of this process, youths must recognize themselves as co-authors of the product.

Trust the Youth /Hands-on methodology – the young person has direct, personal contact with the video equipment or with the computer program that will be used. It may seem strange to people who have easy access to every new gadget that the industry offers, that our decision to put an expensive camera, acquired with such sacrifice, in the hands of youth was considered a crazy one. But we trusted the kids, breaking the taboo that says that sophisticated equipment should be manipulated only by professionals, that is, adults. Our hands-on methodology is an important part of the whole process. Besides learning how to operate a camera, the youngster must learn to take care of it, maintaining the equipment so it is always ready to operate. Everyone is responsible, not just the facilitator or the professional technician. And there is no theory that can match the experience of a hands-on, do-it-yourself methodology. Audiovisual communication media has the potential to amplify globally a given message, and it is important that this message helps to raise the people's awareness. Freire gave us a challenge: We must appropriate the technological knowledge and struggle to put it in practice, creating audiovisual products that have 'the true word' indissolubly linked to 'the true image'. This means that the commitment and ethical responsibility of being truthful when writing must also be applied when producing images.

How it all started

It all started in the late 80s and 90s, when CECIP was working in the periphery of Rio's Metropolitan Region, producing small video documentaries and fiction pieces with the active participation of local people. These products were shown after sundown, in public squares, by the Maxambomba TV, (Maxambomba, a

Cartoon by Claudius Ceccon depicting TV Maxambomba in action, illustrating "How it all started" and reads:
...who said that we only needed a camera in our hand and an idea in our head?

word of African origin, was the ancient name of the region where the screenings took place). The videos were projected on a big screen installed on top of a van. People of all ages left their homes, where they had their own TV sets, missing the evening soap opera episode to watch their image projected on the big screen instead. They did not appear as the TV always showed them, only in connection with some catastrophe or a horrible crime. They were shown as articulate, as they normally are, expressing their views, performing the songs or dances they created or criticizing with sound arguments the local administration, using their sense of humor and reaching out to their community. After each session, a public debate was held with the up to five hundred people who gathered at the square. An open microphone would receive people's comments, criticisms or praise, with their image projected on the big screen. This interaction was key to a process of collective learning: the videos were discussion starters, and whatever information they brought was immediately appropriated by the people present, who would in turn contribute their own vision, knowledge and experience. In an evaluation of how the Maxambomba TV's messages were received, one of the questions asked people to name a TV program that had particularly struck them. We got answers naming videos screened only once, eight years before.

Half of those attending these public screenings were children, adolescents and youths[3]. Therefore, we began to produce videos for them. Some teens were very curious and eager to learn, coming to the community workshops that we began to organize. We then started a project called Neighborhood Reporters. The idea was to have both adults and youngsters working together, making videos on the reality of their neighborhoods. Soon the adolescents and youths took over the project, because they had more time to invest, more interest and were faster learners, eager to put their new abilities immediately into practice.

Maxambomba TV van, with large screen on top "How it all started". Photo: CECIP team

They became responsible for the video productions addressed to youth within the TV Maxambomba screening sessions. It was no longer the case that adults produced videos for children – it was children producing videos about the subjects they cared about, to be showed and discussed by the whole community. When the neighborhood association tried to "use" the teen team to produce what they wanted, this created room for debate – who decides what needs to be said, who is making that decision? And in commercial TV, who makes this decision? What about the schools?

Youths creating, communicating and transforming

In the mid-90s, after one of the regular evaluations of its activity with Maxambomba TV, CECIP decided to reduce the number of neighborhoods involved in our project to work closely with five of the neighborhoods that had shown more vivid interest in our activities. This meant organizing workshops with the population around video production, mostly on weekends, for Saturday was the only free time available.

At a certain point, CECIP was invited by the principals of three schools located in the region to try this methodology with regular students. We had the principals' full support, which is a sine-qua-non condition in a rigid school system. We also had to take into account the daily routine of the teachers, already under pressure to deal with the programs for which they were responsible, with little space left for "modern" methodological principles that demand time to listen to the other, learning to express oneself or being open to new ideas and new visions of reality.

Our idea was to produce messages using video, an activity that cannot be carried on by a solitary genius. It needs teamwork, people gathered around a common objective, division of tasks to be accomplished, decisions taken after open discussions, planning every step to be undertaken, all of them concerned with quality, self-discipline and prevision of actions to guarantee a successful outcome.

It is against this background that our experiences with young people, in and outside the school, must be seen. Here, we mention briefly some of them and will reflect on the social changes with which they are connected.

Video-school project

We were invited by the principal of a school in the poor periphery of Rio's Metropolitan Area to bring a selection of videos previously screened in public squares by the Maxambomba TV. The idea was to use these videos as starting points to encourage the adolescents to discuss subjects that interested them directly. These 14- to 18-year-old adolescents belonged to the working class, to use a European category. This means that they were not among the poorest, but lived in places that offered them little, if any, cultural alternatives and stimulation. At a 40km distance from downtown Rio, most of them had never seen Rio's Central Business District or bathed in the famous Copacabana or Ipanema beaches. The 40 some pupils' class was equally divided between boys and girls. Their horizon wasn't exactly wide, limited as it was by the scarce local opportunities. They were at school mostly because their parents considered, as most of the Brazilian population does, that education might be a way to climb the social scale. But the school curriculum imposed seemed too abstract and had little meaning for them. Free time was appreciated, because it allowed social interaction, but the strict discipline left no room for discussing themes that really interested them. And this is exactly what CECIP was introducing: even more than the contents of our videos, previously produced for a project on adolescent health education, it was the possibility to openly discuss them that attracted their interest. Our videos were made after a study that pointed to many questions that directly affected their lives, such as violence, adolescent pregnancy, HIV-AIDS or drugs, in addition to growth, sexuality and nutrition. No wonder they were interested.

Experimenting

We began by inviting them to discuss our idea. Did these issues have any relationship with their lives? They seemed interested, but at the same time, there was some distance separating interest and enthusiasm. At the beginning, a mixed feeling of curiosity and mistrust was in the air. What was going to happen exactly? Would they be just guinea pigs for another crazy school initiative? After explaining in detail our suggestion, which included videotaping the discussions, their interest seemed to grow. They bought the idea.

We then organized the sessions along different subjects. As no one in our team was a specialist in any of the themes that were going to be discussed, we invited a medical doctor, with experience in working with adolescents, to assist us. She agreed not to intervene in the discussion, unless a question was specifically addressed to her, or if some misinformation had to be clarified.

The first session started with a very brief introduction, immediately followed by the screening of a 15 minutes' video on drugs. The video was performed by four young actors -two couples-, who introduce themselves as a task group that must prepare a theater play on drugs for their colleagues. They are rehearsing in the schools' auditorium and trying to come up with a coherent message. They have books, documents, videos, but they mostly discuss their own ideas about the subject – and they never agree. The video then raises all the questions that are commonly asked about drugs. The actors try to incorporate their ideas into brief skits, but are always interrupted by some disagreement on an exaggerated statement or an idea that is out of place. The scripts of this and other videos were carefully written after many sessions of focal groups with adolescents and the consultancy of experienced specialists. Therefore, it is no wonder they touched the adolescents. In previous sessions, we observed that the videos allowed the students to take on what is called a critical distance attitude. This means that the discussion is facilitated because the adolescent is not discussing his or her own personal problem, but the character's.

In fact, it worked, once more. When the screening was over, it was not necessary to resort to the list, previously prepared, of questions and guidelines to stimulate the discussion that was going to be taped, presuming that the teens would be shy and hesitant to speak in front of the camera. This was a new experience for all, including CECIP's team.

Learning

Our judgment couldn't have been more wrong. The students immediately started discussing what they had just watched. In their interventions, they referred to the characters and situations of the video, but they were in fact eager to speak about themselves, their experiences, their questions. From time to time, we had to ask them to stop, so that we could change tapes. Almost no questions were addressed to our medical doctor, because one adolescent or youth typically provided the answer. The doctor only intervened a few times, to correct possible misinformation. After two hours, under the protests of the students, who wanted to continue to discuss, we closed the session and left.

A week later, we came back with an edited 20-minute video of the two-hour taped session. After the initial surprise of seeing themselves from an absolutely new angle and after lots of laughs and criticisms about everyone's awkwardness in expressing themselves properly, they began to question the concise version we presented: why include that phrase, and not another one, that was more important in their eyes? "Well, the editor made his choice, just like it happens with television" was the answer. That was unfair! A lively discussion followed, until a collective demand was made: why couldn't they choose and edit themselves? And why couldn't they also film, produce, take charge of the whole process?

The next sessions' tapes were edited with the participation of the whole group. It was hectic, but fun. The choices sometimes required long discussions before they were accepted. They wanted to know if the same discussions occurred during the editing of a TV program. How can one guarantee that TV editing is done in all fairness, respecting the original content of the speeches? What are the ethical principles that must guide an editor? Who controls the final product that goes on the air? How can one avoid all sorts of manipulations? The discussion went on and on, with some recalling wrongdoings and dirty tricks perpetrated by this and that television station. Most were dissatisfied with TV contents. A new, critical way of watching TV was developing, together with a new understanding of the power of the medium.

This experience constitutes the roots of a systematized methodology for Media Education, used some time later. We will describe it in detail in section 'Hands on the Media Project'. (see page 312)

The road was open to new experiences. One idea originated from conversations with George Stoney, Professor of Video and Film at NY University. He had worked with US students, "writing" and exchanging video-letters between schools located at some distance from each other. In our experience, adolescents at our school would make videos on their questions and hopes and exchange them with students from another distant school, but in the same region. To do so, they had to plan the production, do the research, read and write a script. They also had to pay attention to their appearance and language: after all they wanted to put their best foot forward. After some exchanges, all were eager to meet the youngsters at the other school. A visit was organized with the official purpose of "exchanging video communication experiences". But, in fact, they really wanted to meet "that funny guy" or "that cute girl".

All this was happening in one class only, out of twenty. Soon, the students from the other classes also wanted to participate. The teachers noticed that the students had become more alert, more interested, and had a different attitude in class. The library, previously an almost empty space, was now filled with interested students.

Informed about what was happening, a group of teachers also asked to have special sessions where they could discuss among themselves. After some negotiation, we started the sessions with them. The issues discussed were their personal experiences, problems and doubts about teaching methodology, learning processes, exams and so on. They soon realized that such discussions had never happened before, either because the official school meetings were limited mostly to administrative, bureaucratic issues or because they were now at ease among colleagues, instead of having to pose as sure of themselves to the school principal.

Connecting young people and adults
Some teachers criticized the students, saying they were passive, uninterested, undisciplined – a common complaint among teachers everywhere. As we had the experience of listening to the same complaints coming from the students, we decided to show each group what the other group thought about it. We were aware of the danger that the idea could go astray and harm, damage the project.

At the beginning of the sessions, each group was outraged by the other's criticism. "Boring teachers", "Lazy students", "Authoritarian attitudes", and so on, seemed to fuel an Armageddon.

We then suggested to the two groups that they have a larger session, in which students and teachers would meet each other and discuss the issues that were, after all, common to both sides. To our surprise, everybody agreed. After a difficult start, little by little the real issues began to emerge. Teachers were ill paid, overworked, had an impossible, outdated curriculum, with themes and subjects imposed from above, poor training, no time to listen, no time to interact with the adolescents, no time to look for solutions, to study, to prepare themselves.

The teachers made their mea culpa, admitting that the adolescents' criticism had enough ground to be consistent. At the same time, students realized that the teachers were also people who had difficulties and limitations but were willing to improve. They admitted that their attitude was far from cooperative or understanding. Slowly, by small, hesitant, careful steps, a common understanding began to emerge. The result was an experiment where for the first time students, teachers and the principal sat together to establish new rules for the school.

According to a joint study carried out by the Ministry of Education and Unicef in 2007, internal dialogue, co-responsibility in school's management, interested teachers and space for student participation are the foundation for improving the quality of learning. It was this school's experience, ten years in advance. The first fundamental change came from the adolescents' concrete experience of being able to speak and having their opinion taken seriously. This had never happened in that school. The opinion of students was non-existent. It was simply not important, and was restricted to being allowed to appeal in case of bad marks. Any initiative to dialogue was cut on grounds of discipline. The violence of this situation – where one side was all powerful, the other oppressed and reduced to silence – eventually produced bursts of conflict, repressed and silenced by authoritarian disciplinary measures. The meeting between adolescent students and their teachers, which enabled both parties to present their points of view, put forward their arguments, and discuss common problems affecting everyone's environment, had features of a revolution. The whole climate of the school changed. Students organized themselves, electing representatives. The school's principal and teachers created space and time that could be used as a forum to solve problems that might arise. Teaching became easier and the interest manifested by students stimulated the teachers to dedicate themselves to preparing better classes. The students were empowered by their increased capacity to express themselves, not only through the videos they were able to prepare, however simple, but also by realizing that the school, after all, had a great deal to offer. Having mastered the technical part of video production, the main challenge became the contents: looking around their own environment, dealing with their own questions, expressing their reality, finding new ways put forward their word.

"Hands on the media" project

This project had its origins in the experience described above. It was clear that it was necessary, for both teachers and young students, to know more about the media, at that time especially television, which was – and still is – the main source of information, leisure and culture. Abramo and Branco's survey reveals that watching TV is the main leisure/cultural activity of Brazilian youth during the week (90%), and the third main activity on the weekend (87% – first is "meeting friends", and second "listening to radio"). Over 90% of the population owns a TV set, and 87% owns a radio, while still only 20% owns a computer.

The media are a powerful pedagogical tool for learning, provided that one masters their logic, specific language and main technical aspects.

Our previous experience showed that adolescents and youths are specially attracted by new technologies. They are eager to learn, and they learn quickly. In our experience, we see that ICT language is avidly appropriated by youngsters, perhaps because it belongs to their historical time. They happily play a trial and error game, in lively competition with each other. This attitude is totally different from their teachers', who are afraid of revealing their technological ignorance, thinking that they cannot make any mistake in the presence of the students, as we learned in the workshops that CECIP has held on media education with high school teachers. It was evident that the teachers' need technical support in order to improve their communication with the students.

Supporting the people who should support youth

At the beginning of those sessions, our concern was to discuss content, meaning, and appropriate coherence between subject and visual language. Although discussions were vivid, we spotted a resistance to the use of video and computers in the classroom, and discovered that it was because the teachers felt insecure, not knowing what to do if the image trembled, the player stopped, or the sound didn't work. We then began the workshops not with a general discussion on media content, but by teaching basic things, like how to make connections be-

Young students acting a "TV program", an exercise of the Hands on the Media methodology. "Supporting the ones who should support youths". *Photo:* CECIP team

tween video player and monitor, how to plug in the sound and the video, and how to fix any problem that might happen. That changed radically the attitude of teachers. One day, a teacher proudly said that her adolescent students were very impressed when she was able to fix the parabolic antenna.

We started by providing 30 hours of training workshops to the teachers in the schools located in the periphery of Rio's Metropolitan Region. During these workshops, the teachers discussed theoretical texts about communication and education, carried out experiments in pedagogical dynamics and were stimulated to put them in practice with their students. They also learned how to operate the equipments most commonly found in schools, namely the video and the TV set. As part of the methodology, we made an appointment one month after the last workshop in order to share the experiences carried out and the difficulties indentified, and to discuss in the group how to overcome them.

The result exceeded our expectations. There was a common line in all the experiences made: the teachers were invariably insecure about the outcomes of their initiatives. One reported that she was terrified when the students asked to operate the camera outside the school premises. She agreed, but was sure that they would bring back the camera in pieces. In fact, she was surprised to see how well they were able to handle it and even more so with what the students were able to do. "I couldn't imagine they would be able to tell a story so well!" she confessed. Another teacher discussed with the students the soap opera that was being screened on TV. They were able to enact a chapter with their own script, very critical to the mores of the original screenplay. Every experience had common points, like the increased participation and interest of the students. Watching TV, something that everybody does, was no longer a danger, an enemy to combat, an enemy so powerful that you felt defeated before the battle. TV became a source of subjects to discuss, to criticize, or to change based on your own point of view. TV as pedagogical matter, as a way to increase media consciousness, was a novelty.

These results were so positive that we were invited by the regional education authorities to share our experience with both teachers of education and university pursuing their teacher training. Since 2004, 500 teachers reaching some 50 thousand students have been trained in Rio de Janeiro only. We decided to systematize our experience by organizing a publication, a tool kit, composed of a booklet, video and posters. It took us more than a year of hard work to produce, but it was worthwhile. After the successful experience with the Regional Authorities, another step was the national distribution, through the Ministry of Education, of 3,500 copies of the publication Hands on the Media. CECIP trained the ministry team that was going to train the teachers responsible for putting the educational toolkit to use. The challenge now is to enlarge this project as a distance project, including the necessary training for its implementation. Brazil being a large country, new technologies and new training methodologies must go hand in hand. Television programs produced in Rio and São Paulo reach the farther villages of the Amazon Region, as well as the periphery of these large metropolitan centers. They exert influence in many ways, some good, some bad – some very bad indeed. A critical eye is not formed by theoretical texts or well-intentioned lessons, but through a mix of theory and practice. That's what we propose with this experience.

We have been using the same toolkit with adolescents in several projects since. The only difference may be the reading of the theoretical texts before discussing their content with the youngsters. The original purpose of this work is to start an awareness-raising process concerning television program watching and the creation of a more critical and creative audience. The methodology is far from just theoretical. What is discussed is put in practice. The production of short (1-minute) video pieces makes a difference. After living this experience, no one ever watches TV in the same way as before. Having learned the principles of video production, if an adolescent or youth is really interested, the door will be open to other experiences. These have to do with the increasing presence of visual communication in our lives, with being able to tell a story with images, organizing the information you want to communicate in a completely different way than the word only. This has consequences for the way in which different kinds of information are absorbed and used in the preparation of a new product. The trained eye and the effort to translate data and facts into a new form of language deeply influence our ability to be aware of the world around us.

"This is our TV" project

This project was part of a larger program called "Schools Networking with the Future". It consisted of training students in video production and in developing micro projects for their schools. The purpose was to link the schools with the surrounding communities. The students who participated in this project organized a study about the history of their neighborhood, called Botafogo. They discovered a treasure that only existed in the memory of the older inhabitants. They were able to interview these people and collect old photos, clippings, articles and many objects and memorabilia that they classified and organized in an exhibition. It was open to the community and officially inaugurated with all the formalities of an important public event. The students also produced a video with the accounts of old and recent inhabitants. Besides the interviews, the documentary showed photos and clippings that were carefully kept among the families' treasures. A comparison was established between that neighborhood and another, by the same name, but located near the seaside in a richer area, close to the well-known Copacabana beach.

The result of this project strengthened links between the students and their community, thus demonstrating how important it is to preserve the memory of what happened years back and showing that changes can be brought about when people join forces. It is difficult to measure self-esteem, an important element that both results from and fuels change. In this case, the signs were spotted in the way parents, teachers and local people reacted to the exhibition of their history. The children – in this case up to 15 years of age – were proud for having been able to tell stories that would otherwise be forgotten. The interest that this project raised was channeled into discussions of the present state of things, and the need to unite to be strong when demanding measures from an indifferent and distant administration. In this process, the leadership was the children's. They could not accept that the things that they had brought to light would remain the same. They didn't listen to the many, among the older inhabitants, who were disenchanted and had become passive in the face of so much to be done. The children set the example for their elders. The project resulted in the beginning of a political reorganization of the locals, who used the school premises as their meeting place. The children succeeded in opening the school to the community, opening a dialogue and transforming the neighborhood from a passive one to a vivid and active one.

Youth and change

When we reflect on these and other experiences we have been developing with adolescents and young people as our partners, we can see with special clarity some particular ways in which Brazilian youth are participating as political actors in the changes that the country is undergoing.

Youth are changing schools

We consider the schools, especially the second grade where the adolescents are, to be a highly strategic place in the process of changing Brazilian society. There are over 200,000 public second grade schools scattered all over the almost 6000 Brazilian municipalities. They are located in places where they represent the only public space in which people from poor communities can meet, practice sports and develop cultural activities. The schools have all sorts of problems, but successful experiences show that amazing things can happen when you have a clear idea of what can be done. And, to the surprise of many, young people frequently have such clear ideas.

Acting in projects such as *Video School, Hands on Media* and *This TV is Ours*, youngsters can transform Brazilian schools from places where there is no collaborative work and students are not heard, to places where students have their word, communicate their views and interact with adults in a horizontal fashion. The youth help teachers in overcoming their resistance to, sometimes "fear" of, dealing with media. It is quite a task to put equipment to work that existed in schools but was not used. It was also difficult to demonstrate to reluctant educators that they could be trusted, and that they could lead educational projects in which media are used to raise community awareness about community members' own strengths and power to improve their quality of life. Video-production methodology being essentially cooperative, young people learn and become able to teach their peers, their teachers and families how to teamwork, how to cooperate to produce things that are both beautiful and useful. It is at this point that the curriculum suddenly becomes interesting, meaningful, close to the real life and interests of the students. By researching, working in groups, looking for information in the school's library or with an older member of the surrounding community, the school becomes a living organization, connected with its social and cultural environment.

Another result of being active within the school premises is a new vision of school management. Through the process, the students experience the feeling that they are really helping to change things around them, including the school itself. They realize that the school doesn't belong to the principal alone, and that they play an important role when they help to improve the school's management.

Most important of all, in this process, young people change their self-image. Their self-esteem grows, and they no longer see themselves as "problems" or as "solutions", but as citizens involved in processes of communication and change, at the same level as other citizens of different ages and experiences.

Youth are changing the media

When youngsters experience producing a video, they undergo a profound change in their attitude towards television as well as other media. They become more critical and are able to understand what is being delivered by the media. They learn through their own practice and realize that images are not neutral, nor do they represent "The Truth", but they are instead a version or interpretation of a reality viewed through someone's eyes, ways of thinking, and also a mixture of feelings and political presuppositions. And they realize that they are able to produce their own images themselves, images that speak about their own ideas, instead of having others speaking about or for them on TV. Open TV in general, and commercial TV in particular, have been disseminating the image of youngsters as brainless beings, superficial, vain, only interested in the brand of their clothes and in their appearance, wanting success without effort. Videos produced by youth in projects such as the ones we have described above show different images. They reveal young people who are not ready-made puppets, but who are instead full of ideas, humor, dreams, and projects that vary according to the different groups and social affiliations of these young individuals. Some of these products are made with digital photo cameras, some with cell phones and others with a varied number of digital video cameras. Their quality varies, but there is always invention, creativity, and novelty in these videos. The Internet is their main spillway channel, but, among us, some make their way to open television, which is looking for ways to attract young viewers. What is most remarkable is that a great deal of these productions in video, music and plastic arts come from those living in the periphery, the poorest ones, who are beginning to be valued

Young students interview a popular character for their video program "Youth is changing the media". *Photo:* CECIP team

and made visible, and who influence middle and upper class youth, reversing what was considered the standard flow of cultural domination -from the top layers of society to the powerless (Tommasi 2008).

Educommunication means education and media working, valuing and trusting our diverse youth. It will make possible a *Brazilian education jump*. We predict that teachers will start to cooperate with young people, seeing them as their partners, as young people are motivated to bring their many cultures and their familiarity with art and the media into the schools. Through the media, students will communicate their support for teachers' struggle for better salaries and work conditions – if students feel connected with and respected and valued by teachers.

• • •

Our mission as an NGO is not to replace the government, or to do what is the responsibility of the public administration, but to demonstrate, through examples of successful projects, that such projects may grow to bigger scales and become public policies. Some of this social technology we've created in collaboration with youngsters has already been incorporated into public policies. But sometimes our dialogue with successive governments looks like a Sisyphus effort of pushing a stone uphill. From time to time, the stone reaches the top and we are able to see concrete and rewarding results of our work, to the benefit of many. Administrative discontinuity may force us to start once more from the bottom of the mountain.

The future is here: change your city, change the world

A project in which we are presently involved is established in a Rio favela, called Morro dos Macacos, and mobilizes 530 young people. They will be qualified as juvenile entrepreneurs by ICT workshops where, besides audiovisual production, they will be involved with digital inclusion, mobilization and marketing, receiving training in management techniques, especially financial ones. The environment will be permeated with discussion of their reality, within the Brazilian youth situation, and of the ways in which they can strengthen their citizenry. The local school is part of the project. It will receive interventions that will help it both retain the young students there and prepare them for successful entry into the labor market. We hope this project will serve as a model that can be multiplied throughout the school system. We are investing all the experience accumulated during these 22 years into this multifaceted project. The project sets an example for projects involving adolescents, youth and their communities by facilitating access to tools that increase their chances not only of surviving in our globalized world, but that enable them to act to change their immediate environment and the world around them.

We believe that youngsters are the main actors in the creation of learning communities. Torres (1999) defines a learning community as: "an organized human community that builds and involves itself in its own educative and cultural project, to educate itself, its children, youths and adults, in an endogenous, cooperative and solidary effort, based on a diagnosis not only of its weaknesses but of its strengths to overcome those weaknesses".

This leads to our conception of the youngster' s role in the city. As one possibility opening up in the future, Attali (2008) sees a development in which the nation-state will become increasingly weaker under the umbrella of a planetary government that aims at a common good. What he calls "altruistic, universal forces" will prevail upon the hypertrophy of market and destructive conflicts . The cities, as spaces of participatory and associative democracy, will become more important than nation-states. There are already some signs of this tendency. The existing network of Educative Cities represents a seed of this possible future. This new concept of a friendly city that educates permanently, as a wide net of pedagogic spaces, both formal (schools, universities, research centers, museums) and informal (homes, plazas, clubs, companies, transportation, media ...), gives scope for new creativity. Through all these spaces, citizens – specially young ones – educate and are educated (Cabezudo 2003, apud Ednir 2006).

In our interaction with young people, we observe that what they learn in the classrooms is only a small fraction of what they learn in their daily lives. Most of their real learning comes from ICT interactions in different spaces of the city, which they occupy and transform through a varied set of manifestations of youth cultures. Circulating through these different spaces, and performing different roles – as family members, students, workers, group/community leaders, artists, performers – young people demonstrate new ways to interact and communicate in a horizontal, inclusive, critical and profoundly democratic way, using a logic that is different from the profit-seeking capitalist one.

The spread of the Internet in Brazil is making it increasingly easy for each youngster to become a producer and disseminator of messages – in images and in text[4], free of charge. In 2007, the Brazilian Government made information labs available in every high school. Soon, every public school in the country will have broadband access to the Internet. LAN (Local Area Network) houses (shops with paid Internet access) are popping up in every neighborhood in Brazilian metropolitan regions including the favelas, making Internet available to their children, adolescents and youths.

The ease with which youngster of all social classes navigate the Web and are able to use spaces of freedom such as Youtube, Joost or Myspace predicts new changes in the near future that, like those in the past, will seem to practically happen instantly, at the same time, everywhere. Television as we know it is already trying desperately to adapt itself in order to survive. Four of the main TV American channels (CBS, ABC, NBC and Fox) have several of their most successful programs in the Internet, for free. Experiences also target the interactivity that makes it possible for part of the programming to be filled with productions made by the audience. This process will increase more and more with new digital technologies. The dichotomy between emission and reception will be replaced by the consumer who is also a producer. The TV screen and the computer screen tend to be the same.

Perhaps one of the main impacts of the digital revolution is the transfer of the mass media power to the individual, who has many ways to access information and has new, unheard of possibilities to spread his/her opinions. As Castells (1999) puts it,[5] there is a new civil global society that is filling the representative void left by traditional institutions. This new scenario legitimizes political action that no longer expresses itself through political parties, or not only through them, but through spontaneous mobilizations that use autonomous systems of communication, the "instant messages" that we call "torpedos".

Increasingly, youth groups in different parts of the cities are connected with each other through the Internet, exchanging messages and cultural products. Cooperation/connections can be enhanced, creating innovative responses to the city's problems and scarcities, in what may be considered a new way to exert one's citizenry.

All these changes are happening now. Tangible results may be revealed earlier than expected.

---

* With the collaboration of Madza Ednir.

Notes

1. The Brazilian population almost quadrupled in the last half century, from 51,944,397 in 1950 to the present 189,612,814 people, according to the 2008 last official estimate.
2. *Pedagogy of the Oppressed*, Herder and Herder, NY, 1970; Editora Paz e Terra, Rio, 1983.
3. Brazilian Children's Law (Estatuto da Criança e do Adolescente – ECA, 1990) considers children from 0 to 11 years old, and adolescents from 12 to 14 years old as *citizens* with rights. Tommasi (2008) points out that the Brazilian Youth Secretariat, created in 2003 by the federal government, consider youths citizens 15 and 29 years of age.
4. Says Tommasi (2008) "(....) the access to computer and Internet is not democratically distributed in Brazilian society: an Ibase – Polis study (2005) reveals that 51% of the interviewed youths do not have access to computers. If we decompose this data, we observe that 80% of the A/B classes claims to have access, while in the C class the index falls to 47.5% and in the D/E classes, to 24.2%".
5. Manuel Castells (2000) 'Technology, Society and Historical Transformation', in Paz e Terra (ed.) *The Information Era: Economy, Society and Culture vol.1. The Society Network.*, Rio de Janeiro, Brazil.

Bibliography

Abramo, Helena Wendel & Branco, Pedro Paulo Martoni, et al. (2005) *Retratos da Juventude brasileira- análise de uma pesquisa nacional*. [Brazilian youth's portraits – analysis of a national research.] Instituto Cidadania, Editora Perseu Abramo.

Abramovay, Miriam & Rua, Maria das Graças (2002) *Violência nas Escolas*. [Violence in schools.] Brasília, Brazil UNESCO.

Attali, Jacques (2008) *Uma Breve História do Futuro*. [A brief history of future.] Novo Século, Brazil.

Cama Rano, M.A (2006) *Transição para a vida adulta ou vida adulta em transição?* [Transition for adult life or adult life in transition?] IPEA, Brazil.

Castells, Manuel (2000) 'Tecnologia, Sociedade e Transformação Histórica' [Technology, society and historical transformation.] in Paz e Terra (ed.) *A era de Informação, Economia, Sociedade e Cultura, vol 1, A Sociedade em Rede* [The information era: Economy, society and culture, vol.1 The networking society.] Rio de Janeiro, Brazil.

Ceccon, Claudius & Ednir, Madza (2008) Plano de Desenvolvimento da Educação-PDE : Educação de Qualidade para Todos [Plan for education's development-PDE : Quality Education for All.] in *Educação 2008 – As mais importantes tendencias na visão dos mais importantes educadores.* [Education 2008 – The most important trends in the most important educationalist's vision.] Multiverso, Brazil.

Ednir, Madza (2008) Entrevista com Claudius Ceccon [Intervieing Claudius Ceccon), in *Projeto Sintonia Jovem*, Fundação Padre Anchieta, São Paulo Brazil, mimeo.

IBGE / Instituto Brasileiro de Geografia e Estatística (2006) [Brazilian institute for geography and statistics census] *Censo 1970, Censo 2000, Censo 2005, PNAD – Pesquisa Nacional de Amostras de Domicílios* [National Home Research Sampling.] Brazil.

Freire, Paulo (1970, 1983) *Pedagogy of the Oppressed*. [Pedagogia do oprimido] Herder and Herder NY, 1970;, Editora Paz e Terra, Rio, Brazil.

IPEA / Instituto de Pesquisas Econômicas Aplicadas (2007) [Institute of applied economic research] Brazil.

Madeira, Felícia (2007) *O impacto da educação básica (ensino médio) nos Jovens*. [The impact of high school education on youths.] Brazil, mimeo.

Moll, Jaqueline (2006) A cidade educadora como possibilidade: apontamentos. [Educative city as a possibility.] apud Ednir, Madza *A aprendizagem da Cooperação: desenvolvendo o potencial de escolas, comunidades e jovens, in Jovens Escolhas em Rede como Futuro* [Learning Cooperation – how to develop school, community and youth's potential in Young Choices- networking with the Future] Credicard Institute, Brazil.

MEC / Ministério da Educação, Cultura e Desporto do Brasil – INEP / Instituto Nacional de Estudos e Pesquisas Educacionais Anísio Teixeira (2007) [Brazilian ministry of education].
OAS / Organization of American States.
Ostrower, Noni et al. (2005) *Botando a Mão na Mídia*. [Hands on the media.] CECIP, Brazil.
Senge, Peter et al. (2000) *Schools that Learn – a Fifth Discipline Resource*. London: Nicholas Brealey Publishing.
Tommasi, Lívia (2008) *Sintonia Jovem – o que pensam e desejam os jovens brasileiros*. [Connecting Youth – what Brazilian youth think and crave for.] Cultura Data/Fundação Padre Anchieta, Brazil.
Torres, Rosa María (2001) Comunidad de Aprendizaje. La educación en función del desarollo local y del aprendizaje, http://www.fronesis.org/immagen/rmt/documentosrmt/ComuApren4.pdf (October 1, 2009).

Communication School for Children
Connecting Caves to the World

José Paulo de Araújo

Abstract
One of the greatest theoretical challenges for those involved in issues of participation is how to measure the level of people's participation accurately. In terms of adolescents' participation, Roger Hart and Antonio Carlos Gomes da Costa have developed assessment tools.

The purpose of the present article is to analyze this participation based on the experience of the Casa Grande Foundation and its Communication School for Children. This program is managed on a daily basis by 33 young people below 26 years of age and is considered by many as a process that works at the highest participatory level. The analysis will attempt to answer the following questions: How has this participatory experience influenced the development of the participants in the long term? How have the city and parents benefitted from this participatory approach? Finally, how are these activities, driven by adolescents, impacting the community?

Welcome to the Casa Grande (Big House)

Mark the correct answer:

A child[1] who belongs to a farmers' family for generations will be:

(a) A farmer

(b) A video maker

(c) An engineer

(d) A musician

(e) Others

All these possibilities could be correct if a child, adolescent[2] or youth[3] participates actively at the Communication School for Children, a program from Casa Grande

Foundation, a non-governmental organization located in the poorest area of Brazil: the Northeast Region. Nova Olinda municipality has 12,077 inhabitants[4] (5,773 below 19 years of age) who basically survive on family farming, mining and small businesses. Ten percent of its children (11 to 17 years of age) are illiterate[5], its Gross Domestic Product/Capita is around US $1,000 and its Human Development Index is 0.637[6].

Casa Grande was the first house in Nova Olinda. Built in 1717, it demarcates the starting point of the colonization period in a region occupied by the Kariri indigenous tribe. Mysteries and legends surrounded the house until 1992, when a couple of musicians (Alemberg Quindins and Rosiane Limaverde) decided to transform it into a museum and a "radio station," which consisted of two loudspeakers on the roof of the old house. At that time, the museum and "radio station" were opened only on weekends, when the founders – who live in another city – came to Nova Olinda. Children's participation was not part of the NGO founders' plan, but the curiosity and desire to participate of three boys and one girl caused the new owners of the house to accept the first children as museum receptionists and radio announcers.

Since then, children and adolescent have occupied it, without fear of ghosts. The Big House demands respect and the children give it in return. The first participants assumed responsibility for maintaining and operating the museum and radio on weekdays – even without the assistance of the couple. The founders decided to call them "managers", because they would be accountable for some activities on a daily basis. By doing so, the NGO became inclusive and participatory. The four "co-founders" – those children who became managers – brought new ideas to attract their peers, including traditional game competitions and "broadcasting" the local football matches. Alemberg and Rosiane accepted not only these initiatives, but also the suggestion of one boy who proposed a TV station. He was fascinated by the cameras that had started registering this experience: his desire came out of the Communication School program.

Developing the activities together, this on-the-job training school is managed daily by 33 children and youth, whose ages vary from 10 to 26 years. The participants include only eight girls, due to the fact that they have more domestic responsibilities. The managers are normally youths, because they have more experience. A group of six youths participate actively, including one of the co-founders (see testimonial in Box 2). A study conducted in early 2008 revealed that the participant families have a similar socio-economic background, with the majority of families from Nova Olinda: their mothers are housekeepers, small farmers or sellers and their fathers are miners, farmers, sellers or migrants in bigger cities. The participants study in public schools, but do not frequent the same places as those who do not participate in the Communication School, as will be highlighted later.

For didactic purposes, Casa Grande Foundation has four programs: Art, Memory, Tourism and Communication. This chapter will concentrate on the Communication School, which embraces eleven production activities and specific libraries. In terms of the production activities, children and youth learn by

> **Box 1.**
>
> Francisco de Assis Junior is 16 years old and is the manager of the Casa Grande Theater. He is also responsible for a daily radio program and produces videos. At the moment he is learning digital lighting. According to his mother, Maria de Fatima Pereira Goncalves, Casa Grande somehow replaced the role of his father, who passed away when Junior was very young: "I have no idea who Junior would be without Casa Grande. He was very aggressive and used to fight with his sister. Junior needed a father. Now he has learned in Casa Grande how to respect others." Junior no longer assists his mother in selling clothes at the open market. On the other hand, Casa Grande helped her to build a guesthouse, which became a source of income for this proud family. On his blog[7], Junior expresses that the best teachers are the children, that the primary need is to communicate, and that the most important people for any person are his/her parents.

> **Box 2.**
>
> "My name is João Paulo Maropo. I study biology and I am 25 years old. My father is a mason and my mother is a housekeeper. I have two sisters and one brother (who is adopted). I had an enviable childhood because I had the freedom to play on the streets without risk of traffic accidents. Curiosity is one of my characteristics. I always like to discover and to create things. Because my father could not afford to buy me toys, I used to make my cars out of slippers, sardine cans and bottle covers. The educational levels of my parents are very low. Both of them always showed us the importance of school and never let us work – a common practice in the camp. I left Nova Olinda in 1991 and returned in 1992. The ghost house I used to play in was being rebuilt. That is when Casa Grande came into my life. Nova Olinda was like an aquarium and Casa Grande became a sea, because it was through it that I could find an outlet for my pent up energy. So I invited myself to Casa Grande. At the beginning I just played and during the weekends we had art courses and listened to Rosiane's radio program. At that time my responsibility was to clean the yard. Now I am studying photography and taking pictures. With the money I got from the photos, I support my family. I hope one day I can approach my parents and say: 'Now I will pay the costs of your house'. Today I am the Administrative Director of Casa Grande and I plan to have a family and have my children playing and learning at Casa Grande.[8]"

practicing how to conceptualize, produce, finalize and disseminate their material through several communication channels. The participants manage:

- A radio station that broadcasts daily programs produced and presented by children and youth from 7:00 until 22:00;
- A video production center with high-level equipment that allows participants to produce special programs for national educational television. In addition they produce video clips and cultural programs. The local production, which is above 100 videos, is shown weekly at the theater, prior to the cinema session;

- Two music bands. One band composes jazz and sound tracks for the cultural videos, and the other one is composed of children below the age of 11 years. This children's band utilizes instruments made of recycled materials produced by the band members themselves. Both bands perform their shows in different parts of Brazil, and the youth band has already performed internationally. They also perform in Casa Grande theater on a regular basis;

- An audio studio, considered the best in the region, where songs produced by children and youth are also recorded by them and transferred to master CDs, which are regularly broadcast through the radio station;

- A publishing department in which children and youth produce CD and DVD covers as well as promotional materials related to shows performed by the children and youth. These promotional materials include posters and banners for shows, as well as comic books depicting the legends of the Kariri indigenous people;

At the publishing department children and youth produce comic books with the legends of the indigenous people who lived in that region. They also produce material to promote their CDs, DVDs and shows.
Photo: João Paulo Maropo

- A theater where plays, videos, shows, cultural seminars and films are organized by the participants;

- An internet department, where youth are responsible for maintaining the website of the Foundation[9];

- The participant blogs[10], which are also used to perform qualitative evaluations based on their investigations and thoughts. Each child and youth has to up-load comments on a book, video, CD or any other cultural material on a monthly basis;

- A project of painting the façades of the traditional local houses. Computers are used by the participants to redefine the colors of the façades prior to its painting;

- The Anthropological Museum in which children are trained to be receptionists and interact with different people through inter-personal communication; and

- Traditional games, which foster the linkage with their traditions and nature, are promoted over electronic games.

As described above, the Communication School integrates many different media to disseminate their culture and the power of children and youth participation.

Besides these production activities, managed by the 33 participants, the Communication School also has different libraries. Each one compiles a variety of cultural products from different nations. Anyone may access to this source of information and knowledge. It includes:

- A comic book library with over 2,600 titles, including the full collection of Will Eisner and Frank Miller;
- A DVD library with over 2,000 films, including the full collection of Andrei Tarkovsky and Akiro Kurosawa;
- A collection of approximately 5,000 CDs and LPs, from rock to traditional Brazilian and African music;
- A library with over 200 books;
- A music room with dozens of instruments, many of them made of recycled materials; and
- An anthropological museum with over 200 pieces.

Casa Grande uses new media to reinforce their local values. The participants replicate famous icons with local elements; instead of video clips with dynamic edition of images, their videos have calm rhythm and are capable of transforming interviews into poems; the website www.youtube.com shows some of their cultural programs; multinational software is used to create comics about the local legends, to record jazz and indigenous music or to make colorful traditional buildings.

Adolescents build their instruments from recycle materials and they make their own songs. It could be the beginning of a long journey. International icons are used to reinforce local culture.
Photo: João Paulo Maropo

The most surprising aspect is that the two adult founders do not live in Nova Olinda nor are there adult teachers in this Communication School[11]. The founders of the NGO transferred the ownership of the organization's projects to the youth and children participants by giving them managerial responsibilities. The participants have the additional benefit of learning how to produce different cultural, artistic and communicational materials as well as of participating in national and international events that disseminate their production. On the other hand, the participants also have the burden of upholding the rules to maintain credibility among parents and the community[12] and of maintaining the premises, which includes cleaning, painting, repairing and other daily activities. The meritocracy system is well established, and with this level of responsibility and discipline, children and adults discuss openly any problems that arise.

This project fits into the definition of education by Paulo Freire: once the children acquire autonomy they are capable of reflecting on their own existence by defining the way they wish to lead their lives. Above this, they obtain the freedom to choose the future according to their skills, aware that they are part of a bigger environment, but without losing the strong connection with the place they are living in. (Acioli 2000: 51)[13]

Research design

Research was conducted in February 2008 to understand how this participatory model implemented at Casa Grande Foundation is perceived by adolescents (12 to 15 years of age) directly involved on the production of communication material (participants) and by those who are not engaged (non-participants).

In the field study, the researcher observed the behavior of both groups in their homes, at school and on the streets. In addition, he investigated the documentation (plan, statute and budget) of the NGO and consulted the Internet to analyze how Casa Grande is perceived by the local media. Four Focus Group Discussions (FGD) were conducted with adolescents not directly involved with production of communication material[14]. Among the adolescents directly involved with the Communication School, two FGD were conducted: One with girls and the other with boys. Among the 33 participants of the Communication School, three were girls and nine were boys between 12 and 15 years of age. All three girls and seven out of the nine boys were part of the other FGD. Beside the FGDs, semi-structure interviews were conducted with the following adults: The parents of four participants; four parents of adolescents not directly involved on the production of communication material; six public school teachers; founders of Casa Grande Foundation and three members of the Tutor Council[15]. Informal interviews were conducted with the responsible official of the education system in the State of Ceará and with 12 former participants of the Communication School. The researcher has been involved with the NGO since 1993.

Because the main subjects were adolescents between the ages of 12 and 15 years, experts[16] recommend a combination of interactive techniques during data collection in order to ensure accuracy and to create a friendly environment. A variety of methods were used during the Focus Group Discussions. These included drawing out their perception of the past, present and future of Nova Olinda and analyzing the connections between the three aspects through: role play, to show their relationships with parents, teachers and peers; and semi-structured interviews, used in FGDs, with adult interviews and with former participants. These varied activities facilitated the validation of the information provided by the adolescents. Video was used only to record the role-play session in order to facilitate analysis of the physical expression of the teens. This decision was taken to avoid inhibition owing to the constant use of video recording.

Moving towards Casa Grande

There is no restriction for any young people[17] from Nova Olinda to join Casa Grande. Therefore the NGO always keeps its gates, playground and libraries open. By playing, studying and observing, children and adolescents initiate their integration, but the newcomer has to show an interest in participating actively. To be a member some rules must be obeyed such as: Observe the schedule, maintain the space, participate in all activities and not only those that he or she enjoys, and follow the orientation of those with more time and experience at Casa Grande.

> Participant Girl 2: Alemberg transferred the responsibility to the older participants and whenever we did something wrong, the youths – those who coordinate the activities – told us what we were doing wrong. If they cannot solve it, they ask Alemberg to solve the problem. Since he is not here everyday, we send him e-mails.

Parents apparently approve of this and consider it the basis of a good relationship:

> Father of Participant 1: At Casa Grande, if a child doesn't behave well, they inform us and we have to do something.

> Mother of Participant 2: If mothers were better informed about Casa Grande, they would let their children participate. If they don't know, they think their children will go there to work. They will not work, they will learn.

> Mother of Participant 3: As a mother, I don't want to see people shouting at my son, but at Casa Grande the rule is that: the younger ones have to obey the older ones. It hurts, but this is part of the rules.

The founders of the NGO consider the discipline and rigor to be part of the pedagogy and their local culture. The rules are clear – although not written – and include respect for people as well as for the environment; no use of drugs, including alcohol; and no involvement in parties that could lead to "bad behavior", such as use of alcohol or involvement in fights.

Climbing the ladder and stair

Communication researchers Eng Eugenia, John Briscoe and Anne Cunningham said: "Participation is not an objective that exists in specific quantities or that can be measured in specific quantities or that can be measured in particular units to be compared over time." (Morris 2005: 126). Roger Hart, professor of Environmental Psychology, challenged this statement and proposed a model to measure children's participation, based on the ladder created by Sherry Arnstein (1969) and used to measure citizen participation. On Hart's ladder there are eight levels of participation for young people. The first three are considered "non-participation", and the others, "degree of participation".

Figure 1. Roger Hart's ladder of young people's participation

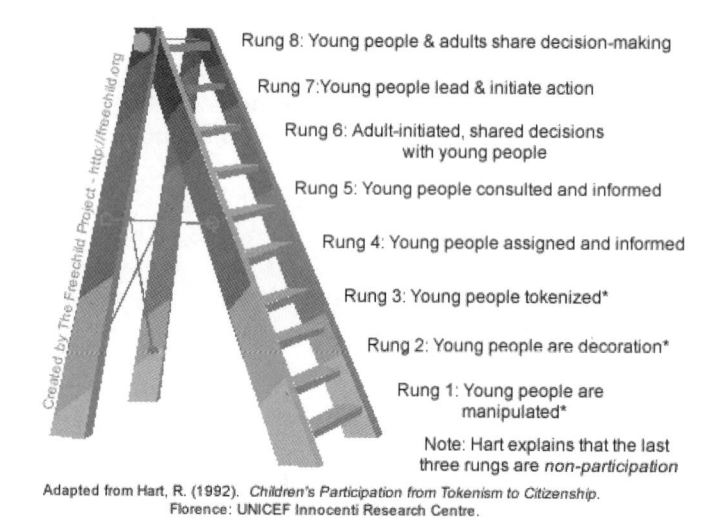

Rung 8: Young people & adults share decision-making
Rung 7: Young people lead & initiate action
Rung 6: Adult-initiated, shared decisions with young people
Rung 5: Young people consulted and informed
Rung 4: Young people assigned and informed
Rung 3: Young people tokenized*
Rung 2: Young people are decoration*
Rung 1: Young people are manipulated*

Note: Hart explains that the last three rungs are *non-participation*

Adapted from Hart, R. (1992). *Children's Participation from Tokenism to Citizenship*. Florence: UNICEF Innocenti Research Centre.

Brazilian professor Antonio Carlos Gomes da Costa identified some inconsistencies in the concept of citizenship in Hart's model, which does not take into consideration other forms of participation such as working or street children. Despite these criticisms, Costa acknowledges the pioneering ideas of Hart and the required partnership with adults. He adapted Hart's model by including the new global scenario and limiting the new model to young people and their educators.

According to Costa, with the end of the Cold War and with globalization, the new Human Being should combine the best of the 1st and 2nd Worlds: "Freedom and solidarity, respectively. Therefore, the new adolescent should be autonomous, have community spirit and be competent, and this can only be achieved in an environment that is conducive to freedom. In developing such an environment, a holistic perspective of development, which includes affection, citizenship and productive lives, is necessary. However, the challenge for schools, parents and

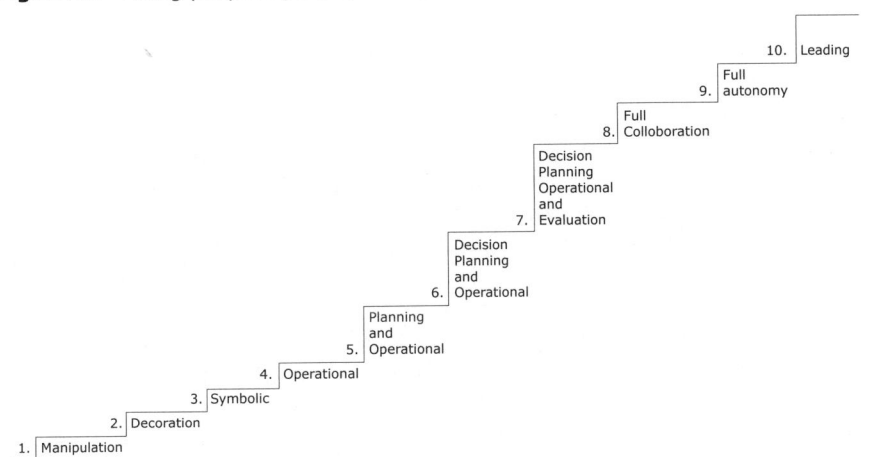

Figure 2. Young people's participation stair

10. Leading
9. Full autonomy
8. Full Colloboration
7. Decision Planning Operational and Evaluation
6. Decision Planning and Operational
5. Planning and Operational
4. Operational
3. Symbolic
2. Decoration
1. Manipulation

developmental organizations is to educate the adolescents with values that fit into their culture and that are suited to the challenges of a global society" (Costa 2000: 101).

The ladder and the stair diagrams limit adolescents' participation to their involvement in structured projects and events. Despite this limitation, these two models were used to measure the level of adolescent participation in this study.

Analyzing the Communication School based on these matrixes, the research observed that:

1. At the initial stage, adolescents proposed and initiated many activities. Now the projects and ideas are more donor oriented. Despite this change, educators and young people discuss how each new intervention will be conducted and monitored.

2. Young people are the primary individuals responsible for the implementation of what has been jointly planned. The founders admitted, during informal conversation, that the adolescents and youth have higher technical skills and are leading the production process.

3. Normally the teenagers are the ones who conduct interviews and travel around to show specific activities or to train other adolescents or even teachers in other parts of Brazil. The founders normally attend large meetings and conferences when the discussion is more theoretical.

Specific to media participation, other authors provide some guidance:

> "The most developed form of participation is self-management. This principle implies the right to participation in the planning and production of media content." (Servaes & Malikhao 2005: 95)

"[Community media] (...) are the media in which the community participates, as planners, producers, and performers. They are the means of expression of the community, rather than for the community" (Berrigan cited by Servaes & Malikhao 2005: 97)

One clear example of this participatory process took place while the author was doing his research. Alemberg came with the news that the music band composed of children below 11 years of age was selected in a national competition and that a CD and DVD would be produced in a studio in São Paulo city. Founders, children and youth decided together to produce both materials and submit directly to the sponsor. They wanted to show their potential not only in composing songs, but also in producing the entire package. They planned together, shared responsibilities and stayed up late at night recording songs; producing pictures and covers of the CD and DVD; and shooting video clips. While these products were being produced by all 33 participants, the founders arranged some shows for the band in São Paulo.

As shown in the above example, the founders of the NGO assume responsibility for fund raising, while young people at the Communication School control the production process and are accountable for delivering products of the required quality, on a daily basis. Thus, the development of the communication material is planned, implemented and monitored by all 33 participants, together with the founders. The participants do not yet guide the adults concerning long-term organizational plan, but they manage the NGO on a daily basis. In other words, adults and adolescents shared decisions after the projects – normally proposed by the founders – has been funded. There are cases in which projects are created based on the talent or interest expressed by adolescents. Almost all activities are a result of "thinking together", as Alemberg says.

Casa Grande FM broadcasts daily programs produced and presented by children and youth, without adult supervision, from 7:00 until 22:00. *Photo:* João Paulo Maropo

Based on this field research and after analyzing all available studies (Acioli and Azevedo), a book (Albanese) and local newspaper articles and stories[18] regarding Casa Grande Foundation, it was easy to identify words, such as "collaboration" and "team building", that were constantly being used to describe children and youth practices. There is clear evidence that the Communication School truly incorporates a participatory "process" – which goes beyond project – and that it is located on the highest steps of Hart's and Costa's models.

The questions now are: How has this participatory experience influenced the development of the participants in the long term? How have the city and parents benefitted from this participatory approach? Finally, how are these activities, driven by adolescents, impacting the community?

Individual changes

After 16 years, Casa Grande has changed a great deal, as has the profile of those who actively participated in their activities. The researcher met with almost all of the youths from the first years of the NGO. They have professions that are quite different from their parents. Amongst those 17 from the "first generation", 11 are at university or have completed their studies, while six completed secondary school. The first generation of Casa Grande participants represent varied professions and include a mining engineer, web designer, electrician, film maker, script writer, photographer, cultural director of a national organization, musical producer, pedagogical manager, teacher, nurse, lawyer, vendor, public servant and health worker. All of them (except one) acknowledge the contribution of Casa Grande to their professional career and personal lives. Ten out of the eleven participants with university degrees still support Casa Grande as volunteers, while only one with a secondary degree continues supporting the organization.

On average, participants of the Communication School perform better than the Brazilian population. According to a 2006 study done by Instituto Nacional de Estudos e Pesquisas Educacionais Anisio Teixeira (INEP)[19], almost 40% of graduate students in Brazil are above the age of 25 years; 54% were outside State capitals; and 87% belonged to middle or upper classes[20]. In 1997, there were less than 2 million university students in a population of 157 million[21] inhabitants. "In Brazil's studies, for example, school attendance peaks at ages 10 to 11, and labour force employment rates begin to climb rapidly at ages 13 to 14, especially for boys" (Boyden and Levison 2000: 29).

In the present field study, children were also observed during weekend nights. All the local bars were full of people, including adolescents, drinking spirits, beer, but also non-alcoholic drinks and ice creams. One study[22] reveals that, in Brazil, alcohol consumption among girls (12-17 years old) almost doubled from 2001 to 2005 – 3.5% to 6% in total. Among boys, the increase was less significant: from 6.9% to 7.3% (12-17 years old). Normally the girls are together along the road that crosses the town, wearing low-necked dresses, while the boys are showing off with bicycles and motorcycles. Wealthy people park their cars in front of the bars and listen to *forró*[23]. In front of Casa Grande, the active members of the organization also meet. Younger children play traditional games, while the adolescents and youths are dating or talking about different issues. They talk about new videos or remember adventures and mistakes they made during the initial stages of the Communication School.

Members of the Tutor Municipal Council and primary school teachers agreed that somehow the lack of family discipline is a result of the deterioration of the family and cultural values, which are leading to the individualistic attitudes of adolescents and their families:

> Member of Nova Olinda Tutor Council 1: One of the major problems is the destruction of family values, which generates a high level of prostitution, as well as a significant number of adolescents and children involved in drugs and alcohol. We are trying to address these problems through the schools, but we are observing that on many occasions the parents transfer their responsibilities to the Tutor Council or to the school and also the school transfers its accountability to other organizations, but the foundation should be the family.

> Primary School Teacher 5: Parents are not ready to guide their children. (...) In our municipality any adolescent can drink anywhere. Some girls start prostituting very early. Many of them think this is the best way of life. Last year I had a student who moved to the night shift and started prostituting. Recently she came to me saying that she was pregnant.

> Primary School Teacher 2: Nowadays we are practically replacing the role of parents in relation to education.

> Primary School Teacher 1: Discipline is the first value that families put aside. When you invite the parents to talk they always say: 'I can't control the situation anymore' and suddenly you discover that the boy they are referring to is 11 years old. The students do not have the perspectives or ambition or objective to develop. They like it the way it is.

Social changes

Nova Olinda is still a low-income municipality (GDP/ capita equivalent to US$ 1,730[24]), but the new adolescent participatory approach has brought curiosity, diversity and tourism to the town and made Casa Grande a powerful institution not only in Nova Olinda, but also in Ceara State.

For the time being, Casa Grande has become a much more complex institution, with many projects, involving not only children, but also their families, and influencing the entire community. For example, parents' income is growing due to its direct participation with the NGO programs. The parents of the participants manage 12 guesthouses, a handicraft store, restaurant and other small businesses using the Casa Grande brand. The organization also influences the social, cultural and economic environment: There is Federal level investment in local tourism[25], the handicraft store next to Casa Grande, the embellishment of schools with replicas of famous Brazilian paintings, and the first private hotel being built in the city, which are just some examples. Casa Grande is becoming a social policy reference to other municipalities and organizations. For instance, the Municipal Education Secretary of Sobral (North of Ceara State) made an agreement with the NGO in order to share with their teachers basic knowledge about adolescents' participation in the school's radio (an internal sound system used by students during the break time). In addition, experiences concerning comics, management of cultural events and revitalization of traditional architecture have been discussed with many municipalities. UNICEF[26] has also used Casa Grande as a benchmark of children's participation. UNICEF Brazil created a quality award for municipalities that developed good policies for children: Selo UNICEF, and the adolescents' participation in Casa Grande became a reference owing to its high quality.

Vision

The study shows that this NGO plays an important role in the city, and this view is almost unanimous among those interviewed and among people in the media.

For the participants, there is a sense of pride over being an actor in the history of Casa Grande.

> Girl 1: In fact this city became known thanks to Casa Grande.

> Girl 3: In the past there was nothing in Nova Olinda, except Casa Grande, so we created theater and other activities that attract children to Casa Grande. (...) Casa Grande shows that this city needs to improve even more.

For young people not directly involved in daily activities, there is a mixture of delight and envy.

> Boy 8: Casa Grande brought us information and this is good. For instance, they brought us theater, which we never heard before (...) They (the participants) learn computer, radio... Everything they have there is good.

> Boy 9: They know a lot about the city, about the tourist places. They brought amusement to this city.

According to almost all parents interviewed, Casa Grande improves children's knowledge and their behavior with parents, and it is a safe place because the participants are in good company.

> Participant Mother 1: Education, respect, communication with others are skills they get there. They learn and share with others. When my son is there I feel safe. I know what he is doing; I know he is not on the streets; there is no bad company there.

Participant Father 1: I think it is very good stuff. The Communication School influences the way the children communicate not only there, but also at home.

Non-participant Mother 1: I think that those who are at Casa Grande become more educated and learn more. Everyday they learn something new.

Non-participant Mother 2: Children from Casa Grande change their behavior because there they get a stronger orientation, while we, as parents, don't have enough time. There, they live with other children who really teach. A child learns more from another child about how to live in a group, how to work together, how to participate in research. I tried to make my son participate, but he is a rebel.

Similar favorable opinions regarding the quality of the services were also reflected in interviews with governmental organizations such as schools or the Tutor Council.

Member of Nova Olinda Tutor Council 1: Casa Grande is a permanent learning space where they learn not the basic (syllabus), but they acquire life skills, which are useful for living in society and achieving a position in the professional market. They learn by practicing. They are learning to be citizens capable of living in society, and they will certainly become able to support themselves. With this solid thinking, children are changing the vision of their parents.

Head Teacher of Primary School: They (participants) are superior in relation to other adolescents in terms of their vision of the world. In Casa Grande they are 500 years ahead.

Primary School Teacher 5: One day I was teaching about the Berlin Wall and I missed one of my students. Their colleagues said: 'He is in Germany.' I was astonished! I would like to be there!

Conclusion

Nova Olinda can be seen as a typical rural and isolated municipality, with very few entertainment and artistic opportunities, monotonous daily life and adults involved in activities that do not require high professional skills. However, the active participation of adolescents at Casa Grande has changed its profile. Casa Grande impacted the life of this community by motivating students; providing recreation and cultural facilities and events; bringing ideas and tourists; and improving the community's income. But the main impact, from the author's point of view, is the development of a new challenging mentality, which shows that any community can change its profile and that young people can, somehow, lead this (r)evolutionary process.

Notes

1. The United Nations Convention on the Rights of the Child in Article 1 defines child as "every human being below the age of eighteen years unless under the law applicable to the child, majority is attained earlier".
2. The World Health Organization defines adolescents as people between 10 to 19 years of age.
3. There is no standard definition of youth globally. For the purpose of this article, youth is defined as 19 – 25 years old.
4. Data based on 2000 National Census. http://www.ibge.gov.br/cidadesat/default.php
5. IPECE – Instituto de Pesquisa e Estrategia Economica do Ceara – Ceara Research and Economic Strategy Institute – http://www.ipece.ce.gov.br/ consulted on 08 March 2008
6. In 2005, Brazil's HDI was 0,800. http://hdrstats.undp.org/countries/country_fact_sheets/cty_fs_BRA.html consulted on 08 March 2008
7. http://juniorfcg.blogspot.com/search/label/eu%20penso
8. Free translation from Joao Paulo Maropo's testimonial.
9. http://www.fundacaocasagrande.org.br
10. http://www.fundacaocasagrande.org.br/blogs.php
11. UNICEF 2002 dedicated one page to this NGO, highlighting it as a benchmark of children's participation.
12. During its 16 years of existence, there has been no reported cases of sexual or drug abuse inside the organization. This, despite the fact that there are bedrooms and participants can sleep there.
13. Free translation.
14. Two FGDs were conducted with boys (10 participants) and an equal number of FGDs with girls (9 participants).
15. The Tutor Municipal Council is an elected body of the municipality responsible for solving individual cases involving the violation of children's rights and for supporting the formulation of municipal policies for children and adolescents.
16. Blagbrough 1998: 35; Johnson, and Ivan-Smith 1998: 54-55 and 65; and Swift 1998: 42
17. For the purpose of this study, the term young people includes children, adolescents and youth.
18. Analysis of the two daily newspapers of the State of Ceara (Diario do Nordeste and O Povo) in relation to Casa Grande Foundation, from 20 October 2005 until 22 March 2008 demonstrates that out of 17 stories and articles, 15 were positive and nine of them refer to the Communication School for Children.
19. National Institute on Educational Research and Studies Anisio Teixeira
20. http://www.universitario.com.br/noticias/noticias_noticia.php?id_noticia=4947 consulted 23 June 2008
21. http://www.ibge.gov.br/english/estatistica/populacao/contagem/brcont96.shtm consulted 12 July 2008.
22. Centro Brasileiro de Informações sobre Drogas Psicotrópicas (Cebrid) da Universidade Federal de São Paulo (Unifesp), 2008.
23. Brazilian North-eastern music emphasizes in its more recent versions lyrical subjects such as parties, alcohol and beautiful girls.
24. Official data for 2004: http://www.ibge.gov.br
25. The Ministry of Tourism includes Nova Olinda on the map of touristic cities and Casa Grande was one of the 50 institutions selected for community-based tourism. http://www.fundacaocasagrande.org.br/novidades_porjeto.php consulted 13 October 2008.
26. Situation of World's Children 1992, page 28; and Situation of World's Children 2008, page 51.

References

Albanese, Mariana (2008) Escola de Sonhos [Dream School] Un-published book.
Acioli, Socorro (2002) *Fundacao Casa Grande: Comunicacao para Educacao.* [Casa Grande Foundation: communication for education.] Social Communication Course Monography – Fortaleza: Universidade Federal do Ceara;
Arnstein, Sherry R. (1969) *A Ladder of Citizen Participation* JAIP, 35(1969)4, July 1969, pp. 216-224, http://lithgow-schmidt.dk/sherry-arnstein/ladder-of-citizen-participation.html consulted on 9 June 2008.
Azevedo, Fabio Giogio Santos (2005) *Tecnologias de Tranmissao Cutural: E Experiencia da "Escola" de Comunicacao Fundacao Casa Grande – Memorial do Homem Kariri.* [Cultural Transmission Tecnologies: and the Experience of the Communication "School" Casa Grande Foundation – Kariri People Memorial], Masters Degree Thesis. Savador: Universidade Federal da Bahia.
Beers, Henk van (2006) *Adults First! An Organizational Training on Children's Participation.* Bangkok: Save The Children Sweden.
Blagbrough, Jonathan (1998) 'Collecting Information from Child Domestic Workers: some Ethical Issues', in Johnson, Victoria & Ivan-Smith, Edda at al., (eds.) *Stepping Forward: Children and Young People's Participation in the Development Process.* London: Intermediate Technology Publications Ltd.
Boal, Augusto (2002) *Theatre of the Oppressed,* 7th ed., New York: Theatre Communications Group.
Boyden, Jo & Levison, Deborah (2000) *Children as Economic and Social Actors in the Development Process.* Working paper EGDI.
Costa, Antonio Carlos Gomes da (2000) *Protagonismo Juvenil: Adolescência, Educação e Participação Democrática* [Youth protagonism: adolescence, education and democratic participation]. Salvador: Fundação Odebrecht.
Freire, Paulo (1993) *Pedagogy of the Oppressed,* 20th ed., New York: The Continuum Publishing Company.
Hart, Roger A. (1992) *Children's Participation: From Tokenism to Citizenship.* Florence: Innocenti essays, no. 4, UNICEF, International Development Centre.
Johnson, Victoria & Ivan-Smith, Edda at al (1998) *Stepping Forward: Children and Young People's Participation in the Development Process.* London: Intermediate Technology Publications Ltd.
Levi, Giovanni & Schmitt, Jean-Claude (1996) *História dos jovens – Da Antiguidade à Era Moderna* [Youth history – from ancient time to modern era]. São Paulo: Companhia das Letras.]
Morris, Nancy (2005) 'The Diffusion and Participatory Models: A Comparative Approach', in Hemer, O. & Tufte, T. (eds.) *Media & Glocal Change: Rethinking Communication for Development* Buenos Aires: Clacso Books; Göteborg: Nordicom.
Norbert, Elias (2000) *Os Estabelecidos e os Outsiders.* Rio de Janeiro: Zahar.
Servaes, Jan & Malikhao, Patchanee (2005) 'Participatory Communication: The New Paradigm?', in Hemer, O. & Tufte, T. (eds.) *Media & Glocal Change: Rethinking Communication for Development.* Buenos Aires: Clacso Books; Göteborg: Nordicom.
Swift, Melinda (1998) 'The Challenge of Keeping Participatory Processes on Track towards the Achievement of Practical Goals', in Johnson, Victoria & Ivan-Smith, Edda et al., (eds.) *Stepping Forward: Children and Young People's Participation in the Development Process.* London: Intermediate Technology Publications Ltd.

The Authors

Ece Algan, Assistant Professor of Communication Studies at California State University, San Bernardino, CA, USA.
E-mail: ealgan@csusb.edu

José Paulo de Araújo is a Brazilian Journalist, with masters in Communication for Development from Malmö University in Sweden. He is currently Deputy Representative, UNICEF Venezuela.
E-mail: jaraujo@unicef.org

Claudius Ceccon is CECIP's Executive Director. Trained as an Architect and Designer in Brazil, with post graduate studies in Town and Regional Planning in Italy and The Netherlands.
E-mail: claudiusceccon@uol.com.br

Aran Corrigan, M.A. in International Relations from Dublin City University. An Irish national, Aran lives and works in Tanzania as Senior Governance Advisor for Irish Aid.
E-mail: aran.corrigan@dfa.ie

Ylva Ekström, Ph.D., is Junior Lecturer in Communication for Development at Malmö University, Malmö, Sweden.
E-mail: ylva.ekstrom@gmail.com

Florencia Enghel holds a degree in Pedagogical Sciences (University of Belgrano, Argentina) and a Master in Communication for Development (Malmö University, Sweden). She is the editor of *Glocal Times* and Ph.D. Candidate at Karlstad University, Sweden.
E-mail: florenghel@gmail.com

Cecilia Flachsland holds a degree in Communication Sciences, University of Buenos Aires, UBA. She is a Lecturer in Communication Sciences at the UBA and a teachers' trainer for the city of Buenos Aires.
E-mail: cflachsland@gmail.com

Minou Fuglesang, Ph.D., is a Media Anthropologist and a Health Promoter. Dr. Fuglesang is the founder and Executive Director of Femina HIP in Tanzania.
E-mail: minou@feminahip.or.tz

Karen Greiner is a Doctoral Candidate in the School of Communication Studies, Scripps College of Communication, Ohio University, Athens, OH, USA.
E-mail: kgreiner@gmail.com

Mette Grøndahl Hansen, M.A., from Roskilde University in International Development Studies and Communication Studies. She currently works in the Communication Department of the NGO ADRA Denmark.
E-mail: methan@adra.dk

Robert Huesca, Ph.D., is Professor in the Department of Communication at Trinity University, San Antonio, TX, USA.
E-mail: rhuesca@trinity.edu

Lise Grauenkær Jensen, M.A. from Roskilde University in International Development Studies and Communications. She is currently employed in the NGO ADRA Denmark as Communications Manager/Coordinator.
E-mail: lisgra@adra.dk

Stine Kromann-Larsen, M.A. from Roskilde University in Cultural Encounters and Communication Studies. Currently, she is employed as Communication Manager and Web Editor at Prescriba .
E-mail: stine@kromann-larsen.dk

Johan Lagerkvist, Ph.D., is a Research Fellow at The Swedish Institute of International Affairs (SIIA), Stockholm, Sweden.
E-mail: johan.lagerkvist@ui.se

Peter Lemish is an Educational Activist, Independent Researcher, and Lecturer in the School of Communications at Sapir College in Israel.
E-mail: plemish@gmail.com

Rashweat Mukundu is a Media Reseacher and Freedom of Expression activist working for the Media Institute of Southern Africa (MISA) Regional Secretariat in Windhoek, Namibia. Rashweayt holds a B.A. from the University of Zimbabwe, a Post graduate Diploma in Journalism and Communications and now completing an M.A. in Media Studies with Rhodes University of South Africa, Grahamstown, South Africa.
E-mail: rashweatm@yahoo.com

Antonieta Muñoz-Navarro, Journalist with a degree from the University of La Frontera, Chile, an M.A. Communication (Universidad Autónoma de Barcelona) and Ph.D. also from UAB. She is currently employed at Universidad Católica de Temuco, Chile.
E-mail: antum75@yahoo.es

Nkosi Martin Ndlela, Ph.D., Associate Professor in Media and Communication Studies at the Department of Business Administration, Social Sciences and Computer Sciences at Hedmark University College, Norway.
E-mail: nkosi.ndlela@hihm.no

Rossana Reguillo is Professor in the Department of Sociocultural Studies at the Instituto de Estudios Superiores de Occidente, ITESO (Western Institute of Advanced Studies), Guadalajara, Mexico.
E-mail: rossana@iteso.mx

Violeta Rosemberg studied journalism at Taller Escuela Agencia and is currently completing her degree in Political Sciences at the University of Buenos Aires, Argentina.
E-mail: violetarosemberg@gmail.com

Datius Rweyemamu, Ph.D., Lecturer at the Department of Sociology and Anthropology, University of Dar es Salaam, Tanzania. Dr. Rweyemamu is also a co-investigator of MEDIeA 2009-2012 (Media Empowerment & Democracy in East Africa) project for Tanzania.
E-mail: datiusr@yahoo.com

Elke Schlote, Dr. phil., works since 2005 for the Internationales Zentralinstitut für das Jugend- und Bildungsfernsehen (IZI) at Bayerischer Rundfunk in Munich, Germany.
E-mail: elke.schlote@brnet.de

Thomas Tufte, Ph.D., Professor in Communication at Roskilde University, Denmark. He is currently co-director of 'Ørecomm – a Communication and Glocal Change Consortium' (http://orecomm.net) and principal investigator on the research project 'Media, Empowerment and Democracy in East Africa' (MEDIeA, 2009-2012).
E-mail: ttufte@ruc.dk

Iryna Vidanava is a former youth activist and frequent commentator on youth issues and 'new media in Belarus. A historian by training, she is a Ph.D. Candidate at Belarus State University, Minsk, Belarus and M.A. in Public Policy from Institute of Policy Studies at Johns Hopkins University, Baltimore, MD, USA.
E-mail: greeneyes2006@mail.com

Jiwon Yoon, Ph.D. Candidate, in the Mass Media and Communication Program and Graduate Research Assistant in the Media Education Lab at Temple University, Philadelphia, PA, USA.
E-mail: jiwony@temple.edu

Ana Zanotti, M.A., in Communication for Development at Malmö University, Malmö, Sweden. Social Anthropology Graduate (National University of Misiones, Argentina, 1996) and documentary filmmaker.
E-mail: anazano@yahoo.com